# THE FATE OF THE AMERICAS

# Interconnections

## THE GLOBAL TWENTIETH CENTURY

Julia F. Irwin, Renata Keller, Christopher McKnight Nichols,
and Jayita Sarkar, editors

This series is home to innovative global, international,
and transregional histories of the long twentieth century.
Our books emphasize interactions and connections
across three principal areas of inquiry: governments,
militaries, and nonstate actors, including businesses;
international organizations, nation-states, and individuals;
and foreign and domestic policies. The series showcases
work that transcends conventional geographic, temporal,
and disciplinary borders, offering fresh and original
perspectives on the making of the contemporary world.

A complete list of books published in the InterConnections
series is available at
https://uncpress.org/series/interconnections-the-global
-20th-century.

# THE FATE OF
# THE AMERICAS

## THE CUBAN
## MISSILE CRISIS
## AND THE
## HEMISPHERIC
## COLD WAR

## Renata Keller

THE UNIVERSITY OF NORTH CAROLINA PRESS CHAPEL HILL

*This book was published with the assistance of the Anniversary Fund of the University of North Carolina Press.*

© 2025 The University of
North Carolina Press

Set in Utopia by codeMantra
Manufactured in the United States
of America

Unless otherwise noted, all translations are the author's.

Material in this book previously appeared in different form in the following articles: "Rockets Here, in Our Pretty Little Cuba: The View from the Epicenter of the Cuban Missile Crisis," *History Today* 72, no. 10 (October 2022): 28–41; "Research Note: The Cuban Missile Crisis and a War of Words in Argentina," *Cold War History* 22, no. 4 (2022): 521–28, www.tandfonline.com; "'Responsibility of the Great Ones': How the Organization of American States and the United Nations Helped Resolve the Cuban Missile Crisis," *Journal of Latin American Studies* 51, no. 4 (November 2019): 883–904; "The Latin American Missile Crisis," *Diplomatic History* 39, no. 2 (April 2015): 195–222.

Cover art: "Briefing Board #13: [Map of Western Hemisphere showing ranges of 1100 and 220 nautical miles]," February 6, 1963, from the Department of Defense Cuban Missile Crisis Briefing Materials collection at the John F. Kennedy Presidential Library and Museum.

Library of Congress
Cataloging-in-Publication Data
Names: Keller, Renata, 1981– author
Title: The fate of the Americas : the Cuban missile crisis and the hemispheric Cold War / Renata Keller.
Other titles: InterConnections
Description: Chapel Hill : The University of North Carolina Press, [2025] | Series: Interconnections : the global 20th century | Includes bibliographical references and index.
Identifiers: LCCN 2025016609 | ISBN 9781469689425 cloth | ISBN 9781469689432 paperback | ISBN 9781469686639 epub | ISBN 9781469689449 pdf
Subjects: LCSH: Cuban Missile Crisis, 1962 | Cold War | Latin America—History—1948-1980 | Latin America—Politics and government—1948-1980 | BISAC: SOCIAL SCIENCE / Ethnic Studies / Caribbean & Latin American Studies | POLITICAL SCIENCE / International Relations / Diplomacy
Classification: LCC F1414.2 .K45 2025 | DDC 972.9106/4—dc23/eng/20250416
LC record available at https://lccn.loc.gov/2025016609

For product safety concerns under the European Union's General Product Safety Regulation (EU GPSR), please contact gpsr@mare-nostrum.co.uk or write to the University of North Carolina Press and Mare Nostrum Group B.V., Mauritskade 21D, 1091 GC Amsterdam, The Netherlands.

*For Cameron*

*After all, it is the fate of the*
*Americas that is at stake, and*
*not just that of the United*
*States.*
— "Sem receios nem
  vacilações," *Folha de*
  *São Paulo*, October 24, 1962

# Contents

# Illustrations

# Preface

*by the editors of the* INTERCONNECTIONS:

THE GLOBAL TWENTIETH CENTURY *series*

*The Fate of the Americas* is the first-ever hemispheric history of the Cuban
Missile Crisis, revealing its immense repercussions throughout the entire
region. In this riveting and groundbreaking account, Renata Keller inno-
vatively combines international and transnational methods with the tools
of microhistory, connecting the local to the national to the hemispheric to
the global. The book examines how individuals, nation-states, and ideologies across Latin America influenced—and were in turn transformed by—
this watershed moment of twentieth-century history. It traces the origins,
progression, and lasting legacies of this nuclear confrontation, showing
how it affected people and governments in every part of the Americas.
Above all, the crisis underscored for Latin Americans that their lives and
political destinies were intimately interconnected.

More than a history of the Cuban Missile Crisis, *The Fate of the Americas*
offers a fresh perspective on the global Cold War. In Latin America, Keller argues, the Cold War was fought on multiple fronts, both between countries and
within them. Keller highlights the shared priorities and values across nations
as well as the debilitating ideological divides that undermined hemispheric
unity. Throughout the region, Keller shows, three vigorously contested sets of
core concerns—security, sovereignty, and solidarity—defined both percep-
tions and realities. Based on extensive archival research—spanning Argentina, Bolivia, Chile, Colombia, Cuba, Guatemala, Mexico, Panama, and the
United States—*The Fate of the Americas* illuminates the history of Latin America's Cold War at its most critical moment while also tracing its deep roots and
long-lasting consequences. "Latin America," Keller definitively demonstrates,
"was at the heart of the Cuban Missile Crisis from the outset."

# Acknowledgments

I started this project on the fiftieth anniversary of the Cuban Missile Crisis, when Bruce Schulman, then-chair of Boston University's History Department, invited me to join a panel that he was organizing to look back at the milestone event. He asked if I wanted to share the research that I had done on Mexico . . . or, he suggested, talk a bit about responses across the Americas. Neither of us knew then that his casual suggestion would set me on a path that would eventually lead to this book. I am grateful to Bruce for reaching out to me, his new colleague, and for unintentionally gifting me such a fascinating project.

While I was still at Boston University, I received intellectual and economic support from numerous sources. The Tertulia group and other colleagues, especially Susan Eckstein, Adela Pineda, Erik Goldstein, Jeff Rubin, Stephen Kinzer, David Carballo, Cornel Ban, Jeremy Menchik, Manjari Chatterjee Miller, Julie Klinger, Anthony Petro, and Mac Marston, offered me opportunities to share my early thoughts and gave me great ideas for developing the project. My research assistants, Ryo Takatsuchi and Zachary Thomas, helped me find sources, and my students in my Freshman Year Experience and US–Latin American Relations courses read some of my first articles and helped me think about expanding them into a book. Boston University and the Pardee School of Global Studies also provided funding for some of my first research trips.

Speaking of research trips—this book required a lot! Friends and colleagues were incredibly generous in their advice as I planned my travel, especially Felipe Cruz, Michael Donoghue, Thomas C. Field Jr., Seth Garfield, Jim Green, Steven Hyland, Robert Karl, Aldo Marchesi, Rachel Nolan, Blake Scott, Carmen Soliz, Dustin Walcher, Eyal Weinberg, and Kirsten Weld. I must thank all the archivists and librarians who helped me navigate their collections as efficiently and effectively as possible. My deep gratitude goes out to the library and archival staff who assisted me, especially Willis Wilder in the Archivo del Ministerio de Relaciones Exteriores de Bolivia; Sonia Martínez and Cecilia Larsen in the Biblioteca Nacional de Argentina; Virginia Castro at CeDInCI;

Jocelyn Jaen at the Biblioteca Simón Bolívar at the Universidad de Panamá; Silvia Rosana Modena Martini at the Arquivo Edgard Leuenroth; Thelma Porres and Reina at CIRMA; Belkis Quesada, Elvis Rodríguez Rodríguez, Luis Montes de Oca Colina, and Rosa Ana Roque Martínez at the Instituto de Historia de Cuba; Jorge Luna, Nulbia Piqueras, Luisa María González, Osvaldo Rodríguez Martínez, Eduardo Rodríguez-Baz, Victor M. Landa Peláez, Ernesto López Alonso, and Luis Enrique González Acosta at Prensa Latina; Ana Hernández and Yanet Granados at the Centro Fidel Castro Ruz; and William, Diano Bello, and Ana Cecilia Ruiz at the Casa de las Américas. Researchers and staff at the National Security Archive and Woodrow Wilson Center have done a huge service to scholars by putting so many documents related to the missile crisis online. I must also give special thanks to the Inter-Library Loan crew at the University of Nevada, Reno (UNR), especially Jennifer Wykoff.

In addition to countless ILL loans, I have received a great deal of support and encouragement from the University of Nevada. My colleagues in the History Department have been extremely helpful, particularly Bruce Moran and Dennis Dworkin, who performed a great mitzvah in bringing me to UNR. Linda Curcio welcomed me as a fellow Latin Americanist, and Greta de Jong wrote me numerous letters of recommendation for funding. Our History Department administrator, Mikki Johnson, was extremely helpful with processing my receipts and shielding me from most of the miseries of Workday, and librarian Rosalind Bucy provided generous teaching and research support. The history junior faculty works-in-progress group, including Christopher Church, Marwan Hanania, Sarah Keyes, Jamie McSpadden, and Cameron Strang, gave me extremely useful feedback on my NEH applications. Students in my Historiography of the Americas class read an early draft of the entire manuscript and offered many helpful suggestions. Friends and colleagues, especially Chris Church, Courtney Church, Mark Lescroart, Valerie Lescroart, Ethan Ris, and Liana Ris, helped make UNR and Reno feel like home. At UNR, I received financial support from the Ozmen Institute for Global Studies, the Vice President of Research and Innovation, the College of Liberal Arts Scholarly and Creative Activities Grant Program, and the John and Marie Noble Fund for Historical Research. I also received funding from outside organizations that allowed me to research and write this book. I am extremely grateful to the American Philosophical Society and the National Endowment for the Humanities for their generous support.

Other organizations and institutions provided permissions to include images and my previously published work in this book. Marcelo Barbosa at *Folha de São Paulo* showed incredible patience, exchanging thirty-nine emails with me to secure permission to publish a political cartoon. Melany J.

Chiari at *El Nuevo Siglo* corresponded almost as much as Marcelo, as did Maria Antonia Bornot Garcell at Prensa Latina. Yang Peiming from the Chinese Propaganda Poster Art Center was extremely helpful in securing a scan and permission, as was Thelma Porres at CIRMA and Magdalena Lanteri at the Comisión por la Memoria. I thank *History Today* for allowing me to include excerpts from my article "Rockets Here, in Our Pretty Little Cuba: The View from the Epicenter of the Cuban Missile Crisis"; *Journal of Cold War History* for permission to include excerpts from "Research Note: The Cuban Missile Crisis and a War of Words in Argentina"; *Journal of Latin American Studies* for permission to include sections of "Responsibility of the Great Ones: How the Organization of American States and the United Nations Helped Resolve the Cuban Missile Crisis"; and *Diplomatic History* for excerpts from "The Latin American Missile Crisis."

I owe a great debt to the friends and colleagues who have discussed this project with me and to those who read all or part of the manuscript. Lorraine Bayard de Volo, Jürgen Buchenau, David Engerman, Vanessa Freije, Virginia Garrard, Paul Gillingham, Tanya Harmer, Andrew Kirkendall, Peter Kornbluh, James Lockhart, Kyle Longley, Casey Lurtz, Achy Obejas, Margaret Power, Rafael Rojas, Mary Roldán, Lars Schoultz, Christy Thornton, Ann Twinam, Charles Walker, and Arne Westad all helped me think through some of my ideas. Aaron Coy Moulton merits special mention for reading the entire manuscript and providing feedback in under twenty-four hours. If anyone else matches that feat, let me know and I will send you a prize! I am also forever in debt to Michelle Chase and Alan McPherson for reading multiple drafts of the entire manuscript and rescuing me from reader-report purgatory. James Hershberg, Robert Alegre, and Michelle Paranzino also read drafts of the full manuscript and provided extremely helpful feedback. Members of my Women's Writing Group read drafts of various chapters—many thanks to all of them for the emotional and intellectual support over the years, and especially to Amelia Kiddle for organizing our group. Ernesto Bohoslavsky, Jonathan Brown, Thomas C. Field Jr., Sarah Foss, Roberto García Ferreira, Jonathan Hunt, Robert Karl, Martín Ribadero, Claudia Rueda, Gustavo Salcedo, Marian Schlotterbeck, Blake Scott, Carmen Soliz, and Greg Weeks all read and commented on sections of the manuscript. I am grateful to my dear friend Juandrea Bates for giving my introduction the Twinam Treatment (and for always being available to talk me off the ledge when I have parenting panic). Roberto García Ferreira, Aaron Coy Moulton, Gustavo Salcedo, and James Shrader all generously shared documents with me from their own research.

I am so glad that this book found a home at the University of North Carolina Press. It has been a pleasure to work with Debbie Gershenowitz again—she really is the best in the business. Her editorial assistant, Alexis Dumain, was extremely helpful and patient, even when I ranted about copyright permissions. My expert copy editor, Steph Attia, made my prose clean and pretty, and Erin Granville did a great job managing the editorial process. The graphic design team did amazing work adapting the Kennedy Library map I gave them for the cover art. I'm also so excited that this book is coming out in our new InterConnections series; working with Julia, Chris, and Jay has been an absolute pleasure, and I thank them for welcoming me and my book.

I must also thank my family and friends. My UHS diaspora kept me sane during COVID and still provide moral support and funny memes on a daily basis. My brother, Kevin, has assisted me so much, from outlining the manuscript with me on a pizza napkin during a writing retreat in New Haven, to hunting down the rights owner of a Chinese poster and helping me pay for it, to reading and commenting on the entire manuscript. My sister, Rachel, continues to be generous with her medical advice and inspirational with her dedication to helping others. My parents, Marion and Peter, have been a constant source of encouragement and motivation; I thank them for a lifetime of love and support. My in-laws, Karol and Bill, have been great cheerleaders and extremely helpful with childcare assistance during many of my travels. My children, James and Alice, have brought so much joy and laughter into my world. Parenting them has been the best challenge of my life.

And finally, the biggest thanks of all go to my husband, Cameron. This book would not exist without him. He has provided endless encouragement while at the same time always pushing me to make my thoughts clearer and my arguments stronger. He has cared for me through the hardest physical times in my life, including pregnancy, childbirth, and the surgeries necessary to put me back together afterward. He enthusiastically agreed, time and again, to watch James and Alice while I galivanted across the Americas. I've lost count of the number of times he read versions of this project, from the first articles to the funding applications to the full manuscript. Cameron's love has been the greatest constant in my life, and I thank him for it.

# THE FATE OF THE AMERICAS

BERMUDA

ATLANTIC
OCEAN

THE
BAHAMAS

CUBA

MEXICO

HAITI

PUERTO
RICO

BELIZE

HONDURAS

JAMAICA

GUADELOUPE

MARTINIQUE

DOMINICAN
REPUBLIC

GUATEMALA

EL SALVADOR

NICARAGUA

GRENADA

TRINIDAD
and TOBAGO

SURINAME

FRENCH GUIANA

VENEZUELA

COSTA RICA

N

PANAMA

COLOMBIA

GUYANA

ECUADOR

PERU

BRAZIL

BOLIVIA

PACIFIC
OCEAN

PARAGUAY

CHILE

URUGUAY

ARGENTINA

| 0 | 500 | 1000 mi |
|---|---|---|
| 0 | 500 1000 | 1500 km |

FALKLAND
ISLANDS

# Introduction

The Bolivian ambassador sat at his desk in Colombia's capital. Perhaps his hand trembled as he clipped stories from the day's news, attached them to blank sheets of paper, and placed them in a file to send back home to the Ministry of Foreign Affairs in La Paz. The ambassador included articles that noted the historical significance of the events he was witnessing: "For the first time since the rise of the Cold War in 1948, the direct threat of being reached by an international conflagration looms for Colombia." He also clipped stories that speculated about what would happen should a nuclear war break out. "Scientists tell us that it would take ten minutes for a bomb launched from Cuba to reach Bogotá"; "A bomb in Panama would bring us a slow death"; "The air itself could be so contaminated that, for a time, special precautions would have to be taken so as not to inhale death." Still other articles emphasized the uncertainty of the moment: "In the current circumstances anything can happen. It is possible that while you are reading this page, the extinction of all human life on the planet is being decided. . . . Only God knows whether the hour of the Apocalypse draws near."[1] The ambassador might have prayed that there would still be a ministry to receive his collection of clippings, that there would still be someone alive to deliver them.

On the evening of October 22, 1962, more than 200 million people across Latin America learned that they were living within reach of nuclear missiles located on the island of Cuba. The news set off an explosion of activity in every part of the region. The presidents of Mexico and Brazil sent messages to Fidel Castro, urging him to give up the catastrophic weapons. Argentine ships steamed from the far southern waters of the Atlantic Ocean to join the Inter-American Quarantine Force in the Caribbean. Cubans readied their island for an invasion. Bolivians, Colombians, Peruvians, and Argentines littered the streets and plastered the walls of their cities with leaflets arguing for peace . . . and for war. Thousands of people marched in demonstrations in Nicaragua, Panama, Costa Rica, Ecuador, Chile, Uruguay, and Brazil. Saboteurs in Venezuela and Argentina set fire to oil fields and launched Molotov cocktails at

US-owned businesses, while protesters in Uruguay and Brazil battled police armed with machine guns. Bolivian demonstrations escalated into a bloody, deadly riot; ultimately more Bolivians than Cubans died in the turmoil surrounding the Cuban Missile Crisis. Latin American citizens and leaders, confronted with the possibility of nuclear war, refused to wait for others to decide the fate of the Americas.

The Cuban Missile Crisis, which brought the world to the brink of Armageddon, has inspired thousands of books and articles. Yet we have not yet come close to telling a complete story of the causes, course, or consequences of this event, one of the most important in modern history.[2] Viewed from the United States, the history of the Cuban Missile Crisis is relatively straightforward: It was a tense confrontation that was resolved peacefully and successfully. Viewed from Latin America, however, it was a battle fought on multiple fronts between and within countries, a struggle with deep roots and long-lasting consequences. Historians have missed both how Latin Americans influenced the crisis and how the crisis changed Latin America. Everyday people and government officials across the Americas helped cause the crisis, worked to end it, and felt its consequences.

Latin America was at the heart of the Cuban Missile Crisis from the outset. The road to October 1962 began with hemispheric reactions to the Cuban Revolution, when Fidel Castro's success in defeating a dictator, wresting Cuba's sovereignty from the United States, and reinventing his country inspired widespread admiration and fear. At the same time as the Cuban Revolution became more radical and as the country's leaders increasingly embraced communism and an alliance with the Soviet Union, their opponents across the Americas also became more radicalized and tried to undermine and isolate the Cuban regime. Right-wing Latin American leaders, Cuban exiles, and the US government worked together to try to get rid of Castro, and most governments in the Americas cooperated to isolate Cuba diplomatically from the inter-American community. These clear threats to the security and sovereignty of Cuba's revolutionary regime were some of the main motivations behind Nikita Khrushchev's idea to offer Castro nuclear missiles and Castro's decision to accept them. The Cuban Missile Crisis, then, began with a tragic irony: Those who were trying to weaken Castro unintentionally inspired the Soviets to offer him stronger weapons than had ever before been introduced into the Western Hemisphere beyond US soil.

Latin American people and governments played important roles in resolving the Cuban Missile Crisis. The Organization of American States (OAS) coordinated a united hemispheric front, while the United Nations (UN) drew on Cuban proposals to help slow the pace of the crisis and open opportunities for a peaceful resolution. Demonstrations of Latin American solidarity embold-ened Castro, while rumors of an impending attack alarmed him. In Washing-ton and Moscow, the days after John F. Kennedy's October 22 demand that Khrushchev remove the missiles were ones of tense stalemate and carefully worded negotiations. Across Latin America, however, the situation was one of constant action, escalating daily, and becoming ever more deadly. Castro sought to gain the upper hand by shutting down US surveillance and stiffen-ing Khrushchev's resolve. These actions backfired and convinced Khrushchev that the crisis was spinning out of his control. Both Kennedy and Castro made Khrushchev blink and withdraw the missiles.

Finally, the Cuban Missile Crisis had enduring consequences for people and states across the Americas. Kennedy's promise not to invade Cuba if Khrushchev removed his nuclear weapons outraged the Cuban exile com-munity and government leaders in the Caribbean Basin, who argued that the greatest threat to their security—Castro—still remained. For them, the blowback of the crisis was unimaginable; instead of removing the commu-nist menace from the hemisphere, Kennedy's promise had provided Castro further protection. After the missile crisis, US support for multilateral inter-vention against Cuba declined precipitously, much to the chagrin of Castro's enemies. The crisis also caused other important international realignments within the hemisphere. It brought the OAS, which had been divided by the Cuba question, back under US leadership, strengthened US relations with countries that aligned with the United States in the crisis, and weakened US ties with those who dared to chart their own path. At the same time, Khrush-chev's decision to withdraw without consulting Castro undermined bilateral relations between the two allies and damaged their reputations among Latin American leftists who had previously looked to Cuba and the Soviet Union for solidarity and security. The crisis was thus a turning point in inter-American relations, helping the United States reestablish its leadership after the desta-bilizing threat of the Cuban Revolution. The full story of the Cuban Missile Crisis is contradictory; it is a history not only of triumph but also of irony and tragedy.

In order to tell a complete story of the Cuban Missile Crisis across the Americas, I have adopted a methodological approach that treats it as both a world-revealing moment and a world-changing event. My history of the crisis is at once a macro-level story that spans an entire hemisphere and a micro-level one that focuses on a single, brief event and the actions of specific people and groups. To span the two levels, I blend international and trans-national methodologies, which emphasize relations between nation-states and the connections that transcend political and ideological borders, with microhistorical analysis, which focuses on the actions of individuals, often everyday men and women.[3] My approach reveals the ways that ordinary people and marginalized countries caused, participated in, and were affected by one of the most famous events in history. It also exposes the values and ideas that motivated their actions. It balances the agency of individual, national, and transnational reactions—voting in the OAS, joining the quarantine, creating propaganda, distributing pamphlets, marching in the streets, sabotaging businesses—with the structures of US imperialism and Cold War ideologies.

In telling a new history of the Cuban Missile Crisis, I also suggest a new way to tell the history of Latin America's Cold War or, as I call it, the "hemispheric Cold War." I use this term to convey the idea of a war that involved people and governments in both Latin America and the United States, a war that was fought both among and within nations.[4] It is no longer enough to define the hemispheric Cold War simply as a confrontation between capitalism and communism or as a proxy war between the United States and the Soviet Union.[5] We must find a new description that balances those traditional concerns with the deeper struggles, diverse actors, and local drivers of the conflicts that took place in this region. Furthermore, most histories of the Cold War in Latin America have been circumscribed by national boundaries, focused on US foreign policy, or limited to actors on either one of the extreme ends of the ideological spectrum.[6] This hemispheric history of the missile crisis moves beyond these confines, bridging histories of left and right-wing activism, while also breaking down the binary between those positions and highlighting the diversity of views. While I emphasize Latin American actions and concerns, I avoid overcorrecting by writing the United States or the Soviet Union out of the story. I do not deny that Kennedy and Khrushchev were central actors in the missile crisis or that the contest between the capitalist and communist camps was important. But I insist that other actors and conflicts were also crucial in shaping the history of the missile crisis and the hemispheric Cold War.

I propose that we tell the story of the Cuban Missile Crisis and the Cold War more broadly not only as a contest between two sides—whether East versus West, North versus South, or capitalists versus communists—but also as a battle within and among societies over how to pursue a distinct set of shared values: security, sovereignty, and solidarity. I argue that these three values shaped the terms of struggle during the Cuban Missile Crisis and the hemispheric Cold War. When Latin Americans sought security, they were looking for safety, whether from nuclear weapons and conventional warfare or from their own citizens and leaders.[7] When they demanded sovereignty, they defended the principles of self-determination and nonintervention, arguing that they should have the full authority to govern within their national territories and determine their own foreign policies. Historically, the threat of intervention in Latin America most often came from the United States; but during the Cold War, many in the region came to perceive the Soviet Union and communist infiltration as significant threats to their sovereignty, too.[8] Solidarity, as both a sentiment and a practice, tended to focus around mutual support, strategic reciprocities, bonds of affection, common causes, and shared experiences. Traditionally emphasized primarily among leftist groups and actors, solidarity emerged as an important value across the political spectrum during the Cold War.[9]

By fighting over the Soviet nuclear missiles in Cuban territory, Latin Americans debated, demonstrated, and transformed their understandings of security, sovereignty, and solidarity. Did Castro have the right to accept Khrushchev's act of solidarity: nuclear weapons that could increase Cuba's security? Or did the advent of atomic warfare put new limits on national sovereignty and countries' rights to possess certain weapons? Did Cuba's neighbors have the right to protect their own security by demanding the removal of the missiles that threatened to set off a nuclear war that could endanger everyone in the region? Were the missiles, in fact, the greatest threat to security in the hemisphere? Or was the greatest threat Castro, or the Soviet Union, or the United States? Could solidarity be a way to strengthen security without sacrificing sovereignty? These questions shaped how people across the Americas reacted to the Cuban Missile Crisis. Furthermore, the crisis changed how many Latin Americans understood their place in the Cold War and the nature of security, the limits of sovereignty, and the value of solidarity.

Reframing the history of the Cuban Missile Crisis and the hemispheric Cold War as a struggle over the shared values of security, sovereignty, and solidarity also offers a new model for global histories of the Cold War. Historians of the Cold War have long recognized the importance of national security concerns in the contest between the United States and the Soviet Union, and they have more recently started turning to issues of individual security and human rights.[10] With the publication of Odd Arne Westad's landmark work, *The Global Cold War*, and other studies that emphasized North-South conflicts, the question of sovereignty in the fights for decolonization in Asia, Africa, and the Middle East became more prominent in histories of this era.[11] Solidarity has recently started to gain more attention, especially as the transnational turn and increasing historical focus on "Third World" projects has encouraged scholars to look beyond nation-state boundaries and government actors.[12] The same three values that drove Latin Americans to action during the missile crisis were thus central to Cold War struggles around the world. We should see contests to defend these three values as a defining feature of the era. Putting security, sovereignty, and solidarity together at the heart of global histories of the Cold War reveals the common concerns that inspired people to act and highlights the shared aims that worked alongside the divisions.

*The Fate of the Americas* tells the story of the Cuban Missile Crisis in Latin America from its origins to its conclusion and consequences. It unfolds chronologically and thematically, following the movement of ideas and action across the Americas. While it begins and ends in Cuba, the epicenter of the crisis, it also crosses national boundaries and geographical scales, from the streets of Havana, Rio de Janeiro, La Paz, Caracas, Buenos Aires, Bogotá, and Mexico City; to the meeting rooms of Cuba's Presidential Palace, the White House, and the Kremlin; to the halls of the OAS and UN. Most chapters combine brief examples from multiple countries with deeper dives into specific places that either best illustrate common patterns or were particularly important at certain moments. I concentrate on the people and places that were most influential or most affected, while still maintaining the geographic breadth and diversity of the story. I also balance my analysis of countries that usually receive a great deal of attention in histories of Latin America's Cold War, such as Cuba, Guatemala, Nicaragua, Argentina, and Brazil, with attention to places that are often left out, such as Mexico, Panama, Colombia, Venezuela, and Bolivia. *The Fate of the Americas* focuses on Latin American people and governments and how they influenced and were affected by Castro, Kennedy, and Khrushchev. These three leaders' decisions were constantly shaped by the hemispheric context in which they acted and by the actions of men and women across the Americas. This book weaves all these stories together to tell a new history of the Cuban Missile Crisis and the hemispheric Cold War.

# PART I CAUSES

# CHAPTER 1
# REVOLUTION AND REACTION

The Cuban Revolution changed the course of Cuban history, US-Cuban relations, and hemispheric politics. The drastic transformations on the Caribbean island inspired people across the Americas to reimagine their own political fates and escalated the hemispheric Cold War by instigating revolutionary and counterrevolutionary movements across the region. Some Latin Americans embraced Cuba's example, as the revolutionary reforms seemed to reflect their own long-standing desires for political sovereignty and economic reform. Others rejected the radicalism of the Cuban Revolution and Castro's embrace of communism. The Cuban Revolution spurred people across the ideological spectrum to take action at home and build international and transnational alliances, providing a common frame of reference to justify their struggles.

## The Cuban Revolution
The roots of the Cuban Revolution go back to 1898, the year the United States intervened in Cuba's war for independence from Spain. With Cuban patriots poised on the cusp of victory, the US Congress and President William McKinley declared war on Spain on the pretext of establishing a stable, responsible government in Cuba. But US intervention not only denied the Cubans their victory; it denied them their sovereignty. After quickly dispatching the Spanish army, the United States began a three-year military occupation that lasted until the new Cuban government agreed to accept the Platt Amendment as an appendix to its 1901 constitution. The amendment severely curtailed Cuban independence by limiting the government's ability to enter treaties or take on debt and by guaranteeing the United States the right to intervene. The amendment also forced the Cuban government to cede territory to establish a US naval base on the island—Guantánamo—further highlighting Cuba's subjected condition and undercutting its sovereignty.

Over the course of the next half century, US leaders consolidated their influence over Latin America in general and Cuba in particular. The US armed forces interceded on numerous occasions; some interventions were brief, others led to long occupations. Even Franklin Roosevelt, Latin America's self-appointed good neighbor, was willing to meddle in Cuban affairs; in 1933, his ambassador, Sumner Welles, undermined a fledgling revolutionary government by cultivating ties with the chief of the army, a young colonel named Fulgencio Batista. Welles helped him stage a coup and organize a new government that was more friendly to US interests. Batista launched a political career that began with union-friendly labor reforms in the 1930s and a progressive constitution in 1940, but the once-populist leader became increasingly authoritarian and seized power on the eve of elections in 1952. Through it all, US leaders supported Batista, even during the years of his dictatorship in the 1950s.

US citizens, investors, and corporations dominated Cuba's economy, and by the 1950s Cuban citizens were suffering severe economic dislocation and hardship. The island's dependence on sugar had long caused economic volatility, which trended more often toward bust than boom. Cubans in the countryside lived in desperate conditions, most without access to education, health care, adequate housing, running water, or electricity. Urban slums encircled Havana, where tens of thousands of people lived in squalor. By 1958, the economy was in a near state of collapse.

Cuba's political situation was equally dire. After his 1952 coup, Fulgencio Batista refused to hold genuine elections, which closed off the political paths to power and drove his opponents into a "vibrant clandestine milieu" of oppositional and insurrectionary groups.[1] The two most prominent insurrectionary groups were the 26th of July Movement, named after the date of the young lawyer Fidel Castro's failed assault on the Moncada army barracks in Santiago de Cuba in 1953, and the Revolutionary Directorate (Directorio Revolucionario), founded by Catholic student leader José Antonio Echeverría.

Cuba's hardships formed the basis of Castro's call for revolution. At his trial after the Moncada assault, Castro gave a speech that was subsequently smuggled out of the country, published, and circulated under the title "History Will Absolve Me." In this manifesto, Castro spoke of Cuba's numerous problems, including unemployment, agrarian stagnation, foreign exploitation, and corruption. He then laid out a program of reforms and revolutionary laws designed to rescue the nation. Castro promised to redistribute land to the farmers that worked it, grant workers a share of the profits of their labor, confiscate any wealth previously gained through fraud, restore civil liberties and political democracy, and demonstrate solidarity with democratic peoples across the Americas.[2]

Cuban communists joined the armed insurrection somewhat belatedly, even though they shared many of Castro's goals. Cuba's Popular Socialist Party (Partido Socialista Popular) had supported Batista during his populist democratic period in the 1940s in exchange for seats in his cabinet, positions in union leadership, and the relatively light censorship of their publications.[3] Despite the fact that Batista outlawed their party soon after returning to power, Cuban communists favored a strategy of mass organizing and mostly refrained from active participation in insurrectionary politics until the late 1950s. Party leadership denounced Castro's attack on the Moncada barracks as "putschism" and "individual terrorism" in 1953 and only slowly, haltingly, started linking up with the 26th of July Movement over the course of 1957 and 1958, under pressure from rank-and-file workers and activists.[4]

Batista waged a merciless war against the insurrection. In the cities of Havana and Santiago, cyclical violence between police and urban militants often spiraled out to claim the lives of innocent bystanders. In the countryside surrounding the Sierra Maestra mountains, where Castro was ensconced, Batista's army tried to root out Castro's guerrilla forces by eliminating his potential collaborators, murdering peasants, squatters, and sugar workers. Batista's security forces and death squads often indulged in spectacular forms of violence, killing prisoners in public and parading their corpses through the streets, or leaving mutilated bodies on display, swinging from trees and lampposts.[5]

Batista's violent methods became so egregious that the US government eventually came to the aid of Cuban revolutionaries—or at least stopped helping Batista fight them. During a pivotal 1957 interview in the Sierra Maestra with *New York Times* reporter Herbert Matthews, Castro complained bitterly about the fact that the United States was supplying Batista with the weapons that he used not only against the guerrillas but also against "all the Cuban people."[6] In March 1958, Washington finally imposed an arms embargo on Batista. The US government also refused to recognize the results of rigged elections that Batista held later that year, and in December of 1958, the State Department sent a secret envoy to Havana to encourage Batista to step down. Cuba's strongman had lost his most powerful international backer and could no longer resist the mounting revolution. Shortly after midnight on January 1, 1959, Fulgencio Batista left Cuba for the last time.

## Early Responses to the Cuban Revolution

People across the Americas responded enthusiastically to the Cuban Revolution. Photos of Fidel Castro, Ernesto "Che" Guevara, and their fellow bearded rebels—*los barbudos*—rolling across Cuba in jeeps and on tanks filled the newspapers. In just the first week following Batista's flight, Mexico's paper of record, *Excélsior*, published almost 100 articles about events in Cuba, the majority of which praised the revolution.[7] In the Nicaraguan capital of Managua, revelers set off fireworks, and youth groups organized a demonstration filled with shouts of "Viva la Libertad," "Viva Cuba Libre," and "Viva Fidel."[8] The romantic story of a small group of dedicated men and women surviving in the mountains long enough to overthrow a cruel tyrant was immensely appealing.

Less than a month after the Cuban rebels seized power, Castro made his first overseas trip. He had accepted an invitation from the residents of Caracas's 23 de Enero neighborhood and the student government of the Central University of Venezuela. A cheering throng of 50,000 people welcomed Castro upon his arrival at the Caracas airport on January 23, 1959. This was a significant date for Venezuelans: the first anniversary of the fall of their own dictator, Gen. Marcos Andrés Pérez Jiménez. The provisional government that had replaced Pérez Jiménez had supported Castro's efforts against Batista, providing asylum to revolutionary leaders and allowing Cuban exiles in Venezuela to send money and weapons to the rebels on the island.[9] In a two-hour speech at the El Silencio plaza in the heart of Caracas, Castro offered his benefactors words of gratitude and solidarity. "From Venezuela we have received only favors . . . you encouraged us during our struggle with your sympathy and affection. . . . I promise you that if Venezuela ever finds itself again under the boot of a tyrant, count on the Cubans, count on the combatants of the Sierra Maestra, count on our men and our arms."[10] To mark Castro's visit and celebrate his revolution, residents of the 23 de Enero renamed the newest sector of their neighborhood the Sierra Maestra.[11]

The passion that Venezuelans showed for the Cuban revolutionaries was unprecedented. A housewife from Caracas, Olga Cecilia Prieto Martínez, told her grandson years later that "the only man apart from your grandfather who got me out of the house was Fidel." On the day of Castro's visit to the university, Olga dutifully prepared her husband's lunch and then left the house in a hurry to see Fidel speak.[12] The Venezuelan congress held a special session to honor the visitor; Deputy Domingo Alberto Rangel gave a speech comparing Castro to the famous leader of Latin American independence and hometown hero Simón Bolívar.[13] Chilean poet Pablo Neruda was in Venezuela at the time of Castro's visit and attended his speeches at the university and in the El Silencio plaza. "I have seen few political receptions more fervent than the one that the Venezuelans gave to the young hero of the Cuban Revolution," Neruda wrote in his memoirs. He recalled, "I was one of the two hundred thousand people who listened, on foot and without interrupting, to that long speech . . . Hearing him speak before that crowd, I understood that a new era had begun for Latin America."[14]

Neruda's words captured the importance of the Cuban Revolution for the rest of the Americas. Castro's stunning success and his bold plans to transform his country ushered in a new era of revolution and—although Neruda and most others did not yet realize it—counterrevolution. Castro seemed poised to deliver to Cubans what so many people across the Americas sought: political and economic sovereignty. Castro also offered solidarity to fellow Latin Americans who opposed their own governments and sought to transform their countries. During his visit to the Venezuelan university, Castro was the first person to contribute money to create a committee to liberate the Dominican Republic from its own cruel tyrant, Rafael Trujillo.[15] The Cuban Revolution gave hope to those who wanted change and offered a new model of revolution that was based on Latin American goals and conditions.

But not everyone in Venezuela was pleased with Castro's visit. Rómulo Betancourt, Venezuela's president-elect and a former revolutionary who had become a respectable politician, immediately clashed with Castro. Even though Betancourt and Castro had both defeated dictators in their respective countries, the two leaders had little else in common. Betancourt was from an older generation; he had been fighting to transform his country into an economically independent, modern democracy since the 1920s, spending much of the first half of his life in the political underground or in exile. A brief exception to his life of opposition politics came in the years from 1945 to 1948, known as the *Trienio*, when Betancourt became president of the Revolutionary Government Junta as a result of a military coup led by Pérez Jiménez in collaboration with Betancourt's Democratic Action (Acción Democrática) party. This brief window of reform and democracy slammed shut on November 24, 1948, when Pérez Jiménez staged yet another military uprising and became, as historian and Kennedy special assistant Arthur Schlesinger Jr. put it, "a rather squalid dictator."[16] Betancourt went back into exile, becoming de facto leader of the international and underground opposition. A blatantly fraudulent plebiscite at the end of 1957—followed by two months of escalating urban protests, military revolts, and a general strike—brought the Pérez Jiménez dictatorship to a sudden end in January 1958. Betancourt returned from exile and, in December of that year, was elected president. By then a senior statesman, Betancourt was the poster boy of gradual reform and liberal democracy in Venezuela and across the Americas.

Castro's visit both highlighted and heightened the differences between the two leaders. Betancourt, a life-long defender of democracy, had initially celebrated the overthrow of Batista but had become dismayed by Castro's reckless behavior. Betancourt represented the old model of political organizing that focused on careful planning and gradual improvement, whereas Castro captured the spirit of a younger generation that embraced bold action and sought quick, profound transformations. According to Neruda's account of Castro's speech in the plaza, the audience booed every time Castro spoke Betancourt's name. Neruda speculated that the speech "sealed a definitive enmity between Betancourt and the Cuban revolutionary. . . . My personal theory is that the speech, Fidel's fiery and brilliant personality, the massive enthusiasm that he awoke, the passion with which the people of Caracas listened to his words, grieved Betancourt, that old-fashioned politician of rhetoric, committees, and closed-door meetings."[17]

In addition to the stylistic contrasts that Neruda observed, ideological and geopolitical disagreements divided Castro and Betancourt. A moderate democratic reformer, Betancourt was an outspoken anti-communist and a loyal ally to the United States. Castro and Betancourt publicly applauded each other's accomplishments, but their private encounter during Castro's visit did not go well. Betancourt later recalled that he briefly postponed their meeting after hearing about Castro's speech at the plaza and his speech in front of the congress, where—as he put it—Castro "launched a virulent diatribe against the armed forces of Latin America and little less than asked the firing squad for their officers." According to Betancourt, "I was so annoyed by the stupid way, deliberate or ingenuously stupid, in which the visitor had behaved in those days that I could not calmly have conducted an interview."[18] When the two men finally sat down together at Betancourt's home, Castro proposed that they "play a masterful game with the gringos," gambling that the Venezuelan leader would side with a fellow Latin American government against the United States. He asked Betancourt to lend him $300 million or the equivalent in crude petroleum. Castro's bet did not pay off in either alliances or money. Betancourt, already unimpressed with his "stupid" visitor, refused.[19] Castro would receive no solidarity, financial or otherwise, from his Venezuelan counterpart. Castro's visit to Venezuela, where he received fervent adulation from some sectors of the public and a cold reception from the president, was an early indication of the variety of ways in which Latin Americans would respond to the Cuban Revolution. It also foreshadowed the political divisions Cuba would exacerbate across the hemisphere.

## Communism and the Cuban Revolution

Even though Castro disavowed any communist leanings during the insurrection, he quickly cozied up to the communists after seizing power. Over the course of his first two years in power, he proceeded to establish close ties with the Soviet Union, radicalize Cuba's revolution, and integrate Cuban communists into positions of leadership throughout the government.

Before the Cuban Revolution, the Soviet Union mostly refrained from direct involvement in Latin American affairs. Instead, the Soviets pursued a pragmatic policy that could be considered diplomatic disruption, seizing opportunities to encourage and exploit anti-US sentiment in Latin America in order to lessen US influence.[20] Their modest program of outreach to Latin America in the first half of the twentieth century mostly consisted of maintaining a few embassies and building trade ties by offering generous lines of credit.[21]

In spite of the Soviet Union's hands-off approach to Latin America, numerous local Marxist-Leninist movements operated across the region. Some of these movements and parties had official ties to the Soviet Comintern; many others did not. Debates over whether to prioritize the interests of the Soviet Union, the international communist movement, or local objectives frequently spawned splinter groups, as did conflicts over whether to favor the strategy of armed struggle or political participation.[22] Internal disagreements were not the only challenge: Latin American communists also faced fierce opposition from both local anti-communists and the United States.

Opposition to communism formed one of the foundations of the inter-American regional security system that US and Latin American officials had built after World War II. At a 1947 conference in Brazil, the nations of the Americas signed a mutual security agreement called the Inter-American Treaty of Reciprocal Assistance, known as the Rio Treaty or Rio Pact. This treaty established a military alliance, declaring that "an armed attack by any State against an American State shall be considered an attack against all the American States."[23] A year later, at the meeting in Bogotá, Colombia, where the OAS was founded, members signed a pledge in which they declared that communism was incompatible with the inter-American system. From its very beginnings, the hemispheric security system was built on a shared understanding that communism posed a significant threat to security and sovereignty in the Americas.

Castro did not share other Latin American leaders' concerns about communism. He knew that his ambitious program of reform required both local support and international assistance and was eager to end Cuba's dependence on the United States. His first order of business was dismantling the old regime. Upon seizing power, Castro dissolved congress, abolished the traditional political parties, and disbanded the army, quickly consolidating power within his 26th of July Movement and, increasingly, the communist party. Castro's provisional government legalized Cuba's communist party mere days after coming to power. Moderates and liberals who initially served in the provisional government, including Prime Minister José Miró Cardona and President Manuel Urrutia, resigned in protest after a few months. Castro replaced Miró Cardona, taking over as prime minister in February, and the Popular Socialist Party's Oswaldo Dorticós Torrado replaced Urrutia in June. By then, other communists had taken up positions of authority, especially in the newly reorganized armed forces under the leadership of Fidel's brother, Raúl Castro.

The Popular Socialist Party's role in Cuba's future remained unsettled in the early years of the revolution. Anti-communism was prominent across broad swaths of Cuban society, including among union leaders, students, Catholic groups, the media, and civil society organizations. In addition to the sectors of society that opposed communism on principle, many on the political left and within the 26th of July Movement held the Popular Socialist Party in contempt for their hesitation in supporting the armed struggle against Batista. As the revolutionary government consolidated power, communist party militants jostled for position with members of the 26th of July Movement, facing off on numerous occasions. While Castro elevated individual communists to positions of authority, he also at times blamed their party for labor unrest and accused its members of "rabble-rousing" and counterrevolutionary activities.[24]

It is likely that much of Castro's public anti-communism in this early period was a calculated attempt to forestall foreign intervention until he had consolidated power at home and established reliable foreign alliances. Some of Castro's closest collaborators—his brother Raúl and Argentine doctor-turned-revolutionary Che Guevara—considered themselves Marxists, and Raúl had long been a sympathizer of Cuba's Popular Socialist Party. In addition to hiding their ties with Cuban communists, Castro and his collaborators were quiet and cautious in their early courtship of the Soviet Union. Raúl had begun putting out feelers even before the rebels seized power; he had become friends with the man who would become the KGB's top Latin America expert, Nikolai Sergeyevich Leonov, at a youth conference in Prague in 1953. In 1955 and 1956, during the Castro brothers' time in exile in Mexico organizing their revolution, they unsuccessfully asked the Soviet embassy for weapons to use against Batista and met regularly with Leonov, who had been sent to Mexico City to improve his Spanish.[25]

Over the course of the first two years of the revolutionary government, the Cubans and Soviets grew closer. Soviet leaders, initially cautious, came to see the Cuban Revolution as a chance to challenge the United States in its own backyard. As Leonov later recalled, "Cuba forced us to take a fresh look at the whole continent."[26] The Soviet Union officially recognized Cuba's new government on January 10, 1959, and in January and February, the 26th of July Movement's newspaper *Revolución* and Fidel Castro both called for the renewal of diplomatic relations with the Soviets.[27] In April, Raúl Castro sent Lázaro Peña, a leading Popular Socialist Party member and labor organizer, to Moscow to ask for military and intelligence advisers.[28]

Military ties laid the groundwork for economic and diplomatic relations, which in turn brought even closer military cooperation. Nikita Khrushchev immediately approved Raúl Castro's request for advisers and sent almost twenty Spanish Civil War veterans and Soviet officers of Spanish ancestry, at no cost, to Cuba.[29] Later that summer and fall, the Soviet Union and Cuba signed their first economic agreements. In October 1959, the Soviet Union sent KGB officer Aleksandr Alekseev as an unofficial envoy to Cuba. Alekseev, who arrived bearing vodka and caviar, told Castro of the Soviet people's great admiration for the Cuban Revolution.[30] The Cuban government invited Soviet first deputy premier Anastas Mikoyan—the second most powerful leader in the Soviet Union—to bring the Soviet Exhibit of Science, Technology, and Culture to Havana after stops in Mexico City and New York. At the end of Mikoyan's visit to Cuba in February 1960, he announced that Soviet and Cuban negotiators had concluded a major aid and trade agreement.[31] In April 1960, the Soviet Union agreed to sell Cuba crude oil at below-market prices. The two countries reestablished formal diplomatic relations that May.

An alliance with the Soviet Union and local communists solved many of Castro's problems, even as it created others. Collaborating with the Cuban communists gave Castro the manpower and organizational expertise he needed to pursue his ambitious reforms, and radicalizing the revolution helped him build an even broader base of support among Cuba's previously dispossessed and oppressed masses. Establishing ties with the Soviet Union— the only nation with enough disposable wealth and geopolitical motivation to challenge the United States—gave Castro a powerful foreign ally. The Soviets, for their part, gained their first toehold in the Americas.

## Two, Three, Many Revolutions

Whereas Castro and his fellow *barbudos* had enjoyed nearly universal acclaim immediately after seizing power, in the years following, their foreign and domestic supporters became fewer but more dedicated. As the revolutionary reforms multiplied and their effects became more tangible, Cuba-watchers realized that they were witnessing a true transformation and not just another change of upper management. Most moderate supporters of the Cuban Revolution followed in the footsteps of Venezuela's Betancourt and became disillusioned with Castro's embrace of communism and betrayal of his democratic promises. Those on the extremes of the ideological spectrum, however, concluded that the Cuban Revolution had ushered in a new era of possibility and were eager to participate.

Most Latin American devotees of the Cuban Revolution limited their efforts to peaceful activities, but an influential minority took steps to follow the Cuban path to power through armed struggle. In May 1960, Che Guevara published his *Guide to Guerrilla Warfare*, an instruction manual on revolution based on his interpretation of the Cuban experience. Guevara's lessons became the essence of the *foco* theory, the idea that a small, mobile band of guerrillas could operate in rural areas to create the conditions necessary to overthrow a repressive government. Guevara's theory was a clear departure from the traditional Marxist gradualist approach of party politics and workers' mobilization. It was immensely appealing to revolutionaries across the Americas who were tired of waiting for their countries to develop industrialized capitalist economies. They jumped at the idea that they could create their own conditions for change.

In Argentina, members of the left wing of the Peronist Party were among those who sought to emulate the Cuban Revolution. Half a generation earlier, in the 1940s and early 1950s, Argentine president Gen. Juan Domingo Perón had posed another influential, if idiosyncratic, challenge to US imperialism. Perón worked to create his own model of economic development, which he described as a Third Position that was neither capitalist nor communist; and he tried repeatedly to block US economic expansion in Argentina and other Latin American markets.[32] A military coup ousted Perón in 1955, but the general and his followers spent the next two decades continuing their efforts to influence the course of Argentine politics and inter-American relations.

A minority faction of the Peronist Party, known as "revolutionary Peronists," hoped to recover their party's anti-imperialist origins and bring Perón back to power by following the insurrectionary example of the Cuban Revolution. In October 1959, a small subgroup of the revolutionary Peronists formed a guerrilla army known as the Uturuncos (tiger or mountain lion in Quechua) in the mountains of the northwestern provinces of Tucumán and Salta. "I read about the triumphs of Fidel Castro, the mountains, the people involved there; and I said 'We can do that,'" one of the Uturunco comandantes recalled.[33] But their attempt to transplant the Cuban Revolution to Argentine soil failed. Most members turned themselves in, were arrested, or fled the country in less than a year.[34] When the Argentine army entered the Uturunco training camps, they found copies of Guevara's guerrilla manual but few remaining guerrillas.[35]

Events in Cuba reawakened a revolutionary movement in Nicaragua as well. Fifty years earlier, the United States had invaded the Central American land of lakes and volcanoes and established a virtual US protectorate backed by the Marines. In the 1920s, Gen. Augusto César Sandino organized an anti-imperialist guerrilla army that battled the US-backed government until the Marines left in 1933. Sandino became a martyr to his cause one year later. After leaving a dinner at the presidential palace, the revolutionary leader was captured and executed by Nicaragua's National Guard, thus ushering in the dictatorship of the Guard's leader, Anastasio Somoza García.[36] Somoza staged a coup in 1936 and built a family dynasty of repressive, exploitative rule. At the time of the Cuban Revolution, Anastasio Somoza's son, Luis Somoza Debayle, had been president for three years following his father's assassination, and his brother, Anastasio Somoza Debayle, was head of the National Guard.

The Cuban Revolution inspired multiple groups of Nicaraguans to revive their own country's revolutionary tradition and turn to armed struggle in their opposition to the Somozas. Carlos Fonseca Amador, a student activist and member of the Nicaraguan Socialist Party—the outlawed communist party in Nicaragua—and Tomás Borge, a former conservative-turned-Marxist student activist who had met Fidel Castro at a Latin American student conference in Colombia in 1948 and whose father had been involved with Sandino, were two of the foremost leaders of a young generation that was especially affected by the Cuban Revolution.[37] Borge recalled that "Fidel was for us the resurrection of Sandino!"[38] Castro's successful guerrilla struggle to overthrow a dictator convinced Fonseca and Borge that their own previous nonviolent efforts to oppose the Somoza dynasty were useless. As Fonseca later wrote, "We Nicaraguans began to recover some notion of ourselves with the outbreak of the new battle for liberation whose first definitive victory [had] as its stage, Cuba."[39] Like people across the Americas, Fonseca reinterpreted his own country's history and future through the lens of the Cuban Revolution. Cubans' success in ousting their dictator—and Castro and Guevara's success in emphasizing the guerrilla operations in the mountains—inspired a new generation to believe that armed struggle was the key to victory.

Fonseca and Borge joined dozens of other Nicaraguans in making the pilgrimage to Cuba after Castro's victory. The Cuban Revolution spurred Fonseca to use Sandino's ideology and image as a nationalist vehicle for his own fight against Somoza. Castro had, in fact, similarly used the legacy of Cuban independence hero José Martí in his war against Batista. Castro's experience had taught Fonseca and Borge that a successful revolution required local roots and a nationalist ideology, not just adherence to Marxist doctrine.[40] Fonseca and Borge decided to launch a new revolutionary political movement to re-vive Sandino's legacy and free Nicaragua from the Somozas. They joined with other members of the opposition to become the Sandinista Front of National Liberation (Frente Sandinista de Liberación Nacional) in 1961. "We are the *fidelista* generation," Fonseca declared, promising to establish in Nicaragua "the second free territory of the Americas."[41]

The Cuban government provided the Nicaraguan revolutionaries with fi-nancial support and training and encouraged some veterans of the Cuban Revolution to join them. Che Guevara helped organize disparate factions of Nicaraguan exiles into a group called the Nicaraguan Revolutionary Move-ment and appointed Nicaraguan exile and former National Guard officer Ra-fael Somarriba as leader. In June 1959, Somarriba's motley assemblage of sixty revolutionaries attempted to launch an invasion of Nicaragua from neighbor-ing Honduras, but they were routed by Honduran soldiers working with the Nicaraguan National Guard. Six members of the guerrilla group were killed, three others were captured and executed, fifteen were wounded—including Carlos Fonseca, who was shot in the lung—and the rest surrendered. Fonseca was brought back to Cuba to recover in a Havana hospital, and after recuper-ating, he continued to plot and train with Borge and Guevara.[42]

Argentine and Nicaraguan revolutionaries were just some of the thousands of Latin Americans who received Cuban training and other forms of support and solidarity in their efforts to reproduce the Cuban Revolution in their own countries. In 1959 alone, Cubans participated in and supported three addi-tional failed revolutions against the governments of Panama, Haiti, and the Dominican Republic.[43] Thousands of would-be guerrillas, mostly young men, traveled to the island in the early 1960s, and many matriculated in Cuban schools for ideological indoctrination and military training. French diplomats reporting from Havana estimated that between 1,000 and 1,500 Latin Amer-icans received revolutionary training in the year 1962 alone.[44] Of that total, the largest number of trainees came from Venezuela (approximately 200), while most of the others came from Peru, Bolivia, Ecuador, Argentina, British Guiana, and various parts of Africa. Latin American revolutionaries who man-aged to gain acceptance into the Cuban training schools and who finished the rigorous courses returned to their home countries ready to spread the gospel of the Cuban Revolution.

## Counterrevolution

The Cuban Revolution inspired equally powerful reactions among its ene-mies. Opposition started early, when revolutionary tribunals publicly exe-cuted former Batista henchmen, and it increased as Castro's government became less democratic, promoted revolution in neighboring countries, and moved further into the Soviet orbit. Cubans themselves were among the first and loudest to protest the extremist turn of their government and its increasing alignment with the Soviet Union.

The first anti-communist demonstrations within Cuba took place in response to Soviet first deputy premier Anastas Mikoyan's visit to the island in February 1960. On the morning of February 5, Mikoyan stopped by Havana's Central Park to pay his respects at the monument to the leader of Cuba's independence movement, José Martí, and deposited a floral offering of a giant globe adorned with a hammer and sickle. After Mikoyan left the park, a group of about 100 young protesters marched to the monument with a counteroffering of a Cuban flag made of flowers, bearing a banner that read: "To you, our Apostle—to make amends for the visit of the assassin Mikoyan."[45] The students' protest devolved into a bloody confrontation with revolutionary police and militia members.

Some of the organizers of the anti-communist demonstration fled into hiding in Cuba and into exile in the following months and went on to form the Revolutionary Student Directorate (Directorio Revolucionario Estudiantil) in the fall of 1960. This group adopted the name of the earlier, pro-Catholic Revolutionary Directorate that had participated in the struggle against Batista. The name symbolized their goal to reclaim what they saw as the original nature of the Cuban Revolution as a nationalist, democratic struggle.[46] Members of the Revolutionary Student Directorate in exile linked up with the Central Intelligence Agency and used the CIA's generous funding of thousands of dollars a month to build a vast transnational network of offices, with delegations in seventeen countries by mid-1962. The organization published and distributed anti-Castro propaganda through its radio programs and bulletin *Trinchera* (trench). The directorate also had a paramilitary branch that operated without CIA funding—and sometimes in direct contradiction to US policy—whose clandestine activities included launching commando raids on Cuban coastal targets.[47] In the summer of 1962, the group condemned what it saw as Kennedy's weak stance on Cuba and its Soviet allies in a headline on the cover of *Trinchera*: "Peaceful coexistence, No! War, Yes!"[48]

The Revolutionary Student Directorate was one among many organizations that operated within Cuba and, more often, from exile, in opposition to Castro's government. Anti-Castro groups ran the ideological gamut from the Anti-Communist Legion of the Caribbean on the far right, to the moderate liberal democratic umbrella group Democratic Revolutionary Front (Frente Revolucionario Democrático), to the noncommunist leftist People's Revolutionary Movement, founded by disillusioned veterans of the insurrection who had briefly served in the revolutionary government. These opposition groups varied widely in political ideology and tactics, but all agreed that Cuba's ties with the Soviet Union and their country's transformation into a communist state were unacceptable.

The foes of Castro's government, denied elections, voted with their feet. Cuban émigrés thought their exile would be temporary, a brief escape until Uncle Sam sent in the cavalry—or the CIA or the Marines—to remove Castro. More than 200,000 Cubans who left for political and economic reasons formed the first wave of exiles between 1959 and 1962. This exodus began with Batista's supporters, or *batistianos*, who left immediately after the dictator's departure, followed soon thereafter by members of the upper and middle classes who had lost their jobs, properties, and investments to government expropriations and nationalizations, or who had been Castro supporters and were now disheartened with the radical turn of the revolution.[49] As Castro's government became increasingly intolerant of political dissent, more and more of his opponents turned to emigration as a last resort. Most, but not all, moved to Miami, where many of these upper- and middle-class Cubans already had long-standing social, economic, and cultural ties.[50] The US government eased visa restrictions and provided this largely privileged, white, Catholic group an extraordinarily enthusiastic welcome, especially as the wave of emigration was politically embarrassing for Castro. The Cuban government, meanwhile, grudgingly allowed political opponents to leave as a sort of safety valve to release domestic discontent.

The Cuban exodus had enormous ramifications in both Cuba and the United States. The presence of hundreds of thousands of Cubans on US soil aided both countries' intelligence efforts: Castro's spies infiltrated the exile community, and the CIA offices in Miami became the largest outside of its headquarters in Langley, Virginia. The relocation of most of Castro's critics from the island to the mainland cemented the impression within Cuba that the main threat to its national security came from outside the country. The reduction of local opposition allowed Castro to further consolidate his regime, leaving the remaining opposition isolated and confined largely to the countryside. At the same time, the wave of exiles also weakened Cuba's economy and society, constituting a brain drain of the experts and experienced professionals who could have facilitated, and perhaps even moderated, the revolution's reforms. In the United States, the Cuban exiles utterly transformed Miami, where they eventually outnumbered US-born residents and paved the way for more Latin American immigration, earning Miami the nickname of "the northernmost Latin American city."[51] Cuban exiles formed a vocal— and eventually very powerful—political bloc that pushed relentlessly for an aggressive foreign policy against Castro. The most ambitious among them became the latest in a long tradition of Cuban and other Latin American exiles to plot revolution—or counterrevolution—from the relative safety of foreign soil.

In addition to inspiring counterrevolutionary movements among Cubans, the repudiation of Castro's revolution also energized anti-communists and radicalized moderates in other parts of Latin America. Foes of the Cuban Revolution organized across national lines, within their countries, and at the grassroots levels. Just like in Cuba, opposition to the Cuban Revolution could be found across the political spectrum, from the authoritarian far right to the liberal, democratic left. And just like in Cuba, opposition took many forms, from political organizing to public denunciations to paramilitary violence. The Cuban *foco* theory inspired not only those who sought to promote revolution but also those who worked to prevent it. In Mexico, for example, new organizations grew out of alliances between conservative students, Church authorities, businessmen, the right wing of the ruling Institutional Revolutionary Party (Partido Revolucionario Institucional), and the conservative National Action Party. One of the most influential of these groups, the University Movement of Renovating Orientation (Movimiento Universitario de Renovadora Orientación [MURO]), emerged after a violent confrontation between pro-Castro and anti-communist students on the campus of the National Autonomous University of Mexico on July 26, 1961. Members of this semi-clandestine paramilitary Catholic student organization were focused predominantly on Mexican politics but also indulged in the occasional burning of Castro effigies. Mexican intelligence agents reported that members of MURO attended secret training camps where the young men studied sabotage and read Che Guevara's *Guide to Guerrilla Warfare* while the women trained in espionage.[52]

And while some groups and individuals across Latin America used the example of the Cuban Revolution to push for change in their own countries, many others clung to stability and continuity. In Argentina, a French colonel who had spent two years advising the Argentine army published an article in the *Magazine of the Superior War School* in February 1962 in which he warned: "The most effective and insidious 'transmission belt' of communism in Argentina is clearly *fidelismo*, which can take advantage of the permanence of an old anti-American sentiment and the availability of a Peronist mass." The colonel further explained that the Cuban experience showed that communists could "capture" a nationalist party, and that even a small group of intellectuals could spark a revolution. "After enlisting the masses under a nationalist banner, they can, more or less progressively, divert the movement towards Castroism, popular democracy and communism."[53] The colonel interpreted nationalism—or the struggle for sovereignty—and popular democracy as facades behind which to hide communist penetration in the Americas. He congratulated his Argentine hosts on the strides that they had already made in combating the communist threat, pointing to the elimination of the revolutionary Peronist Uturuncos as a particular success. He encouraged his hosts to continue working on improving civilian-military coordination, cooperation among the various branches of the Argentine armed forces, and intelligence sharing among the governments of the Americas in the fight against revolution.

## Conclusion

The Cuban Revolution ushered in a new phase of the hemispheric Cold War. The revolution responded to both immediate and long-standing problems within Cuba and in Cuban-US relations. Fidel Castro and other Cuban revolutionaries fought first and foremost to oust US-backed dictator Fulgencio Batista, but they also promised to bring political sovereignty and economic security to the island. Castro knew that the kind of deep reforms he envisioned—massive redistributions of property and wealth—would no doubt meet significant resistance among Cuba's upper class and in the United States. He found local partners among Cuban communists and an external ally in the Soviet Union. For the first time since World War II, a Latin American government began cultivating close military ties with a foreign power outside the hemisphere, and everyone took notice.

# CHAPTER 2
# COUNTERREVOLUTION
# AND CONTAINMENT

The Cuban Revolution's destabilizing effects posed a serious challenge to governments across the hemisphere. US and Latin American leaders agreed that having a member of the inter-American community join the Soviet bloc was undesirable. Where they failed to find common ground was in their responses. Some political leaders advocated for a policy of forbearance. They argued that even though the radical turn of the Cuban Revolution was hardly ideal, the rest of the Americas needed to respect the sovereignty of the Cuban people by allowing them to solve their own problems and determine their own fate. Others claimed that Castro's exporting of revolution and his alliance with the Soviets threatened the security of the entire hemisphere; in their eyes, Castro's encouragement of other Latin American revolutionaries posed an internal threat, while his relations with the Soviet Union opened the hemisphere to external intervention. These opponents of the Cuban Revolution pushed for a military solution. Still others advocated for multilateral diplomatic actions, arguing that whereas intervention violated the foundational principles of inter-American relations, isolation would help contain the Cuban Revolution and perhaps even strangle it. Government officials in the United States, long accustomed to seeing themselves as regional leaders, found that their failure to establish a coherent US foreign policy toward Castro's Cuba undermined their ability to orchestrate an effective, unified hemispheric response.

## Self-Determination and Nonintervention

The leaders of two of the largest and most powerful countries in the Americas started off as vocal defenders of the Cuban Revolution. At least in public, government officials in Mexico and Brazil celebrated the Cuban Revolution and its reform efforts.[1] As Castro's government moved ever further into the Soviet sphere, Mexico and Brazil's leaders muted their praise but still defended the Cuban people's right to self-determination and nonintervention—in other words, their right to sovereignty.

At the time of the Cuban Revolution, Mexico was preparing to celebrate the fiftieth anniversary of its own revolution, and the events on the neighboring island inspired many Mexican citizens to reflect on whether their country had abandoned its celebrated legacy. Critics, including former president Lázaro Cárdenas, accused their government of betraying the nationalist, populist roots of the Mexican Revolution and the radical Constitution of 1917, and they pointed out that the nation's leaders had become much more economically and politically conservative since Cárdenas left office in 1940. President Adolfo López Mateos, a member of Mexico's semi-authoritarian Institutional Revolutionary Party, sought to use his country's solidarity with Cuba to keep his party's left wing in check and bolster Mexico's revolutionary image. Furthermore, relations with Cuba were part of López Mateos's larger "global pivot," a geopolitical strategy that sought to counterbalance US influence through political and economic engagement with other potential partners and movements.[2]

In the first years after Castro's victory, President López Mateos publicly embraced the Cuban Revolution and its leaders. When Cuban president Oswaldo Dorticós visited Mexico as part of a presidential tour of Latin America in June 1960, López Mateos gave him the warmest reception of his journey, declaring in his welcome speech, "We, who have travelled similar paths, understand and value the transformative effort that Cuba is undertaking."[3]

López Mateos's declarations of solidarity became more muted after Castro announced that his government was communist, but Mexican diplomats still defended Cuban sovereignty by resisting the use of force or multilateral actions against Cuba. In May 1961, Mexico's foreign minister Manuel Tello held a private meeting with the US ambassador to Mexico, Thomas C. Mann, in which the two men debated the nature of the Cuban threat and appropriate responses. When Mann argued in favor of direct intervention to dislodge Castro, Tello vehemently disagreed, countering that "external attacks against Cuba's revolutionary government would do nothing but strengthen it and its sympathizers in Latin America. The Cubans should be left to solve their own problems." When Mann then floated the idea of international sanctions through the Organization of American States (OAS), Tello also rejected that approach and offered instead to mediate between the United States and Cuba.[4] Half a year later, at the January 1962 OAS meeting in Punta del Este, Uruguay, Tello followed through on his conversation with Mann and abstained from voting on resolutions that applied sanctions on Cuba and expelled the country from the organization. He claimed that his actions were based on Mexico's traditional dedication to the principles of self-determination and nonintervention.[5]

Brazilian leaders also praised Castro's government and defended Cuban sovereignty. At the time of the Cuban Revolution, Brazilian politics were in a state of transition. As President Juscelino Kubitschek's term was coming to an end, the eccentric, charismatic governor of the state of São Paulo, Jânio Quadros, campaigned to replace him. Political outsider Quadros ran on an anti-corruption and anti-inflation platform symbolized by a broom and gained support from numerous parties across the political spectrum. Quadros indicated that he planned to make significant changes to Brazilian foreign policy. Instead of traveling to Washington, DC, during his campaign, as was the tradition for Brazilian politicians, Quadros accepted an invitation from Fidel Castro to visit Havana in March 1960. There, Quadros was received as an important state guest; held meetings with Castro, Guevara, and Dorticós; and deposited a wreath at the tomb of José Martí. Quadros was accompanied by a large entourage, including some of the leaders of Brazil's Peasant Leagues (Ligas Camponesas), an autonomous rural social movement, led by revolutionary communist lawyer Francisco Julião, that fought for radical agrarian reform in the impoverished northeastern region of the country. The Ligas representatives made contact with the Cuban communist party during the visit, and thereafter the Peasant Leagues began establishing committees of solidarity with Cuba, and the Cuban government began supporting the Ligas.[6] Upon his return to Brazil, Quadros told reporters that "the reforms undertaken by Prime Minister Fidel Castro are contributing to the construction of a New World that is awakening now in America. Our duty is to protect the Cuban Government and people."[7]

Soon after Quadros swept the elections and became president in January 1961, his effusive celebration of Cuba's revolutionary leaders caused him trouble at home. That August, Quadros arranged for Che Guevara to stop by Brasília on his way back to Cuba from the OAS meeting in Punta del Este, Uruguay.[8] Quadros presented the revolutionary hero with the Order of the Southern Cross (Cruzeiro do Sul), the highest Brazilian award conferred on foreign dignitaries. The fact that Brazil's president bestowed such honors on a communist rabble-rouser outraged Brazilian conservatives. The same day that Quadros decorated Guevara, top conservative politician and governor of Guanabara Carlos Lacerda, known as the "destroyer of presidents," held his own ceremony in which he presented Cuban exile leader and longtime anti-communist politician Manuel Antonio 'Tony' Varona with the keys to the city of Rio de Janeiro.[9]

Quadros's decision to honor Guevara may have been the last straw for his already strained political coalition. The president's economic austerity policies had alienated the popular classes and the left wing of Brazil's political spectrum, while his self-described "independent" foreign policy—especially his friendly relations with Cuba, Yugoslavia, and the Soviet Union—had angered conservatives.[10] A few days after Guevara left Brazil, Quadros abruptly resigned from the presidency; in a cryptic letter of explanation, he blamed the "terrible" internal and foreign reactionary forces.[11] Correspondents from Cuba's Prensa Latina news agency speculated that a conspiracy among the CIA, Carlos Lacerda, and "a group of fascist military personnel" had pushed Quadros out.[12] The most common explanation, however, was that Quadros had expected that the public would protest his departure and demand his return; after all, that ploy had worked for Fidel Castro when he had briefly resigned as prime minister in July 1959, and it had worked for Quadros himself when he temporarily resigned as presidential candidate in November 1959.[13] He probably calculated that even his vocal conservative critics like Lacerda would change their tune and that the military would intervene to assure his return, especially considering that the alternative was his vice president, João Goulart, a leftist politician from the Brazilian Labor Party (Partido Trabalhista Brasileiro). But Quadros's gambit failed. After ten days of crisis and uncertainty, the Brazilian congress and military agreed to allow Goulart to become president after passing a constitutional amendment that established a parliamentary system that severely curtailed presidential powers.

After Quadros's tumultuous departure, his successor, Goulart, maintained Brazil's solidarity with Cuba. When Goulart's ambassador to Washington, moderate economist Roberto de Oliveira Campos, presented his credentials to Kennedy in October 1961, he advised the US president to avoid using force against Castro and to instead pursue a strategy of "hopeful vigilance."[14] At the January 1962 OAS meeting, Brazil joined Mexico in abstaining from voting on resolutions that expelled Cuba from the organization and instituted sanctions against the island. Brazilian foreign minister San Tiago Dantas pushed instead for a "constructive solution" to the Cuban problem, warning that the members of the OAS "would destroy the inter-American system the day that we consider armed intervention as a means capable . . . of eliminating a political regime."[15] He argued that Cuba should be brought back into the inter-American community, not ostracized and pushed further into the Soviet bloc. To that end, the Brazilian government joined the Mexican government at various moments in trying to mediate between Cuba and the United States, with little success.

## The Interventionists

In stark contrast to Mexican and Brazilian leaders' defense of Cuba's sovereignty, other Latin American government officials argued that the Cuban threat required a more drastic solution. Some, such as Nicaraguan dictator Luis Somoza Debayle, Haitian despot François "Papa Doc" Duvalier, and Dominican strongman Rafael Trujillo, clashed with Castro immediately and violently. Castro's long-standing involvement with Caribbean Basin anti-dictatorial efforts made these leaders early opponents of the Cuban Revolution, even before their fellow tyrant Fulgencio Batista fled in disgrace. Trujillo had provided weapons to Batista when he was still in power and in asylum, after his fall. Trujillo also sheltered many of Batista's followers after Castro took over, and he teamed up with Duvalier in solidarity with Cuban exile efforts to retake power.[16]

However, to the surprise of many observers, the first government targeted in Cubans' export of revolution was not any of these three notorious dictatorships but the nominally democratic government of Panama. In Panama, a small group of families was struggling to maintain oligarchical hold over the nation's politics through personal ties, fraudulent elections, and the occasional coup and assassination.[17] Ernesto de la Guardia, Panama's president at the time of the Cuban Revolution, was trying, like many of his predecessors, to negotiate more favorable arrangements with the United States regarding the Panama Canal. He had seen little progress, and in 1958, Panamanian students engaging in Operation Sovereignty planted sixty-five Panamanian flags in the US-controlled Canal Zone and held demonstrations demanding more schools and financial aid, which led to deadly clashes between the demonstrators and Panama's National Guard.[18] The following year, unrest over the question of the Canal Zone increased on November 3, the anniversary of Panamanian independence, when a group of politicians and students led a protest march and once again tried to fly the Panamanian flag in the Canal Zone. Army units, Zone police, and the National Guard injured numerous demonstrators, who in turn burned US buildings.[19]

While President de la Guardia was trying to control this internal turmoil, he faced threats from both Cuban-inspired and Cuban-supported Panamanian revolutionaries. In April 1959, a group of young men calling themselves the Movement of Revolutionary Action (Movimiento de Acción Revolucionario) tried to establish a guerrilla base in the mountains of western Panama. These would-be revolutionaries proclaimed that their goals were to end US control of the Canal Zone, improve Panama's educational system, and overthrow Panama's corrupt government. The head of Panama's National Guard put a young officer, Omar Torrijos, in charge of a task force assigned to root out the guerrilla group.[20] Torrijos's men made quick work of the ill-prepared and poorly organized revolutionaries, though Torrijos did suffer some injuries in a firefight. The guerrillas scattered; some were killed, others were captured, and most made it to Panama City and took refuge in foreign embassies. Later that same month, two cousins of President de la Guardia launched a separate revolutionary effort from Cuban shores. This attempt to overthrow the

Panamanian government also failed in a matter of days, despite the support and manpower provided by Cuban revolutionaries. President de la Guardia sent out the National Guard and appealed to the OAS and US Caribbean Command in the Canal Zone for support. The Guatemalan government showed solidarity by sending weapons and airplanes to aid in their neighbor's defense, and the governments of Colombia and Ecuador promised assistance as well. Fidel Castro, who was concluding a tour of North America at the time, denied involvement and condemned the invasion, but the fact that Cubans outnumbered Panamanians more than ten to one in the expedition made Cuban participation hard to ignore.[21]

Cuban solidarity with other Latin American revolutionary groups, alongside Cuba's guerrilla training program, gave Castro's opponents plenty of evidence that the new Cuban government threatened the security and stability of the hemisphere. Nicaraguan and Dominican officials broke diplomatic relations with Cuba, brought numerous complaints against Cuba before the OAS, and protested when the organization failed to take decisive action.[22] The OAS held two emergency meetings in San José, Costa Rica, in August 1960. The second meeting produced the "Declaration of San José," which denounced "the intervention or the threat of intervention by an extracontinental power in the affairs of the American republics" but did not specifically call out Cuba or apply any sanctions.[23] Panama's foreign minister, Galileo Solís, reported that the meeting "gave the depressing impression of a lack of character and decision to face a problem that everyone could clearly see."[24] Guatemalan leaders took matters into their own hands and threatened to declare war on Cuba in November 1960 after accusing Castro's government of supporting a local uprising.[25] Nicaragua's Somoza also warned that "if our lethargy continues, we will awaken someday to a Red Central America."[26] Guatemalan and Nicaraguan requests for aid in the fight against Castro pushed President Dwight Eisenhower into action; he responded by sending US Navy warships to patrol the Caribbean, the first public US military attempt to contain the spread of the Cuban Revolution.[27]

## The Bay of Pigs Invasion

By the time that the Eisenhower administration sent Navy ships to the Caribbean, it was already deeply involved in a covert operation to overthrow Fidel Castro. After a period of uncertainty following Castro's initial victory, US leaders began to embrace more forceful policies by the end of 1959. Cuba's increasingly close ties with the Soviet Union were part of the problem, as was the nationalization of businesses and other properties owned by US investors and corporations. When Cuban exiles who had fled to the

United States began taking to the skies and dropping leaflets and bombs in Cuba, Castro used that as evidence that the Cuban Revolution was under attack. On October 26, 1959, the revolutionary government announced the formation of a people's militia (what would become the National Revolutionary Militia, or Milicia Nacional Revolucionaria) and called for a mass rally to protest the "foreign aggression." At the rally, Castro waved a rifle while electrifying the audience of some 400,000 angry Cubans by exclaiming: "Every day our enemies are more insolent and audacious, and we must defend ourselves. The world must know that the Cubans will die fighting against any internal or foreign enemies."[28]

After the rally, US leaders had had enough. Even one of the most dedicated proponents of moderation and patience in US policy, the ambassador to Cuba, Philip Bonsal, recalled that "Castro's performance of October 26 on the 'bombing' spelled the end of my hope for rational relations between Cuba and the United States."[29] Two weeks after the rally, Secretary of State Christian Herter sent Eisenhower a proposal to end the US strategy of forbearance and cooperation and instead begin "a step-by-step development of coherent opposition" to the Castro regime.[30] The new year began with an exchange of protest notes between the US and Cuban governments over expropriations and exile attacks, and then news of the Soviet-Cuban trade agreement and resumption of diplomatic relations struck another blow.

US-Cuban relations became even more strained after the French ship *La Coubre*, loaded with Belgian weapons, exploded at the Havana docks on March 4, 1960. There were, in fact, two explosions: a small first blast, followed thirty minutes later by a much larger one. "At first I thought it was an atomic bomb, it scared the life out of me," Cuban police captain Juan Luís Rodríguez Infante, who lost a leg in the aftermath of the explosions, recalled years later.[31] The skies blackened over Havana, ash rained down for days, and nearly all the windows in the neighborhood surrounding the harbor were shattered. The explosions killed at least seventy-five crewmembers, dockworkers, first responders, and civilians who had rushed to the scene to help, and injured hundreds more. The cause of the disaster became a matter of intense controversy. US authorities blamed careless Cuban dockworkers; Cuban authorities claimed that terrorists had planted bombs on board the ship when it stopped in Miami on its way to Cuba.[32] At the funeral for the victims, Castro gave a rousing speech in which he claimed that the explosions were the result of sabotage, part of US efforts to keep Cuba unarmed and defenseless. He also spoke the words that became the Cuban Revolution's new slogan: "Patria o Muerte" (Homeland or Death).[33] Huge crowds cheered, and photographer Alberto Korda snapped what would become an iconic photograph—now a staple of T-shirts, posters, and album covers—of a solemn, determined Che Guevara gazing out at the scene. The terrifying detonations fueled the sense among Cubans that they were under attack.

Two weeks after the *La Coubre* explosions, Eisenhower approved a top-secret CIA Program of Covert Action to undermine Castro's government. The proposal included launching a propaganda offensive, creating a civilian op-position outside the island, strengthening the anti-Castro underground move-ment within Cuba, and developing a "small paramilitary force" that would be "introduced" into Cuba to organize, train, and lead resistance groups.[34] The plan was modeled on the CIA's successful operation to overthrow Jacobo Ar-benz's government in Guatemala in 1954, and various veterans of the Guate-malan intervention were assigned to lead the operation against Castro.

Although directed and funded by the CIA and the White House, the coun-terrevolutionary expedition that would become known as Operation Zapata was a multinational affair. After receiving Eisenhower's blessing, the CIA brought together several Cuban exile factions to form the Democratic Revolu-tionary Front (Frente Revolucionario Democrático), began screening recruits in April 1960, and set up a training camp at US Army installations in Panama.[35] Eventually the group came to include Cubans recruited from exile communi-ties across the Americas—New York, Miami, Mexico, Panama, Guatemala, and Venezuela.[36] The Guatemalan and Nicaraguan governments had volunteered to participate in US-led covert counterrevolutionary programs even before Eisenhower approved the plans, and the CIA accepted their offers and shifted most of the operation to training camps in Retalhuleu, Guatemala, and to airstrips and docking facilities in Nicaragua.[37] Secrecy was particularly hard to maintain in Guatemala: The Guatemalan newspaper *La Hora* leaked news of the training camps as early as October 1960, describing rumors among Cuban exiles that the preparations were "well under way."[38] US newspapers also re-ported on invasion preparations around the same time, providing specific details about the training camps in Guatemala.[39] A CIA postmortem report concluded that "the project had lost its covert nature by November 1960."[40]

By the time that Kennedy was elected president and learned the details of the plans, preparations were well underway for a full-scale military inter-vention. Over the course of 1960, the operation had ballooned from the in-troduction of small two- or three-man paramilitary units to the creation of a 1,400-man amphibious assault force known as Brigade 2506. Correspond-ingly, emphasis among the planners shifted from strengthening Cuba's coun-terrevolutionary guerrilla groups and other internal opposition to building a strike force capable of securing a beachhead and establishing a liberated zone from which a new provisional government could wage a civil war against

Castro.[41] In the weeks leading up to Kennedy's inauguration on January 20, 1961, Eisenhower broke diplomatic relations with Cuba and advised his successor, "We cannot have the present government [in Cuba] go on."[42] During Kennedy's first White House briefing, CIA director Allen Dulles filled him in on the plan's progress and warned the new president that the window for action was closing because Castro's control over the island was becoming ever tighter, and his regime was continuing to receive arms shipments from the Eastern Bloc. Simultaneously, a brief mutiny among the Cuban trainees in Guatemala over the political line of the brigade and the inclusion of former Batista loyalists sent the message that the uneasy alliance among the exile groups would not hold much longer.[43] Kennedy continued to allow the plans to proceed, despite warnings from numerous advisers. During Kennedy's first briefing, the chairman of the Joint Chiefs of Staff questioned the military viability of the operation, and Secretary of State Dean Rusk predicted the potentially disastrous effect such a brazen intervention could have on the United States' reputation in Latin America.[44] As the final preparations took place over the next two months, Kennedy insisted on changes that would ostensibly hide the United States' guiding hand in the operation, but he passed up every opportunity to cancel what he must have seen as his best chance to remove Castro.

The Bay of Pigs invasion would go down in history not only as one of Kennedy's biggest mistakes but also as one of the greatest failures of US foreign policy. On the morning of April 15, eight B-26 airplanes piloted by Cuban exiles took off from Nicaragua; their aim was to wipe out Castro's air force ahead of the invasion. The results of the air raid were disappointing: U-2 reconnaissance photos taken the next day revealed that the raid had disabled at most half of the Cuban government's planes. As the brigade's convoy of ships approached Cuba, Kennedy, still determined to conceal the United States' role, made the controversial decision to cancel two follow-up rounds of air strikes. Nicaragua's small air force volunteered to send its own planes to aid the Cuban exiles, but the US government prevented this by refusing to allow Nicaraguan planes to refuel in Key West.[45]

From that inauspicious start, things continued to get worse for the members of Brigade 2506. When they arrived at Playa Girón and the nearby Playa Larga in the predawn hours of April 17, they encountered unexpected coral reefs, lost their surprise entry in shootouts with local militia, and struggled with their own rusty and poorly prepared equipment. Castro's still very lethal air force targeted the brigade's ships, managing to sink one, blow up another that carried most of the brigade's supplies, and drive away the rest before they could unload much of their cargo. A few Cuban and US pilots flying sorties out of Nicaragua eventually provided some air cover, but it was not enough. The exile troops that managed to make it to land were significantly outgunned and outmanned, marooned on a narrow beachhead, and in urgent need of ammunition and medical supplies. They held off Castro's forces for two days before being overrun on the afternoon of April 19. The majority were eventually captured, marched in front of cameras, interrogated, and imprisoned.

Though there were multiple US errors that contributed to the failure of the Bay of Pigs invasion, it is also important to recognize that Castro and the Cuban people worked hard to win their David versus Goliath victory. The Cuban government was ready for the coming attack, thanks to its extensive network of counterintelligence agents and the detailed reports in the US press. In December 1960, the founder and director of Cuba's news agency Prensa Latina, Argentine revolutionary Jorge Masetti, discovered and decoded detailed plans for the invasion hidden within wire cable communications between the United States and Guatemala.[46] In February 1961, the Cuban minister of foreign relations sent a memorandum to all the governments of the hemisphere in which he denounced the imminent invasion.[47] The Cuban military was also closely tracking the activities of its US counterparts and issued detailed reports, such as one from March 1961 that described the movements of three destroyers between Florida and Panama and warned "they are preparing some kind of attack on our island."[48]

In the days and months before the invasion, the Cuban government and Cuban people wasted no time preparing. Committees for the Defense of the Revolution (militant neighborhood watch groups) and government officials rounded up as many as 100,000 potential and suspected political opponents to prevent a popular uprising, while Castro fortified the coasts and put his army and militia on high alert.[49] The day after the air strikes, he held a funeral for the seven victims. During his speech, he compared the air attack to Pearl Harbor and prepared his audience of 10,000 for war, warning them that the real battle was still to come. "The United States sponsored the attack because it cannot forgive us for achieving a socialist revolution under their noses," he told his listeners, publicly describing the Cuban Revolution as socialist for the first time.[50] Castro also criticized the "lackey" governments of Central America that had provided their national territory for air bases and training.[51]

During the invasion, Cubans and supporters of the Cuban Revolution rallied to the defense of the island. Some 20,000 Cuban troops, pilots, and militia members fought on the beaches and in the swamps of the Bay of Pigs, and as many as 5,000 lost their lives in the process.[52] Soviet military supplies aided their efforts. In the waning months of 1960, the US embassy in Havana had noticed that Soviet bloc weapons, including small arms, light artillery, tanks, aircraft, and truck-mounted rocket launchers, were "pouring" into Cuba.[53] Raúl Castro later recalled that the Soviet supplies arrived just in time to help save Cuba's revolutionary government. "There were tankers and artillerymen who learned how to maneuver with these weapons on their way from Havana to Playa Girón," he recounted.[54] Fidel Castro and Oswaldo Dorticós issued a call to "the people of the Americas and the world," asking for solidarity. They made a special exhortation "to our Latin American brothers: make the North American imperialists feel the incontestable force of your action."[55]

Across Latin America, people outraged by the invasion were quick to answer Castro's call. The secretary-general of Chile's communist party, Luis Corvalán, flew to Cuba in the middle of the invasion to help defend the revolution.[56] In Lima, Peru, protesters held three demonstrations at San Marcos University; at one of these gatherings, US journalist Carleton Beals—who was famous for, among other things, interviewing Augusto Sandino—denounced the "US imperialist invasion" and warned the 500 people gathered there that it could lead to World War III.[57] In Bolivia, the invasion set off violent riots among students and workers. Protesters burned American flags, stoned the US and Guatemalan embassies, and lined up to donate blood to the Cuban army.[58] Police in Montevideo, Uruguay, used tear gas to disperse a demonstration of 3,000 people, while police in Bogotá, Colombia, fired their rifles and advanced with bayonets to defend the US embassy from a crowd of 1,500 people shouting, "Cuba sí, Yankees no!" In Recife, Brazil, Francisco Julião gathered a crowd of 2,000 in front of the US consulate and gave a stirring speech in which he blamed the invasion on "the imperialist bandit Kennedy and Wall Street."[59] One student in Caracas, Venezuela, was killed in a confrontation with police, and in Maracaibo, Venezuela, another student and a police officer were killed.[60] Guatemalan university students marching in protest of their country's involvement in the Bay of Pigs invasion came under fire from a group of well-armed anti-communists, who killed three of the demonstrators and injured numerous others.[61]

The Bay of Pigs invasion and the wave of fury that it unleashed had serious repercussions for inter-American relations and for Kennedy's and Castro's reputations. After initially trying to hide US involvement, Kennedy changed course and owned his defeat. Less than a week after the invasion, the White House put out a statement that "President Kennedy has stated from the beginning that he bears sole responsibility for the events of the past days."[62] The fact that the United States had organized and funded the invasion of a neighboring country fanned nationalist and anti-imperialist sentiment across the region. Eight thousand people from across the political spectrum gathered for the largest demonstration that Montevideo had seen in years to protest a speech that Kennedy gave on April 20, in which he asserted the US right to defend the hemisphere from communist aggression. The demonstrators interpreted the speech and the invasion as a renewed US policy of intervention, and speakers from political parties on both the left and the right called Kennedy "the worst imperialist in fifty years."[63] At the same time, proponents of intervention such as Cuban exiles and Nicaragua's Anastasio Somoza called Kennedy weak and never forgave him for betraying the members of Brigade 2506. "If the United States had maintained its commitment to the invaders of the Bay of Pigs, Castro would not exist today," Somoza told a biographer almost twenty years later.[64]

Castro and other Cuban leaders, by contrast, reveled in their victory and used the opportunity to consolidate their control at home and their popularity abroad. In the days after the invasion, Castro took foreign journalists on tours of the battlefields and gave numerous speeches and interviews on how the heroic Cuban people had defended their sovereignty against the imperialists and their mercenaries.[65] During the televised interrogations of the Bay of Pigs prisoners, journalists dug into all the details of the preparations for the invasion, including the fact that Guatemalan president Miguel Ydígoras Fuentes had visited the training camps on two occasions and described Brigade 2506 as "the security of Guatemala."[66] According to the prisoners, Kennedy was not the only president who had been counting on the Cuban exile forces. Four months after the invasion, Che Guevara thanked—and taunted—White House aide Richard Goodwin in a top-secret meeting in Montevideo, Uruguay. Guevara told Goodwin that the revolutionaries' hold on Cuba "had been a little shaky, but the invasion allowed the leadership to consolidate most of the major elements of the country around Fidel."[67]

After the spectacular failure of intervention, Kennedy and other opponents of the Cuban Revolution pivoted to covert, economic, and diplomatic strategies. As another direct military invasion was temporarily off the table, Kennedy turned to quieter forms of covert intervention and, in November 1961, approved a new joint CIA-Pentagon effort codenamed Operation Mongoose. This new operation, designed to "help Cuba overthrow the communist regime," encompassed intelligence collection, counterrevolutionary organizing, the infiltration of small paramilitary teams, sabotage, assassination attempts, and preparations for US military intervention.[68] Soviet and Cuban leaders knew about Operation Mongoose and the threat it posed to Cuban security. As Khrushchev later recalled, "We were quite certain that the invasion was only the beginning."[69] Publicly, Kennedy promoted his new Alliance for Progress, a massive aid program that he had announced just a month before the invasion, calling it "an example to all the world that liberty and progress walk hand in hand."[70] Modeled on former Brazilian president Juscelino Kubitschek's Operation Pan America and the earlier US Marshall Plan to rebuild Europe after World War II, the Alliance for Progress was designed to modernize Latin America and support economic development in order to encourage democratic governance and relieve social pressures for more Cuban-style revolutions.[71] The Alliance also increased US funding and training for Latin American militaries that were expected to combat internal threats—especially Cuba-inspired revolutionary groups—and take a lead role in development efforts.[72] This significant increase in aid for the rest of Latin America contrasted sharply with the economic embargo against Cuba that Eisenhower had initiated and that Kennedy tightened and formalized in February 1962.[73] And finally, US leaders worked with their Latin American counterparts on a diplomatic track, hoping that multilateral cooperation could contain Castro.

## The Multilateral Approach

Some prominent leaders in Latin America saw the Cuba question as an opportunity to strengthen the region's multilateral institutions, especially the OAS. One of the most strenuous advocates for a multilateral approach was Colombian president Alberto Lleras Camargo. Lleras and other Colombian leaders argued that a hemispheric response to the Cuban Revolution coordinated through the proper organizational channels could demonstrate the utility and effectiveness of international institutions like the OAS, and thus contribute to long-term peace, democratic governance, and cooperation in the region.[74]

As an elder statesman from Colombia's Liberal Party, Lleras had a great deal of experience building political bridges both within Colombia and in the inter-American community. After Colombians had overthrown their own dictator, Gen. Gustavo Rojas Pinilla, in a wave of mass protests in 1957, Lleras led the effort to create the National Front (Frente Nacional), a power-sharing coalition between liberals and conservatives that promised an end to the authoritarian years and a resolution to the extremely violent antagonism between members of the two traditional political parties. In the previous decade, conflicts between the two parties had intersected with simmering regional, cultural, religious, ethnic, racial, and socioeconomic tensions. These overlapping conflicts led to such a tremendous amount of brutality, bloodshed, death, displacement, and state-sponsored terror that historians have designated the period of undeclared civil war from the late-1940s to the late-1950s

"La Violencia."[75] Lleras and other members of the National Front sought to revive and strengthen Colombia's democratic institutions and encourage dialogue between the traditional political parties through a process they called *convivencia*, or coexistence.[76]

Lleras's commitment to peace and democracy in Colombia translated on the international level into his dedication to multilateralism in inter-American affairs. During his brief time as Colombia's minister of foreign relations in 1945, he represented his country at the Inter-American Conference on Problems of War and Peace, or the Chapultepec Conference, in Mexico City. There, he proposed that the nations of the hemisphere adopt an expansive definition of collective security. Lleras also paved the way for the transformation of the Pan-American Union into the stronger OAS. He did so both in his participation at the founding meeting of the United Nations (UN) in San Francisco in 1945, where he argued effectively for the coexistence of regional and global organizations, and in his role as director of the Pan-American Union, where in 1947 he helped initiate the effort to transform the union into the OAS. He became the first secretary-general of the new OAS in 1948 and served in that role until 1954.

Lleras's push for a multilateral answer to the Cuba question sought to balance his national and international agendas. At the time of the Cuban Revolution, Colombia's National Front government was pursuing an ambitious program of political, economic, and social reform. Lleras's administration introduced austerity measures as an immediate way to stabilize the country's economy and gain much-needed international aid and investments. He also had long-term developmental goals, such as land and tax reform, that required further foreign support.[77] At the same time, the political situation in Colombia was tenuous as Lleras tried to shift the political culture away from "violence-as-practice" to "peaceful democratic consolidation" while also dealing with social unrest unleashed by the economic austerity measures and resistance from the business community to the government's wider economic reforms. Lleras recognized the danger that events in Cuba posed to Colombia's newfound peace, as he faced left-wing insurgencies that, according to his intelligence agents, received support from the Cuban government.[78] He tried to neutralize the Cuban threat in such a way as to avoid inflaming the increasingly polarized pro- and anti-Castro passions in Colombia or the wider inter-American community.

As Castro's regime became more clearly authoritarian and communist, the Colombian government led the effort to coordinate a multilateral response. After the colossal failure of the Bay of Pigs invasion, Colombian officials working with President Lleras composed a memorandum addressed to Latin

American and US leaders in which they proposed a two-part approach to "avert risks of the Cold War and prevent Communism's advance, penetration, and infiltration in the rest of the hemisphere." The Colombians recommended delaying immediate action on Cuba to allow the "very bad impression caused by the frustrated invasion" to dissipate, during which time a meeting of economic and foreign ministers should be held to establish the Alliance for Progress that Kennedy had proposed before the Bay of Pigs. The Alliance would create a public impression of "revitalization and progress which would permit governments to obtain a generous response from their people for better fulfillment of their national and international obligations." Then, a separate meeting could be held under the auspices of the Rio Treaty (the 1947 Inter-American Treaty of Reciprocal Assistance) to deal directly with Cuba and coordinate a hemispheric response to protect against communist threats. "It is not too late to adopt a line of conduct wedded to the principles that have made the OAS an admirable experiment," the Colombian proposal concluded.[79] Venezuelan president Rómulo Betancourt, who had been pushing for a meeting of foreign ministers to impose sanctions on Cuba, reviewed the Colombians' proposal and was convinced by their recommendation to delay any action until after the economic meeting.[80]

US officials agreed with the Colombian proposal for a multistep, multilateral approach. That August (1961), a meeting of economic ministers and other government officials took place in Punta del Este, Uruguay, to establish the Alliance for Progress. US representatives pledged to immediately contribute $1 billion of public funds to Latin American development and to secure $20 billion in aid from private investors and international lenders over the following decade.[81] The Colombian government, in particular, received a great deal of aid through the Alliance for Progress; after Brazil, it was the second-highest recipient of aid over the course of the 1960s, and it was treated as a showcase of the Alliance's potential to transform Latin American economies.[82] US economic aid was, in part, a reward for Colombia's leadership in the multilateral effort to oppose Castro.[83]

In the waning months of 1961, the Peruvian and Colombian governments began campaigning for a meeting of foreign ministers to deal with the Cuban threat. It was unclear whether enough other countries would approve—that is, until Castro took the stage before a live television and radio audience on the night of December 1. In a characteristically expansive speech in which he recalled the political and military development of the Cuban Revolution, equated capitalism with imperialism, and heaped praise upon the Soviet Union, Castro declared: "I am a Marxist-Leninist, and I shall be a Marxist-Leninist to the end of my life." In the same speech, Castro also announced that he was establishing a single party to run the Cuban government, thus officially putting an end to any pretenses at democratic governance.[84] In another speech a few days later, Castro specifically targeted Colombia's leaders, calling them "miserable traitors" for proposing a meeting of foreign ministers. He declared that Cuba was not interested in maintaining relations with "Judas and blackmailers." President Lleras cut diplomatic relations with Cuba the day after Castro's insults were aired, and he reissued his call for a hemispheric meeting, now armed with clear evidence of Castro's communist, antidemocratic orientation.[85] Castro's words galvanized the rest of the hemisphere's leaders, who approved Colombia's request for an OAS meeting in January 1962.[86]

Foreign ministers from across the Americas gathered in Punta del Este on January 22, 1962, to debate the hemispheric response to the Cuban threat. Unlike the meeting in San José, Costa Rica, in 1960, this gathering was convened under the Rio Treaty rather than under the OAS Charter, giving the participants greater authority to take concrete measures in the name of hemispheric security. Colombia's representative spoke of the importance of the inter-American system of collective security, arguing that the system was not interventionist and that failure to take a multilateral approach could result in unilateral action. He pointed out that thirteen countries of the Americas had already cut diplomatic and economic relations with Cuba, and he proposed that the remaining countries cut ties as well. Guatemala's representative went even further, calling on the member countries to expel Cuba from the OAS. Oswaldo Dorticós, the head of Cuba's delegation, countered that the OAS should include all the nations of the Americas, regardless of their political orientations, or risk becoming "a private preserve of Washington, governed in the manner of a Ministry of Colonies." In response to Dorticós's speech, the Honduran representative argued that Cuba's president no longer spoke for the Cuban people. "The Cuban Revolution was radically liquidated by the international Marxist-Leninist revolution," he declared. "The American voice of Cuba can no longer be heard. Now resounds the loud, threatening, and violent cry of the Muscovite bear."[87] According to the Honduran representative, Castro's rejection of democratic norms and his turn to the Soviets denied the Cuban public their sovereignty and endangered the entire region's security.

After a week of speeches and three days of closed-door meetings, the delegates voted to decide Cuba's place in the inter-American system. Everyone present, except for the Cuban delegation, agreed with the first resolution, that "the continental unity and the democratic institutions of the hemisphere" were in danger, and that the principles of communism were incompatible with the inter-American system. The majority of the delegates also approved resolutions to exclude Cuba from all organizations of the inter-American system and to impose an arms embargo on the island. But representatives of many of the region's largest and most important countries, including Mexico, Brazil, Argentina, Ecuador, Chile, and Bolivia, abstained from voting on exclusion. Secretary of State Dean Rusk, reporting back to Kennedy about the meeting, conveyed his "keenest disappointment" with the abstaining countries.[88] Though the OAS meeting accomplished its primary goals of condemning Castro's turn to communism and expelling Cuba from the organization, it also highlighted the continuing differences among the nations of the hemisphere over how to answer the Cuba question. The countries that conspicuously abstained from approving actions against Cuba did not believe that Castro posed a great enough threat to the region to justify infringing upon Cuba's sovereignty.

## Conclusion

Public responses to the Cuban Revolution, both among Latin American revolutionaries and counterrevolutionaries, pushed governments across the region to take a variety of actions to contain the fallout. Some Latin American governments, like those in Mexico and Brazil, argued for a hands-off approach to Cuba; but they were in the minority. The United States and most other countries in the region insisted that something had to be done about Castro. Cuba's neighbors worked together and separately to weaken Castro's communist regime and isolate it from the rest of the inter-American community. Through the Bay of Pigs invasion and Operation Mongoose, US and Latin American governments worked together with Cuban exiles to directly attack Castro's government. The Alliance for Progress attempted to undercut the popular appeal of the Cuban Revolution by offering an alternative path to economic reform and development. Multilateral measures in the OAS isolated Cuba from the rest of the inter-American community. Cuban and Soviet leaders interpreted these actions as a clear threat to the security of Castro's regime and decided that something had to be done to protect Cuba.

# PART II CRISIS

# CHAPTER 3
# DECISIONS

The Bay of Pigs invasion, Operation Mongoose, and Cuba's increasing isolation in the inter-American system all sent a clear message that Cuba's neighbors did not intend to tolerate Fidel Castro's regime. In the spring of 1962, Nikita Khrushchev decided it was time for a dramatic demonstration of solidarity with his Latin American ally: He would offer to station Soviet nuclear missiles in Cuba. Khrushchev's decision set off a chain reaction of decisions on the other side of the world. Castro had to decide whether to accept Khrushchev's offer. Castro's neighbors had to decide how to interpret confusing reports that an increasing Soviet military presence in Cuba threatened hemispheric security. John F. Kennedy, after learning that the Soviets were installing nuclear weapons in Cuban territory, had to decide how to respond. Combined, all these decisions had the unintended result of bringing the world the closest it had ever come to nuclear war.

## A Soviet Arsenal in the Caribbean

On the morning of May 29, 1962, Cuba's leaders welcomed a delegation of hydrotechnic specialists from the Soviet Union. To the Cubans' surprise, embedded within the Soviet scientific delegation were top military leaders who had come to make an extraordinary offer: nuclear missiles.[1] The Soviet Union had already sent thousands of weapons and other war material—planes, tanks, ships, guns, men—to the island, but this time was different. This time, Khrushchev's representatives proposed to provide a full arsenal of medium-range and intermediate-range ballistic missiles. During a visit to Bulgaria earlier that month, the Soviet premier had struck upon the idea as a solution to two problems: Cuba's vulnerability and the Soviet Union's missile gap with the United States.[2] The Soviets requested an immediate meeting with Castro and laid out their top-secret proposal.

Khrushchev's representatives opened by expressing concern over the increasing threats to Castro's government. Domestic unrest was on the rise thanks to the political turmoil following Castro's embrace of communism and severe shortages caused by a combination of government mismanagement and the US embargo. The United States and its Central American and Cuban exile partners had already attempted one invasion and were reportedly planning another. These same conspirators were also continuing their efforts to undermine Castro through Operation Mongoose. More than 200 Cuban exile groups continued to stage raids on the island and plot counterrevolution from abroad.[3] Cuba's neighbors had declared that Cuba's political system was incompatible with the rest of the hemisphere and had expelled the country from the inter-American community. Soviet and Cuban intelligence officers were uncovering multiple plots—involving Cuban exiles and the US, Costa Rican, Guatemalan, and Venezuelan governments—to assassinate Castro and other top Cuban officials.[4]

When the Soviet delegates asked Castro what he thought should be done, he seized the opportunity to request something he had long desired: a mutual security agreement with the Soviet Union. He argued: "If the United States knows that an invasion of Cuba would imply war with the Soviet Union, then, in my view, that would be the best way to prevent an invasion of Cuba."[5] One of the Soviet delegates responded that such an agreement would need something concrete to be effective; the delegate then declared, "The government of the USSR is prepared to help Cuba strengthen its defensive capability by all possible means, up to considering the question of installing intermediate-range missiles on its territory."[6] Offering to use nuclear weapons to defend Cuba's security was the most dramatic demonstration of solidarity that a foreign power had ever made to a Latin American ally.

The Soviet offer caught Castro by surprise and put him in a tough position. For more than a year, he had been pushing and cajoling the Soviets to provide more conventional weapons, and suddenly they were offering nuclear missiles. The Cuban leader later recalled that he interpreted the proposal primarily as a way to improve the Soviet Union's geopolitical position. "In my view, there was a clear desire [on their part] to obtain an improvement in the balance of power between the USSR and the United States." Although Castro was eager to help his new ally and patron, he remembered feeling "none too happy about the presence of those weapons in Cuba, given our interest in avoiding the image of Cuba as a Soviet base, especially [as we might be seen in that way by] Latin America."[7] What was more, accepting Soviet missiles would clearly put Cuba in the Soviet camp, thus endangering Castro's ambitions to establish a position of leadership alongside other Third World leaders in Africa and Asia in the burgeoning Non-Aligned Movement.[8] Castro had to weigh the benefits of gaining greater military security against the cost of sacrificing some of Cuba's hard-won sovereignty and the solidarity that it had received from supporters across the region and around the globe.

Castro's concern about Latin American public opinion was a significant hurdle. He had been working hard to gain support for the Cuban Revolution in general and especially for his campaign against foreign bases in the Americas—especially Guantánamo. The main Soviet representative in Cuba, Aleksandr Alekseev, had warned Khrushchev that Castro might reject the missiles, observing that "Fidel Castro is trying to build security, the defense of the Cuban Revolution, by mobilizing Latin American public opinion."[9] Alekseev argued that military measures were not the only means of providing security: Solidarity could also offer protection. But Khrushchev correctly anticipated that Castro's fear of further attacks and invasions—his desire for military security—would overshadow his worries about national sovereignty and his search for hemispheric solidarity. Castro listened to the Soviet proposal and then replied that he had to consult with his inner circle on such an important matter. After meeting with his brother Raúl, Che Guevara, and a few others, Castro told the Soviet representatives that he would accept their offer. "If this will strengthen the socialist camp and also—and this is in the second place— contribute to the defense of Cuba, we are willing to accept all of the missiles that may be necessary," Castro determined.[10] By portraying his acceptance of the missiles as a selfless gesture of solidarity, Castro tried to soften the blow that the Soviet missile bases represented to Cuba's sovereignty and its reputation in the Americas.

After Castro gave his verbal agreement to accept the missiles, there were many important details that remained to be decided. Chief among them was whether to undertake the transfer of weapons openly or in secret. The Cubans wanted a public military agreement, and they argued that just the announcement of such a pact would deter attacks against their country. They also contended that it was their sovereign right to obtain any weapons they deemed necessary for self-defense, and that moving the missiles in secret would make them look guilty. Immediately after the meeting with the Soviet delegation, Raúl Castro confided to Fidel that he doubted whether it would even be possible to keep such an immense operation hidden, given Cuba's terrain and the size of the missiles.[11] Raúl spent the first two weeks of July 1962 in Moscow, ironing out details of the arrangement. He brought with him a draft of a mutual security agreement that Fidel had written by hand, and he urged Khrushchev to make the agreement and the missile transfer public. Khrushchev insisted that he wanted to keep the security agreement and the missiles a secret until the launch sites were finished. Khrushchev told Raúl that he planned to travel to Cuba himself in December 1962. He would make a big show of revealing the missiles, and then he and Fidel would publicly sign the mutual security agreement.[12] When Che Guevara made his own trip

Acuerdo entre el Gobierno de la República
de Cuba y el Gobierno de la Unión de Repúblicas
Socialistas Soviéticas, de cooperación militar
para la defensa del territorio nacional de Cuba
en caso de agresión

———

Acuerdo entre el Gobierno de la República de
Cuba y el Gobierno de la Unión de Repúblicas
Socialistas Soviéticas de cooperación militar
y defensa mutua.

———

Acuerdo entre el Gobierno de la República de Cuba y el Gobierno de la Unión de
Repúblicas Socialistas Soviéticas sobre apoyo
militar de las Fuerzas Armadas Soviéticas
a la defensa del territorio nacional de Cuba
en caso de agresión

( de emplear cualquiera de los tres títulos
anteriores )

El Gobierno de la República de Cuba y el
Gobierno de la Unión de Repúblicas Socialistas
Soviéticas.

Guiándose por los principios y objetivos
del Estatuto de la Organización de Naciones
Unidas.

The first page of Fidel Castro's handwritten draft of the mutual defense agreement that the Cubans and Soviets were negotiating in 1962. (Courtesy of the Instituto de Historia de Cuba. Used by permission.)

to Moscow at the end of August, he also tried to convince the Soviets of the merits of transparency. Khrushchev ignored these repeated recommendations and continued to insist on complete secrecy. When Khrushchev vowed that he would "send the Baltic fleet" if the United States discovered the missile bases before they were operational, Guevara and his travel companion looked at each other with raised eyebrows.[13]

Starting in August 1962, Soviet personnel and weapons flooded the island. The Soviet forces included five nuclear regiments—three with medium-range missiles that could travel as far as 1,050 miles and two with intermediate-range missiles that could go twice as far—four motorized regiments, two tank battalions, forty MiG-21 fighter planes, forty-two Il-28 light bombers, and two cruise missile regiments armed with nuclear warheads.[14] The Soviets sent the antiaircraft missiles ahead of the nuclear missiles to deter American U-2 spy planes from getting a good look at the military buildup.[15] All told, eighty-five ships from the Soviet merchant marine made 185 trips, protected by seven nuclear-armed submarines, transporting weapons, supplies, and 42,000 troops.[16] By late October 1962, a total of 162 nuclear warheads had arrived in Cuba, each with seventy times more power than the bomb detonated over Hiroshima.[17]

The Soviets and Cubans went to great lengths to hide their massive undertaking. The Soviets gave the operation a misleading codename: Anadyr, a river in Siberia. Soviet leaders told the troops called up for the expedition that they were going to a cold location, and outfitted them with skis and fleece-lined parkas.[18] The men deployed on the ships to Cuba, even the captains, did not learn their real destination until they began to cross the Atlantic Ocean; then they spent most of the trip crowded belowdecks to avoid detection.[19] In order to keep the nuclear weapons a secret once they arrived in Cuba, caravans of trucks transported the tarp-covered missiles from the docks to the island's interior under the cover of night.[20] "Must be importing palm trees, judging by the shape," the locals joked.[21] All Cubans outside Castro's small inner circle were forbidden from entering the Soviet bases. Anyone who went beyond jokes and confessed to knowing or seeing anything about the missiles was locked away in strict isolation; as Castro later put it, "If you knew something, you were infected, so you were in quarantine."[22] Fidel and Raúl Castro later claimed that "a constant stream of people would come up to us and say: 'Hey, lock me away because I know about this, that and the other. This Soviet guy so-and-so told me . . . '" The Castro brothers described these men and women as "self-interned prisoners" who, for lack of a better solution, had to be locked up on a base on the outskirts of Havana.[23]

Despite all these measures, the Cuban public knew something was going on. Many years later, Fidel Castro called the operation "the best-kept secret in history, because several million Cubans knew about it."[24] Cuban journalist Carlos Franqui, the editor of the newspaper *Revolución* at the time, described the missiles as "a public secret." "No one spoke about them," he later explained, "but all knew."[25] Hundreds of farms and families were relocated to make room for the missile bases; residents of the small town of Santa Cruz de los Pinos recalled that one house on a street corner had to be evacuated in the middle of the night so that soldiers could demolish the building to enable the long missile transport vehicles to make the tight turn.[26] Those living near the bases had the clearest view of the transformation of their country into a nuclear arsenal. Though the bases themselves were off limits, the locals were able to interact with the Soviet technicians and soldiers who ventured out in search of alcohol and entertainment. Some struck up friendships and romances with the soldiers, others exchanged Cuban rum for Soviet knives, clothes, soap, and wristwatches. Residents of Santa Cruz de los Pinos also noted US airplanes flying low over their village, and they worried that war could break out at any moment.[27] For Cubans across the island, especially those living on the edge of the bases, it was clear that they were entering a new period of heightened danger and uncertainty.

## Watching and Waiting

Cuban citizens were not the only ones watching and waiting: As the Cuban government had warned from the first days of Operation Anadyr, it was impossible to hide such a large military undertaking. While the Soviets did manage to conceal the scale of the buildup and the transfer of the nuclear missiles, they could not keep all the ships, men, trucks, planes, helicopters, and tanks under wraps. As early as mid-August 1962, Cuban exiles in Miami were claiming that their homeland was becoming "a big, unsinkable, missile platform, with hidden launching pads."[28] On August 25, the same day that the *New York Times* published reports from unnamed US officials that the Soviets were "pouring" some 3,000 to 5,000 technicians into Cuba and possibly providing surface-to-air missiles, the Colombian newspaper *El Tiempo* ran an editorial claiming that Cuba was becoming a Soviet base.[29] "Russian tanks, planes, and soldiers at the continental gates themselves, are both a challenge and a threat," the Colombian editors warned; "the hemisphere cannot remain indifferent to this bridgehead, from which Soviet cannons are starting to point in all directions."[30]

These alarming reports of a Soviet buildup in Cuba demanded an official response, and Kennedy provided a provisional answer along with a warning.

On September 4, President Kennedy put out a public statement confirming the rumors of increased deliveries of Soviet equipment to Cuba, including antiaircraft missiles, but denied that there was any evidence of a "significant offensive capability" in Cuban hands. He drew an implicit distinction between "offensive" weapons—missiles capable of reaching a great distance—and "defensive" weapons, or ones that could only be used at close range to defend against an invasion. Kennedy warned, however, that the US government was watching closely, and if the Cubans did gain offensive weapons, "the gravest issues would arise" and the United States would use whatever means necessary to prevent Castro from threatening any part of the Western Hemisphere.[31]

Kennedy was not the only national leader who had to respond to the Soviet buildup in Cuba. Mexican president Adolfo López Mateos drew a distinction like Kennedy's between offensive and defensive weapons. He told reporters in early October that his sources indicated that "all the weapons that Cuba possessed were of a defensive nature, that do not endanger the peace of the continent." Like Kennedy, López Mateos left the door open for a change of policy based on the category of arms. "However," López Mateos continued, "if the type of weapon changed, we would reconsider our attitude toward that nation."[32] Other Latin American leaders pushed for more decisive action. Nicaraguan president Luis Somoza told reporters that if the Organization of American States (OAS) continued to fail to act, "the governments of the nations of the Caribbean must address these military measures as quickly as possible."[33]

Panamanian officials did everything within their power to convince the rest of the Americas that Cuba posed a political, economic, even existential threat to their security. Panama's finance minister Gilberto Arias warned that the establishment of a Soviet base in Cuba could threaten private investment in the Caribbean region. Arias publicly proposed forming a Latin American military alliance modeled on the North Atlantic Treaty Organization, "for defensive as well as offensive purposes, if such need arises." He called for a meeting of ten nations that "stood in the path of Communist aggression," identifying Panama, Guatemala, El Salvador, Honduras, Nicaragua, Costa Rica, Colombia, Venezuela, the Dominican Republic, and Haiti as "the countries closest to Cuba and those most exposed to its evil influence."[34] Costa Rica's president Francisco José Orlich Bolmarcich seconded Arias's proposal and issued a formal invitation to those nations to gather in Costa Rica to discuss such an alliance.[35] Panama's foreign minister Galileo Solís painted an even more explicit—and prophetic—picture of the threat that Cuba posed. In his annual report before his country's congress on October 1, 1962, Solís warned that "Russia has converted Cuba into a gigantic war arsenal." "The Cuban danger has ceased to be exclusively a continental danger to become also a universal danger," Solís argued. "If the Sino-Soviet communist insistence on intervening in intra-continental affairs endangers the internal defense of the United States—and this has already begun to occur—then the need to contain the communist advance in America may lead to the outbreak of a Third World War whose apocalyptic consequences are unforeseeable."[36]

Some Latin American leaders looked to the OAS to coordinate a hemispheric response to the Soviet military buildup. In late August 1962, the Guatemalan government contemplated calling a meeting of foreign ministers to invoke the Rio Treaty. But when the Guatemalan ambassador to the United States approached Edwin Martin, the assistant secretary of state for inter-American affairs, about the idea, Martin dissuaded him. Martin argued that even though the Soviets had sent defensive military equipment and technicians to Cuba, the lack of hard evidence of the presence of Soviet troops meant that the OAS could take no enforcement action.[37]

Disagreements over the nature of the Cuban threat and the appropriate level of response made the OAS an unlikely venue for organizing decisive action. As the Soviet military buildup proceeded throughout the month of September, the CIA reported that while some Latin American countries with firm anti-communist foreign policies, including the nations of Central America, the Dominican Republic, Venezuela, Colombia, and Argentina, preferred a formal meeting of ministers capable of initiating forceful joint action, others like Brazil, Mexico, and Haiti would likely agree to participate only in an informal meeting and would not endorse direct intervention in what they perceived as Cuba's internal affairs.[38] To add to the complications, some of the Latin American leaders who were spearheading the efforts to coordinate hemispheric action against Cuba drew the line at military intervention. Venezuela's Rómulo Betancourt told scholar Robert Alexander in August 1962 that he was "absolutely against United States armed intervention" and wanted to continue the policy of diplomatic and economic isolation.[39]

When the OAS eventually decided to address the issue in early October, it was at an informal meeting where the only action the members could take was to issue a press communiqué calling for further action. The OAS declared that "the most urgent of the serious problems that face the hemisphere is the Sino-Soviet intervention in Cuba as an attempt to convert the island into an armed base for communist penetration of the Americas and further the subversion of the democratic institutions of this hemisphere." At that point, communist penetration—not nuclear attack—still appeared to be the main threat to security. The OAS left it up to future meetings and individual countries to decide how best to counter the communist menace. The organization did, however, "note the desirability of intensifying surveillance of the delivery of arms and war supplies to the communist regime in Cuba" in order to warn the nations of the Americas "about the secret accumulation on that island of weapons that can be used offensively against the hemisphere." [40] The State Department's confidential report on the meeting acknowledged that the "phraseology [was] not as strong or specific as we would have preferred."[41] Without clear evidence that Cuba posed a military threat to the security of the hemisphere, government officials in the United States and many parts of Latin America were unwilling to take direct action against Castro's government.

## Discoveries and Deliberations

On October 14, 1962, a U-2 spy plane flew over Cuba, taking almost a thousand photographs of the western half of the island. US intelligence sources had been reporting the possible arrival of nuclear missiles in Cuba ever since mid-September, but this was the first flight over Cuba since then, thanks to political concerns about losing planes to Soviet antiaircraft fire and unfavorable weather conditions. On the afternoon of October 15, analysts in Washington reviewing photos from the U-2 flight found evidence of medium-range ballistic missiles in a field near Santa Cruz de los Pinos, an area also known as San Cristóbal. The analysts immediately reported their discovery to the deputy director of the CIA, who informed National Security Adviser McGeorge Bundy, Secretary of State Dean Rusk, and other top Kennedy administration officials. The next morning, Bundy alerted President Kennedy. Kennedy quickly formed a group of close advisers who later became known as the ExComm, short for the Executive Committee of the National Security Council.[42]

Kennedy and the ExComm spent the next week engaged in urgent, top-secret deliberations to decide how best to respond to the discovery of Soviet nuclear missile bases in Cuba. On Tuesday, October 16, during Kennedy's first meeting with the ExComm, Secretary of State Dean Rusk opened the debate by framing it as a choice between two options: a quick strike to eliminate the bases or a somewhat slower combination of diplomatic and military maneuvers designed to convince the Cubans or Soviets to remove the missiles. Rusk pushed for the diplomatic option and recommended convening a meeting of the OAS "to make it quite clear that the entire hemisphere considers that the Rio Pact has been violated." He warned that a quick strike could easily escalate into general war and urged Kennedy: "We have an obligation to do what has to be done, but do it in a way that gives everybody a chance to pull away from it before it gets too hard."[43] Rusk provided additional arguments against a first strike in the second ExComm meeting later that evening. He warned that an unannounced attack on Cuba could have serious repercussions off the island. "If we strike those missiles, we would expect, I think, maximum communist reaction in Latin America," he predicted. "In the case of about six of those governments, unless the heads of government had some intimation requiring some preparatory steps from the security point of view, one or another of those governments could easily be overthrown." Rusk pointed to the governments of Venezuela, Guatemala, Bolivia, Chile, and "possibly even Mexico" as particularly vulnerable to violent internal reactions.[44] Rusk's point was that missiles were not the only threat to peace and security in Latin America.

The president and his brother, Attorney General Robert F. Kennedy, worried that nuclear missiles in Cuba could affect the balance of power in the Americas. Robert warned that if Castro were allowed to keep his new weapons, he could use them to deter US action in other parts of the region. "Say some problem arises in Venezuela," he posited. "And you've got Castro saying 'You move troops down into that part of Venezuela, we're going to fire these missiles.'" President Kennedy, echoing his brother's fears, fretted, "It makes them look like they're coequal with us."[45] The missiles were not only a military threat but a political and psychological one. The possibility that the Cubans could challenge US freedom of action in the Americas and behave with equal authority was unacceptable.

Hemispheric security and inter-American relations also topped the list of concerns for the head of the CIA, John McCone. In a memorandum that he presented to the ExComm, McCone acknowledged the importance of geopolitical considerations like the status of Berlin and NATO alliances but contended that "maintaining the maximum security and safety of the United States and of the Western Hemisphere, cementing Western Hemisphere relationships, and reversing the growth of communism in the Western Hemisphere represent our most important national interest and must be our overriding concern." According to McCone, the United States could not tolerate the presence in Cuba of nuclear weapons "capable of striking the United States, the Panama Canal, and most Latin American countries." He also warned that if Castro and the Soviets were allowed to keep the weapons, their apparent victory would encourage "dissident" groups across the region. "It is my personal opinion," the CIA director argued, "that this will result in Latin American countries from Mexico in the north to Argentina in the south seeking ever closer ties with the Soviet Union because of demonstrated Soviet strength and power." If Kennedy did not take aggressive action, McCone maintained, "these Latin Americans will move away from dependence upon the United States because of our own demonstrated weakness and lack of resolution."[46] Like Rusk and the Kennedy brothers, McCone was concerned about the psychological fallout events in

Cuba could have on the rest of the Americas. US leaders immediately looked beyond the military aspects of the missiles to the broader impact they could have on US prospects for winning the hemispheric Cold War.

McCone contended that a blockade—one of the possible strategies that was emerging in the ExComm's deliberations—was an insufficient solution, since the weapons were already on the island and any delays would only allow the Soviets and Cubans to make them operational. He also predicted that a blockade would give the US and Latin American public enough time to realize the danger they were in, resulting in "great fear and distress" and "disenchantment with our policies." The CIA director recommended that Kennedy issue an ultimatum to Castro and Khrushchev, demanding that they remove all offensive weapons and Soviet military personnel. Once the Soviets were warned and out of the way, McCone proposed, "we should take over Cuba by military means, remove the threat and also remove the Castro-Communist government and establish in Cuba a government which will serve the interests of the Cuban people and become a member of the Western Hemisphere community of nations." The CIA director saw the missile crisis as an opportunity to finally get rid of a government that had been causing trouble for the United States and the rest of the nations of the Americas. By the time McCone submitted his recommendations, however, Kennedy and other members of the ExComm had already begun turning away from the military option and were looking for alternatives that would reflect more favorably on the United States in both the court of world opinion and the history books.

As a military approach became less appealing, the prospect of working with Latin American allies reemerged in the ExComm's discussions. Initially, Rusk's recommendation of cooperating with the OAS had fallen flat. This was, after all, the organization that *Washington Post* columnist Drew Peterson had, just that September, called "a namby-pamby conclave of diplomats."[47] Vice President Lyndon Johnson, who had spent the previous weekend with the ambassadors of the OAS, feared trusting them with such an important responsibility. "I think this organization is fine," Johnson told the rest of the committee, "but I don't think, I don't rely on them much for any strength in anything like this."[48] Kennedy was even more dismissive, declaring, "I don't think we ought to do the OAS. I think that's a waste of time."[49] This knee-jerk, trivializing attitude toward the OAS betrayed a deep and long-standing distrust of both the organization itself and its member states. It also stemmed from the fact that OAS members had remained deeply divided on the Cuba question up to that point, and some of its most influential members, including Mexico and Brazil, had steadfastly refused to take action against Castro.

But Secretary Rusk continued to push for a coordinated inter-American approach. On October 18, he argued that "the Rio Pact is, I think clearly, our strongest legal basis for whatever action we need to take."[50] When discussion turned to the possibility of a blockade or quarantine around Cuba, most of the ExComm members argued that such action would require a declaration of war. Rusk again piped up: "You could have a blockade imposed under Article 8 of the Rio Treaty."[51] Undersecretary of State George Ball and Soviet expert Ambassador Llewellyn Thompson predicted that Khrushchev and the rest of the legalistic Soviets would be more likely to respect a blockade if it were established according to international law.[52] After a long day of meetings, Kennedy returned alone to the Oval Office, turned on the tape recorder that he had hidden there, and dictated his thoughts. "I was most anxious that we not have to announce a state of war," he reflected, "because it would obviously be bad to have the word go out that we were having a war rather than that it was a limited blockade for a limited purpose."[53] Over the course of the October 18 discussions, it became clear to the president that the OAS could serve as a useful partner in providing a legal, limited response to the Soviet provocation.

On October 20, after five days of intense deliberation, President Kennedy decided to pursue a two-pronged strategy. The United States and its Latin American partners would establish a quarantine around Cuba to prevent the delivery of additional weapons, and Kennedy would issue an ultimatum to Khrushchev to remove the missiles already on the island. Lawyers from the Justice and State Departments had weighed in by that point and advised Kennedy that under the United Nations (UN) Charter, the OAS could legally authorize a blockade.[54] Officially, Kennedy was careful to call the action a quarantine rather than a blockade in order to avoid thorny legal questions.[55] Secretary Rusk also pointed out that using the term "quarantine" avoided unflattering comparisons with the Soviets' blockade of Berlin in 1948, one of the first major international crises of the Cold War.[56] And, as Rusk had proposed, the OAS would play a crucial role in laying the legal foundations for the quarantine.

One question about the OAS remained, even as Kennedy prepared to make his speech to the world on October 22: Would the United States get enough votes to approve the quarantine? In calling the meeting and proposing the quarantine, the United States was setting the agenda for the OAS, but it was up to the Latin American members to approve or reject the US proposal. Dean Rusk and Edwin Martin were confident that they could get the two-thirds required—fourteen member countries—to pass a resolution invoking the Rio Treaty, but others were not so sure. In the October 18 ExComm deliberations,

Kennedy had predicted that Latin Americans would view the whole situation as an overreaction, "a mad act by the United States."[57] Robert Kennedy warned that a failed attempt to get OAS approval would be politically disastrous.[58] In the final meeting to decide the US actions on October 20, the president expressed particular concern about whether the Latin American countries would see a blockade as an appropriate response.[59] On the afternoon of October 22, Kennedy elaborated further in a conversation with congressional leadership, explaining to Senator Richard Russell, the influential chairman of the Armed Services Committee who was pushing for an invasion or a first strike, "We're going to do the blockade in any case, Senator. The legality of the blockade depends—if it's a peacetime blockade—upon the endorsement, under the Rio Treaty, of the OAS, which meets tomorrow morning." Kennedy also told the senator of his contingency plan: "If they don't give us the 14 votes, the two-thirds vote, then we're going to do it anyway. But in that case, we are going to have to have what's legally an illegal blockade or a declaration of war."[60] Therein lay the importance of the OAS: The organization did not determine US policy—Kennedy was going to move forward with the quarantine either way—but if enough of its member countries voted to support a quarantine, they could help the United States avoid declaring war.

In order to head off the possibility of losing the vote in the OAS, the State Department sent top-secret instructions on October 21 to US ambassadors across Latin America to coordinate the hemispheric response. The instructions told the ambassadors to wait until they received another message with the single word "GO" and the date and time of Kennedy's speech. Then, the ambassadors were to set up meetings with the heads of state of their host countries half an hour before the speech on October 22. At those meetings, they would deliver a letter from Kennedy along with the text of his speech. Kennedy's letter to his fellow national leaders opened with a stirring call for cooperation: "We face the necessity and the opportunity in this hemisphere of determining by the wisdom of our joint action in the next few days what may be the whole future of man on this earth." The instructions to the US ambassadors noted, "You should also reinforce the President's request for [OAS] support . . . you should make clear that this is a first vital step to deal with a major threat by the USSR to the peace and security not only of this hemisphere but the whole free world." The State Department told the ambassadors to "strongly emphasize" the importance of passing an OAS resolution "as promptly as possible, and very preferably on the same day, agreeing that the governments of the Hemisphere should take all actions they may deem necessary against Cuba as provided for in Article 8 of the Rio Pact."[61] Through this coordinated approach, the State Department and White House sought to balance the need for secrecy with the equally compelling desire for support from the rest of the Americas.

## The Big Reveal

At 7 p.m. Eastern time on the evening of Monday, October 22, President Kennedy sat at his desk in the White House and revealed to a live international television and radio audience that the Soviet Union had secretly placed nuclear missiles in Cuba. "Within this past week," he began in a somber tone, "unmistakable evidence has established the fact that a series of offensive missile sites is now in preparation on that imprisoned island. The purpose of these bases can be none other than to provide a nuclear strike capability against the Western Hemisphere."[62]

From the opening lines and throughout his entire speech, Kennedy consistently emphasized that the missiles threatened the security not just of the United States but of the entire hemisphere. He explained that aerial surveillance had discovered the presence of two types of missiles: medium-range ones "capable of striking Washington D.C., the Panama Canal, Cape Canaveral, Mexico City, or any other city in the Southeastern part of the United States, in Central America, or in the Caribbean area"; and intermediate-range missiles able to travel twice as far "and thus capable of striking most of the major cities in the Western Hemisphere, ranging as far North as Hudson's Bay, Canada, and as far South as Lima, Peru." Kennedy described the arsenal in Cuba as "an explicit threat to the peace and security of all the Americas," and he argued that whereas US citizens "have become adjusted to living daily on the bull's eye of Soviet missiles located inside the USSR or in submarines," this was the first time that the nations of Latin America had been subjected to a potential nuclear threat. Kennedy argued that Cuba's leaders—he never referred to Castro by name—had put their own country in grave danger by transforming it into "the first Latin American country to become a target for nuclear war, the first Latin American country to have these weapons on its soil." According to Kennedy, the Soviet missiles brought Cuba more danger, not security.

In addition to pointing out the hemispheric nature of the threat, Kennedy also laid out the role that the hemispheric and global community would play in their removal. He argued that the sudden transformation of Cuba into a strategic base of weapons of mass destruction was "in flagrant and deliberate defiance of the Rio Pact" and that a nuclear missile launched from Cuba toward any nation in the Western Hemisphere would be considered an attack by the Soviet Union on the United States, "requiring a full retaliatory response upon the Soviet Union." He announced that the US government was calling for an immediate meeting of the Organ of Consultation of the OAS to officially invoke the Rio Treaty "in support of all necessary action," as well as an emergency meeting of the Security Council of the UN to call for the prompt dismantling and withdrawal of all offensive weapons from Cuba. Kennedy made clear his desire to work with international organizations and hemispheric partners to find a peaceful solution to the crisis.

## Conclusion

Watching from afar as his new ally and Latin America's first communist government struggled to survive in a hostile hemisphere, Nikita Khruschev decided that the time had come for a powerful display of solidarity. He answered Fidel Castro's pleas for weaponry and a mutual security agreement with what he thought would be an even better way to protect Cuba's security: nuclear missiles. Castro decided to accept Khrushchev's offer, despite his misgivings that opening Cuban territory to Soviet missile bases would make his own government appear less sovereign and cost him the solidarity of some of his supporters in Latin America and the rest of the developing world. Ultimately, security took priority over sovereignty and solidarity. As a result of these decisions, the island of Cuba was transformed over a matter of a few short months into a Soviet nuclear arsenal in the Caribbean.

Castro's neighbors watched with dread, trying to figure out just what was happening in Cuba under the cover of darkness. On October 15, photos from a U-2 surveillance flight confirmed the rumors that the Soviets were stationing nuclear weapons in Cuba. Kennedy had to decide how to answer Khrushchev's and Castro's challenge. From the beginning of the deliberations in the ExComm, Kennedy and other US leaders demonstrated significant concern for Latin American responses and for the potential impact of the missiles on inter-American relations. Finally, they decided that a hemispheric threat required a hemispheric response. Kennedy called upon the OAS to invoke its own mutual defense treaty and demanded that Khrushchev remove the missiles. Now the question remained: Would the rest of the nations of the Americas answer Kennedy's call?

# CHAPTER 4
# FIRST RESPONDERS

The revelation of Soviet nuclear missile bases in Cuba launched Latin American leaders and citizens into action. In the first hours and days of the crisis, people across the Americas had to decide how to respond to the new threat to their security and survival. The fact that the missiles could reach almost any target in the region made it clear that Latin Americans had a stake in the outcome of the crisis. National leaders and journalists turned to international organizations, hoping to find a collective solution to a collective danger. The members of the Organization of American States (OAS) had to decide—on extremely short notice—whether to finally come together on the Cuba question and establish the legal foundations for the quarantine. Such action would require a greater level of cooperation than the nations of Latin America had achieved since World War II. The United Nations (UN) also reacted immediately to the news of the missiles, as the UN secretary-general used the organization's moral authority to fight for the cause of world peace. At the same time, a couple of Latin America's most influential national leaders, worried that multilateral responses were not enough, took it upon themselves to work to prevent the horrific prospect of a nuclear war.

## Breaking News

Latin American journalists immediately recognized the profound danger posed by the crisis in the Caribbean. The front page of *Última Hora* in Rio de Janeiro warned of "World War by a Thread!"[1] Newspapers published maps of the Americas showing the locations and reach of the missiles. Journalists in countries that President Kennedy had specifically mentioned in his speech highlighted the threat that the missiles posed to local residents. The front page of Peru's *El Comercio* noted that Lima was "within the zone threatened by the intermediate-range missiles installed by the Russians."[2] A headline on the front page of Panama City's *La Hora* warned, "The First Bomb Could Fall in Panama."[3]

Political cartoonists across the region mocked Castro, depicting him as ignorant and impotent. A cartoon in *El Diario* of La Paz showed Fidel Castro clapping his hands and grinning idiotically while Mars, the ancient Roman god of war, launched a missile at the United States.[4] A cartoon in *Folha de São Paulo* depicted Kennedy and Khrushchev playing a game of chess with missiles, while a frightened, childlike Castro watched over Khrushchev's shoulder.[5] These cartoons emphasized the threat of nuclear warfare, while the grins, smiles, and smirks on the faces of Mars, Castro, Kennedy, and Khrushchev suggested that the people in charge were carelessly toying with the lives of millions for their own entertainment. A cartoonist in Bogotá had a slightly different take on the situation in a comic he drew for *El Tiempo*. This cartoon portrayed Castro as a black sheep, an outcast and misfit, that Kennedy was forced to protect inside a fence labeled "Blockade." "I'm sorry," Kennedy told Castro in the comic, "even though you are the black sheep, I don't want the wolf to eat you."[6] The Colombian cartoon showed Kennedy acting in a protective capacity, whereas the Brazilian one portrayed him as one of two men endangering the world. The different depictions suggested that not all Latin American observers approved of US actions. But all three cartoonists did concur in their depictions of Castro as powerless: He was either an enthusiastic observer or a child, or a helpless sheep that had to rely on others for security and protection. As Castro had feared, the news of the missiles immediately damaged his reputation in the rest of the Americas.

Editorialists debated how to react to the crisis. Most lined up in support of Kennedy's proposal for a quarantine, arguing that strong measures were necessary to eliminate the nuclear threat. An editorial in Bogotá's *El Tiempo*, titled "Solidarity in the Face of Obvious Provocation," praised US policy as "infinitely responsible and unalterably sensible." The fawning editorial described Kennedy as "firm, sure, with a head clear of prejudices or exaggerations," and it celebrated how "he resisted everything and faced everything bravely, with clear intelligence and a vigorous conscience."[7] Other editorialists, however, spoke out in Cuba's defense. An article titled "With Cuba against the Crime," in Montevideo's leftist newspaper *Época* called the quarantine "a criminal decision resulting from the fear and impotence of a regime that cannot overcome its own contradictions." It portrayed the crisis as a deadly game between Kennedy and Khrushchev and warned that if the Soviet Union had to play the card of defending Cuba, "we are without a way out before the gloomy prospect of a catastrophe, a true prelude to hell." Like the Brazilian cartoonist, the editorial in *Época* argued that Kennedy and Khrushchev were playing reckless geopolitical games. The author of the piece suggested that Latin Americans should look beyond the interests of the two superpower blocs and their nuclear showdown. "Latin Americans care about the destiny and the right of a brother people to freely choose their path," the

Political cartoon of Kennedy and Khrushchev playing a game of chess with missiles while a frightened, childish Castro watches. *Folha de São Paulo*, October 26, 1962. (Cartoon by Orlando Mattos / Folhapress. Used by permission.)

editorial claimed.[8] This article touched on all three of the main themes of the crisis: security, sovereignty, and solidarity. The author showed solidarity with Cuba and argued that Cubans had the sovereign right to choose their own destiny. By denying Cubans that right, Kennedy and Castro's other enemies were endangering the security of the entire hemisphere.

Still other editorials and political cartoonists argued that world leaders should look beyond the Cold War divide to find multilateral solutions to the crisis. Bogotá's *El Tiempo* published a cartoon on October 26 showing a cowering cherub hiding beneath the umbrella of the UN as the skeletal hand of death dangled a grenade over the Earth, suggesting that the global organization was the only thing shielding humanity from destruction. An editorial in the same newspaper described October 22—the day of Kennedy's speech—as Latin America's "long day's journey into night," alluding to Eugene O'Neill's famous play. The author pleaded for a peaceful solution: "An agreement that prevents the bloody disaster that would engulf us all. An agreement that could put an end to that long and anxious day that began on Monday."[9] On October 25, *El Diario* newspaper in La Paz, Bolivia, published an editorial titled

"Responsibility of the Great Ones." The "great ones" that the article referred to were not the usual suspects. The author was not calling on the Cold War superpowers to resolve the crisis; instead, the article emphasized the importance of multinational organizations. "We have the United Nations on the one hand and the Organization of American States on the other. . . . These are the entities that should be speaking out about the dangers that lie in wait for men and threaten their peace and their lives."[10] In looking to these multinational organizations instead of to the United States or the Soviet Union, the editorials and cartoon put forth two arguments. First, that the Cuban Missile Crisis was a global crisis, thanks to the shared danger of nuclear war. And second, that because the missile crisis was a global problem, international organizations should help resolve it. The collective threat of the Cuban Missile Crisis required a collective response, which gave multilateral organizations the responsibility to defend world peace and an opportunity to prove their worth.

## The OAS Confronts the Crisis

Kennedy's speech on the evening of October 22 jolted the OAS into action. At the time of his speech, the OAS's Inter-American Economic and Social Council had just begun a conference in Mexico City about the Alliance for Progress. Kennedy's announcement prompted a mad rush for the exits, as diplomats and functionaries hurried to the airport and crowded onto planes in order to get to Washington, DC, in time for the next morning's emergency meeting. One flight delayed its departure to wait for the secretary-general of the OAS, José Antonio Mora, and the president of the Council of the OAS, Alberto Zuleta, as they raced from the conference hotel to the airport.[11] Many of the diplomats arrived in Washington exhausted after flying overnight. The Argentine ambassador to the OAS could not find a seat on an airplane and had to be replaced at the last minute by the Argentine ambassador to the United States, Roberto T. Alemann.[12] Venezuela and Uruguay also had to send substitute representatives; but one way or another, every OAS member country answered Kennedy's call to action. Even Bolivia, which had suspended its participation in the organization in protest over the United States' tin dumping and the lack of OAS attention to its conflict with Chile over the Lauca River, sent a representative to the emergency meeting about the missile crisis.

When the Council of the OAS convened its extraordinary session on the morning of October 23, Dean Rusk wasted no time in laying out the United States' proposal and the stakes of the OAS's decision. He asked, first, that the council constitute itself provisionally as an Organ of Consultation and, second, that it establish the quarantine and issue a call for the immediate dismantling and removal of all missiles and other weapons with offensive capabilities.[13] The second part of the proposal, if passed, would be the most forceful action that the OAS had ever undertaken. "All the world will be watching how wisely, how resolutely, how unitedly this Council acts to meet a challenge within our Hemisphere," Rusk urged. "The future of peace and freedom in the world has never before been so dependent upon the inter-American system as it is today."[14]

Latin American representatives whose governments were already pursuing anti-Castro foreign policies responded enthusiastically. The first to speak up, Argentina's ambassador Alemann, declared that his country, as an "indivisible part of the West," would comply with the commitments of the inter-American system and the Rio Treaty. The Guatemalan ambassador, whose government had advocated unsuccessfully for OAS action against the Soviet buildup back in August, declared that "faced with the lethal danger that threatens us all equally, categorical definitions must prevail. This is no time for half measures and lukewarm responses." Venezuela's representative launched into a tirade against the Cuban government, accusing Fidel Castro of being a counterrevolutionary who "wanted to drag the American republics back to their former colonial condition." In his view, the presence of the missiles proved what his government had long argued, that Cuba had surrendered its sovereignty and become a Soviet satellite. The Nicaraguan ambassador took an especially internationalist stance when he stated, "Last night we listened with Pan-American emotion to President Kennedy's speech. . . . The continent should respond with collective action to the Soviet provocation, putting our hemispheric solidarity to work." Nicaragua's ambassador and the other participants in the OAS meeting emphasized the shared nature of the threat and the need for solidarity in the form of a cooperative response. In their eyes, Castro had sacrificed Cuba's sovereignty to the Soviets, so concerns about respecting Cuba's self-determination by avoiding intervention no longer carried any weight. The leaders of these nations had already been pushing for stronger multilateral actions against Cuba and saw the crisis as an opportunity to rid the hemisphere of Castro once and for all.

Furthermore, some argued that the US proposal for a quarantine was not enough to defend against the greater communist threat. The Salvadoran representative explained that "for us, the danger does not end with the missiles. Cuba's subversive activities in our countries, with the terrorist hordes that it is unleashing, are impeding our governments from doing the work necessary to help our people." He urged the council to look beyond the immediate danger of the missiles and put an end to Cuba's other destabilizing activities as well. Peru's representative spoke up next, reviewing the long history of inter-American security cooperation and, specifically, the multiple charges of communist intervention that the government of Peru had recently brought against Cuba in the OAS. He argued that the current crisis only proved the wisdom of those concerns, and that Cuba, as the base of operations for communism's war against the free world, "posed the greatest threat to peace and security that America had ever confronted." According to the Salvadoran representative and others, a quarantine was a good start but not enough to resolve the overall threat that Cuba and communism posed to the region. In their view, Castro's efforts to destabilize their governments were just as great an existential threat as the Soviet missiles. Castro was the one who failed to respect his neighbors' national sovereignty. Their statements demonstrated that collective action against Castro was not simply a US policy imposed on Latin America or the Organization of American States but in fact a goal shared by many member governments.

After voting to invoke the Rio Treaty, the OAS voted on the specific measures that should be taken to guarantee the security of the hemisphere. The resolution that the United States had proposed included a paragraph that stated that the Council of the OAS would

> recommend to the member states, in conformity with Articles 6 and
> 8 of the Rio Treaty, that they adopt all the individual and collective
> measures, *including the use of armed force*, that they consider
> necessary to assure that the Government of Cuba will no longer be able
> to receive from the Sino-Soviet powers military supplies and provisions
> that threaten the peace and security of the Continent, and to prevent
> the missiles with offensive capacity in Cuba from being converted
> at any moment into an active threat to the peace and security of the
> Continent.[15]

The vote on the resolution passed unanimously.[16] The quarantine around Cuba would be a collective measure established in accordance with the Rio Treaty of the OAS.

When Dean Rusk brought the results of the OAS meeting to the rest of the members of Kennedy's ExComm, the relief was palpable. "They're really rallying around," Rusk reported, amid general exclamations of "Wonderful!" and "Terrific!" Deputy Undersecretary for Political Affairs U. Alexis Johnson remarked, "If the OAS has acted before the [United Nations] Security Council, oh, that's going to be a big help. Our diplomacy is working . . . That's great. That's terrific. Oh, that's great news."[17] Kennedy wasted no time in incorporating the OAS resolution into the last sentence of the ultimatum that he sent to Khrushchev on the evening of October 23. He warned the Soviet leader, "I hope that you will issue immediately the necessary instructions to your ships to observe the terms of the quarantine, the basis of which was established by the vote of the Organization of American States."[18] Robert Kennedy congratulated his brother in private later that evening: "You got all those South American countries and Central American countries to vote unanimously. When they've been kicking us in the ass for two years, and they vote unanimously for this."[19] When he wrote his account of the missile crisis a few years later, Robert Kennedy used less colorful language to describe the importance of the OAS vote. "The diplomatic effort was of great significance," he recalled. "We were able to establish a firm legal foundation for our action under the OAS Charter, and our position around the world was greatly strengthened . . . the Soviet Union and Cuba faced the united action of the whole Western Hemisphere."[20]

South American diplomats also celebrated the OAS action. A summary of the missile crisis from Uruguay's embassy in Washington called the OAS vote "the clearest demonstration of hemispheric unity since World War II."[21] A secret report that Argentina's OAS representative sent back to Buenos Aires claimed that US embassies in Europe and Africa observed that the united front presented by the OAS had made a great impression on the other side of the Atlantic. "The action of the regional organization played a preponderant role in defining the support of some European allies," the Argentine representative claimed. Furthermore, it had silenced potential criticism from neutralist countries in Africa "prone to considering the Cuban question as a controversy between a great power and a smaller country formerly subject to its sphere of influence."[22] The OAS response demonstrated that the United States was not the only country in the Americas that was worried about the repercussions of the Cuban Revolution or the danger of nuclear missiles in Cuba. By limiting debate within the Americas and quickly agreeing upon a single hemispheric response to the crisis, the OAS may very well have discouraged debates in other parts of the world.

The OAS resolution was transformative. Instead of being a unilateral US act of war against Cuba, the quarantine gained official standing as a multilateral action in defense of hemispheric security. If the OAS had rejected the US proposal, or if the larger countries had broken ranks (as they had in Punta del Este the previous January), the crisis could have appeared to be an overreaction on the part of the United States. By unanimously approving the US resolution, the countries of Latin America signaled to the rest of the world that they, too, considered the missiles an existential threat to the entire hemisphere. This was not a conflict just between Cuba and the United States, or even between the

United States and the Soviet Union; the OAS resolution sent a clear message that all the members considered themselves participants in the crisis. What was more, the unanimous OAS vote not only transformed the quarantine but also transformed the OAS. The missile crisis marked the height of OAS cooperative action during the Cold War. In previous meetings, some of the largest and most powerful countries in the region had refused to sacrifice any of their own sovereignty or Cuba's to act against Castro. The missile crisis forced these countries to choose between security and sovereignty; all opted for security.

## The United Nations Steps In

The OAS vote also influenced the response of the UN. Immediately after the conclusion of the October 23 meeting, the secretary-general of the OAS, José A. Mora, sent the text of the resolution to UN secretary-general U Thant.[23] That same day, Adlai Stevenson informed the other members of the UN Security Council that the OAS had adopted a resolution calling for the removal of the missiles. Venezuela's representative in the UN, who was serving as a temporary member of the Security Council at the time of the crisis, reminded the council of the OAS's action at the next day's meeting on October 24. Claiming to speak "on behalf of all Latin American countries in voicing their serious concern over the installation of rocket bases and nuclear missiles in Cuba," the Venezuelan announced that the OAS had already adopted a resolution that reflected Latin Americans' security concerns. He told his fellow UN representatives that he "considered it imperative that the Security Council take measures to stop nuclear weapons from arriving in Cuba and to ensure the dismantling of the existing bases."[24]

In his account of the Cuban Missile Crisis written years after the fact, U Thant expressed conflicting feelings about the juridical basis of the OAS resolution, especially the part that authorized the use of armed force. He described the UN's failure to request that the International Court of Justice issue an advisory opinion on the question of regional enforcement action earlier in 1962 as "a tragedy."[25] "By this *non-action*," Thant reflected, "the Security Council implicitly endorse[d] 'Monroe Doctrines' everywhere on Earth."[26] Thant interpreted the quarantine not as a multilateral effort but as a continuation of the United States' long-standing effort to dominate hemispheric politics and keep other foreign competitors out. Furthermore, Thant personally sympathized with the Cubans. He recalled later, "My judgment was that Cuba was fully within its rights to ask for and receive the missiles and bombers from a Big Power, in the same way that Turkey, Pakistan, Thailand, and Japan, on the perimeters of communist countries, were fully within their rights to act similarly."[27] The only difference that Thant saw was that Cuba had received the weapons in secret. But the secretary-general believed that his hands were tied; the UN had to accept the quarantine because refusal would have infringed on the regional sovereignty of the OAS.

Even though Thant had to accept the OAS quarantine, there was still a great deal of room for the UN to determine its own reaction to the Cuban Missile Crisis. Thant had received slightly more advance notice than most other world leaders and the public about the missiles in Cuba, giving him a little more time to formulate his response. On Saturday, October 20, Thant's military adviser, Brig. Gen. Indar Jit Rikhye, told him that leaders in Washington had "definite proof" of the presence of Soviet missiles in Cuba. That same day, Thant received a call from the UN representative in Washington, who reported that President Kennedy believed that the evidence of the missiles was irrefutable.[28] By the time that Kennedy made his televised address on the evening of October 22, Thant was ready to use his position at the helm of the UN to fight for peace.

Representatives of countries around the world wanted the global organization and its leader, U Thant, to take an active role in resolving the nuclear showdown. On the morning of October 24, forty-five member states—mostly nonaligned countries led by Algeria, the United Arab Republic, Morocco, Mali, Guinea, and Ghana—petitioned the secretary-general to intervene in the conflict. Specifically, they asked Thant to appeal to the United States, the Soviet Union, and Cuba "to take no action that would 'exacerbate' the crisis."[29] The secretary-general, who had been involved with the Non-Aligned Movement and its nuclear nonproliferation efforts since its origins at the 1955 Bandung Conference, told the diplomats who presented the petition that he planned to speak at the Security Council meeting that very evening. Even before the meeting, however, Thant acted upon their request. During the annual concert held in the General Assembly Hall to celebrate United Nations Day, Thant retreated to his office on the thirty-eighth floor of the UN building to write identical messages to Kennedy and Khrushchev. He opened by explaining:

> I have been asked by the Permanent Representatives of a large number of Member Governments of the United Nations to address an urgent appeal to you in the present critical situation. These Representatives feel that in the interest of international peace and security, all concerned should refrain from any action which may aggravate the situation and bring with it the risk of war. In their view, it is important that time should be given to enable the parties concerned to get together with a view to resolving the present crisis peacefully and normalizing the situation in the Caribbean.[30]

By framing his message as a request from multiple member countries, Thant used the numerical weight of the UN to pressure the superpowers to consider the global implications of their actions.

Thant appeared to have listened to the petitions of the UN ambassadors when he spoke to the Security Council at its televised meeting on the evening of October 24. He opened by reminding those gathered that "what is at stake is not just the interests of the parties directly involved, nor just the interests of all member states, but the very fate of mankind." He then read the text of the message he had sent earlier in the day to Kennedy and Khrushchev, and even though he had not sent the initial message to Osvaldo Dorticós or Fidel Castro, he belatedly included the Cuban leaders in his efforts. "I should like also to take this occasion to address an urgent appeal to the president and prime minister of the Revolutionary Government of Cuba," Thant stated. He reminded the Cubans of President Oswaldo Dorticós's own proposal at the October 8 meeting of the UN General Assembly: that if the United States would give assurances not to commit acts of aggression against Cuba, then Cuba would have no need for weapons. Thant suggested that this offer could be the basis for a peaceful resolution to the crisis and asked the Cubans to suspend construction on the missile installations to allow for a period of negotiations. The secretary-general closed his remarks with the hope that "not only in the Council Chamber but in the world outside, good sense and understanding will be placed above the anger of the moment or the pride of nations."[31]

After his speech to the Security Council, U Thant continued to work in public and behind the scenes to find a peaceful resolution to the crisis. The most urgent danger when Thant sent his messages and gave his speech on October 24 was the fact that Soviet ships were steaming toward the quarantine zone. But on the afternoon of October 25, Thant received a reply from Khrushchev in which the Soviet leader welcomed Thant's initiative and agreed to his proposed suspension of activities to allow for a period of negotiations. "I understand your concern over the situation which [sic] has arisen in the Caribbean, for the Soviet Government too regards it as highly dangerous and as requiring immediate intervention by the United Nations," the message read.[32] That same day, Thant received a somewhat more tepid reply from Kennedy in which the US president also agreed to the prospect of initial talks. Thant then sent two more rounds of messages to the two leaders in which he set a time for preliminary negotiations and asked Khrushchev to instruct his ships to avoid the quarantine zone and Kennedy to instruct his ships to do everything possible to avoid confrontation with the Soviets.[33] Both parties agreed. Thant's intervention allowed the US and Soviet leaders to back a small step away from the brink while still saving face, and it elevated Cuban proposals and advocated on behalf of the countries and people around the world who were shut out from the negotiations while still dependent on their outcome.

## Missions and Messages of Peace

The leaders of two of Latin America's most powerful countries went beyond multilateral actions to pursue their own unilateral efforts to find a peaceful solution to the crisis. Mexican president Adolfo López Mateos, who was on a tour of Asia when the news of the missiles broke, cut his trip short to return home and manage his country's response. Before he left the Philippines for Mexico, López Mateos hedged his bets and stated that Mexico's reaction would depend on the nature of the weapons in Cuba. Mexico would comply with the Rio Treaty and wait to do anything until the OAS and UN had seen proof and decided on a course of action, the president told reporters.[34]

On his way back to Mexico, President López Mateos took the initiative to reach out personally to his US and Cuban counterparts. In messages to both Kennedy and Cuban president Oswaldo Dorticós, López Mateos called for peace. He made a special appeal to the Cuban president, "in the name of the friendly relations that unite and have united our countries." "I consider that the possible existence of the installations . . . could constitute a serious threat not only to the security to the peoples of the American continent, but for the peace of the world," the Mexican president warned. He ended his message by stating that he believed it was his duty "in the name of peace which all Mexicans have the wish to preserve," to "cordially call upon your government so that those bases are not used in any form whatsoever and the offensive weapons are withdrawn from Cuban territory."[35] In reaching out directly to Dorticós, López Mateos tried to use the friendly relationship that he had established with the Cuban president during his visit to Mexico two years earlier as well as Mexico's unique ties with its Cuban neighbors. Furthermore, the Mexican president was treating Cuban leaders as full participants in the crisis on their island, not as mere victims, puppets, or observers.

Upon his return to Mexico on October 24, López Mateos went straight to the National Palace to present Mexico's response to the nation's public and the rest of the world. In an improvised speech from the balcony to the crowds gathered below, the president emphasized his country's pacifist position. He described Mexico's stance on international relations in the nuclear age: "We are supporters of peace, of complete disarmament, of the prohibition of nuclear testing for warlike purposes, of the use and possession of atomic weapons." López Mateos made an appeal "on behalf of the Mexican people, lovers of peace," to the global leaders directly responsible for the situation. "Let us strive to find suitable solutions. Let us strive so that peace and human tranquility are not broken," he urged.[36] He also appealed directly to the Mexican people: "Let us hope that this crisis may be resolved in favor of the people and in favor of peace." López Mateos closed by vowing, "We are in the ranks of democracy: We will fight for peace and for liberty."[37] The Mexican president's speech was a plea for peace, but it also made clear that he sided with those who denied that the Cuban government had the right to obtain nuclear weapons. Mexico's previous solidarity with Cuba and defense of Cuban sovereignty was not a blank check. When it came to questions of hemispheric security, Mexico would both support multilateral efforts to get the missiles out of Cuba and would take its own steps to encourage Cuban leaders to participate in a peaceful solution.

Brazilian president João Goulart and other Brazilian officials made even more elaborate efforts in favor of peace. Goulart's defense of peace was not an instinctive reaction to the news of the missiles. When US ambassador Lincoln Gordon and military attaché Vernon Walters met with President Goulart in the hours before Kennedy's speech, the Brazilian leader was "visibly shocked." He interrupted Gordon to point out that only a few weeks prior, US officials had insisted that the Soviets were providing only defensive weapons to Cuba. "If the offensive buildup [is] true," Goulart told the ambassador, there could be "no doubt about Brazil's solidarity with the United States." The Brazilian president seemed surprised about the "mildness" of the quarantine and argued that "even stronger language should be used with the Soviets, who are always harshly threatening others." At one point in the conversation, he even asked, "Why don't you blow the whole island out of the water?" When Ambassador Gordon explained that Kennedy had designed the quarantine to avoid killing innocent Cuban civilians, Goulart retorted, "What, and let Americans get killed instead?"[38]

The Brazilian president insisted that he would need to see proof of the bases before taking a strong stance, especially since he would need to justify the change in his policy to the Brazilian public. He was managing a precarious political situation at home, and solidarity with Cuba and defense of Cuban sovereignty had been key elements of Brazil's new independent foreign policy that his popular predecessor, Jânio Quadros, had established. "The previous Brazilian position supported the right of any nation to defend itself against aggression, including Cuban defense against attack by exiles or others," Goulart told Gordon. "But Russian offensive bases in Cuba, constituting a clear danger of aggression against other American nations" were a "wholly different matter." At the end of the meeting, Ambassador Gordon asked President Goulart to instruct his representatives at the OAS and UN to support US initiatives, and Goulart promised to do so. Goulart's initial response to the news of the missiles indicated that he would be willing to change his country's defense of Cuba in light of the revelations of the new nuclear threat.

Brazil's public position on inter-American action against Cuba was less clear than Goulart's initial reactions in his private conversations with US officials. President Goulart struggled to defend both hemispheric security and Cuban sovereignty. After Brazil's OAS representative, Ilmar Penna Marinho, voted in favor of the resolution, Brazil's prime minister and acting foreign minister, socialist Hermes Lima, recalled him to Rio de Janeiro for consultation. The Brazilian press speculated whether Penna Marinho's summons meant that he had disobeyed his instructions by approving OAS action against Cuba.[39] Leonel Brizola, the influential leftist governor of Rio Grande do Sul and Goulart's brother-in-law, gave a two-hour speech over radio and television in which he claimed that Penna Marinho had disobeyed his orders and, by approving the OAS resolution, had violated Brazil's foreign policy of opposing any violence against Cuba.[40] Goulart hesitated to clarify what instructions he had given his representative, merely issuing a statement that described rather than explained Penna Marinho's vote.[41] The Brazilian ambassador to the United States, Roberto Campos, claimed in his memoirs that when he had consulted with Goulart before the OAS meeting, the Brazilian president had told him, "You are authorized to promise Brazil's vote."[42] Brazil's foreign ministry archives contain a telegram to Penna Marinho from Foreign Minister Lima instructing the ambassador to participate in voting only if the resolution could be broken into parts to allow Brazil to approve the quarantine and reject the use of armed intervention—which is what Brazil's OAS representative did.[43] The most likely explanation for the rumors, then, is that Goulart used them to pacify leftist sectors and pin responsibility for Brazil's diplomatic abandonment of Cuba on the OAS representative, thereby avoiding taking a potentially controversial position of his own.[44]

The rumors about Brazil's rogue OAS representative reflected President Goulart's overall approach to the missile crisis: a messy attempt to appease all groups that ended up satisfying very few. Three days after Goulart expressed shock over the presence of Soviet missiles in Cuba and suggested that Kennedy blow the island out of the water, he held a meeting with the acting Soviet ambassador to Brazil. In a long conservation with the Soviet diplomat, Goulart awkwardly defended his country's vote in the OAS, called the quarantine a serious threat to world peace, and claimed that "monopolist circles in the United States" wished for the outbreak of war.[45] Venezuela's ambassador in Rio noted Goulart's uncertain loyalties, observing that "the Brazilian government has attempted once again to take its traditional and characteristic intermediate position." He explained that Brazil's leaders were seeking "to combine a formula that at the same time avoids displeasing the United States too much, which sends so many dollars to this country, to maintain the coherence of the internal demagoguery, to ratify before the world the classic 'independence' of Brazil, and above all to satisfy its conscience about the attachment to 'principles.'"[46]

The main strategy that Goulart used in this effort to please all sides was a multifaceted campaign on behalf of peace. Goulart used international diplomatic gatherings to promote his pacifist plans. On October 24, Goulart expounded on the theme of peace in his inaugural address to the fifty-first annual meeting of the Inter-Parliamentary Council in Brasília. He told the legislators from forty-seven countries in attendance that his government applauded and supported all measures that they might come up with for the preservation of world peace. "Events have placed at the head of the agenda of this meeting calm consideration of the situation facing us, and the efforts of all peoples, and above all of their leaders, toward coexistence, which is the essential and imperative condition for the preservation of peace," he urged them.[47] The conference attendees took Goulart's words to heart and unanimously agreed to send a resolution appealing to the governments of the United States and Soviet Union "to avoid henceforth taking any action which might lead to the catastrophe of general conflict for the peoples of the world." They also encouraged the UN "to take urgently, in the spirit of the Charter, all appropriate measures which would contribute to the maintenance of peace."[48] Goulart and the legislators gathered in Brasília urged Kennedy and other global leaders and organizations to look beyond the Cold War divide to resolve a dangerous, potentially catastrophic, situation.

Goulart and other Brazilian officials also attempted to use their special relations with the Cuban government to slow the pace of the crisis. After learning about the missiles, Goulart secretly reached out to Cuban leaders through his ambassador in Havana, Luís Bastián Pinto, and the Cuban ambassador in Rio de Janeiro, Joaquim Hernández Armas. Through these channels, he tried to convince the Cubans to open their territory to an investigative UN commission. The presence of "independent" investigators would presumably prevent US military action until the claims about offensive missile bases could be confirmed. Brazil's UN delegate also raised the idea of an investigative commission in a private conversation with Cuba's UN representative, Mario García Incháustegui, who responded that he would be relieved if such a commission would force the United States to suspend its blockade.[49] But Castro did not give any indication of interest in Brazil's proffered commission, and the question of inspections faded into the background, at least temporarily.

Another way that Brazilian officials fought for peace was by trying to revive their efforts to designate Latin America a nuclear weapons–free zone. Numerous Latin American officials had been pushing since the late 1950s to establish a nuclear-free zone in the Americas. The idea of "nuclear-free zones" actually came from Polish leaders, who first proposed the creation of such areas in 1956 as an adaptation of the use of demilitarized zones in conventional warfare.[50] The United States encouraged disarmament and nonproliferation initiatives in Latin America, especially through the OAS and the Atoms for Peace program in the UN.[51] Costa Rican, Chilean, and Mexican government officials floated various ideas for the creation of diplomatic commissions and agencies to pursue the goal of nonproliferation through the late 1950s and early 1960s.[52] On September 20, 1962, the Brazilian representative to the UN, Afonso Arinas Melo Franco, was the first person to officially raise the possibility of creating a nuclear-free zone in Latin America.[53] In his memoirs, Melo Franco recalled that "Brazil, represented by me, was not bound by the orders of either side of the Cold War. It voted freely and honestly in favor of disarmament and peace."[54] A month later, just a few days before the missile crisis broke out, the Mexican representative to the UN, Luis Padilla Nervo, followed up on Melo Franco's statements and presented his own resolution about limiting nuclear tests.[55]

Ambassador Roberto Campos in Washington was the first to float the idea of reviving the nuclear-free zone proposal. On October 23, in an extremely urgent cable to Foreign Minister Lima, Campos suggested that the denuclearization proposal that Brazil's representative to the UN had made back in September could be revisited as a way to resolve the missile crisis. "A UN decision to internationalize the question would permit Cuba [and the] Soviet Union to save face, diminishing the dangerous direct confrontation," Campos advised.[56] The ambassador again pushed for the denuclearization proposal in another message to his foreign ministry the following day, arguing, "There is an urgent necessity for creative formulas that, avoiding humiliation for both sides, reduce the tension."[57] Brazil's representative in the United Nations, Afonso Arinos de Melo Franco, agreed with Campos, and on October 24 circulated a draft denuclearization resolution to the member delegations of the UN Security Council for their consideration.[58] Chile's UN representative, who occupied one of the temporary seats on the Security Council, expressed support for the resolution. The Chilean diplomat told reporters that Brazil's proposal demonstrated the intense worry that the Latin American countries felt over the problem of atomic weapons and "the anxiety that we feel when we hear that such weapons already exist in one of the republics of our continent."[59]

Secretary of State Rusk was also receptive to the idea of reviving Brazil's denuclearization resolution. When Kennedy's ExComm met on the evening of October 25, Rusk mentioned that one way the UN could get more involved would be if the Latin American members were to propose the creation of a nuclear-free zone in the region. Rusk predicted that many Latin American countries would support such a resolution, and that the Soviets would have a difficult time opposing it.[60] Declaring Latin America a nuclear-free zone could solve the short-term goal of getting the missiles out of Cuba while also accomplishing a goal the Brazilians and others had been pursuing for years: protecting the Americas from the global nuclear arms race.

At the same meeting, Rusk raised the possibility of another, top-secret way that the Brazilian government could help by serving as a mediator between the United States and Cuba. He suggested that US leaders ask the Brazilian ambassador in Havana, Luís Bastián Pinto, to meet with Castro in order to convince him that there were few benefits for Cuba in being tied permanently with the Soviet Union.[61] Rusk had actually suggested reaching out to Castro through a third-party intermediary during the second ExComm meeting on October 16, inspired by comments that the previous Brazilian foreign minister, San Tiago Dantas, had made about Cuban neutralization at the January 1962 OAS meeting. But at that point his idea was dismissed because contacting Castro would have prevented the United States from launching a surprise attack.[62] By October 26, Rusk was fully committed to the idea of negotiating Cuba's neutralization and was ready to present the rest of the ExComm members with a draft of a cable that he wanted to send to the Brazilians. The cable outlined a covert approach to Castro with the goal of convincing him to break with the Soviets.

Kennedy gave his approval and, that afternoon, Rusk sent his secret message to Ambassador Gordon in Rio:

> We believe [the] time has come for [a] representative [from a] friendly
> country to discuss with Castro alone [the] predicament in which
> Soviet actions have placed him. We also believe [that the] Brazilian
> Ambassador in Havana is [the] best person to do this and therefore
> wish you to see Hermes Lima as soon as possible to secure his
> agreement to instruction [sic] to their Ambassador along following
> lines. This approach to Castro should be handled in such a way as [to]
> make absolutely clear to Castro [that] it is solely [a] Brazilian initiative.
> Naturally we would hope [this] matter could be handled by [the]
> Brazilians with [the] greatest discretion. In this connection we feel
> strongly that [the] need for complete secrecy between [Foreign Minister

Lima] and Ambassador [Bastián Pinto] in Havana only, and absolute accuracy, is so great that the instructions should be taken to Havana by special courier in [a] special airplane as soon as possible.[63]

Rusk's message to Gordon also laid out very specific arguments that US leaders wanted the Brazilian ambassador to make in his talks with Castro. Bastián Pinto was to point out that the presence of Soviet missiles in Cuba had put the Cuban people and Castro's government in great danger, and that the rest of the countries of the Americas had unanimously called for the missiles' removal. The Brazilian ambassador was also supposed to advise Castro that the Soviets were unreliable allies who were already turning around their ships and reaching out to NATO countries with offers to trade concessions in Cuba for advantages in other parts of the world. "You are not only being used for purposes of no interest to any Cuban, but deserted and threatened by betrayal," the message warned. Bastián Pinto was also supposed to make a thinly veiled threat that the rest of the countries of the Americas could no longer sit by and watch as the missile sites became operational and as the danger of nuclear war increased: "Further steps will have to be taken against Cuba and very soon."

The message concluded with an olive branch. The Brazilian envoy was to suggest that giving up the missiles could be the first step in improving Cuba's relations with its neighbors: "From such actions many changes in the relations between Cuba and the OAS countries, including the U.S., could flow." The message concluded with an offer for a pledge of nonintervention. "If Castro tries to rationalize the presence of the missiles as due to Cuban fear of a U.S. invasion, Ambassador Bastián should reply that he is confident that the OAS would not accept an invasion of Cuba once the missiles were removed and that the U.S. would not risk upsetting hemispheric solidarity by invading a Cuba clearly committed to a peaceful course."[64] Rusk's plan to have the Brazilians send a secret communication to Castro was yet another attempt to find a peaceful resolution to the crisis.

Goulart was more than ready to play the role of mediator in the Cuban Missile Crisis. In April 1962, Goulart had approved a similar effort spearheaded by his then-foreign minister, San Tiago Dantas, to have Ambassador Bastián Pinto secretly approach Castro to try to pry him away from the Soviets and old-line Cuban communists. Even though that initiative stalled after Castro received Bastián Pinto but avoided accepting to his offer to mediate between Havana and Washington, Goulart and other Brazilian officials remained dedicated to the idea of negotiation.[65] On October 25, the same day that Rusk revived his secret Brazilian envoy scheme, Goulart sent a letter to Kennedy criticizing the US and OAS responses. "I will not conceal from your excellency my apprehension and the dissatisfaction of the Brazilian people at the manner in which there was sought and obtained a decision of the Council of the Organization of American States without there being carried out, or even discussed, an on-the-spot investigation," Goulart contended. He warned that hasty OAS actions such as the one taken against Cuba ran the risk of converting the inter-American organization into an "uncompromising ideological bloc." The Brazilian president also decried the lack of "any attempt by means of negotiation, such as we proposed last February, to obtain the disarmament of Cuba with a mutual guarantee of non-invasion."[66] He offered Brazil's "sincere collaboration" in "everything which [sic] may represent an effort to preserve peace."[67] Both through his diplomats and his personal communications, Goulart was pushing for UN inspections and a negotiated solution to the crisis.

Brazilian officials did not agree with their US counterparts on how to negotiate with Castro. Instead of making a top-secret approach through Washington's preferred intermediary, Ambassador Bastián Pinto, Goulart followed Foreign Minister Hermes Lima's advice and chose as his emissary Gen. Albino Silva, the new chief of the presidential military staff, whom US officials regarded as pro-communist and anti-American.[68] Sending the leftist general also contributed to frictions within Brazil's military, where the conservative majority of officers likely took it as a sign that pro-Castro elements were gaining influence.[69] Furthermore, instead of keeping the mission a secret, Brazilian officials boasted about it in the local and international press and leaked all the mission's details except for the crucial aspect of US involvement. A headline on the front page of *O Jornal do Brasil* announced, "Goulart Sends an Emissary to Havana," while the front page of *Folha de São Paulo* quoted Hermes Lima that "Brazil Initiates More Effective Action in the Crisis."[70] Far from being a secret approach, Goulart used the mission as a way to gain recognition for his government's efforts to serve as an intermediary capable of bridging the Cold War divide.

Contrary to Brazilian claims and US hopes, Goulart's special mission failed to influence Cuban behavior. The Brazilian emissary spent three days on the island, during which time he reportedly held private meetings with both Castro and UN secretary-general U Thant, who was on his own mission to Cuba. *Diario Carioca* announced that General Silva returned home in the early morning hours of November 1 claiming that Brazil was victorious in its mission.[71] He boasted to reporters that "Brazil is the first country to dedicate itself to a mission of peace and understanding in the Cuban-American crisis given that we are dedicated supporters of peace in our Hemisphere." Silva showed off a large box of cigars that Castro had gifted him, which Brazilian journalists quipped were "peace cigars."[72] Though Silva made it clear that he did not return to Brazil entirely empty-handed, what he left unsaid was that he was unable to get the Cuban leader to change his position on anything, including his alliance with the Soviets or his resistance to UN inspections. Silva's mission to Havana did, however, allow Goulart to portray his government to domestic audiences as a central player in world affairs, capable of defending both hemispheric security and Cuban sovereignty.

## Conclusion

Latin Americans wanted to avoid a nuclear war on their doorstep. They encouraged and enabled the peaceful resolution of the Cuban Missile Crisis through the mechanisms of the OAS and the UN as well as through independent missions and messages of peace. Member countries of the OAS that had resisted action against Cuba were so impressed by the nuclear threat to hemispheric security, they decided to sacrifice their traditional defense of the principle of sovereignty. The two international organizations rose to the occasion and served their foundational purpose of using diplomacy and strength in numbers to help resolve international conflicts. National leaders in Mexico and Brazil, two countries that had shown solidarity with the Cuban Revolution and maintained special relationships with Castro, also took the initiative to send their own messages of peace. Mexico and Brazil's independent responses served a dual purpose: They portrayed their countries as important participants in global affairs and allowed them to defend both hemispheric security and Cuban sovereignty. Latin Americans' first responses to the missile crisis offered hopeful signs that most people in the Americas wanted to find a way to step back from the brink.

# CHAPTER 5
# HEMISPHERIC SECURITY

After the Organization of American States (OAS) voted to establish a quarantine around Cuba, it was time for member countries to step up and make good on their calls for collective action. In the days following the OAS meeting on October 23, the representatives of numerous Latin American governments sent messages to the secretary-general of the OAS offering their cooperation in hemispheric security measures. Most of the leaders of the countries participating in the quarantine were eager to use the missile crisis as an opportunity to demonstrate their solidarity with the United States and, ideally, oust Fidel Castro and put an end to the Cuban Revolution.

## The Inter-American Quarantine Force

Numerous Latin American countries joined in the effort to establish a quarantine around Cuba. Argentina and the Dominican Republic promised naval cooperation; Costa Rica and Haiti made their port facilities available; Guatemala, Nicaragua, and Honduras offered their air and naval bases; and Colombia promised "all necessary and possible collaboration."[1] Ecuadorean navy officials contacted the US embassy in Quito to offer intelligence about shipping, while other countries like Venezuela and Argentina pledged their support in public declarations.[2] Even non-member countries contributed to the OAS quarantine; the government of Trinidad and Tobago offered the use of Chaguaramas Naval Base to warships of any OAS nation.[3] The combined forces of the OAS member countries formed the Inter-American Quarantine Task Force 137 under the direction of the commander of the South Atlantic Force based in Trinidad. From November 12 until the end of the quarantine on November 20, this combined naval force patrolled the seas around the Lesser Antilles, forming the southern-most part of the quarantine line.[4]

The leaders of the Dominican Republic found themselves in a strategic location on the front lines of the quarantine operation. After a period of political turmoil following the May 1961 assassination of its longtime dictator Rafael Trujillo, the country had regained tenuous stability under US supervision and with the transitional leadership of President Rafael F. Bonnelly and a seven-man Council of State. The US ambassador, journalist John Bartlow Martin, met with Bonnelly and the council on the afternoon of October 22 to reveal Kennedy's plans to remove the missiles. Council member Antonio Imbert Barrera, one of the men who had collaborated in the assassination of Trujillo, was the first to react. "I want more," he demanded. Imbert told the ambassador that he wanted war; he wanted to invade Cuba, kill Castro, and end the Cuba question once and for all. When Martin reminded the councilman that an invasion could lead to thermonuclear war and argued that Castro was not worth the risk, Imbert conceded and replied, "Anyway, at last we're doing something."[5]

As they waited somewhat impatiently for their war, the leaders of the Dominican Republic settled for participating in the quarantine. In the first few days of the crisis, the council offered one fleet unit; but by early November, it had expanded that number; the council pulled two frigates off coastal patrol operations and began reprovisioning them to join the quarantine line.[6] At their own expense, the Dominicans also relocated an old oil tanker to Puerto Plata to supply Dominican and US quarantine ships.[7] On November 14, the *Gregorio Luperón* and the *Captain General Pedro Santana* set sail to join the Inter-American Quarantine Force (gathered in Trinidad), with a planned stop in San Juan, Puerto Rico, for minor repairs and final instructions.[8] The Dominican contribution to the quarantine effort had an inglorious conclusion, however. Ambassador Martin recalled that the two frigates soon developed technical difficulties and "limped into Puerto Rico." According to Martin, the United States spent about $100,000 repairing the ships and paying the crew members, who demonstrated their inter-American solidarity by stealing 300 lightbulbs that US repairmen had installed and smuggling 82 refrigerators back to the Dominican Republic. "Despite all this, I thought a show of hemispheric solidarity worth the price," Martin reflected in his memoirs.[9]

Guatemalan leaders were also eager to join the inter-American effort to remove the missiles, and like the Dominicans, they hoped that the quarantine would be the first step in removing Castro. Years before, Guatemala had been the first battleground of the hemispheric Cold War. There, popular demonstrations drove US-backed dictator Jorge Ubico to resign in 1944, ushering in a period of revolution and reform known as the October Revolution and the Decade of Spring. Democratically elected presidents Juan José Arévalo (1945–51) and Jacobo Arbenz (1951–54) introduced a host of reforms. Arévalo's moderate administration passed a Labor Code in 1947 that legalized unions and guaranteed the right to strike, and his government protected political freedoms including the right to vote and freedom of expression. Arbenz went even further. Working closely with communist collaborators, Arbenz passed an Agrarian

Reform Law in 1952 that redistributed uncultivated land from large estates to peasant families. As a result of the reform, over one-quarter of Guatemala's arable land changed hands, including almost 75 percent of the United Fruit Company's property in the country.[10]

Arbenz's double sin of embracing—or at least tolerating—communism and redistributing property prompted fierce domestic and international backlash. Within Guatemala, elite landowners, conservative political parties, and Catholic Church leaders united with university students and market women to wage a cross-class campaign of so-called Christian opposition under the banner of anticommunism.[11] Counterrevolutionary exiles and governments from around the Caribbean Basin—Guatemala, Nicaragua, Costa Rica, Colombia, Venezuela, and the Dominican Republic—formed transnational networks independent of and in collaboration with the United States to oust Arbenz.[12] The United Fruit Company hired lobbyists and publicists to convince the US government and public that Arbenz was a communist and "irresponsible and recklessly anti-American."[13] The Soviet Union, a potential ally, refused to provide meaningful support beyond allowing Czechoslovakia to sell Arbenz a secret shipment of captured Nazi weapons, intended for use by the Guatemalan army and workers' militias.[14] The arms shipment—the first such provision of Eastern Bloc weapons to Latin America—backfired spectacularly when the secret spilled, providing the perfect pretext for an armed intervention that had been years in the making. Under the combined weight of local opposition, diplomatic isolation, military unrest, and a CIA-organized invasion and campaign of psychological warfare, Arbenz resigned on June 27, 1954.

By the time of the missile crisis, Guatemala was being run by some of the fiercest opponents of the Decade of Spring, men who were determined to prevent their country from further experiments with communism and revolution. The president, Gen. Miguel Ydígoras Fuentes, was a strident anti-communist who had run against Jacobo Arbenz in 1950 and then tried to overthrow him.[15] Ydígoras was elected president in 1958 and soon became extremely unpopular for his corruption and incompetence. In November 1960, 150 military officials organized a nationalist rebellion to protest his leadership and his decision to allow the US government to use Guatemalan territory as a training ground for the Bay of Pigs invasion. Ydígoras put down the rebellion with the help of the CIA and the US Army and Cuban exile troops who were training in Retalhuleu.[16] Though the coup attempt failed, some of its leaders fled into exile and began organizing the 13th of November Revolutionary Movement (Movimiento Revolucionario 13 de Noviembre), named after the date of their uprising.[17] Ydígoras blamed Castro for the revolt and threatened to declare war on Cuba.[18] In addition to military uprisings, Ydígoras was struggling against right- and left-wing guerrilla and paramilitary groups in the countryside and student-led protests that in March 1962 devolved into six weeks of riots and pitched battles against police in Guatemala City.[19]

While most of the opposition that Ydígoras faced was the result of his own poor leadership and antidemocratic practices and of the long-standing divisions within Guatemala, the Cuban Revolution also provided inspiration, with the Cuban territory serving as training grounds and haven. The Cuban Revolution was popular among many of Ydígoras's critics, especially among students.[20] Jacobo Arbenz took up residence in Havana in 1960, as did José Manuel Fortuny, the former head of Guatemala's communist party and Arbenz's closest collaborator.[21] Che Guevara had been in Guatemala during the waning months of Arbenz's presidency and had grown close to some of his Guatemalan hosts; those ties became tighter as Guevara and Arbenz's supporters fled into exile after the coup. One of Che's closest Guatemalan exile friends, Julio Roberto Cáceres, had followed him first to Mexico and then to Cuba, and then had gone on to participate in Guatemala's first revolutionary guerrilla group. Cáceres died in the group's failed uprising in March 1962.[22] In early 1962, according to CIA estimates, the Cuban government began providing material assistance to Guatemalan guerrilla groups.[23] Cuba played host country for a meeting in December 1962 between young members of the Guatemalan communist party (who had traveled to the island on educational scholarships and secretly received guerrilla training), veterans of the student protests of the previous spring, and the leaders of the 13th of November Revolutionary Movement. In Havana, the three groups decided to create the Rebel Armed Forces (Fuerzas Armadas Rebeldes), an armed wing of the Guatemalan communist party.[24] If Cuba would not become another Guatemala, as Che Guevara and others liked to declare in their thinly veiled slights against Arbenz's 1954 resignation, then perhaps Guatemala could become another Cuba.

When Ydígoras learned of the presence of the Soviet missiles in Cuba, he felt vindicated. He had spent the past two years claiming that Castro's government posed a threat to Guatemala and to the rest of the Americas, and the news about the missiles seemed to be a pretty clear confirmation. "President Kennedy's speech tells us that the giant finally woke up and that it will abandon its paralysis and lack of foresight," he commented. Ydígoras declared that the Guatemalan army was ready to honor its commitments under the Rio Treaty and to "resolve by arms what has not been able to be resolved within the assigned peace that our countries, enemies of war and of aggression, deserve."[25] Newspapers carried photos of warships accompanied by headlines proclaiming, "We Are on the Brink of Going to War." The use of the word "we"

A LA EXPECTATIVA
ESTAMOS AL BORDE
DE IR A LA GUERRA

A photograph of warships and aircraft carriers participating in the quarantine around Cuba, with the headline "We are on the brink of going to war." *El Gráfico de Jueves* (Guatemala City), October 25, 1962, 4. (Centro de Investigaciones Regionales de Mesoamérica. Used by permission.)

in the headline emphasized the idea that a war against Cuba would involve Guatemala and the Guatemalan people. A Guatemalan frigate, the *Burrunida*, which was undergoing repairs in a Miami shipyard, was placed at the disposition of the United States for quarantine use.[26] Guatemala's OAS representative offered to make Guatemala's air bases and ports available to US forces and even volunteered to host missile sites anywhere in Guatemala. Ydígoras had actually already made the offer on October 16, during a meeting in which he had warned the US ambassador to Guatemala that the Soviet Union was building nuclear weapons bases and undertaking "alarming warlike preparations of an offensive nature" in Cuba.[27] Even before Kennedy had decided on the quarantine, Ydígoras had been offering solidarity in war.

Nicaraguan dictator Luis Somoza Debayle, like his Guatemalan counterpart, seized upon the missile crisis as an opportunity to reiterate his calls for action against Castro. The situation was ideal: The United States could bear the military and financial burden, and he could reap the political rewards. An article on the front page of the Somocista newspaper *Novedades* on October 23 reminded readers that Somoza had repeatedly called for stronger measures against Fidel Castro.[28] An editorial in *Novedades* the next day argued that the only language "the masters of the Kremlin" understood was force.[29] The following day, October 25, another editorial responded to Kennedy's words (that the cost of freedom was always high but that Americans always paid it) with the claim that "the two hundred million Latin Americans who want to go on living as free men have said that we will not hesitate to pay with our lives and blood the cost of dignity and heroism."[30] *Novedades* published a front-page article that same day describing a Somocista Youth rally in Managua in support of the quarantine in which 3,000 people reportedly demanded weapons so that they could take part in the liberation of Cuba. One of the speakers at the rally, Cuban exile leader Luis Manuel Martínez, told the cheering audience: "Ending the blockade at a conference table, accepting as legitimate the genocidal and conspiratorial regime of Fidel Castro, would be a vile capitulation and a show of absolute contempt for the members of the Organization of American States."[31] The articles and editorials in the official government newspaper and the speeches at the pro-government rally helped disseminate Somoza's position that forceful actions were necessary and that Nicaraguans were eager to participate in those actions.

Somoza himself waited until October 26 to make an official statement at an international press conference. He began by reminding the press that his government had warned about the Cuban threat to hemispheric security on multiple occasions and that he had repeatedly called for collective action to put a stop to it. "Nicaragua considers that President Kennedy's decision, supported unanimously by the Organization of American States, is fully justified by the circumstances," Somoza declared. He then continued: "But we also consider at the same time, that [the quarantine] is only a provisional measure, that by itself is not enough to solve the Cuban problem in a definitive way." He argued that, with or without the missile bases, the Soviet-dominated regime in Cuba would continue to pose a threat to the inter-American system and to the security of the hemisphere. "The people and governments of the Americas should resolutely assume the responsibilities that correspond to them in this decisive hour and share whatever future action becomes necessary to defend the independence and sovereignty of our countries," Somoza concluded. He agreed with his Guatemalan and Dominican counterparts that coordinated action against Castro was long overdue and that the quarantine alone was not enough to protect hemispheric security.

## Reluctant Warrior

Rómulo Betancourt's government in Venezuela, eager to support a multilateral solution to the threat of the missiles, also participated in the

Inter-American Quarantine Force. Betancourt had spent the years leading up to the missile crisis pushing for diplomatic, coordinated responses to the Cuba question on the international level while carefully managing domestic unrest and the local repercussions of the Cuban Revolution. The Communist Party of Venezuela (Partido Comunista de Venezuela [PCV]) was one of the most influential communist parties in Latin America when Betancourt began his term. The communists had gained prestige from their participation in the joint efforts to overthrow the dictatorship of Marcos Pérez Jiménez and then enjoyed a surprisingly strong showing in the elections of 1958. But relations between Betancourt and the communist party started out tense and quickly deteriorated. The president excluded the communists from his coalition administration, and they responded by supporting demonstrations and strikes and, in November 1960, by calling for a "popular rebellion" against his government.[32] Meanwhile, earlier in 1960, most of the younger members of Betancourt's Democratic Action party had split—or were expelled—from the party and created the Movement of the Revolutionary Left (Movimiento de la Izquierda Revolucionaria [MIR]), a group that was even further to the left than the traditional communist party.[33] Starting in November 1960, Betancourt's administration began curtailing the activities of both leftist groups, suspending constitutional guarantees on occasion. At the beginning of 1962, the communists and MIR members responded by embracing armed struggle, waging guerrilla warfare in Venezuela's rural areas, and launching a campaign of urban terrorism in the cities. Members of the leftist parties also participated in two failed military uprisings: a relatively small, abortive one in Carúpano in May 1962, and a larger, extremely violent one in Puerto Cabello the following month.[34] Leftist officers and soldiers who fled the military in the aftermath of the uprisings swelled the ranks of Venezuela's guerrilla groups.[35] A CIA intelligence estimate from October 1962 called Venezuela's guerrilla movement the most active in Latin America with the greatest potential in terms of organization, equipment, and finances.[36]

Venezuelan leftists became more radical in the early 1960s in response to both Betancourt's anti-communist politics and the Cuban Revolution. The leaders of the Movement of the Revolutionary Left and the younger generation within the communist party admired the uncompromising militancy of the Cuban Revolution and the sweeping changes that it had brought in such a short time. As one guerrilla leader, Luben Petkoff, recalled, "When we took to the mountains for the first time we were more than a little taken with the idea that our war was going to be a Cuban-style war, or very similar to the Cuban guerrilla war."[37] Another communist commander, Alfredo Maneiro, described the violence in Venezuela as "inexplicable, unimaginable, without the magic of the Cuban Revolution, without the magic of the guerrillas."[38] One of the leaders of the Movement of the Revolutionary Left, Jorge Dager, later told an interviewer that "In the MIR, everyone wanted to make a revolution modeled on the Cuban Revolution . . . we all wanted to be Fidel Castro."[39] Castro, meanwhile, offered verbal encouragement and guerrilla training to Venezuela's armed opposition.[40] In speeches broadcast over Radio Havana, Castro called Betancourt a traitor and an imperialist and accused him of worshipping the interests of foreign oil companies, the US State Department, and the Venezuelan military.[41]

Betancourt was indeed careful to cultivate good relations with his military in order to preserve Venezuela's recent return to civilian rule. He maintained open, friendly lines of communication with his armed forces; the US ambassador to Venezuela, Charles Allen Stewart, recalled that Betancourt kept Thursday afternoons free for meetings with any member of the military who wanted to stop by his office. The president would listen to any problem or question they raised, personal or political, and try to help solve the problem or answer the question.[42] These meetings helped Betancourt build up loyalty within the armed forces and enabled him to identify smart, dedicated officers to place in key posts. Furthermore, the president offered tangible rewards for loyalty; under his administration, military salaries increased, and better housing, low-cost loans, and professional training became available.[43] Finally, Betancourt's firmly anti-communist policies appeased the military and assuaged suspicions that he might have lingering communist sympathies from his younger days. Betancourt made it clear that he was a moderate reformer and Venezuela's best hope for avoiding revolution or a military dictatorship.

Despite Betancourt's efforts to maintain domestic stability, tensions in Venezuela were high in the weeks leading up to the missile crisis. At the end of September, terrorists launched a new offensive in and around Caracas. They murdered several military and police officials, assaulted a military transport, set off a bomb in a hotel, and burned the Dominican and Polish embassies. Betancourt responded forcefully on October 7; he blamed the Communist Party and Movement of the Revolutionary Left, announced a partial suspension of constitutional guarantees, and imposed general censorship. Security forces rounded up more than 400 suspected terrorists, mostly civilians in left-wing political groups with some 60 members of the military and police forces in the mix, but the violence continued. The military gave Betancourt an ultimatum: ban the Communist Party and the Movement of the Revolutionary Left or face a coup.[44] The Bolivian ambassador to Venezuela described the confrontation as "one of the most acute crises of the entire constitutional period"; and on October 12 he reported that he feared a right-wing military coup was "imminent." The ambassador also speculated that Betancourt might be the target of a "double conspiracy," under attack from both the left and right wings of the opposition who wanted to see the military overthrow him.[45] On October 15, Betancourt announced plans to petition the Supreme Court to outlaw the Communist Party and the Movement of the Revolutionary Left and to strip their representatives in congress of their political immunity so that they could be arrested for civil rebellion. He called the authors of the violence "agents of Khrushchev and Castro," and made no mention of military or right-wing threats to his government.[46] Betancourt's decision to suspend constitutional guarantees and begin the process of outlawing the parties of the extreme left appeared to appease the military and resolve the immediate crisis, but his actions drew condemnation from opposition political parties and created tensions within his governing coalition.[47]

When the news broke about the Soviet missiles, all eyes in Venezuela turned away from the unrest at home and looked across the Caribbean to Cuba. A US anthropologist who was living in La Laja, a poor barrio in Ciudad Guayana, described seeing groups of people all over the neighborhood sitting around their radios, listening intently to news of the crisis. She asked one of her neighbors, a housewife who was usually consumed with childcare and household duties, "What's new around here?" The neighbor responded: "Nothing, except this terrible situation in Cuba." The anthropologist observed that the crisis was the main topic of general conversation, even though most residents of the neighborhood usually showed very little interest in international events. She guessed that the missile crisis attracted so much attention in La Laja because residents saw it as an extension of their usual interest in national and local politics. "Venezuelan politics is seen as developing between two opposing poles represented by the United States and by Cuban Castroism," she concluded.[48]

While the North American anthropologist saw the missile crisis as an extension of national politics, other observers interpreted it as a well-timed distraction. Bolivia's ambassador to Venezuela, observing the events in his host country, described the missile crisis as a "life raft" for the embattled Venezuelan government.[49] Kennedy's speech came just a week after Venezuela's latest political crisis, and Betancourt was primed for action. Immediately, on October 23, Betancourt's foreign minister Marcos Falcón Briceño announced the country's support for hemispheric defense efforts. Coalition party leaders who had been criticizing Betancourt's handling of the domestic crisis earlier in the month lined up in agreement. The Christian Democrat party (Comité de Organización Política Electoral Independiente [COPEI]), a member of the governing coalition that had resisted Betancourt's mid-October efforts to directly outlaw the communists and Movement of the Revolutionary Left, issued a call for national unity the same day that Foreign Minister Falcón Briceño announced Venezuela's stance. "Venezuela's position should be categorical," the Christian Democrats declared; "we call upon all the political, social, and economic forces of the nation to demonstrate unity in civil and military defense so that we can prepare with determination and efficiency."[50] On October 27, Betancourt became the first Latin American president to order a full-scale mobilization of his armed forces in response to the crisis. "I have no reason to hide the fact that we face a difficult and dangerous situation," Betancourt declared, underscoring in particular the threat that the missiles posed to Venezuela's cities and oilfields. "My government will comply with each and every one of its international compromises, not only out of loyalty to written agreements in treaties that impose inevitable obligations, but also out of a sense of national survival," he explained.[51]

In order to fulfill Venezuela's international obligations and to protect hemispheric security, Betancourt contributed to the Inter-American Quarantine Force in the Caribbean. By October 31, two Venezuelan destroyers, *Nueva Esparta* and *Zulia*, had reported to the South Atlantic Force, ready to join the Inter-American Quarantine Force.[52] Betancourt's government also sent airplanes and Venezuela's only submarine to participate in the quarantine effort.[53] The US embassy noted approvingly that the Cuban Missile Crisis was the first time in modern Venezuelan history that Venezuelan forces had participated in international military actions.[54] At the end of the crisis, Dean Rusk sent a message to the Venezuelans thanking them for "the eloquent demonstration of your government's full assumption of its responsibilities to defend the Western Hemisphere."[55]

Betancourt turned internal security over to the military. The Venezuelan armed forces divided the country into four zones under military jurisdiction in order to prevent any demonstrations or acts of violence.[56] The press censorship imposed earlier in the month remained in effect, and the police and military officials continued arresting members of leftist groups.[57] Observers in the US embassy described how "quietly by stages, Caracas and Venezuela slipped into an undeclared but reasonably effective state of martial law."[58] The Cuban newspaper *Revolución* described Venezuela's capital as a city under occupation. "All the bridges, factories, electric power plants and public service units, road junctions and telephone services are controlled by soldiers and police. Caracas today appears to be a city invaded by its own army."[59]

Betancourt's decisive action on both international and domestic fronts took advantage of the missile crisis to further his long-term goals of opposing Castro and stabilizing Venezuela. His participation in the quarantine earned his country the enthusiastic gratitude of US leaders, who were pleased to see the Venezuelans participating in multilateral military actions for the first time in their country's history. Splitting the country into zones under military commands—and designating which leaders would command in those zones—also allowed Betancourt to shift more power within the armed forces to loyalists, who further helped him consolidate domestic stability.

## Forces from Afar

When news broke of the missiles in Cuba, Argentina was in the midst of a political, social, and economic crisis. A few years earlier, lawyer and intellectual Arturo Frondizi had been elected president on a vague economic nationalist platform; but once in office, he had undertaken a developmentalist program funded by a series of controversial reforms and unpopular austerity measures. In order to gain the foreign investment, loans, and other aid that he saw as necessary for Argentina's economic development and industrialization, Frondizi opened his country's petroleum industry to foreign partnerships and adopted a drastic stabilization program recommended by the International Monetary Fund.[60] But Frondizi's economic reforms proved unable to revive Argentina's stagnant economy, inflation and the cost of living continued to soar, and the foreign loans that he took on to pursue development added to the country's balance-of-payments problems. Furthermore, the methods that Frondizi used to gain power and pursue his economic program—deception, secrecy, and double-dealing— gave the president a reputation as a Machiavellian politician who could not be trusted.[61]

Over the course of Frondizi's time in office, Argentina's armed forces had become increasingly dissatisfied. In the military's eyes, the president was guilty of numerous sins, chief among them his refusal to take a strong stance against communism, Fidel Castro, or Juan Perón. Members of the Argentine military accused Frondizi of harboring communist sympathies and interpreted his state-led development efforts as evidence of communist infiltration in the government.[62] In August 1961, Argentine military leaders unsuccessfully pressured Frondizi to resign after learning that he had held a secret meeting with Che Guevara; and in January 1962, they tried, again unsuccessfully, to convince Frondizi to vote to exclude Cuba from the OAS.[63] Infuriated by their country's abstention in the OAS meeting, the military leaders made clear to the president, the press, and US observers that they were "prepared to go all the way and overthrow Frondizi's government" if he did not agree to cut relations with Cuba.[64] The president caved and cut relations with Cuba at the beginning of February 1962, and the threat of a coup temporarily receded.

But the military's top priority was preventing the Peronists from returning to power in Argentina, and they were already suspicious of Frondizi thanks to the rumors about the secret pact he had made with Perón to get elected in 1958. Frondizi's decision to allow Peronist participation in gubernatorial and legislative elections in March 1962 was the final straw. After Peronist candidates had a surprisingly strong showing and won numerous congressional seats and several governorships, including the powerful governorship of Buenos Aires, Frondizi desperately annulled the results of the elections. On March 29, the military staged a much-anticipated coup, arrested Frondizi, and closed the congress.[65] The president of the senate, José María Guido, a lawyer and career politician whom the US embassy described as "colorless, taciturn, and cautious," became the new interim president.[66] An unelected, uninspiring leader, Guido was entirely dependent upon the armed forces for both his promotion to and his continuation in power.

Frondizi's ouster was not enough to settle the conflicts within Argentina's armed forces. Military leaders were divided into two factions that clashed over the role that the armed forces should play in promoting modernization, protecting democratic rule, and fighting communism and Peronism. Both groups opposed communism and Peronism, but the legalist *azules* (blues) took a relatively moderate approach and sought to preserve civilian rule, while the more extremist *colorados* (reds) were pushing for military rule and had, in fact, spearheaded the coup against Frondizi.[67] The two factions' fundamental disagreement over the role of the military in national governance was a conflict that would bring them to blows on multiple occasions in the early 1960s and that would haunt civilian-military relations across Latin America throughout the Cold War.

Argentina's nominally civilian government and its military backers responded immediately and enthusiastically to Kennedy's call for hemispheric action to remove the missiles in Cuba. When US ambassador Robert McClintock visited the office of Argentine foreign minister Carlos Muñiz the night of October 22, the minister told him that interim president José María Guido and his cabinet had carefully discussed Kennedy's revelations. Muñiz, who had been in his position for less than a month, was, according to McClintock, an energetic and "forceful character" who had immediately asserted complete and exclusive control over all matters of foreign policy.[68] "The Minister said that not only in the COAS [Council of the Organization of American States] but throughout this crisis we could count on total, repeat total, Argentine support," McClintock reported.[69] Muñiz reminisced decades later that he had felt no doubts about Argentina's stance during his meeting with McClintock. The foreign minister considered the crisis "an event that affected our own security

. . . there were no options. If a war had been declared, Argentina would not have been able to remain neutral."[70] Muñiz issued a public statement about the crisis in the pre-dawn hours of October 23.[71] "Argentina will adopt a clear and conclusive position in defense of the principles of the free world. It will decisively comply with the commitments made and will be united with the other countries of the continent in the battle against communism," the foreign minister declared.[72] Muñiz's words left no doubt: Argentina would show solidarity with any actions that the United States and the OAS decided to take against Cuba.

What was more, Argentina's leaders went significantly further than those of most other nations of the Americas in delivering on their promises. A spokesman for Argentina's navy told reporters on the afternoon of October 23 that the navy was ready to act on any orders it received.[73] That evening, Foreign Minister Muñiz announced that, as a first concrete step, Argentina's navy would cooperate in the hemispheric defense effort.[74] The naval bases in Puerto Belgrano and Mar del Plata began preparing two *Fletcher*-class destroyers, the *Rosales* and the *Espora*, that the navy had acquired from the United States the previous June. Both ships had seen action against Japan in World War II's Pacific theater and were armed with anti-submarine and antiaircraft capabilities as well as with updated radar equipment. On October 27, President Guido visited the base at Puerto Belgrano to give a simple farewell toast in the commander's quarters of the *Espora*. "I wish you good luck. To the Navy and to the Country," he told his officers.[75]

The ships left the following evening, their fresh coats of paint shining in the setting sun. The orders for departure were read aloud from the deck of the *Rosales* and broadcast over loudspeakers. "It has corresponded to our institution, and very particularly to you, the distinguished honor that the homeland entrusts you with the first task in the effective defense of the peoples of America," the orders read. They offered stirring words of encouragement that reminded the sailors of Argentina's historic role in fighting on behalf of its neighbors' independence in the first decades of the nineteenth century. "Set sail safe in the knowledge that behind you there is a Republic that supports you with history, as at the dawn of our nationality, when Argentine arms fought on American soil defending the cause of freedom." The nearly 600 sailors on board were maintaining their country's proud tradition of solidarity: "Today you leave to collaborate, as then, with our brothers of America in the face of the threat of those who seek to subjugate them." Darkness had fallen by the time the ships set sail, and the crowds that had gathered on the docks to bid them farewell raised their handkerchiefs in silent salute.[76]

Argentina's contribution to the defense of hemispheric security earned vigorous praise from the nation's press. An editorial in *Clarín* declared that

Argentina was ready to make the sacrifices required to prevent the universal pain of a war that could be humanity's last, and to defend against the oppression of "the materialism that has no more horizons or prospects than a world of robots, with uniform gestures and voices in the obedience of slavery." "The peace of America is inseparable from the peace of the world," the editorial declared. "We are not an island, men are not islands, and in expressing solidarity with the democratic concerns of the West, we defend all the people of the world, especially those who live in denial or ignorance of liberty." The author's celebration of the West's tradition of democracy made no mention of the recent military coup at home, nor of the ongoing struggles in Argentina over the merits of civilian rule or free elections. "We are protagonists in a decisive moment in the history of the world," the editorial concluded, showing intense pride in the active role that Argentina's leaders had decided to take in the missile crisis.[77]

The decision to send the destroyers to participate in the quarantine inspired substantial jealousy among other branches of Argentina's armed forces. Even before the naval actions were announced on October 23, Brigadier General Cayo Alsina, a *colorado* and the commander of Argentina's air force, took it upon himself to send a message to the commanders of other Latin American air forces in which he declared that Argentina's airmen were ready for action and suggested that the others could join in cooperative measures "in defense of Western Christian Civilization." Alsina released the text of this message to the public and sent a similar offer of cooperation to Gen. Curtis LeMay in Washington. LeMay responded immediately, thanking Alsina for expressing the Argentine Air Force's support in "our common cause."[78] On October 24, Brig. Gen. Juan Carlos Onganía, leader of the *azules* faction and commander in chief of the army, issued orders to prepare for immediate action, either within Argentina or in "a continental or extra-continental theater of operations, either in joint actions with the navy or air force or with the armed forces of the world."[79]

The enthusiastic expressions of hemispheric solidarity from members of the armed forces worried Argentina's civilian leaders. Foreign Minister Muñiz summoned US ambassador McClintock to his office that same day to request that all contact between US and Argentine officials to coordinate military efforts be handled exclusively between the two of them. "Specifically, Muñiz did not wish our service attachés to discuss with Argentine opposite numbers [the] details of Argentine participation in the joint Council of Organization of American States effort," the ambassador reported. McClintock, agreeing with the minister's assessment that it was critical for Argentina's government to speak with one voice and for the civilians in power to get the armed forces under control, promised to run all communications between the embassy and the foreign ministry.[80]

After the Argentine government spent the first week of the missile crisis solidifying its chain of command and focusing on the naval effort, it turned to the matter of the members of the other armed services and their desire to participate in hemispheric action. On November 2, Muñiz and McClintock discussed the air force's informal offer of the use of two SA-16 aircraft and five crews. Muñiz explained that Cayo Alsina wanted the United States to make a formal request for assistance as it had done with the naval destroyers. "What we have is another case of inter-service rivalry," he told McClintock.[81] On November 5, General Onganía approached the chief of the US Army mission in Argentina to offer army participation in a potential land forces deployment in the Caribbean. McClintock, informed of the offer, commented, "Obviously the Argentine army, jealous of its two sister services, wishes to get into the act."[82] Muñiz "begged" McClintock to follow the same procedures with the army as he had with the air force: have the United States indicate its readiness to accept assistance, if necessary, to which the government of Argentina would give immediate agreement.[83] As a result of these negotiations, on November 4, two Argentine air force amphibious aircraft reported to MacDill Air Force Base in Tampa, Florida, for combined operations with the US Air Force in the Caribbean; and three additional Argentine crews departed their country on November 7 for training with US forces. General Onganía announced the same day that the army would organize a brigade of 3,000 men to send to the Caribbean, if required. Ambassador McClintock observed that all of this military cooperation marked the first time that US and Argentine forces had participated in combined operations.[84]

Members of the Argentine armed forces would pay a price for their inter-American solidarity. In mid-November, nine Argentine Air Force pilots died in Panama in a flight connected to the quarantine. Ambassador McClintock met with Foreign Minister Muñiz to express Secretary of State Dean Rusk's "deep regret for the most unfortunate accident."[85] President Kennedy followed up with a letter to President Guido after the crisis was fully resolved, thanking him for the "prompt and resolute manner in which Argentina contributed to the carrying out of the decision of the OAS," and conveying his grief over the deaths of the Argentine pilots.[86]

## Conclusion

The Inter-American Quarantine Force was mostly symbolic—the vast majority of the ships and men involved in the quarantine were from the United States—but during the Cuban Missile Crisis symbolism mattered.

The quarantine temporarily satisfied some of Castro's most dedicated enemies, who hoped that it would be the first step in finally ousting the revolutionary leader. Participating in the quarantine offered an opportunity for Latin American leaders to demonstrate their anti-communist zeal to domestic audiences and to show solidarity with the United States and the rest of the hemisphere. It helped vulnerable civilian leaders in Venezuela and Argentina consolidate power at home against threats of civil unrest, political divisions, and military encroachment.

The fact that so many Latin American nations showed solidarity with and participated in the quarantine also sent a clear message to Castro and his Soviet allies. Soviet general Anatoli Gribkov recalled years later that the Soviets had received intelligence reports that "among the six or seven divisions that were getting ready to attack Cuba, there were Argentine forces, Venezuelan forces, and forces from the Dominican Republic, and military support was ready to come from Ecuador, Colombia, Costa Rica, Peru, Honduras, Haiti, Guatemala, and Nicaragua."[87] The coordinated efforts of multiple Latin American countries and their joint participation in the quarantine gave the Soviets the impression that Cuba was surrounded by enemies that were ready to strike. Just as the earlier multilateral efforts to attack and isolate Castro helped cause the missile crisis by threatening Cuba's government, the Inter-American Quarantine Force helped increase global tensions at the height of the crisis. Soviet and Cuban leaders realized they faced an entire hemisphere of countries united against them.

# CHAPTER 6
# HOMELAND SECURITY

While national leaders in the Caribbean Basin and Argentina were participating in hemispheric security efforts, in other parts of Latin America people were preparing to defend themselves and their countries. Cubans, at the epicenter of the crisis, prepared to repel an invasion. Even though they were the ones with the nuclear weapons, Cubans saw themselves in a defensive role, protecting their national security and sovereignty against outside aggression. In Panama, local authorities worked with US and Canal Zone officials to protect one of the most likely targets of the Soviet missiles: the Panama Canal. The representatives of both countries temporarily put aside their long-standing conflicts over sovereignty in the Canal Zone to operate in tandem to defend the security of the strategically valuable territory. In neighboring Colombia, terrifying media coverage of the crisis pushed members of the public to make their own calculations about how to defend their personal security. Faced with a shared question—How do you defend against a nuclear war?—people and governments in some of Latin America's most vulnerable countries came up with a wide variety of answers.

## A Las Armas!
Even before Kennedy's broadcast, Fidel Castro was sure that a confrontation was coming. He had repeatedly warned Khrushchev that the weapons could not remain hidden for long. Inter-American tensions over the Soviet military buildup had been increasing over the course of the fall, and Castro certainly would have noticed the enormous military mobilization—supposedly in preparation for yet another practice invasion of Cuba with the comically transparent codename Operation ORTSAC ("Castro" spelled backward)—that took place in mid-October while Kennedy was secretly meeting with the ExComm. The US mobilization included reinforcing the Guantánamo Bay Naval Base in Cuba with three additional Marine battalions, doubling the total number of men stationed there to 16,000.[1] Spies infiltrated among the Cuban workers on the base warned Castro about the Marine reinforcements.[2] Castro, in turn, pressed the Soviet military command to speed up

construction on the missile installations. The troops worked day and night. On October 16, none of the installations were ready; by October 18, there were eight operational launch pads; on October 20, there were thirteen; and by the October 21, there were twenty.[3] The US mobilization had put Castro on high alert, and the days that Kennedy took to decide upon a course of action gave the Soviets the crucial time that they needed to finish preparing at least some of their weapons.

Events in Cuba moved quickly in the hours leading up to Kennedy's speech. On the morning of October 22, the newspaper *Revolución* ran the headline "Preparations for Yankee Aggression."[4] At noon, Marines began evacuating almost 3,000 US dependents—women and children—from the Guantánamo Bay Naval Base.[5] Once again, Castro's spies at the base alerted him of this development. At 3:50 p.m. local time in Havana, Castro placed Cuba's Revolutionary Armed Forces on combat alert, and less than two hours later—twenty minutes before Kennedy's speech—Castro issued a combat alarm. The alarm mobilized all of Cuba's available troops: 56 infantry divisions, 4 brigades of tanks and artillery, 10 anti-landing battalions, 6 battalions of defensive artillery, 20 naval units, 118 antiaircraft batteries, and 47 combat aircraft. All told, nearly 400,000 active service personnel, reservists, militia members, and participants in People's Defense Units reported for duty, ready to defend their homeland.[6]

The Cuban leadership divided the island into three defensive zones. Raúl Castro took command of the eastern zone, where he could monitor Guantánamo. Che Guevara established his headquarters in a cave system, la Cueva de los Portales, in order to lead the defense of the western zone, where most of the missile sites were located and where a US invasion would most likely come. The army chief of staff and revolutionary veteran Juan Almeida commanded the central zone from the city of Santa Clara. Fidel remained at the helm in Havana, able to travel freely between the zones and coordinate the island's defenses.[7]

The Cuban public learned the reason for the massive mobilization as soon as Kennedy gave his speech. Ten private Florida radio stations had coordinated to broadcast Kennedy's words live to Cuba, along with a simultaneous Spanish translation.[8] Cubans had to wait until the next morning for Castro's response; but in the meantime, a few hours after Kennedy's speech, Spanish Cuban journalist Luis Gómez Wangüemert appeared before the cameras on Havana's CMQ television network. "This is nothing more than a machination by the US government against Cuba," Wangüemert told viewers, describing Kennedy's speech as "a series of lies about Cuba whose aim seems to be no other than to prepare US opinion for the acceptance of other direct aggressive

A woman hanging a poster calling the Cuban people to arms. *Noticias de Hoy* (Havana), October 26, 1962, 3.

steps toward our country." Wangüemert ended his broadcast with a reminder that Cuba had friends and allies: "We must also remember that we are not alone!"[9]

The day after Kennedy's speech, the Cuban government continued rallying public support. By the morning of October 23, the walls of Havana were covered with thousands of copies of a bright red poster with a photograph of a militia member holding a machine gun over his head during the Bay of Pigs invasion.[10] "A Las Armas!"—to arms—the poster exhorted, as it reminded Cubans of their earlier victory over invading forces. The propaganda coordinator of Cuba's Communist Youth Union, Juan Ayús García, created another poster with the message "Commander in Chief: At Your Orders!" superimposed over a photo of Fidel Castro gazing out from the peaks of the Sierra Maestra. The photograph was one taken by Alberto Díaz, or "Korda," the man who also shot the famous image of Che Guevara. Ayús recalled being inspired by seeing the patriotic message painted on a wall at the University of Havana: "They wrote it raw, quickly, without capital letters or punctuation. The author may have been a young student, a worker, a professional, or a soldier. It stuck with me."[11] The posters used photographs that hearkened back to Cubans' previous military triumphs to encourage the public to both take up arms and follow the instructions of their fearless leader.

On the evening of October 23, twenty-four hours after Kennedy's speech, Fidel Castro took to the radio and television airwaves to give his much-anticipated response. Earlier in the day he had received a reassuring letter from Khrushchev in which the Soviet leader had denounced Kennedy's actions as "pirate-like, perfidious, and aggressive." Khruschev also informed Castro that he had ordered Soviet troops in Cuba to adopt the necessary measures to be completely ready for combat. Castro took the letter as a promise that Khrushchev would stand strong and refuse to retreat.[12] In his first televised speech about the crisis, Castro read portions of Kennedy's broadcast in a mocking tone, interjecting his own commentary. To Kennedy's claim that Cuban leaders were "puppets and agents of an international conspiracy who have turned Cuba against your friends and neighbors," Castro countered: "It is they who have compelled the neighbors to break with us; that is, to turn them into our enemies." He then proceeded to put forth his own interpretations of the meaning of sovereignty, international law, and the ethics of international relations. "They try to tell us what measures we should take, what steps we should take to defend ourselves? The victim must consult with the assassins as to how he is going to defend himself?" Castro demanded. He insisted that the Cuban government had the right to gain weapons and that it did not have to report its plans to anyone. "Whoever said that we are obliged to render accounts to the imperialists—to the aggressors—of the measures and of the weapons we are taking for our defense?" Castro asked. He also rejected any attempts at supervision or inspections. "Within our frontiers, we are the ones who rule, and we are the ones who do the inspecting. . . . Anyone who tries to come and inspect Cuba must know that he will have to come equipped for war," he warned. Castro claimed that his country was facing the threat with a serene, confident attitude. He addressed his closing words of reassurance to the Cuban people: "All of us, men and women, young and old, we are all united in this hour of danger, and ours, the fate of all the revolutionaries and the patriots, will be the same fate, and the victory will belong to all."[13]

Castro's speech set off a wave of patriotic fervor. A Chilean journalist who was in Cuba described how the entire nation was glued to their radios and television sets as Castro spoke. "There was not a soul in the streets and Havana seemed like a deserted city," he reported. As soon as Castro concluded his speech, the residents of Havana flooded into the streets and began improvising torches and singing. The Chilean journalist described the moving scene, as "starting from the thousands and thousands of points of light of the torches, the sounds of the Cuban national anthem rose in waves."[14] "Do not fear a glorious death, for to die for the Fatherland is to live," thousands of Cuban voices sang in unison.[15] Another foreign observer also described an atmosphere of nationalist fervor. Argentine journalist and scholar Adolfo Gilly, at the time a member of the Trotskyist fringe offshoot Posadist party who was spending a year in Cuba studying the revolutionary transformation, wrote, "It was as if a long-contained tension relaxed, as if the whole country had said as one: 'At last!'" Gilly recounted, "There was not the slightest fear or alarm." He claimed, "Cuba was one man and his rifle." According to Gilly, taking up rifles and joining militias gave Cubans a sense of control over their fate. "There was no waiting with empty hands for a battle that others decide some place where one cannot intervene," he recalled. "In Cuba, everyone felt he had the means with which to decide the outcome."[16]

As Gilly reported, Cubans took up their weapons and prepared for battle. Members of the armed forces mounted machine guns on the roofs of the tallest buildings and antiaircraft batteries along Havana's Malecón, the iconic roadway, esplanade, and seawall whose construction had begun during the early twentieth-century US occupation. Young boys stuck butcher knives, meat cleavers, and machetes in their belts.[17] Teenagers, boys of thirteen and fourteen years, carried rifles, manned antiaircraft guns, and commanded tanks.[18] Professors at the University of Havana distributed rifles to students.[19] A student later recalled watching as one of his humanities professors—whom he described as "an apolitical man, certainly no friend of Castro and the revolution"—put on his best suit, gathered several of his favorite books, and walked slowly and calmly to the trenches, "a ghostly and surreal sight, in order to be with his people at their moment of truth."[20] Members of militias who were not sent to the trenches reported to work in their uniforms, weapons at their sides, in order to maintain production levels.[21]

Even critics of the Cuban government answered to the call to arms. Carlos Moore—an Afro-Cuban of Jamaican descent who had initially been so excited by the promise of the Cuban Revolution that he returned to Cuba in June 1961 from his family's exile in the United States—was nineteen at the time of the missile crisis. He was working in the Ministry of Communications, having previously served time in prison and at a work camp for questioning the Cuban government's racial policies. Moore set aside his grievances and rallied to his country's defense. He was issued a rifle and assigned to an improvised rampart in an open field beside the ministry. Moore recalled, "I was unafraid, prepared to defend my country's sovereignty." Moore considered himself a nationalist—not a *fidelista* like many of his compatriots—and decided that defending Cuba's security and sovereignty in its hour of need took priority over criticizing its leaders. Moore also remembered his excitement at learning that Cuba had acquired nuclear weapons: "We were jubilant. We finally had real power. The Caribbean midget . . . could fell the giant United States." Moore and other Cubans saw the nuclear weapons as a great equalizer; while they had been defending against threats including invasion and sabotage for

Young Cuban militia members arming antiaircraft weapons.
(Photograph by Roberto Salas. Courtesy of Prensa Latina. Used by permission.)

years, now everyone in the hemisphere faced the prospect of a nuclear war. As Moore put it, "Fear would become a democratic affair."[22]

The Cuban government provided detailed instructions to the public on how to defend themselves and prepare for an attack. Authorities put out a long informative bulletin, which was published in *Bohemia* magazine and distributed by the Federation of Cuban Women (Federación de Mujeres Cubanas [FMC]). It recommended that because constructing air raid shelters would take too much time, residents should instead find other locations that could serve the same purpose such as the basements and interior rooms of houses and businesses. The bulletin advised those who planned to shelter in their homes that they should reinforce the walls with sandbags and the ceilings with strong wooden beams, and it provided instructions to calculate the air and space requirements for each person. In the event of an air strike, the bulletin told Cubans to "remain calm and act with confidence and poise." They should follow the instructions of the authorities and keep the streets and phone lines clear. Instead of trying to call friends and family members to check on them during an attack, the public should trust the authorities to take care of their loved ones. "Phone calls do not stop bombs," the bulletin cautioned. It explained that in case of explosions, people should take cover under doorways, tables, or beds, and remain crouched or on all fours. "It is not advisable to lie on the floor," the bulletin warned, "due to the violent shakes that explosions produce in the structures and that can cause serious injuries.

In such cases, it is recommended to place a piece of wood or hard rubber between the teeth." Residents should stock up on sand to put out fires but not on food because that would cause shortages.[23] The government bulletin presented Cuban citizens with both practical advice to protect themselves and patriotic exhortations to protect their country.

Cuban women stepped up to contribute their sweat and blood to the defense effort. In a televised speech on October 24, Vilma Espín, president of the Federation of Cuban Women, informed women of all the ways they could participate. She advised women to take up positions in health brigades, in the military, and in factories and fields. "Don't let production decline!" she exhorted. "For every mobilized man there must be a woman to take his place at the machine or the furrows."[24] Espín also encouraged Cuban women to donate blood, and they responded enthusiastically, waiting in line for hours to donate. Even more donors showed up to hospitals and the blood bank during the missile crisis than during the Bay of Pigs invasion, and medical staff had to work extra hours to keep up with the Cuban public's desire to contribute.[25]

Cuban women also rushed to keep their country's machines humming. One fifty-year-old Afro-Cuban former domestic worker, Cristina Llerena Flores, a member of the Federation of Cuban Women, took up her son Félix's place in the Augusto César Sandino carpentry workshop when his militia was called up to duty. Félix's coworkers tried to turn Cristina away, telling her they could cover for him, but she stood firm. "I have come here to substitute for my son," she insisted. Cristina told a reporter from *Hoy* newspaper that she and her children had suffered from poverty and racial discrimination before the revolution and that she was proud that her children now had good educations and respectable jobs. "Kennedy wants to re-enslave us!" she exclaimed. "But just like Fidel said, they will first have to make us disappear from the face of the earth."[26] Cristina was one of many women who did their part during the crisis by keeping Cuba's factories producing. Their labor—and the importance that the government and media placed on it—revealed that invasions and nuclear attacks were not the only threats to Cuban security. Shortages were also dangerous, and working to prevent scarcity was one way for Cuban women to demonstrate solidarity and participate in their country's defense efforts.

Cuban artists and writers contributed their labor to the defense effort as well. Poet and singer Jesús Orta Ruiz, who went by the name El Indio Naborí and was a longtime member of the Cuban communist party and supporter of Fidel Castro, joined a military unit in Pinar del Rio province. He also composed some verses for the occasion. "If you attack my peaceful and pleasant sands," his poem warned, "you will find your graves where you sink your boots." We might all wind up dead, Orta Ruiz concluded, "You, with the dirty

Cuban women working in a factory to maintain production during the missile crisis. (Courtesy of Prensa Latina. Used by permission.)

death of pirates; Us, with the clean death of patriots."[27] Photographer Korda also entertained thoughts of death but kept the mood light by going around Havana making jokes that he wanted to know where to stand to get the best shot of the mushroom cloud.[28] The National Union of Writers and Artists of Cuba (Unión Nacional de Escritores y Artistas de Cuba [UNEAC]), founded by poet Nicolás Guillén in 1961, embraced the call for production. The group inaugurated its new workshop on October 25 and 26 with a marathon gathering of two consecutive days and nights to produce creative material in defense of the country. Graphic artists designed propaganda posters, writers penned essays, and poets wrote lyrics to songs that were then put to music by composers.[29] Kennedy's name featured prominently in a song that Guillén wrote, titled simply "Son" in reference to the traditional Afro-Cuban son musical style:

Kennedy con su bloqueo
nos quiere cerrar el mar,
    Quenedí, quenedá
Afeitar a los barbudos,
Volvernos a esclavizar.
    Quenedí, quenedá,

¡qué bruto que es el Tío Sam!
    Quenedá.

Ni un paso atrás, compañeros,
amigos, ni un paso atrás,
    Quenedí, quenedá,
plomo y plomo al enemigo,
plomo y plomo y nada más.
    Quenedí, quenedá,
¡qué bruto que es el Tío Sam!
    Quenedá.

Kennedy with his blockade,
wants to close the sea to us,
    Quenedí, quenedá,
Shave the bearded
Enslave us again.
    Quenedí, quenedá.
What a brute Uncle Sam is!
    Quenedá.

Not one step back, comrades,
friends, not one step back,
    Quenedí, quenedá.
lead and lead to the enemy
lead and lead and nothing else
    Quenedí, quenedá,
What a brute Uncle Sam is!
    Quenedá.

The song mocked Kennedy and accused him of wanting to isolate and re-enslave Cubans. The threat of returning to the era of slavery that cast a dark shadow over both Cuban and US history was a common—and powerful—trope during the missile crisis. Guillén, like volunteer factory worker Cristina Llerena Flores, portrayed attacks on Cuba's sovereignty as an attempt to enslave the island and its people, many of whom were descended from enslaved workers. Guillén emboldened his fellow patriots to stand their ground together and trust in their weapons. The songs, posters, and essays that the Cuban artists created helped boost public morale and reinforced Cuban leaders' calls to action and their claims that the country was united and ready to fight to the death.

Posters created by graphic artists in the National Union of Writers and Artists of Cuba (Unión Nacional de Escritores y Artistas de Cuba [UNEAC]) during the missile crisis. They read, "We will overcome" and "Cuba is not alone." (Photograph by Roberto Salas. Courtesy of Prensa Latina. Used by permission.)

Foreign supporters and observers of the Cuban Revolution who found themselves on the island during the crisis also joined the defense effort. *Revolución* newspaper reported that citizens of twenty-two countries formed their own combat brigade to reject "the violation of international law by Yankee imperialism." Members of the foreign brigade hailed from East and West Germany, Algeria, Ethiopia, Senegal, South Africa, Argentina, Bolivia, Brazil, Colombia, Costa Rica, Ecuador, El Salvador, Guatemala, British Guiana, Nicaragua, Panama, Paraguay, the Dominican Republic, Venezuela, the Soviet Union, and Vietnam.[30] This cooperative effort brought together people from countries on both sides of the Cold War divide who were ready to risk their lives for the cause of revolutionary solidarity. Nicaraguan revolutionary Carlos Fonseca, who was in Cuba getting support for his fledgling Sandinista Front of National Liberation at the time of the missile crisis, participated in the mobilizations by leading a group of Nicaraguans who manned two machine guns in the Mariel military unit.[31] Armida Mármol, a Venezuelan who worked in Cuba's Casa de las Américas and joined a militia unit, told reporters from *Bohemia* that she was honored to help defend the island because Cubans and Venezuelans were one and the same. "What an honor for me, a Venezuelan, to feel like a daughter of Cuba, and to live as a daughter of Cuba, to fight as a daughter of Cuba, at this crucial and glorious moment of her destiny!"[32]

Mármol and the other members of the international brigades saw the missile crisis as an opportunity to defend the revolution that had given them hope and inspiration.

One foreign fighter who found himself in Cuba during the missile crisis had a bird's eye view of the events from his bed on the tenth floor of the Cuban Armed Forces Hospital. Argentine revolutionary Ciro Bustos, who was in Cuba training with *Prensa Latina* founder Jorge Masetti and Che Guevara for their guerrilla campaign in Argentina, spent most of the crisis in the hospital in Havana undergoing treatment for a bronchial infection. The rest of his training group had departed for Pinar del Rio province to help Guevara with the defense effort, but Bustos could only watch from the window of his hospital room as US warships dropped anchor at the edge of the international waters and US airplanes flew overhead. He found solace in the courage of his fellow patients, wounded soldiers who begged to have their uniforms and weapons back so that they could help defend their country. Bustos was elated when he recovered from his infection in time to rejoin his group in western Cuba by the end of the week.[33]

Just as Bustos found inspiration in the dedication of Cuban soldiers, Cubans were encouraged by demonstrations of solidarity in other parts of the Americas and around the world. Newspaper pages were filled with stories of protests and declarations, bearing headlines such as "Cuba Is Supported by the Solidarity of the Entire World" and "The World Increasingly Rejects the Yankee Provocation."[34] Chilean journalist Sergio Pineda described Cuban factory workers' reactions as they listened to reports on loudspeakers of popular demonstrations in Montevideo, Rio de Janeiro, and Buenos Aires. "People raise their heads, listen, and return to work with more energy, with a kind of furious joy, their rifle just there within reach," he observed. Cuban workers were heartened by the news that they were not alone in their hour of need.

It is important to remember, however, that there could have been a significant difference between how Cuban people responded publicly to the missile crisis and how they responded privately. It is also crucial to recognize that journalists chose to highlight the most extreme examples of patriotism, as by that time most of the media was under tight government control. Other sources suggest that while the Cuban public did maintain at least an outward appearance of composure, the response was not as unified or as defiant as Cuban newspapers and leaders claimed. A British diplomat stationed in Havana at the time described a scene of "unnatural calm here as on the edge of a cyclone." But whereas Cuban leaders claimed that the calm atmosphere was a sign of confidence, the British diplomat attributed it to a "mood of dazed anxiety." "We have nothing to suggest," he pointed out, "that the average man and woman—very many of them now in militia uniform—has a burning desire to die for the cause."[35]

Likely, Huber Matos's jailer on the Isle of Pines was suffering from a "mood of dazed anxiety" when he forgot to lock the door to the political prisoner's cell one afternoon during the crisis. Matos was a former commander in Castro's July 26th Movement who, in the fall of 1959, had had the temerity to criticize Castro's turn to the communists and accuse him of "burying the revolution."[36] During the missile crisis, Matos watched, mystified, through the bars of his small window as Cuban troops began to gather in the woods beyond his cell. He noted the increasing number of airplanes flying overhead and concluded that something big was about to happen. Matos also noticed a change in his jailer's behavior; instead of coming three times daily he cut his visits to once a day, and "walked as if he were very worried." Other prison guards, clearly on edge, snapped at Matos and his cellmate when they tried to turn on their light. "No! You cannot turn on the light! If you do, we will shoot!" For days, Matos was kept literally and figuratively in the dark, unable to go out into the prison's courtyard and uninformed about the dangerous confrontation mounting outside the prison walls. When he learned from another prisoner two months later about the missiles, Matos reflected: "I find it ironic to consider that if war had broken out, we would have disappeared without knowing what was happening."[37] Everyone at the prison, the guards and the inmates alike, spent the missile crisis going through their daily motions in a combination of fear, distraction, and ignorance.

Cuban writer Edmundo Desnoes was another person who found himself on the front lines of the crisis without a burning desire to sacrifice himself for the cause. During the crisis, Desnoes served as a member of a delegation of Cuban intellectuals who were dispatched to the San Cristóbal base to report any possible attacks to the Soviet bombers waiting there.[38] Desnoes spent the night at the airbase on a cot in the infirmary, resting next to empty gurneys that had been prepared for the corpses that were expected to arrive at any minute.[39] Three years later, Desnoes published a semi-autobiographical novel titled *Inconsolable Memories*, which served as the basis for the seminal 1968 Cuban film *Memories of Underdevelopment*.[40] The novel's protagonist, an alienated bourgeois intellectual, describes listening to Kennedy's speech on the radio and feeling numb with shock. "I suppose the yanquis will invade us, the Marines, they will bomb Havana first. I can't believe it, rockets here, in our pretty little Cuba." "I was scared to death," he described, "my lungs heaving with anguish." The narrator contrasted his own terror with what he saw while wandering the streets of Havana over the following days. "People talk and move about . . . as if war were a game," he marveled. "They don't know what can happen to them. They're fools."[41] Desnoes later elaborated that "Cubans, those committed to the revolution, had no understanding of the horrors of a nuclear war. Faith in the promise of social justice blinded them to the cruel facts."[42]

In further contrast to other Cubans' desire to do whatever they could to help the cause, Desnoes's narrator describes feeling helpless and impotent. "Others are deciding my life. I can do nothing. I control nothing. If I lie down to sleep, I may never get up again." He muses that by acquiring nuclear weapons, Cuba has become a modern country. "Today we have entered history. . . . Our power to destroy makes us the equal for a moment of the two great powers. . . . We have never been more important or more miserable." As the novel closes, the threat of death makes Desnoes's narrator realize that he does not want grandeur, that he would rather remain in an underdeveloped country than in an important one. "I am not interested, or attracted to a destiny that must confront death every minute in order to survive," he reflects.[43] It is impossible to say how many other Cubans would have agreed with Desnoes and his narrator and shared his feelings of terror and impotence. But the fact that his story exists, was published in Cuba, and became a popular and celebrated film, suggests that there was a greater variety of responses than the Cuban media and leaders claimed.

## Prime Target

Panamanian officials and citizens were quick to note that the presence of the US-controlled canal in the middle of their country made them a probable ground zero for a nuclear assault. Kennedy had, after all, listed the Panama Canal as the second most likely target in his speech to the world on October 22, right after Washington, DC, and Castro had already demonstrated his willingness to support attacks against Panama's government in previous years. The canal itself was indeed an attractive strategic target; destroying or damaging it would significantly complicate military and commercial transportation between the Atlantic and Pacific oceans. Furthermore, the US military facilities within the Canal Zone, known as the US Caribbean Command, included the Pentagon's most important training centers for its Latin American partners—the Inter-American Air Force Academy and the US Army Caribbean School (which would later become the infamous School of the Americas)—as well as the Pentagon's premier jungle training center for US special forces. The command post in the Canal Zone also housed all the largest telecommunication and satellite-radar facilities for monitoring Central America, South America, and the Caribbean. A nuclear attack on the Panama Canal could wipe out the US military's most important outpost in Latin America.[44]

Panama's top officials immediately expressed enthusiastic support for the United States and multilateral efforts to remove the missiles, as they had long been pushing for more aggressive measures against Castro. On October 23, Panama's foreign minister, Galileo Solís, praised Kennedy's speech and his request for OAS action. He remarked that no one following the course of events in the region should have been surprised because "sooner or later the time would come when immediate action became necessary, and that moment has now arrived."[45] After the OAS established the quarantine, President Roberto Chiari voiced his strong support and vowed that Panama would adopt any measures required to strengthen the hemisphere's defenses. "The time has come for all the countries of the Americas to have a clear vision of what this common danger means," he declared.[46]

Panamanian and US officials hurried to defend both the canal and the surrounding territory. US military commanders mobilized all their troops in the Canal Zone and exercised their authority to rush US warships through the canal's locks, ahead of commercial vessels. US residents of the Canal Zone—known as Zonians—lined up with their children along the edges of the canal to watch the parade of ships, an impressive demonstration of their country's naval power. This was the first time in a generation that the Zonians and their military garrison had felt a real sense of importance, of strategic purpose, and they were excited to play their part.[47] The Chilean ambassador to Panama also went out to the Port of Balboa—the Pacific port of the canal near the Bridge of the Americas in Panama City—to count the number of US warships making their way from the Pacific Fleet to join the quarantine in the Caribbean.[48] President Chiari regretfully informed the US ambassador when they met on October 22, before Kennedy's speech, that since Panama lacked an army and navy, his country would be unable to collaborate in any military efforts. Foreign Minister Solís did promise, however, to use Panama's national guard units to strengthen the Canal Zone's defenses, protect US citizens and property, and maintain peace in the rest of the country.[49] In addition, Panama Canal authorities announced that Soviet ships passing through the canal would be subjected to heightened security measures, comparable to the inspections required of Soviet ships seeking to pass the quarantine line established around Cuba.[50] In taking this step, Panama Canal authorities in effect extended the quarantine line to Panamanian territory.

Panama's minister of government, Marcos A. Robles, used the need to strengthen his country's security as an opportunity to silence local opposition. On October 25, he gave a televised speech to the nation in which he first stoked fears and then tried to calm them. Robles warned his viewers that "the power thirst and insanity of one man, Fidel Castro, combined with the

Soviet Union and international communism's limitless ambition to subdue the world's free nations," had brought the nations of the Americas to "the brink of a war which, if it should come, undoubtedly would lead to the use of nuclear weapons with catastrophic bloodshed, mourning, sickness, misery, and sorrow." Robles then assured Panamanians that their government was fully aware of the danger of the situation and ready to face it with courage, decisiveness, and patriotism. He urged citizens that they should not let hysteria or pessimism rule their emotions but instead calmly await instructions from the authorities. To ensure the public's cooperation, Robles specifically issued a warning to "communist agitators" that he would not tolerate any propaganda, meetings, or other activities. "I will act drastically against those agitators if they try to carry out subversive acts; and I warn them that I fully know of the violence and terroristic acts used by international communism and I will not under any circumstances permit them to hide under the immunity of any political position to pursue their deplorable ends," the minister threatened.[51] He concluded by asking Panamanians to pray to God for peace on behalf of their president, their country, the world, and humanity as a whole.

Robles and other Panamanian officials created a new National Civil Defense Commission to coordinate their efforts. Robles announced the creation of this organization in his October 25 speech, arguing that the country was "in diapers" in its preparations and that thoughts and prayers were not enough to protect citizens against attack. The committee to organize this commission brought together representatives from a wide variety of organizations: hospitals, the Red Cross, the fire departments, the National Guard, the Ministries of Social Welfare and Education, the Public Roads Department and Chamber of Transports, the Amateur Radio Association and Government Information Service, and US officials from the Canal Zone. The committee's top priority at its first meeting was public communication. It called for an immediate campaign among all media outlets to help prevent hysteria and inform the public that within twenty-four hours, they could expect to receive instructions on how to defend themselves in case there was insufficient time to wait for government measures. The committee announced that it was issuing instructions to the chief of radios that commentators who presented alarming information to the public should be removed from their microphones. In case of a loss of electricity in the nation's capital, the committee approved the creation of an independent radio communication system operated by amateurs.[52]

The civil defense commission issued a bulletin containing simple, brief instructions on how to respond to a nuclear assault. The bulletin provided two alarm codes to listen for: a continuous tone lasting three to five minutes would indicate that an attack was expected, whereas a three-minute intermittent chime told listeners "ENEMY ATTACK IMMINENT, TAKE SHELTER IMMEDIATELY WHERE YOU CAN." The bulletin instructed readers that the best place to seek shelter was in an interior room on the ground floor of a building. If they found themselves in a car during an attack, they should roll down the windows and crouch on the floor. If they were outside, they should lie flat on the ground. The final directive on the bulletin was that Panamanians should follow the instructions of the Civil Defense Commission only, which their favorite radio station would transmit when necessary.[53] The commission distributed the bulletin through posters in public places and in Panama's newspapers, telling readers to cut out and save the instructions.

US authorities who were in charge of securing the Canal Zone coordinated with Panama's National Civil Defense Commission but distributed their own informational pamphlet in the zone's retail stores. These pamphlets were more detailed than the ones published outside the zone, and contained information on emergency first aid, protection from radioactive fallout, and food recommendations for emergency shelters. Canal Zone newspapers reported that there had been high public demand for the pamphlets ever since the quarantine was announced.[54] A sign placed in a veterans' club in the zone reportedly offered more concise advice on what to do in the event of a nuclear attack: "First: keep calm, do not lose your composure. Second: pay your bill. Third: run like hell."[55] A clothing store in Panama City, Almacen Manhattan, took a similarly tongue-in-cheek approach to the crisis, running a full-page ad claiming that it was closing its doors and liquidating all its merchandise because war had broken out. The advertisement featured images of missiles, warplanes, submarines, and exploding bombs.

Panamanian legislators took the crisis seriously and challenged Minister Robles, accusing him of relying upon amateur groups and infringing upon civil liberties and professional protections. On October 25, immediately after Robles gave his speech about defensive measures, Panama's National Assembly summoned him to testify about his statements and plans. Deputy José Pablo Velásquez argued that the US military should be the ones responsible for protecting Panama from a nuclear attack, since it was the presence of the canal that made Panama a prime target. "The US military with its technicians and its millions of dollars should be in charge of Panama's civil defense," Velásquez argued. He vehemently criticized the motley composition of Robles's civil defense committee, declaring that "with such a committee, we should consider ourselves as good as dead."[56]

Other deputies took Robles to task for his claim that political immunity would not protect "agitators" from prosecution. Robles fumbled around and tried to backpedal his defiant declaration. He explained that his statements

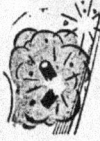
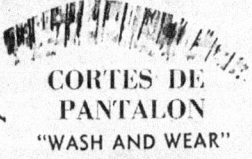

Full-page advertisement for Almacen Manhattan's liquidation sale, featuring the words "War Broke Out!" and images of missiles, warplanes, and exploding bombs. *La Hora* (Panama City), October 26, 1962.

were not directed toward the members of the assembly, national deputies who actually had immunity, but that he had used the words *supposed immunity* "to refer to counselors who believe themselves immune to everything, which is an error, because immunity has its limits."[57] In this clarification, Robles tried to draw a distinction between what national deputies could say and do with impunity and what city councillors could do. Robles may have been referring to reports in Panama's newspapers about a Cuban radio broadcast that claimed that a member of the Panama City Council had cabled Fidel Castro to pledge, "We will hurl ourselves into the streets to shed Panamanian blood in defense of the Cubans."[58] Robles may also have been referring to the actions of leaders of the Panama University Students Union, who had put out a statement blaming the United States and the members of the OAS for the crisis and calling the governments of Latin America "accomplices of a possible third world war." The two-page mimeographed declaration exhorted students to close ranks and demand world peace, the neutralization of the Panama Canal, and the dismantling of all US military bases in Panama. Minister Robles was not the only one trying to use the missile crisis to gain political advantages, but while he was concerned with domestic politics, the students had the more ambitious goals of regaining Panama's canal and its national sovereignty. The students also accused "the irresponsible and servile Panamanian oligarchy" of turning their country into a possible field of thermonuclear action. "It is evident that Panama can well disappear from the world scene," they warned.[59]

One prominent national deputy, Thelma King, walked a fine line between supporting and criticizing her government's response to the missile crisis. King was a nationalist politician who used her radio program, newspaper columns, and political platform to oppose US control of the Panama Canal and occupation of the Canal Zone. In her 1961 book, *The Problem of Sovereignty in the Relations between Panama and the United States of America*, King described Panama as "the country that was divided to unite the world."[60] Her criticism of US imperialism and her leftist politics made her a natural ally of Fidel Castro, and she made multiple trips to the island after he seized power. In January 1960, King was invited to Havana to celebrate the first anniversary of Castro's victory, and she was given a seat at the head table with Castro, Che, and other leftist luminaries. King also made an eight-day visit to Cuba in July 1962 on her way home from the World Peace Conference in Moscow.[61] Clearly annoyed by Robles's threats about limiting political immunity—threats that many observers assumed were directed at her—King retorted during the minister's visit to the National Assembly that Panama was not prepared to defend itself from atomic war but instead prepared only to throw people in jail.

King took the opportunity to defend both her country's security and her personal politics. She called upon Panamanians to stand together in defense of their country: "We cannot be split into hatreds or rancors just because of a handful of paid and bribed anti-communist charlatans, as if they owned loyalty and love for Panama." She also claimed that a moment of crisis was not the time to focus on individual political agendas. King declared that even though she personally sympathized with Cuba's revolutionaries, "over and above Fidel Castro, and over and above all the revolutions stands Panama." She argued that no one could deny her or anyone else the right to their personal sympathies as long as they fought for their country in its time of need. Furthermore, even though the canal was theoretically neutral, world circumstances made it impossible for any nations to be neutral. "The fact that for good or bad we have a canal here obliges us, all us Panamanians, to each one take our place within our physical possibilities and also, to do our part, which only the Panamanian government will assign at the opportune moment," she explained. "With all the sympathies I have for Fidel Castro, if tomorrow the president of Panama declares that we are at war with Cuba, what will I do? I must be on the side of Panama."[62] According to King, the crisis was a moment when the people of Panama had to put aside their personal and political differences to defend their country. The danger of the nuclear weapons was so great that even King, one of Panama's most important nationalist politicians and Castro's most influential ally in the country, argued that security had to take priority over concerns of sovereignty and solidarity.

## Collateral Damage?

In neighboring Colombia, a new presidential administration had to respond to the missile crisis only two months after coming into office. Guillermo León Valencia, a member of the nation's Conservative Party, had just replaced Liberal president Alberto Lleras Camargo in August 1962, as part of the National Front's power-sharing *convivencia* agreement. Valencia faced mounting social tensions, an economic crisis, and increasing violence among paramilitary and guerrilla groups in rural parts of the country. Colombia's economy was on the brink of collapse; declining market prices for coffee, Colombia's main export, combined with the National Front's ambitious development program, were threatening to bankrupt the country. The government was also struggling to pay off loans it had taken out in earlier efforts to end La Violencia.[63] Finally, Valencia was facing political opposition from a new party under the leadership of former military dictator Gustavo Rojas Pinilla and from within his own administration, especially from his minister of war, Gen. Alberto Ruiz Novoa. Ruiz Novoa was a veteran of the Korean War and a progressive modernizer who believed that the military should dedicate itself to economic and social development and rural peacekeeping.[64]

Kennedy's revelation of the missiles and request for hemispheric support sparked a heated, top-secret debate among Colombia's leaders. Valencia had spent the two weeks before the crisis bedridden with a bronchial infection but roused himself on the afternoon of October 22 to receive US ambassador Fulton Freeman, who had returned to Colombia at midnight to deliver the text of Kennedy's speech.[65] After Freeman left, Valencia summoned his ministers to discuss how to respond. General Ruiz Novoa wanted to reject Kennedy's request for military assistance, arguing that Colombia always supported the United States—as in Korea—without seeing any benefit. "The United States doesn't need any help from us," General Ruiz Novoa insisted. Furthermore, he warned, military cooperation with the United States would provoke communist and pro-Cuban groups within Colombia. Valencia countered that the people who had voted him into office had done so expressly because he was anti-communist, and therefore, he did not owe anything to "the nation's enemies, the communists and crypto-communists." Minister of Finance Carlos Sanz de Santamaría pointed out that the United States had in fact provided Colombia with a great deal of military support, especially under the auspices of the Alliance for Progress. He argued that Colombia needed to cooperate with the quarantine because US support was critical to Colombia's plans to resolve its economic problems.[66] Their debate reflected an adage from the early years of the twentieth century: "Colombia is a country of peculiar things: Civilians make war, and the military peace."[67] The minister of war wanted to stay out of the fight against Cuba, while the country's civilian leaders were eager to join the hemispheric defense effort.

Colombian authorities ultimately decided to provide the United States with political and diplomatic, but not military, support. On October 22, Colombia's foreign minister, José Antonio Montalvo, issued a brief statement expressing his country's "irrevocable adhesion" to the Rio Treaty and the OAS Charter.[68] Colombia's armed forces were put on alert, but General Ruiz Novoa denied rumors that Colombia had offered to participate in the naval quarantine, explaining that the country would fulfill its international commitments by maintaining order and preventing more weapons from reaching Cuba.[69] The CIA reported that Ruiz Novoa had threatened to resign if his government sent land forces at a time when Colombia faced serious internal security problems.[70] On October 27, Foreign Minister Montalvo gave a public address about his country's position. "Colombia is obliged by legal commitments, for moral reasons, for national honor, and for its own convenience to comply in this case with the Inter-American Treaty of Reciprocal Assistance," he declared. Montalvo explained that compliance "implies the solidarity of all the nations of the Americas in the current emergency, and therefore the moral and material support to the extent possible, to the collective action of the Americas in defense of the continent and of universal peace."[71] Montalvo's declaration explained that Colombia sided with the United States and the OAS resolutions, while his use of the hedging term "to the extent possible" suggested that the actual solidarity and support that his country could offer would be rather limited.

Members of the press focused immediately on the danger that the nuclear weapons posed to homeland security. On October 23, the liberal newspaper *El Espectador* published a map of the missile range with the headline "Bogotá under Nuclear Threat." The following afternoon, October 24, *El Espectador* zeroed in on a more plausible threat—the danger represented by the proximity of the Panama Canal. Recognizing that Colombia itself was not a likely target, the newspaper postulated in a front-page headline that "A Bomb in Panama Would Bring Us a Slow Death." That morning, reporters from the paper had interviewed Father Jesús Ramírez, the rector of the Universidad Javeriana and the founding director of the Geophysical Institute of the Colombian Andes. The Jesuit scientist told the interviewers that while an explosion in Panama would not have immediate repercussions in Colombia, the release of radioactive contamination would pass from the air into the soil and water. Animals and plants would then absorb the contamination; cows would transmit it in their milk, and children drinking that milk would absorb the radioactive particles into their bones and develop leukemia. He concluded the interview warning the reporters, "The only defense we would have in our country against an atomic explosion would be the mines and natural caves or underground refuges or shelters. That is where we should flee in the case of an atomic attack."[72]

Father Ramírez was not the only one telling Colombians to seek shelter in underground refuges. On October 24, the same day that *El Espectador* published the article about the slow death that could arrive from an attack on the Panama Canal, *El Tiempo* published an article informing the public about what precautions to take. "If an atomic bomb of 10 megatons were to explode in the center of Bogotá, the destruction of the city would be total," the newspaper warned. "Even so, residents of the city might have a chance to save themselves if they quickly, within five or ten minutes, find refuge in special locations underground."[73] The same day, *El Espectador* also published information obtained from an interview with a member of Bogotá's Civil Defense

Corps, a civic organization directed by the captain of police and composed of approximately seventy engineers, architects, doctors, and lawyers. The civil defense group encouraged families to construct emergency shelters in their homes—and *El Espectador* helped by publishing diagrams of how to build such shelters. The instructions accompanying the diagrams told readers to seek refuge immediately in case of attack: "You have to think only of yourselves. You cannot wait for your friends. The situation is a little inhumane, but there is no way around it. The only justified wait is for children, parents, or other close family members. Any delay may be fatal."[74] The instructions made clear that during a nuclear war personal security was more important than solidarity.

Some residents of Bogotá resented newspapers' alarmist coverage. One citizen of Bogotá, Luis Santacruz, was so distressed by the coverage in *El Tiempo* that he wrote a letter to the editor. "At last, we can breathe a sigh of relief," he remarked sarcastically, "thanks to this stupendous, ingenious, angelic article." He mocked the article's recommendation that families build shelters under their homes and equip them with radios so that they could follow the news aboveground and know when it was safe to emerge, pointing out that an atomic bomb would destroy the city's radio transmitters, rendering the radios useless. "In any case, señor Director," Santacruz concluded, "give your reporter my congratulations for his acuity, concern, and altruism . . . tell him that we now feel relieved and safe."[75]

Other residents of Bogotá expressed mixed feelings about their safety. A reporter from *El Tiempo* conducted an informal public survey, which offered insight into how everyday Colombians interpreted the news they were reading and how they perceived the missile crisis. Juan Manuel de Tovar told the reporter, "I believe there will be war and they will wipe us out with one stroke." Rancher Francisco Izquierdo disagreed, stating: "Reporters are doing nothing but alarming their poor readers. By now, the *bogotanos* believe that nuclear war is going to erase them from the map. But no one should be afraid because there will be no war." Housewife Marina Duarte de Sánchez also held out hope for peace, predicting, "Frankly, according to what I've heard on the radio, I don't believe that there will be a war. If the situation gets worse, the intervention of the Church will be decisive. I don't think the United States will refuse to negotiate over Cuba, knowing that a cold war would be the end of the world, terrible for everyone."[76] Colombians' confessions to the reporter ran the emotional gamut from terror to exasperation to hope, based on whether they believed that world leaders would step back from the brink. They all agreed, however, that their fates were in the hands of others.

While some readers believed that individual efforts at self-preservation were futile, *El Tiempo* continued to offer advice about personal and communal responses to atomic attack. In case war broke out, the newspaper reported, Bogotá's Civil Defense Corps had announced plans to enlist half a million volunteers across the country to serve as first responders. "Wherever an atomic bomb falls," the group explained in a bulletin, "everyone who has not been killed or incapacitated, and all the hospitals and barracks that have not been destroyed, must dedicate themselves to caring for those injured by the bomb." *Tiempo*'s article also accused *El Espectador* of publishing "alarmist news," in a not-so-subtle dig at their competitor newspaper. The author claimed that sources from the Geophysical Institute of the Andes had corrected a "alarmist report published in an afternoon newspaper" based on statements from Father Jesús Ramírez about the danger of bombs in Panama. *El Tiempo* reassured its readers that the only way bombs in Panama would endanger Colombia was if "so many bombs exploded that the world became oversaturated with radioactive particles." Furthermore, a different organization, the Institute of Nuclear Matters (Instituto de Asuntos Nucleares), had also issued a "serious explanation" of the actual danger facing Colombians. The main threat, in the Institute's view, was that radioactive particles from a nuclear explosion could spread through the rain into the ground and water, and from there into plants, animals, and humans.[77]

*El Tiempo* was not the only newspaper calling out its competitors for publishing alarmist news while at the same time indulging in sensationalist coverage on its own pages. The conservative newspaper *La República* published an editorial on October 25 accusing *El Espectador* of "atomic terrorism." *El Espectador* fired back in its own editorial pages the next day, pointing out that *La República* had, on the same day that it made accusations of atomic terrorism, been engaging in that very activity.[78] *La República* had, in fact, published another editorial on October 25 titled "Would There Be Survivors?" This editorial opened by warning readers: "It is possible that while you are reading these lines, someone will have determined the extinction of all human life on Earth." Most of the editorial, however, consisted of speculation that the real beneficiaries of a nuclear war between the United States and the Soviet Union would be the Chinese. "It is possible that, after a universal conflagration, millions of Chinese would remain alive . . . nor would it be strange for some people in Patagonia or tribes in Africa to survive. This would mean the future predominance of the yellow race," *La República* warned.[79] The editorial's interpretation of the missile crisis through the lens of racial competition, while jarring, was not the first time that *República* writers had used racist imagery to scare readers.[80] The warning about Chinese predominance also demonstrates Colombian readers' and journalists' awareness of the Sino-Soviet split and the shifting balance of power across the Third World or Global South. The missile crisis thus provided an opportunity for some Colombian journalists to spread racist ideas about civilizational competition.

As journalists speculated and warned about the possible consequences of nuclear war, their alarmist coverage had actual, immediate consequences. Colombian newspapers' dramatic coverage created a climate of fear that sent their readers into a heightened state of alarm. Scenes of panic played out throughout the country. People worried about their financial security rushed to banks to either take out or deposit their life savings, while others who prioritized their spiritual security flooded the churches.[81] On October 24 in Bogotá, a power outage caused by a falling tree limb drove hundreds of terrified residents of the neighborhood of San Cristóbal to seek refuge in churches. Across Bogotá, the number of people trying to make confession reportedly reached such unprecedented heights that there were not enough priests to hear them all. A group of Catholic women in Bogotá convinced the papal nuncio to deliver a special mass in front of Foreign Minister Montalvo and the diplomatic corps. The nuncio, Archbishop Giuseppe Paupini, reminded the congregation of the importance of faith in moments of crisis: "Nations pass, kingdoms fall, and towns can turn to dust in the Satanic fury of nuclear weapons. There is only one reign that does not fall or end, because it is eternal: the Reign of Christ."[82] One can imagine that the archbishop's description of nations falling and towns turning to dust did not do much to dampen fears. *El Tiempo*'s local correspondent in the town of La Dorada reported that people were trying to build shelters by digging caves in ditches along the banks of the Magdalena River. Other residents of the same town were digging holes in the streets to create shelters. Schoolteachers in La Dorada were instructing their pupils that, upon catching sight of a red light in space, they should throw themselves facedown "as recommended by instructions in the national press."[83] The state of panic in Colombia was so widespread that it caught the attention of the international press. The Buenos Aires newspaper *El Mundo* carried a report from Agence France-Presse stating, "In Bogotá, where an excessive nervousness made people believe that a US invasion of Cuba was imminent, the sensation was increased as a result of information attributed to a local radio station that 'bombs were raining down over Cuba.' And thus was created psychosis."[84]

Colombian observers also used the term "psychosis" to describe the public's reaction to the crisis. On October 24, photos on the front page of *El Siglo* showed residents of Bogotá looking fearfully into the heavens. The caption,

Photographs from the front page of *El Siglo* (Bogotá), October 24, 1962, showing residents looking fearfully up at the skies. (El Nuevo Siglo. Used by permission.)

—Dorotea, Dorotea! Estoy oyendo ruido no sé si de cohete o de proyectil!

Political cartoon from *El Siglo* (Bogotá), October 29, 1962, showing a terrified man mistaking a fly for a missile. (El Nuevo Siglo. Used by permission.)

under the heading "Psychosis of Nuclear Danger," explained that international reports and local radio broadcasts had caused widespread concern. "Faced with any natural phenomenon, many residents of Bogotá, as can be seen in these photos, were looking at the sky, worried about an approaching threat of modern weapons in the face of the serious international situation due to the US blockade of Cuba," the caption explained.[85] On October 28, just as the height of the crisis passed, an article in *El Tiempo* described the reaction in Colombia to the missile crisis as "a nuclear explosion in the nervous system of every human being."[86] A political cartoon in *El Siglo* titled "Psychosis of Panic" showed a frightened man mistaking the buzzing of a fly for the sound of a missile.[87] *El Tiempo* also published a political cartoon mocking the widespread "psychosis" in the country. The cartoon showed people digging shelters in their backyards while trying to avoid paying their bills, stores holding "end of the world"–themed liquidation sales, and bosses giving last-minute raises that they would not have to pay since the world was about to end. The cartoon suggested that fear and opportunism operated hand in hand. Colombia's communist party paper, *Voz de la Democracia*, used a similar term—"hysteria"—to describe the public reaction. The communists blamed the "publicity organs of the capitalists" for unleashing "criminal war propaganda." According to the communist party paper, "thousands of citizens who take literally the fables of the bourgeois newspapers flocked to the confessionals, dedicated themselves to hoarding canned food and even building picturesque shelters against the atomic bombs that were going to rain down on us from Cuba."[88] In the communists' view, local capitalists in league with the United States were using the major newspapers to drum up war fever and were provoking the public to take selfish (and useless) actions like hoarding and building private shelters.

Colombians' "psychotic" reactions to the Cuban Missile Crisis were in part a response to their historical experience. They were already living in a heightened state of fear thanks to the resurgence of political and social violence. Their recent experiences of extreme violence and trauma from the 1940s and 1950s prepared them to jump to the worst possible conclusions. Some of the responsibility for the widespread state of psychosis in Colombia during the missile crisis also belonged to the civil organizations, institutions, and individuals who were feeding the frightening and contradictory information to the media. Father Jesús Ramírez of the Geophysical Institute of the Colombian Andes, members of the Civil Defense Corps, and the Institute of Nuclear Matters were actively promoting the idea that the missiles in Cuba threatened Colombia, likely as a way to increase the influence of their own organizations. The newspapers, in turn, probably saw these experts' alarming bulletins, statements, and predictions as a chance to increase their own readership. By using the Cuban Missile Crisis as an opportunity for individual or organizational gain, journalists, politicians, scientists, intellectuals, and professionals worked together to inflict atomic terrorism upon the Colombian public.

## Conclusion

How do you defend your homeland against a nuclear war? In Cuba, where most people saw an invasion and shortages as the most likely dangers, the entire country mobilized to man the barricades and keep the factories humming. In Panama, where US and local leaders worried about an attack on the canal, authorities worked together to protect the strategic target and prepare the public. Some—though not all—of the most adamant critics of US ownership of the canal temporarily put aside their demands for national sovereignty. In Colombia, a deluge of terrifying newspaper coverage focused the public's attention on their personal security, causing nationwide panic and even psychosis. For people in Cuba, Panama, and Colombia, the missile crisis was not just a distant matter of superpower politics and brinksmanship but also a matter of their individual and national survival. As Carlos Moore put it, the missile crisis made fear a democratic affair. And yet, Latin Americans' shared sense of danger generated a widely varied range of reactions based on their local and national conditions.

# CHAPTER 7
# WAR OF WORDS

Latin American officials reacted quickly and decisively to the Cuban Missile Crisis. Kennedy's call upon the Organization of American States (OAS) to establish the quarantine had forced all member countries to choose sides. Mexican and Brazilian leaders took individual initiatives to fight for peace, authorities in the Caribbean Basin and Argentina participated in hemispheric security efforts, and governments in Cuba, Panama, and Colombia prepared for defense.

Members of the Latin American public and officials outside the military and executive branches also reacted quickly and decisively to the crisis. Furthermore, they often staked out positions in direct opposition to their respective national authorities. Politicians, workers, students, intellectuals, and everyday men and women from across the region raised their voices and took their own stances. Through their debates and declarations, Latin American citizens engaged in a war of words. They saw themselves as protagonists in the crisis and were not resigned to let Kennedy, Khrushchev, Castro, or even their own national authorities decide their fates. Their arguments reveal the grassroots responses to the Cuban Missile Crisis in Latin America.

## Congressional Debates

Politicians in two of Latin America's proudest democracies took advantage of their professional platforms to weigh in on the Cuban Missile Crisis. In Chile, a nation that enjoyed an exceptionally strong democratic tradition with stable civilian leadership and widespread respect for constitutional norms, senators challenged their country's international position in the crisis. The president at the time, Jorge Alessandri, an independent politician whose right-wing ideological leanings aligned with the Conservative and Liberal Parties, had only narrowly defeated the leftist candidate, socialist Salvador Allende, in the election of 1958, with the centrist Christian Democrat candidate following close behind. Chileans across the political spectrum valued their country's democratic traditions and showed a consistent preference for constitutional processes over the use of force, at both national and international levels.

Chileans' respect for democratic norms shaped their relations with Cuba. While Allende and other leftists in Chile celebrated and showed solidarity with the Cuban Revolution, they did not see a need to emulate it. Most Chilean leftist leaders rejected Guevara's *foco* theory and sought political power through peaceful methods—what Allende would call "the Chilean road to socialism" when he finally won the presidential elections on his fourth try in 1970—and Cuban leaders respected that preference and refrained from providing the types of support for violent revolution that they offered to opposition groups in other countries.[1] Chilean officials, in turn, had refrained from joining the hemispheric campaign against Cuba before the missile crisis. Chile's representative abstained from voting for the January 1962 OAS resolution that excluded Cuba from the inter-American community, and at the time of the missile crisis, Chile was one of only five Latin American countries that still maintained relations with Cuba.[2]

The presence of nuclear missiles in Cuba changed the Chilean government's calculations about both security and solidarity. In response to Kennedy's speech, Chilean foreign minister Carlos Martínez Sotomayor issued a statement in which he called the missiles in Cuba "a grave danger for the peace of the Americas." He promised to honor Chile's commitment to international agreements and explained that, whereas Chilean leaders had resisted invoking the Rio Treaty earlier in the year because they had not considered the danger great enough to warrant such action, the presence of Soviet nuclear weapons on Cuban territory changed the situation. "Chile is a peaceful, democratic, and progressive country," the foreign minister insisted. "It would not and should not shirk its responsibilities, and for that reason will support, within its serene and fair judgement, measures that are conducive to guaranteeing the defense and the security of the hemisphere."[3] Chile thus would no longer stand in solidarity with Cuba and defend its sovereignty now that the Cuban government had allowed the Soviets to install weapons that put the security of the entire hemisphere at risk.

Chilean representatives in the OAS and the United Nations (UN) implemented the new policy on Cuba. Following Foreign Minister Martínez's instructions, Chile's OAS representative voted to approve the collective measures.[4] Chile's representative in the UN, who occupied one of the temporary seats on the Security Council at the time, declared that while his country had always defended the principle of nonintervention, the question was no longer about whether Cuba and its neighbors were intervening in each other's affairs. "Unfortunately, in Cuba, an extra-continental power has found an open door to intervene in our hemisphere and threaten our security, trying to transform the Caribbean island into a base for war," he told the UN assembly. Chile would no longer defend Cuba's political sovereignty now that it was clear that Cuban leaders had already surrendered it and were threatening the security of the rest of the hemisphere. He expressed particular alarm at the clandestine introduction of nuclear weapons into Latin America, a region where they had never before been placed or used, and he reminded the assembly that the Chilean delegation had only recently pushed for a resolution against nuclear testing. He encouraged the United Nations to pursue the creation of denuclearized zones and called upon the Cuban government to accept a delegation of UN inspectors. "This call is made by Chile," he entreated, "whose people feel connected to the Cuban people by sacred and indestructible ties. It is made by a country that cannot be accused of bad faith or accused of any other goal than that of finding solutions that prevent the tragedy that can result from the aggravation of the conflict."[5] The Chilean representative's heartfelt plea for peace and inspections put the blame for the situation squarely on Cuba and the Soviet Union, but it also encouraged the Cuban government to help resolve the crisis. The representative argued that his country's stance was not based on partisan politics or ideology: Nuclear warfare posed a universal threat that no one could ignore.

Not everyone in Chile agreed with their country's new stance. Chilean senators responded to the missile crisis in a special session on the morning of October 23. Senator Luis Corvalán, the secretary-general of Chile's Communist Party, was one of the first to speak. He declared that Kennedy's quarantine, not Khrushchev's missiles, had put the world in grave danger and that peace was hanging by a thread. He argued that the stakes were higher than the question of the fate of the Cuban Revolution. "Right now, something much greater is in play," Corvalán told his fellow senators, "something that can unite all Chileans, over and above their differences: nonintervention, the sovereignty of each and every nation of Latin America, and world peace." What happened in Cuba would set a precedent for the rest of the region, Corvalán warned. He accused the United States of believing itself "owner of the oceans . . . the policeman of the seas," of believing that it could dictate which ships were allowed to go where, and which countries were allowed to arm themselves. He argued that if the rest of the world allowed the United States to use imperialist methods in violation of international law, then the international system would crumble, and the law of the jungle would prevail.[6]

Socialist senator Salvador Allende piled on more criticism of the United States. He argued that the crisis was the latest example of weapons manufacturers and the capitalist imperialist politicians who represented them waging a war for profit. He proceeded to review all the times that the United States had attacked and humiliated Chile and the many times it had intervened in other Latin American countries. In providing his fellow senators with this extensive history lesson, Allende sought to drive home the point that the United States was to blame for the crisis because it had spent more than a century creating a climate of intervention and insecurity for all the countries of the Americas. Allende viewed the confrontation through the lens of North versus South conflicts, not East versus West. The missile crisis was the latest example of an imperialist country in the Global North attacking a weaker one in the Global South. He closed his remarks with additional criticism for his own government and for how the foreign minister had failed to consult the senate before abandoning Chile's policy of defending Cuban sovereignty. "Unfortunately, the arrogant attitude of the United States has managed to devastate and demolish that worthy position in which we had placed ourselves," Allende concluded.[7]

The communist and socialist senators' remarks sparked a wide-ranging debate in the Chilean senate over the principle of sovereignty and the stakes of a nuclear war. The next day, Corvalán again raised the issue of the missile crisis during the senate's incidental time, an hour set aside for senators to speak on any topic. He argued that Chileans could not remain neutral or use their geographic isolation as an excuse to avoid participation in the crisis. He pointed out that if nuclear war were to break out, the radiation could reach Chile, the US markets for Chilean exports would be wiped out, and millions of lives would be lost. There were thus multiple types of security—physical and economic—at stake in the crisis, he argued. According to Corvalán, Chileans were morally obligated to side not with the United States but with the cause of peace. Like Allende the day before, Corvalán criticized his government for abandoning its traditional dedication to the principles of peace, nonintervention, and self-determination.

Other senators challenged the communist representative's interpretation of sovereignty and the related concepts of nonintervention and self-determination. Conservative senator Pedro Ibáñez from the Liberal Party asked whether Corvalán, in his enthusiastic promotion of nonintervention, had considered whether training guerrillas and sending them to other countries to subvert public order constituted intervention. Ibáñez pointed out that Venezuela's widely respected democratic leader Rómulo Betancourt had denounced the presence in his country of guerrilla groups from Cuba, and he reminded the senators that invasions of Panama, Nicaragua, and the Dominican Republic had also been launched from Cuban shores. "Intervention is no longer the formal act that it was in the nineteenth century, when a ship would sail into a port and notify the authorities that they would be bombarded unless they complied with all demands," Ibáñez argued. In the modern era, intervention was much more insidious and, thus, more dangerous. The senator then turned to the question of self-determination, which he argued had become similarly muddied since its original establishment as a tenet of international law. He offered examples of multiple methods that governments had used to claim the mantle of self-determination, comparing democratic elections like those in Chile with "the more efficient system of Mr. Fidel Castro, who self-determines himself as long as he is not self-determined from Moscow." He agreed with Corvalán that Chileans could not be neutral but argued that they should applaud the United States for its "realist and virile" attitude in defense of the free world.[8]

On the other side of the continent, in Betancourt's Venezuela, members of congress also held a heated debate over both their country's response to the Cuban Missile Crisis and the wider principles of international relations. After Venezuela's foreign minister Marcos Falcón Briceño expressed immediate and enthusiastic support for hemispheric defense efforts, the foreign relations committee of the Chamber of Deputies summoned him to explain the country's position. On the morning of October 26, Falcón Briceño stood before the fifteen members of the committee and opened with a twenty-minute presentation on Venezuelan foreign policy. He placed the government's opposition to Castro within the larger context of its campaign in favor of democratic rule and reminded the senators that Venezuela had also proposed multilateral sanctions against the Dominican tyrant Rafael Trujillo, who had tried to assassinate their president. He concluded by explaining that the Rio Treaty allowed its members to use force to defend against threats to hemispheric security but that it did not require them to do so. Just because Venezuela had voted to invoke the treaty and establish a quarantine did not mean that the country was obligated to commit its own armed forces.[9]

Many deputies expressed strong condemnation of their government's position. José Herrera Oropeza of the center-left Democratic Republican Union party (Unión Republicana Demócrata), was the first to challenge the foreign minister. His party had enjoyed the second-strongest showing in the elections of 1958 after Betancourt's Democratic Action party and had split from Betancourt's coalition over Venezuela's foreign policy and its efforts to exclude Cuba from the OAS.[10] Herrera Oropeza argued that the whole situation was the fault of the United States, whose hostile attitude toward the Cuban Revolution had forced Cuban leaders to arm and defend themselves. He also claimed that the use of the OAS to wage a multilateral campaign against Cuba had converted the organization into an instrument destined to wound the people and the countries of Latin America. Revolutionary Left (Movimiento de la Izquierda Revolucionaria) deputy Raúl Lugo Rojas, who had been arrested earlier that year in connection with the Puerto Cabello military revolt, accused Betancourt of participating in "an international commitment of grave proportions."[11] "The government will be responsible for the deaths that occur as a result of sending Venezuelan troops to serve a cause that is not their own," he warned. Lugo argued that Venezuela should have adopted a pacifist position in the crisis instead of supporting what he characterized as an illegal US blockade. Deputy Servando García Ponce of the Communist Party continued the chorus of criticism, accusing the Venezuelan government of "submissive obedience" to the United States. García Ponce asked the foreign minister whether Venezuela's current position was in keeping with its traditional defense of nonintervention and the peaceful resolution of disputes, and whether the unwelcome presence of a US military base at Guantánamo Bay was a violation of Cuba's sovereignty. If Venezuelan leaders were so opposed to intervention, why did they not invoke the Rio Treaty during the Bay of Pigs invasion, he wondered.

Not all members of the committee vehemently opposed Venezuela's international stance, however. José María Machín from the "old guard" (*guardia vieja*) wing of Betancourt's Democratic Action party leaped to the government's defense. He called his fellow deputies' earlier statements "false and off-topic" and insisted that the Soviet missile bases in Cuba posed a clear threat to the rest of the Americas. He defended his government's position and asserted that the US actions could in no way be considered a violation of international law.

When Foreign Minister Falcón Briceño was given a chance to respond to the deputies' questions, he reiterated his position that Venezuela was complying with its commitments to hemispheric security. He pointed out that while the deputies had found much to discuss regarding the question of nonintervention, they had overlooked the critical issue of security. "When a great or small country believes that its security is at risk . . . the least that country can do is take the defensive measures that it considers prudent," he argued. He insisted that the actions that Venezuela was supporting were not acts of war but defensive measures that were legal according to sections of the OAS Charter dealing with collective security. The foreign minister denied that anyone had offered Venezuela's armed forces for an invasion of Cuba or that Venezuela's foreign policy was beholden to the United States. He explained that Venezuela continued to oppose unilateral intervention and had voted in favor of the quarantine because it was a multilateral action. He hedged on the question of whether Venezuela planned to employ the use of armed force against Cuba and merely reiterated that the OAS Charter and Rio Treaty could authorize but not require the government to do so. Falcón Briceño closed his remarks to the deputies by reassuring them that their government had sought and would continue to seek peaceful solutions to the crisis. "It is better to negotiate than fight," he concluded.[12] He had listened to their arguments and answered their questions, but he would not change Venezuela's stance of strong support for multilateral action against Cuba.

In Chile and Venezuela, politicians took advantage of their respective countries' democratic traditions and freedom of speech to publicly debate their countries' international positions in the crisis. On the international level, the Chilean and Venezuelan governments spoke with one voice and sided with the United States. At home, however, politicians were much more divided. Some showed solidarity with Cuba and accused their governments of abandoning their traditional defense of sovereignty. Others countered that the legal principles of self-determination and nonintervention that had underpinned sovereignty in earlier eras had lost all precision in the era of the Cuban Revolution. According to Senator Ibañez, Deputy Machín, and other like-minded politicians, national and international security had to take priority, especially when the status of Cuba's own sovereignty and its leaders' respect for the principles of self-determination and nonintervention had become so uncertain. Whereas the question of sovereignty had become murky, the Soviet nuclear missiles in Cuba provided the clearest evidence yet for those who argued that Fidel Castro and international communism threatened the security of the Americas.

## Word on the Street

While Latin American legislators and other politicians had professional forums in which to air their views and debate the missile crisis, members of the public found other ways to be heard. Chilean poet Pablo Neruda made international news by hoisting the Cuban flag above his seaside home in Isla Negra.[13] Brazilian intellectuals including architect Oscar Niemeyer, poet Vinicius de Moraes, and writer Beatriz Bandeira issued a declaration of solidarity with Cuba in which they called the quarantine a threat to world peace.[14] Political groups inspired by the Cuban Revolution issued public declarations and sent messages to Castro. The Sandinistas in Nicaragua put out a statement calling on their countrymen to mobilize in support of Cuba, declaring, "The Cuban Revolution is the example that shows both the people of Nicaragua and the other oppressed peoples of Latin America and the world that it is possible to fight victoriously against Yankee imperialism." They pledged, "We Nicaraguans are resolved to give our lives if necessary in defense of the Cuban Revolution."[15]

Opponents of the Cuban government made public declarations as well. Brazil's conservative governor of Guanabara, Carlos Lacerda, who was in

Berlin when the news about the missiles broke, sent an open telegram to President Kennedy. "On behalf of my family and my people, I congratulate you on your courageous and prudent decision on Cuba," the governor wrote. "On behalf of Brazil and the free people of the entire world, I ask God to bless you for trying to put an end to this conquest without war."[16] In Costa Rica, the Christian Democratic youth group (Juventud Costarricense Demócrata Cristiana) collected more than 100,000 signatures for their declaration of approval of their country's support for the quarantine.[17]

Groups and individuals across the Americas—and across the ideological spectrum—distributed pamphlets and other written materials to make their voices heard. Sometimes these little slips of paper served as effective ways to communicate political positions, other times, they were useful weapons in a war of disinformation and intrigue. Local police and diplomatic officials collected and preserved this ephemera, creating a uniquely rich archive of grassroots activism that reveals how various groups across the Americas interpreted and participated in the Cuban Missile Crisis.

In Peru, the mysterious appearance of some particularly threatening pro-Cuban pamphlets caused an uproar. There, the Cuban-inspired National Liberation Front (Frente de Liberación Nacional [FLN]) political party was one of many groups struggling against a military junta that had seized power in July 1962 to prevent the president-elect, Víctor Raúl Haya de la Torre, from taking office.[18] The liberation front had requested and received permission from local authorities in Arequipa to hold a rally in the city's main square, the Plaza de Armas, on the night of October 27. The day before the rally, someone spread leaflets around the city. The police collected copies, one of which read: "In the face of the Criminal Aggression that the Imperialist Yankee Dogs attempt against Cuba, we must raise our fists in order to punish these miserable Yankees which we have here. Let us burn their houses, their factories! Let us kill their wives and their children, just as they do with our Comrades. LET US AVENGE CUBA!"[19] Another flier proclaimed: "LET US DEFEND CUBA: There are now *Yankee insects* in our slum areas who have come to poison our families. Let us defend Cuba by hanging these bugs—then let's burn them with gasoline so they will not infect our soil. DEATH TO THE YANKEES! LONG LIVE CUBA!"[20] Local authorities responded to the threatening leaflets by canceling the rally, and the inspector-general of the police warned the US consulate that he was especially concerned about the safety of Peace Corps volunteers living in the city's poorer neighborhoods. The consulate considered evacuating the volunteers, and it held several hurried meetings with the police and regional military commanders. The area's prefect conspicuously strengthened the Civil Guard presence in the city, putting his men in battle dress on horseback, in

A pro-Castro flyer distributed by a communist youth group in La Paz, Bolivia, during the missile crisis. (Courtesy of the National Archives and Records Administration.)

mobile units, and on foot patrol. The liberation front, in the meantime, issued a declaration denying that they had authored the leaflets, claiming that the offending messages had been printed and distributed by "agents in the service of Imperialism and the National Oligarchy." They denounced the cancellation of their rally as a violation of their rights of free assembly and free expression, but they complied with the authorities' orders and instructed their members to avoid participation in any demonstrations. It seems possible that the over-the-top leaflets were, in fact, a plant by anti-communist groups or even by police, as they ultimately served to silence and discredit pro-Castro groups in Arequipa.

Pro-Castro flyers distributed in La Paz, Bolivia, on October 26, 1962. These examples were collected and preserved by the US Embassy. (Courtesy of the National Archives and Records Administration.)

Various leftist groups distributed leaflets in Bolivia, too, to drum up support for Cuba. These messages were less aggressive than those in Arequipa but equally alarming since many of them emphasized the dangers of nuclear war. The National Front in Defense of the Cuban Revolution circulated a pamphlet that warned, "The nuclear war that imperialism wants to unleash against Cuba will also make the Latin American countries suffer all the same hardships and disasters."[21] A women's committee distributed a declaration at the teachers' training college that made a universal plea for peace based on their identity as mothers. "We have all brought children into this world for peace, not for war . . . if Cuba is attacked, many mothers will lose their children. Thousands of Cuban and American children, white, blonde, black, and mulatto will perish innocently in the fratricidal fire of war," the women warned.[22] The pro-communist weekly newspaper *El Pueblo* put out a special issue with the headlines "J. Kennedy Wants to Burn the World," and "750 Million People Would Die!"[23] The Communist Party decreed a state of emergency, warning, "There is no safe place on Earth, there are no safe distances, there will be no differences between soldiers and civilians, no people or nation will be able to escape a thermonuclear war."[24] These pamphlets, similar to the terrifying newspaper coverage in Colombia, argued that even in places far from Cuba, no one was safe from the danger of nuclear war.

Many leftist declarations directly criticized the United States. The Communist Youth created a flyer with a drawing of Fidel Castro containing the famous Cuban slogan: "Fidel, seguro, a los Yanquis dales duro!" (Fidel, for sure, give the Yankees hell!)[25] Other Castro supporters distributed tiny, bright pink pieces of paper with short declarations like: "The Bolivian people should support revolutionary Cuba because otherwise they are condemned to be subjugated and enslaved forever. Yesterday it was Guatemala, today it is Cuba, tomorrow it will be Bolivia."[26] The La Paz regional committee of the youth wing of the governing party, the Revolutionary Nationalist Movement (Movimiento Nacionalista Revolucionario [MNR]) distributed a manifesto that included a quote from Simón Bolívar, in which the nineteenth-century independence hero observed, "Providence seems to have ordered the United States to plague Latin America with misery in the name of freedom." The authors of the manifesto warned that if the US efforts against Cuba were not contained, all Latin America would be submerged in a dark era of capitalist slavery.[27] The Trotskyist Revolutionary Workers' Party proposed taking US diplomats and spies hostage for as long as the quarantine continued.[28] In defense of the Cuban Revolution and world peace, the national federation of unions, the Bolivian Workers' Central (Central Obrera Boliviana), decreed a state of emergency for the workers in the country and ordered the mobilization of all union militias "in order to repel any provocative acts of counterrevolutionary elements."[29] The miners' federation was holding a national conference when the news of the quarantine broke. They passed a strongly worded denunciation of "the warlike attitude of Washington" and its "belligerent blockade against Cuba."[30] These pamphlets and declarations were clear acts of solidarity with Cuba, created by groups whose members believed that the United States posed the greatest threat to hemispheric security.

Anti-communist groups in La Paz distributed their own declarations. The Bolivian Front in Defense of Liberty published a message in the conservative newspapers *El Diario* and *Presencia* calling Khrushchev the "Attila of the Century" and commanding the front's members "to remain alert to repress any outbreak of violence that the Creole communists try to unleash in support of their masters in Moscow and Havana."[31] The Front of Anti-Communist Youth Groups of Bolivia circulated a pamphlet that praised the quarantine as a unanimous OAS effort to defend the security and peace of the hemisphere. The pamphlet concluded: "Down with Soviet meddling in America!"[32] Another pamphlet by the same group attacked the manhood of Bolivian labor organizers who supported Castro. "They don't deserve to call themselves workers' leaders or even Bolivians, as they are simply vulgar traitors and eunuchs at the service of Soviet imperialism," the anti-communist youths claimed.[33] The anti-communist groups argued that Cuban leaders had already forfeited their national sovereignty to Soviet imperialism, and that Castro's supporters in Bolivia were trying to follow the same path. In their view, Bolivian workers who showed solidarity with Cuba were sacrificing their own country and masculinity.

A poet in La Paz writing under the name Juan José proposed a creative resolution to the nuclear standoff in a poem published in the ruling party's newspaper, *La Nación*.

AN ORIGINAL SOLUTION AGAINST WORLD WAR
These are suicidal jokes.
Come to a scary party!
That they are throwing in honor of the birthday
Of the United Nations.

How they congratulate her:
Telegram.—In one second
We can erase the world.
(Signed) Kennedy and Nikita.

It doesn't matter who started it,
What's wrong is wrong.
Who can say, completely:
"I am the owner of the world"?

They can have,
The same as I,
Their children and wife,
But not the Earth.

It is said that it took God,
Seven days to create the Earth,
And today they want to blow it up
In two minutes of war!

There is nothing that justifies
A nuclear war.
They are going to sink us
With their battle, into the ocean.

As this is rushing to a conclusion,
I propose a solution:
That John Kennedy and Nikita
Have a grand meeting.

Let them put on their boxing gloves
And use punches
And resolve like men
This fierce contest.[34]

The poet portrayed the crisis as an ironic, suicidal joke that Kennedy and Khrushchev were playing on the UN, threatening to blow up the entire world on the anniversary of the creation of the peacekeeping organization. The poem went on to argue that nothing could justify a nuclear war, regardless of who started the fight. Juan José's solution? That Kennedy and Khrushchev put on boxing gloves and resolve their contest like real men. The poem used dark humor to put forth a biting criticism of the leaders of both superpowers, who were endangering all of humanity for the sake of their fragile male egos. The fact that the poem was published in the governing party's official newspaper suggests that Bolivia's leaders may have shared the poet's dismay and disgust with both Kennedy and Khrushchev.

In Colombia, numerous communist party committees distributed their own leaflets. Some of the pamphlets, such as one created by the National

Youth Directorate, compared the quarantine around Cuba to past US attacks on Colombian sovereignty. "Let us remember that it was precisely a kind of naval blockade by the Yankees that prevented the Colombian navy from intervening to protect Panama from the maneuver intended to take over the Canal in 1903," the authors of the leaflet reminded the public.[35] The Colombian nation had lost an important part of its national territory when the United States had first encouraged and intervened in the Panamanian independence movement in the early years of the twentieth century and then seized control over the canal zone; why, the authors of these pamphlets wondered, should Colombians support a similar attack on another Latin American nation?

In Argentina, communist and other leftist groups undertook a particularly vigorous pamphlet campaign to make their declarations. Throughout the missile crisis, they distributed their tracts in lightning protest meetings on street corners, hung them on the walls of public buildings, snuck them into workplaces and universities, handed them out during demonstrations, and scattered them on sidewalks, roadways, and train platforms.[36] Creating pamphlets was a way for these opposition groups—many of which were outlawed and operating clandestinely—to show solidarity with Cuba and to promote their interpretations of both the immediate crisis and wider issues of national and international politics. In their view, the missile crisis was a moment of great danger and great opportunity. They called upon the public to come together, take to the streets, and challenge their government and its reaction to the crisis.

Almost all Argentina's leftist fliers depicted the crisis as a North-South conflict, the latest episode in a long history of US imperialism. They criticized the United States and accused US leaders of risking or even seeking world war. One activist from the San Nicolás Commission of Solidarity with Cuba claimed that "the attitude of the United States of North America—that once again wants to police the world—has brought all of mankind to the brink of war."[37] A branch of the Communist Party in Villa Ballester in Buenos Aires province distributed a pamphlet that began: "The hysterical, maniac, warlike Yankees THREATEN WORLD PEACE. They want to impose their reactionary politics even at the cost of unleashing a WAR."[38] The authors of the pamphlets argued that the missile crisis was just the latest attempt by the US government to "police" or control other countries, violate their sovereignty, and impose its political system on the world. The more moderate pamphlets accused US leaders of being willing to risk war to gain power, while the more extreme ones claimed that war was the ultimate goal.

The authors of the leftist pamphlets showed just as much contempt for their own government as they did for the United States. The National Commission of Solidarity with the Cuban Revolution exhorted their fellow Argentines to "openly condemn the foreign policy of [interim President] Guido ... who puts our country at the service of the gangster politics of the State Department that violate the principles of nonintervention, sovereignty, and self-determination, and endangers our security by pledging himself unconditionally to the risky policies of the darkest forces of global reactionaries."[39] In their view, the United States and its allies in the Argentine government were threatening Argentina's security and sovereignty by attacking Cuba. The Communist Party of the city of Junín called their government a "lackey of imperialism," while the communist youths of Bahía Blanca referred to their country's leaders as fascists.[40] The Communist Party of Morón in Buenos Aires province argued that what the "Yankee monopolies and national oligarchies" feared was that the Cuban Revolution would be repeated in "countries like our own that suffer from governments that no one elected, that represent oligarchic minorities, that starve and leave our people without work, that hand over our riches to the Yankees, that hold hundreds of political prisoners, that torture and assassinate."[41] The authors of the pamphlets combined their criticism of their government's foreign and domestic policies, and denied its very legitimacy as an undemocratic imposition by foreign and domestic economic elites.

The pamphlets demonstrated particularly vehement opposition to the Argentine government's decision to participate in the quarantine. The young communists of Bahía Blanca declared that "the people of Argentina will NOT serve as a mercenary force for the Yankee warmongers," while the communist-led Movement of Unity and Trade Union Coordination insisted that Argentina would not contribute anything to the war against Cuba: "Not the blood of our soldiers, nor weapons, nor the food of our people ... NOTHING for Yankee imperialism!"[42] The Argentine Peace Council warned that their government's promise to support US measures signified "the entry of Argentina into the war." They contrasted the government's stance with the country's supposedly pacifist traditions and former defense of the principles of self-determination and nonintervention. The peace council accused the government of "trying to convince Argentines to sacrifice themselves in the service of the same warlike North American monopolies that oppress and exploit them, that ignore and violate [Argentine] national sovereignty." They warned that if the people of Argentina did not resist these efforts, "Argentine homes will be submerged in blood and tears."[43]

Some of the pamphleteers saw the Cuban Missile Crisis as the ideal opportunity for Argentines to unite across political divisions and overthrow their own government. The Communist Party branch in the Floresta neighborhood of Buenos Aires called for "unity among the people of Argentina to topple the government that does not represent popular interests and [that] maintains illiquidity, hunger, and unemployment for its own people but does not hesitate to mobilize millions of pesos a day to put its marines and air force at the disposal of the State Department of the Yankee warmongers!"[44] The Communist Party branch of Mar del Plata distributed a pamphlet demanding that "Argentina's current government, that has become a criminal accomplice of the bloodthirsty warriors, that has put our armed forces at the service of aggression, must go!"[45] The Communist Party branch of the Liniers neighborhood of Buenos Aires issued a tract calling for the removal of Argentina's "warlike government." It called the government a "servile lackey of Yankee imperialism" that was "sending destroyers and preparing to use our soldiers as cannon fodder." The authors of the pamphlet protested the undemocratic process by which only a handful of people had decided that Argentina would follow the US plans. The communists of Buenos Aires claimed that the Argentine people wanted peace, bread, and work, and "a peaceful, democratic, and popular government that would be led by the working class." They concluded their pamphlet by calling for combative unity in the streets "to remove these minions of the Pentagon." "This warlike government must go!" they insisted.[46] The authors of these pamphlets hoped that Argentina's close cooperation with the United States in the missile crisis would convince patriotic nationalists that Guido's government served US interests, not those of Argentina.

The authors of the pamphlets emphasized that Argentines needed to work together to remove their antidemocratic government and defend Cuba and world peace. Though most of the pamphleteers were members of communist or communist-affiliated organizations, a small but influential sector of the population, they addressed their words to a much wider audience.[47] The Mar del Plata branch of the Argentine Women's Union, a leftist organization loosely affiliated with the communist party, summoned Argentine mothers to form commissions in defense of peace, "so that our sons will not be massacred in defense of outside interests." The women's group criticized their "puppet government" that was "tied to Yankee imperialism" and argued that "the same people who want to attack Cuba are the ones to blame for the lack of basic food in our country due to the tremendous scarcity that the Argentine people endure, for the lack of land for those who work it, and for the low wages of teachers, retirees, and public workers."[48] A collection of leftist groups in the city of San Nicolás addressed a plea to the soldiers and lower-level officials of the local army base who were being mobilized to participate in the quarantine. The pamphlet described the Argentine government as a "civilian-military dictatorship," saying, "It isn't enough for them to hand over the economy of our country to the IMF [International Monetary Fund]; now, after sending two destroyers and aviators, they have decided to also send a brigade of 3,000 army men to the Caribbean, of which approximately 200 will be from the Battalion of Engineers of San Nicolás." The authors of the pamphlet warned the Argentine soldiers: "Brothers in the Armed Forces: Don't let yourselves be blinded by a few blood-soaked dollars that the Yankee butchers promise you . . . because you won't have a chance to enjoy these rewards. The 'lucky winners' will be bodies on the beaches of Cuba, just like the invaders at Playa Girón." The leftist groups went on to warn the soldiers that Argentina could be the next target: "If tomorrow we elect a government that does not please the imperialists, they will use the same methods that today they are trying to employ in Cuba."[49]

Quite a few of the pamphlets spoke directly to Peronists, trying to convince them that, as another oppressed group, they should work together in defense of Cuba and in opposition to the Argentine government. The Communist Party of San Martín called upon "Peronists, Radicals, Socialists, Catholics and Protestants, civilians and members of the military, men and women" to mobilize to avoid war.[50] The Communist Party of Buenos Aires addressed its message to all "patriots of our country: communists, Peronists, socialists, men and women of all tendencies." Their pamphlet insisted, "We cannot let our common enemy divide us. We must repudiate anticommunism! We must unite to defend the cause of Cuba that is also our own cause!"[51] The Communist Party of the Liniers neighborhood claimed that "the same people who overthrew Perón want to bring down Fidel Castro."[52]

The authors of the pamphlets also appealed to nationalist sentiments that transcended party affiliation. "When we defend Cuba, we are in fact at the same time fighting for our own independence, for our own rights to self-determination and for respect for our own sovereignty," the National Commission of Solidarity with the Cuban Revolution argued.[53] "To defend Cuba is to defend our own right to liberation!!!" the San Nicolás Commission of Solidarity with Cuba declared.[54] The pamphlets' nationalist rhetoric challenged the popular impression that communists were loyal to the Soviet Union above their own country. They argued that Argentines who showed solidarity with Cuba were defending the sovereignty of both nations.

Anti-communist groups and government agents in Argentina conducted their own pamphlet campaigns during the missile crisis. In the city of San Martín on October 25, police and anti-communist groups undertook a cooperative, secret "campaign of anti-communist psychological action." To prevent communist elements in their jurisdiction from organizing lightning demonstrations regarding the missile crisis, the police reached out to their informants and collaborators in anti-communist groups to learn in advance what

**FUERA COMUNISTAS DE AMERICA**

ORGANIZACION NACIONAL ANTICOMUNISTA

.¡ MAÑANA PUEDE SER ARGENTINA !
¡.. UNETE HOY A LA LUCHA CONTRA EL COMUNISMO !!

Centro Juv. Anticomun.
San Martin

COLABOREMOS A SACAR AL COMUNISMO DE AMERICA
APOYEMOS A E.E.U.U. ....
¡CUBA VOLVERA A SER LIBRE!

Centro Juv. Anticomun
San Martin

LA JUVENTUD ARGENTINA ESTA AL LADO DE OCCIDENTE EN SU LUCHA CONTRA EL FEROZ ASESINO ROJO
E.E.U.U ES LA SALVACION ¡Resiste.

¡ANTES QUE SEA TARDE !
LUCHEMOS CONTRA EL COMUNISMO OPRESOR y ASESINO !
E.E.U.U. NOS DA EL EJEMPLO
¡ UNAMONOS !

CENTRO JUVENIL ANTICOMUN
SAN MARTIN

LOS COMUNISTAS SON HOMBRES SIN PATRIA Y SIN DIOS
COMBATELOS !
¡HECHEMOSLOS DE AMERICA.

Centro Juv. Anticomun
San Martin

ARGENTINO!
¡DEFIENDE TU FAMILIA !
¡LUCHA CONTRA EL COMUNISMO !

Centro Juv. Anticomun
San Martin

PARA QUE EL INFIERNO ROJO NO LLEGUE A NOSOTROS
¡¡ APOYE A E.E.U.U. EN SU Lucha contra el Comunismo !!

Centro Juv. Anticomun
SAN MARTIN

Handwritten anti-communist pamphlets from the National Anti-Communist Organization and San Martín Anti-Communist Youth Organizations. (Courtesy of the Comision Provincial por la Memoria, Centro de Documentacion, Registro y Archivo. Used by permission.)

the communists were planning. "Finding said collaborators already active, we have proceeded to get ahead of the communists in terms of propaganda, and using the services of anti-communist organizations, today we proceeded to distribute throughout the city the attached flyers," the police reported.[55]

The anti-communist youth of San Martín and the National Anti-communist Organization fired off broadsides that consisted of simple, hand-scrawled messages that viewed the crisis through the lens of West-East conflict, in stark contrast to the lengthy tracts on US imperialism put out by the leftist groups. The anti-communists made clear, direct appeals: "Get the communists out of America," and "Let's work together to get communism out of America. Let's support the United States. Cuba will be free again!!"[56] Whereas the leftist pamphlets criticized the US government and praised Cuba's heroic leaders, these messages called the communists "men without homeland or God" and argued that Argentines should emulate and join the United States.[57] "Before it is too late! Let us fight against oppressive and murderous communism! The United States gives us the example! Let us unite!" and "The youth of Argentina are on the side of the West in its battle against the ferocious red assassin! The United States is the salvation!" they exhorted.[58] They also made emotional appeals that resembled those in the leftist pamphlets, calling on Argentines to defend their families and warning that Argentina could be next. "So that the red hell does not reach us," they insisted, "support the United States in its fight against communism!"[59] Instead of portraying the US and Argentine governments and nuclear war as the main threats to the security of Argentine families, these messages focused exclusively on the communist menace.

The police of San Martín acted alone in another top-secret pamphlet campaign during the Cuban Missile Crisis. On the same day that they distributed the simple flyers made by the youth groups, the police also created and distributed 20,000 copies of a more professional looking pamphlet. This one was signed by an imaginary group called the Argentine Revolutionary Anticommunist Movement (Movimiento Argentino Revolucionario Anticomunista [MARA]). In their report about the operation, the police agents explained that the MARA was "a non-existent entity that is used for distraction," and that the goal was to "bring confusion to the communist ranks."[60] The pamphlet that the police secretly distributed warned Argentines that their country was in danger and that communists were trying to take over important government posts. The fake group claimed that communists would be allowed to take power in Argentina only "over our dead bodies." They argued that the moment had come when everyone must choose between liberty and communism, and they threatened that anyone caught engaging in communist propaganda or other activities would be put to death after a secret and summary trial. "For

CUBA: NUESTRO PROBLEMA

EL GOBIERNO TRAIDOR DE FIDEL CASTRO, VENDIDO A LOS
COMUNISTAS RUSOS, AMENAZA LA PAZ AMERICANA. NO
HABRA SEGURIDAD, TRANQUILIDAD, PROGRESO, DESARROLLO
ECONOMICO, PARA EL PUEBLO ARGENTINO MIENTRAS QUE
EL ENEMIGO COMUN -EL IMPERIALISMO COMUNISTA-RUSO-
NO SEA RECHAZADO TOTALMENTE
                    FUERA DE CUBA!
COMUNISTAS    FUERA DE ARGENTINA!
                    FUERA DE AMERICA!

An anti-communist pamphlet showing a Soviet bear reaching for Argentina. (Courtesy of the Comision Provincial por la Memoria, Centro de Documentacion, Registro y Archivo. Used by permission.)

every Cuban that they shoot in their country, we will execute five communists in Argentina," the pamphlet warned, referring to Castro's execution of Batista allies and other enemies of the revolutionary regime in the early months of 1959. The operation demonstrated that Argentine authorities, like the leftist groups who were trying to oust President Guido, decided to use the missile crisis as an opportunity to strike a blow against local opponents. The pamphlet drew an explicit connection between events in Cuba and Argentina, showing that its authors in the police forces saw the countries' fates as intimately connected. Security officials were worried about communist propaganda efforts and were using the same propagandistic methods of communication, albeit in a much more deceptive and manipulative manner. Anti-communist groups also produced some very artistic pamphlets. Police in La Plata found a flyer, titled "Cuba: Our Problem," littering a plaza after a gathering on November 21. It showed a bear with the claws of one paw already grasping Cuba, reaching with its other paw for Argentina. The text below the drawing warned, "The treacherous government of Fidel Castro, sold to the Russian communists, threatens the peace of the Americas." It claimed that there would be no security, tranquility, or economic development for Argentina until Russian-communist imperialism had been completely defeated. "Communists: Out of Cuba! Out of Argentina! Out of America!" the pamphlet demanded. On the back side, the authors of the pamphlet argued that Castro should leave Cuba along with the Russians and their missiles. "If not," the flyer warned, "America is in danger of new betrayals." Russian imperialism still posed a threat to Argentina: "Where their rockets do not reach, they will reach with their hatred, corruption, and subversion." The flyer called upon Argentines to unite in the face of their common enemy and liberate the Cuban people. "Get the Russian bear out of Cuba!" it exhorted.[61] The pamphlet's words and images made a compelling case that even without their missiles, the Soviet Union still maintained a toehold in Cuba from which it could threaten the rest of the Americas. Argentines could not ignore what happened on the distant Caribbean island; Cuba was their problem; Cuba's fate could be their fate.

## Conclusion

The urgency of the Cuban Missile Crisis pushed people across the Americas to voice their perspectives on international relations, national politics, and the Cold War. Through their debates and declarations, Latin Americans engaged in a war of words over principles and policies. Many also sought to use the crisis to pursue practical political goals, ranging from silencing their opponents to uniting disparate political groups, to overthrowing the government. Their arguments made strategic use of the ideas of sovereignty, security, and solidarity. They debated the source of the greatest threat to security, the limits of national sovereignty, and the potential rewards and risks of solidarity. But there was one thing that everyone who responded to the missile crisis could agree on: Their own fates were intimately connected to the fate of Cuba. Beyond the fact that a nuclear war could endanger the entire world, Latin Americans pointed out that events in Cuba set a precedent. The Cuban Missile Crisis mattered outside of Cuba because, whatever happened, other countries could be next. They could fall to nuclear radiation or be the next victims of US or Soviet imperialism. Latin Americans were not content to let their national leaders decide their fates or that of Cuba—they demanded the right to be heard.

# CHAPTER 8
# EXPLOSIONS

In the days following Kennedy's speech, as the missile crisis continued without resolution, tensions across Latin America increased. Latin American governments and militaries had geared up for war and defense, while members of the public had participated in the crisis through their debates and declarations. The latent threat of violence started escalating into bloody battles. Police and soldiers employed brutal containment methods to respond to demonstrations. Saboteurs used the crisis as an opportunity to unleash a wave of destruction, attacking symbols of government oppression and of US economic imperialism in their countries. Finally, in Bolivia, groups on both sides of the ideological divide clashed in a bloody, chaotic riot that cost five people their lives. Just like the wider hemispheric Cold War, the Cuban Missile Crisis in Latin America was less of a standoff and more of a deadly, heated conflict that took a significant toll in lives and livelihoods.

## Demonstrations

In addition to using the power of the pen, people across Latin America and across the political spectrum took to the streets to make their voices heard. In Panama City, nuns and priests led thousands of people dressed in white in an orderly procession from the Church of Christ the King, calling on the faithful to pray for peace.[1] In León, Nicaragua, more than 400 university students held a pro-Castro demonstration, risking heavy reprisals from the Somoza dictatorship.[2] Thousands of Costa Rican students marched through downtown San José to denounce Castro's threat to world peace. President Francisco Orlich greeted them and promised that his government would support all measures necessary to eliminate "this attack on liberty."[3] In Chile, thousands of people gathered along Avenida Bernardo O'Higgins—Santiago's main avenue—for a pro-Cuba demonstration organized by students and workers. Senators Salvador Allende and Luis Corvalán attended the rally, called for world peace, and criticized the United States. When the demonstration ended and 500 of the attendees tried to march to the Cuban embassy, carabinero police units intercepted them with tear gas and batons.[4]

Photograph of representatives of the Arhuaco Indigenous group participating in a workers' demonstration and protesting the blockade of Cuba. *El Espectador* (Bogotá), October 27, 1962.

In Colombia, representatives of the Arhuaco Indigenous group from the Sierra Nevada de Santa Marta and the city of Valledupar demonstrated to make their voices heard on both national and international issues. At the height of the missile crisis, Arhuaco representatives traveled to Bogotá to participate in a campesino conference. They marched along Bogotá's main avenue and to the Plaza de Bolívar in an opening event to the conference. Some of the Arhuaco representatives carried signs calling for workers' rights in the countryside, while other signs condemned the "Yankee aggression against Cuba."[5] During the demonstration in the Plaza de Bolívar, other attendees burned a US flag to show their solidarity with Cuba.[6]

Ecuadorean officials struggled to prevent public demonstrations. On October 24, the National Congress, after issuing a unanimous declaration in support of the quarantine, approved a motion calling on the minister of the interior to forbid any "anti–North American" protests. The Ecuadorean congress argued that street demonstrations taking place in Quito and Guayaquil were illegal and should be quashed by the police.[7] That afternoon, police in Quito arrested five students who were driving around the city making declarations over a loudspeaker and distributing flyers that criticized the quarantine. The busy authorities of the capital city also broke up an anti-communist student demonstration that same afternoon.[8] Police in the port city of Guayaquil had a harder time of it the next evening, when university students and leftist groups held a pro-Cuba demonstration that took over four blocks surrounding the campus. The student protesters of Guayaquil broadcast speeches and revolutionary Cuban music over a loudspeaker and destroyed several vehicles, one of which still had occupants inside. Police deployed tear gas and smoke bombs as the students answered with a barrage of empty gasoline canisters, iron benches, and rocks.[9] Agence France-Presse described the confrontation in Guayaquil as a "pitched battle" that resulted in four injuries.[10] Ecuador's president, Carlos Julio Arosemena, an ambiguously leftist politician who struggled with alcoholism, was indisposed on what was rumored to have been a fourteen-day drinking binge while politicians in congress were taking steps to provide support for Kennedy and the police battled local Castro supporters.

In Uruguay, Cuban solidarity groups, students, and workers organized multiple demonstrations. Uruguay was one of the places where the Cuban Revolution enjoyed the greatest popularity; during Fidel Castro's brief visit as part of his South American tour in May 1959, he gave a speech to a crowd of 20,000 people in downtown Montevideo and, according to some accounts, left the Uruguayan capital with 2,000 letters and telegrams of support.[11] When Che Guevara attended the meeting of the Organization of American States (OAS) economic ministers in Punta del Este in 1961, he was received as a celebrity and mobbed by supporters and reporters wherever he went.[12] Uruguayan communists sought to capitalize on this popular enthusiasm for the Cuban Revolution by creating a coalition called the Leftist Liberation Front (Frente Izquierda de Liberación, or FIdeL) in preparation for the national elections of November 1962.[13] Uruguay's democratic government, headed by a nine-person National Governing Council—described as "a nine-headed monster" by a disparaging Chilean ambassador—was one of the few governments that still maintained relations with Cuba.[14] Uruguay's OAS representative had taken a rather confusing position at the October 23 meeting, initially abstaining from all voting out of a lack of instructions. After reviewing the evidence of the missile bases and consulting with their political parties, the members of the National Governing Council voted unanimously the next day in support of the quarantine but maintained their abstention on the part of the OAS resolution regarding the use of force.[15] Council member Eduardo Victor Haedo of the National Party, who had hosted a picnic luncheon in Che's honor and shared a gourd of mate with the revolutionary hero during his 1961 visit to Uruguay, justified his support for the quarantine by stating that "non-intervention does not mean passiveness in the face of aggression."[16] Solidarity with Cuba had its limits.

The first few major pro-Cuba rallies in Montevideo ended peacefully. On the evening of October 24, as many as 20,000 people gathered in front of the University of the Republic. Speakers from workers unions and student organizations expressed solidarity with the Cuban Revolution and criticized their own government. The final speaker, a representative from the Federation of University Students, declared: "Here we are, the youth, the people; there, in the Government House are those who betray the popular classes, selling our country's sovereignty to imperialism and conspiring against the Cuban Revolution."[17] After the speeches concluded, the crowd began a noisy but peaceful march down Montevideo's main avenue.[18] Three blocks away from the US embassy, police officers and a small troop of cavalry intercepted the marchers. The leaders of the demonstration, indicating that they did not want any trouble, formed a cordon to contain the rest of the participants and encouraged the crowd to disperse. Two other rallies in downtown Montevideo organized by the communist-led Leftist Liberation Front and the socialist-led Popular Union party on the night of October 27 also attracted large crowds and ended peacefully. The fact that simultaneous but separate demonstrations took place showed that even though numerous Uruguayans wanted to show solidarity with Cuba during the crisis, enthusiasm for the Cuban Revolution was not enough to bridge the divisions among different groups on the left.

A final large pro-Cuba demonstration at the national university on the night of October 29 ended in a violent clash between security officials and protesters. Before this demonstration, rumors that Castro had ordered his followers in Latin America to undertake acts of sabotage had sent government officials into a state of high alert.[19] The October 29 march proceeded much like the earlier ones, with chants and songs and speeches, until the protesters reached a police barricade. It was unclear who threw the first blow or stone, but the demonstration quickly descended into chaos. For more than two hours, 1,000 police officers assailed the 6,000 demonstrators with tear gas, water cannons, and bayonets. Soldiers with trucks and tanks and a cavalry platoon lent a hand in the fighting, as did members of paramilitary anticommunist student groups.[20] Some of the demonstrators departed extremely frustrated at the abrupt conclusion to their march, including a young man named Eleuterio Fernández Huidobro who in the following months would go on to become one of the leaders of the Cuban-inspired urban guerrilla group later known as the Tupamaros. In his memoirs, he emphasized the divisions among the leftist groups in their responses to the brutal repression of their demonstration and recalled that "for the first time—and it would not be the last—our glorious revolutionary project had been shattered."[21]

In Brazil, President João Goulart's ambiguous response to the missile crisis invited criticism from all sides. On October 23, as Brazil's OAS delegate voted to approve the quarantine, Foreign Minister Hermes Lima stepped in front of a crowd of 500 workers and students that had gathered at the foreign ministry headquarters, known as Itamaraty Palace, in Rio de Janeiro. The protesters carried signs that warned, "Intervention in Cuba Today, in Brazil Tomorrow," arguing that Brazil's government was supporting tactics that could later be used against it.[22] A group from the National Union of Students sang a samba about how Brazil was at war but wanted peace. A spokesman for the workers, the secretary-general of the newly organized General Command of Workers (Comando Geral dos Trabalhadores) and president of the National Confederation of Stevedores, called Kennedy irresponsible for risking a third world war and criticized the Brazilian government for supporting US intervention against Cuba. He also warned that "while Cuba is being attacked today, tomorrow it could be us."[23] Foreign Minister Lima appeased the protesters by agreeing with them. He argued that the presence of a socialist regime in Cuba did not mean that such a regime was "un-American," thus indirectly challenging the January 1962 OAS resolution that a communist government was incompatible with the inter-American system. The foreign minister declared: "What must be defended in Cuba is the right of its government to carry out the political experiment it is carrying out, since that government results from the self-determination of the people."[24] He urged the demonstrators to support the Brazilian government's efforts on behalf of peace. The demonstration concluded without any incidents, and the crowd left, apparently satisfied with Lima's statements.[25]

The next afternoon, the foreign minister had to answer to a considerably less friendly audience assembled outside his office doors. About 100 people, mostly members of a recently formed Catholic conservative group called the Brazilian Women's Campaign for Democracy (Campanha da Mulher pela Democracia) gathered in the lobby of Itamaraty Palace, singing the national anthem and bearing signs that read "We Don't Want Communist Forces in American Territories!" and "We Should Comply with the Treaty of Rio de Janeiro!"[26] One woman who claimed to speak on behalf of Brazilian mothers said that she was ready to give her life in defense of democracy, while a student from the Catholic University Vanguard (Vanguarda Universitaria Católica) accused Brazil's government of following a crazy foreign policy. Lima listened patiently, then responded that the fact that two vastly different demonstrations could take place in the foreign ministry within a mere twenty-four hours showed that the government respected ideological diversity and freedom of expression. He argued that Brazil's position in the missile crisis was not one of weakness or insecurity but was instead consistent with the country's long-standing defense of peace and pursuit of nuclear nonproliferation. Brazil supported the defensive measure of the quarantine but condemned intervention. Lima tried to continue speaking but was drowned out by angry cries from the demonstrators. Visibly upset by the disturbance, the foreign minister demanded that the women show him the same respect that he had shown them. "If this commission has come with antidemocratic intolerance, I will order it to evacuate the premises," he threatened. Shouting to be heard over the racket, Lima concluded, "We voted without hesitation and freely against the accumulation of nuclear material in America. What we did not vote [for] and will not vote [for] is condemnation of the Cuban regime or authorization of an invasion. . . . This government will never support the application of measures of force."[27] Even before Lima finished his remarks, the demonstrators tried to leave the ministry in disgust, hurling insults. They were blocked by a crowd of some 200 pro-Cuba counter-protesters who had gathered at the front gates. Most of the women retreated into Itamaraty Palace to wait until a police escort arrived. Others remained in the courtyard, arguing through the bars of the ministry's gates with the crowd on the street.

A few hours after the anti-communist women harangued the foreign minister in Rio, the military police broke up Castro ally Francisco Julião's demonstration in Recife. The Pernambuco state deputy and founder of the Ligas Camponesas in Northeastern Brazil had organized a solidarity rally in Recife's central plaza and declared before the small crowd in attendance that "guaranteeing Cuba's integrity is protecting Brazil and the future of its people."[28] He also issued a threat to the US president: "Kennedy, do not come to Brazil. Do not come to Pernambuco, do not come to Recife, hammer of freedom, to confront our people with your Pharisee smile and loot the riches of our homeland."[29] Julião combined his criticism of Kennedy's treatment of Cuba with condemnation of US economic imperialism and extractive behavior. He told the enthusiastic audience that protecting Cuba's sovereignty was critical to protecting their own. Military police armed with machine guns, tear gas, and steel batons broke up the demonstration, and some of the protesters, including Julião, sought sanctuary in a nearby church.[30] Julião reportedly wet down his hair with holy water and turned up his collar to disguise himself, then fled down a side street when the police violated the sanctity of the church.[31]

The following day, police in Rio de Janeiro broke up another, much larger, pro-Castro demonstration. On the afternoon of October 25, 4,000 people gathered on the steps of the Legislative Assembly for three hours to protest the quarantine and show solidarity with Cuba. A federal deputy for the Brazilian Labor Party (Partido Trabalhista Brasileiro) spoke to the crowd, saying that the Brazilian people were engaged in a symbolic war with the United States for its cowardly aggression against Cuba. "The Brazilian government must never condone this act of betrayal of the ideals of democracy and self-determination, an act that was part of an international plan to restrain any progressive movement in Latin America and that also poses a constant threat to the integrity of Brazil," he declared. When 2,000 of the protesters tried to march on the US embassy, police intercepted them with batons, tear gas, pistols, and machine guns. The police also took the opportunity to debut a new anti-riot weapon called the *brucutu*, a truck outfitted with a water cannon. The demonstrators, mostly students and workers, fought back with stones and managed to wound two police officers. One woman who had participated in the protest was shot in the leg, and seventy other protesters were arrested. Reporters covering the police's violent repression of the demonstration dubbed it the "Lacerdão," after the conservative governor of Rio, Carlos Lacerda.[32]

Across Latin America, thousands upon thousands of people took to the streets to declare their positions in the Cuban Missile Crisis. Some demanded peace, others showed solidarity with Cuba, and still others supported the United States. As the crisis went on without a resolution and as nuclear war seemed increasingly likely, demonstrators' demands became more urgent—and local authorities' responses became more violent. The latent violence of marches and chants escalated into bloody battles, especially in places like Uruguay and Brazil where political tensions were already high. The missile crisis lit a match to the dry kindling of Cold War politics across the hemisphere.

## Bombs

Or perhaps instead of lighting a match, detonating a bomb would be a better metaphor. In Argentina and Venezuela, while some protesters devoted their energies to writing pamphlets, others found more extreme ways to show their displeasure with their governments and their alliances with the United States. They attacked newspapers, office buildings, and US businesses, using rocks and Molotov cocktails to break windows and set fires. The acts of sabotage were so many and so widespread that the police could not protect all the possible targets.

The elegant streets of Argentina's capital city became an urban battleground during the missile crisis. Night after night, police chased protesters through Buenos Aires and neighboring cities, leaving broken windows and clouds of tear gas in their wake. A little before midnight on October 23, police confronted members of the Commission of Solidarity with Cuba who were hanging pro-Castro posters on city walls. When the police tried to arrest them, the Castro supporters answered with gunfire. Both groups shot at each other without hitting their marks, and police eventually arrested three of the protesters.[33] In nearby La Plata, a Jeep full of Castro sympathizers shouting "Viva Cuba!" shattered the windows of the offices of the newspaper *El Día*.[34] The next evening, saboteurs threw Molotov cocktails at a Pepsi-Cola bottling plant, a Ford dealership, a supermarket, a Parker Pen factory, and a Bona-fide coffee shop. At a theater where the US embassy was showing a movie as part of an exhibit about the Alliance for Progress, five young protesters set off homemade flash smoke bombs. The bombs scorched some curtains and injured several spectators, one of whom needed treatment for cuts and burns on his leg.[35] At 3 a.m., four Molotov cocktails hit the residence of the deputy cultural attaché of the US embassy, setting fire to the front door.[36] On the evening of October 25, saboteurs shattered the windows of the central offices of the newspapers *Clarín* and *La Nación*, the local IBM headquarters, and the Singer office building; they burned six trucks by throwing incendiary bombs over the fence of the General Motors factory; they fired shots at the offices of the public electric company; and they lobbed Molotov cocktails that damaged equipment in the laboratories of the Parke-Davis and Johnson & Johnson pharmaceutical companies.[37] The *Clarín* office in the neighboring city of Lanus was also attacked. Just before midnight, protesters threw two Molotov cocktails at the newspaper's offices, breaking a window, damaging a door and some furniture, and setting fire to the curtains. Police found a paper reading "North Americans leave Cuba alone" inside the office.[38] A subsequent editorial in *Clarín* quipped that Castro's followers in Argentina were "turning themselves into launching bases for Molotov bombs."[39]

Argentina's Molotov-missile launchers were not done yet. They targeted the American Club the next afternoon, October 26, scorching the outer walls of the building with more incendiary bombs. A few hours later, a group of Castro sympathizers gathered in front of the offices of *La Razón*, where a crowd was reading about the day's events on newspapers posted in the windows. The demonstrators chanted some pro-Cuba slogans, heaved stones at the windows, and then fled. Truckloads of police patrolled the streets of downtown Buenos Aires, using tear gas and batons to break up other small "lightning" protests. Two police officers who were chasing a suspicious man accidentally ran into a crowd of pro-Castro protesters, who punched and kicked them until the officers fired their guns toward the sky to summon help. When 1,000 people gathered for a larger demonstration on the Avenida de Mayo and started marching toward the Palace of the Argentine National Congress chanting

"Viva Cuba!" and "Death to the Yankees," police filled the air with more tear gas and spent an hour chasing down the protesters. As they fled, the demonstrators hurled stones at the police and at the windows of nearby buildings. A second demonstration in a different part of downtown Buenos Aires met a similar fate an hour later. By the end of the night, seven people, including protesters and police officers, had been wounded by bullets and blows to the head.[40]

On the night of Saturday, October 27, as tensions in the Caribbean reached a climax, the violence and terror in Argentina also mounted. Two movie theaters took advantage of the pervasive fear and held a special midnight showing of the 1961 Japanese apocalyptic film *The Last War*. The advertisement for the special screening featured a giant mushroom cloud and promised "a terrifying taste of the thermonuclear cataclysm that may explode right now!" It tantalized viewers with descriptions of 100-megton bombs, secret launchpads for guided rockets, nuclear submarines, and the destruction of the world's major cities, including New York, Paris, and Moscow.[41] Science fiction apparently helped some film fans come to terms with their equally terrifying reality. Perhaps on their way to the theater some of the moviegoers saw the damage left behind by the incendiary bombings that had taken place at six businesses throughout the city that night.[42]

Even after the news broke that Khrushchev would withdraw his missiles from Cuba, the violence in Argentina continued. On the evening of October 28, a group of twenty teenagers shouting pro-Castro slogans and strewing pro-communist pamphlets threw rocks at the windows of the newspaper *La Nación* and Molotov cocktails at the information booth of the United States Information Service library.[43] On the night of October 29, Buenos Aires police exchanged gunfire with two separate groups of protesters who were holding unauthorized demonstrations and painting slogans on city walls. On October 30, a group of fifty women whose relatives were political prisoners gathered in the Plaza de Mayo, where they were joined by a group chanting in favor of Castro. Police hurled tear gas grenades to clear the plaza and injured some bystanders in their haste to capture the protesters.[44] This would not be the last time that Argentine women gathered in the nation's main plaza to make their voices heard, nor would it be the last time that security officials would spill innocent blood in attempts to silence them. The women's demonstration foreshadowed by fifteen years the actions of the famous Mothers of the Plaza de Mayo, who launched a global human rights movement in search of their disappeared loved ones and who suffered violent repression for their efforts.[45]

While Argentine leftist groups were responsible for most of the sabotage and property damage connected to the missile crisis, and while police shared

Advertisement for a special midnight showing of the apocalyptic movie *The Last War* at two Buenos Aires movie theaters. *La Razón* (Buenos Aires), October 27, 1962.

responsibility for the injuries, the extremist right-wing nationalist group Tacuara contributed to the climate of violence. In a special edition of their bulletin published in November 1962, the Tacuaras criticized the Argentine government for putting its armed forces "unconditionally under the orders of a country [the United States] that until 1945 was allied with Soviet communism." The nationalist group also complained that Argentine lives were being put at risk for the sake of US security and blamed US imperialism for the rise of Fidel Castro. They pointed out that interim President José María

Guido's hasty offer of military aid to the United States coincided with the OAS meeting of economic ministers in Mexico, where Argentine officials "begged for loans that will mortgage our national sovereignty." The Tacuara bulletin called the choice between Yankee imperialism and Soviet imperialism a false dichotomy and concluded, "Neither Yankees nor Marxists: Nationalists!"[46] On November 20, a day that Argentine nationalists had declared Sovereignty Day, members of Tacuara tried to stage a prohibited mass meeting. When "energetic" police forces dispersed the gathering, the nationalist protesters broke the windows of more than thirty businesses as they evaded capture. That evening, unidentified shooters suspected of belonging to Tacuara opened fire with a machine gun on the Soviet embassy and on US ambassador Robert McClintock's residence, wounding a police guard posted at the latter.[47]

Argentina was not the only country where the threat of nuclear war set off more traditional explosions. In Venezuela, the rash of violence around Caracas in early October had already put the Venezuelan government on high alert, and President Rómulo Betancourt's mobilization of his armed forces prevented the sort of major outbreak of urban violence that Argentina experienced. Betancourt was especially attuned to threats to his country's oil industry and to US businesses. Immediately after Kennedy's speech on the night of October 22, Betancourt sent out an order to the police in all oil-producing areas of the country: "Fill up the jails." He also instructed the police and National Guard to protect US-owned companies and property, particularly the oil fields, as well as the US embassy.[48]

Betancourt's preparations could not prevent all acts of sabotage and terror. The US embassy received anonymous phone calls from outraged people threatening to kill one American in Venezuela for every Cuban who died as a result of Yankee aggression.[49] A little before midnight on October 24, a bomb exploded in front of a branch of the National City Bank. Betancourt told the US ambassador the next day that he had had the bank's guards arrested for leaving their posts for a coffee break and then circulated the news of their arrests to other police forces as a warning to stay on high alert.[50] On October 26, three men armed with machine guns attacked a Goodyear Tires warehouse, forcing employees to the floor and burning the stock of tires. Other saboteurs set off a bomb in the downtown Caracas headquarters of Pan American Airlines that same afternoon. The next afternoon, a loud bomb went off across the street from the US embassy.[51] Betancourt censored local news coverage of these incidents to avoid alarming the public, but the Cuban newspaper *Revolución* described how hundreds of people fled into the streets after the explosion at the airline office, afraid that war had broken out.[52] While the residents of Caracas had been exposed to other acts of terrorism before the Cuban Missile

Crisis, explosions that took place during those tense days were especially distressing because of the additional threat of nuclear war.

On October 27, President Betancourt took drastic steps to respond to the heightened sense of danger. Venezuela's interior minister informed the US ambassador that morning that the government had intercepted messages from Cuba instructing local communist groups to begin all-out acts of terrorism against US installations and citizens. A few hours later, Betancourt told the ambassador that he had held an emergency meeting of the National Defense Council to discuss this increased level of danger and had laid out plans to integrate all armed forces, including the army and National Guard, into law-and-order operations.[53] In his address to the nation that evening, Betancourt focused on the threat to Venezuela's oil industry, the black lifeblood of the national economy. He warned, "Everyone knows the importance of petroleum as a basic raw material to mobilize the industrial and military machinery of modern states." Because of oil's strategic importance, he went on, "the existence of nuclear weapons in Cuba thus threatens not only the vital centers of industry in the United States but also the oil fields and cities in the East and West of our country."[54] Betancourt was right to be concerned; oil exports provided about 90 percent of Venezuela's exchange earnings at the time.[55] Any damage to the oil industry would harm both Venezuela's economy and its ability to provide a crucial strategic resource to the United States.

Venezuelan opposition groups were well aware of the importance of their country's precious oil industry. Shortly before midnight on October 27—the same night that Betancourt ordered a full-scale mobilization of his armed forces—saboteurs dynamited the installations of the Standard Oil subsidiary Creole Petroleum Corporation in Lake Maracaibo, almost completely destroying four power substations. Observers at the US embassy described the attack as "one of the most successful sabotage acts in Venezuelan history."[56] A spokesperson for Creole characterized the explosions as "expert sabotage, carefully coordinated," and identified one of the authors of the attack as a former company employee.[57] A guerrilla group composed of members of the Communist Party of Venezuela and the Movement of the Revolutionary Left took credit for the bombing. They issued a statement that their attack on the oil fields was "in response to the order of military mobilization decreed by Betancourt in support of the United States."[58] The international media reported that Castro had issued orders to Venezuelan communists to target their country's oil production just hours before the explosions.[59] Less than a week later, saboteurs staged another attack on Venezuela's oil industry. On the night of November 2, three oil and gas pipelines near the port city of Puerto la Cruz belonging to the Mene Grande, Texaco, and Mobil companies exploded.

This second incident caused less damage than the first but was still unsettling and disruptive.[60]

The Venezuelan government requested an emergency meeting of the OAS in early November to address the attacks. The Venezuelan representative formally accused the Cuban government of instigating the bombings as part of a general plan of sabotage and subversion. He also read a cable that he claimed that the Venezuelan government had intercepted on October 27 from Cuba's Federation of University Students to fellow students in Caracas. "The increasing movement of North American troops in the Caribbean and the stubborn actions of Kennedy indicate that there will be an imminent imperialist military attack against our country," the telegram warned. The Cubans requested "immediate concrete and effective acts against the imperialist aggressors, against North American embassies and consulates in every country." The telegram promised that the Cuban people and their government, for their part, would "resist and reject the imperialist attack."[61] The Cuban government, already expelled from the inter-American system, could not answer these charges in a formal manner but anticipated and denied the Venezuelan accusations, calling them "another farce by the Yankee lackeys."[62] Cuban state-controlled media had, however, celebrated the attacks; a huge headline about the explosions in Venezuela shared top billing in *Revolución* with the news that Khrushchev had decided to remove his missiles.[63]

The attack on the Creole oil installations was an extremely costly act of sabotage both for its target and for its perpetrators. The explosions set Creole back more than half a million barrels a day—about a sixth of Venezuela's total daily production—for almost a week. Creole lost as much as $10 million in total between repairs and lost production.[64] The cost was even higher for the saboteurs themselves. Of the four men who staged the attacks, the one who provided and set up the dynamite, Rafael Camejo, died in the explosions, while another, Tulio Peña, died a few days later of burns he sustained when the boat that the men used to travel between the substations caught fire. National Guard officials captured Peña and a third saboteur, also injured, as they clung to the base of an oil derrick near one of the explosions. The fourth man escaped. The government-sponsored newspaper *El Nacional* splashed across its front pages photos of Camejo's body, floating in the lake, and of Peña's, covered with burns, a none-too-subtle warning to other aspiring pyrotechnicians.[65] The arrested member of the group was interrogated and sent to a military court, as Betancourt had expanded military jurisdiction during the crisis.[66]

In Argentina and Venezuela, the line between activism and terrorism became extremely blurry during the Cuban Missile Crisis. Groups that were prevented from expressing their positions peacefully—the Communist Party was already outlawed in Argentina and under threat of being banned in Venezuela—resorted to illegal, violent methods to make their voices heard. Both countries already had significant opposition movements that were forming guerrilla groups, and the missile crisis added an additional layer of tension and terror to the situation. The bombings and other acts of sabotage certainly succeeded in gaining attention and further added to a climate of fear that was already near a breaking point.

## Bullets

It was in Bolivia, a land-locked Andean nation far from the tropical shores of the Caribbean, where the wave of violence inspired by the Cuban Missile Crisis crested and crashed. Groups on both extremes of the ideological spectrum organized demonstrations in La Paz on Friday, October 26, to voice their positions in the crisis. Factory workers summoned the public to a "combative but peaceful" demonstration to take place in the afternoon.[67] The Front of Anti-Communist Youth Groups of Bolivia, meanwhile, convened the "good Catholics" and students of Bolivia for a counter-demonstration on Friday morning. With the announcement of competing pro- and anti-Castro demonstrations on the same day, the stage was set for violence.

Anti-communist students were the first to take to the streets of downtown La Paz on the morning of Friday, October 26. Around 10:30 a.m., some 2,000 high school students, led by representatives from the venerable Colegio Ayacucho, marched through the highest capital city in the world. As they went, they shouted pro-US and anti-Castro slogans and called on their government to break relations with Cuba. Some particularly raucous participants attacked a truck in which people with a loudspeaker were advertising the pro-Cuba demonstration to be held in the afternoon, then the anti-communist protesters broke into and ransacked a communist-friendly bookstore. Two police officers were injured when the students stoned the offices of the weekly pro-communist newspaper *El Pueblo* and the offices of a radio station, Excélsior, owned by the construction workers' union.[68]

Then it was time for the supporters of the Cuban Revolution to take their turn. Their march of around 500 workers and students down the Paseo del Prado, the most important avenue in La Paz, got underway a little before five in the evening. Popular communist miners' union leaders Federico Escóbar Zapata and Irineo Pimentel—both closely affiliated with the Cuban embassy—participated in the demonstration, as did a man that newspapers dubbed "the Assassin in Blue," who carried a rifle that he fired into the air every few minutes.[69] The march ended in front of the headquarters of the miners' federation and the Central Obrera Boliviana, where some 2,000 to 3,000 people had gathered to hear speeches from union leaders. As the speeches got underway, someone in the crowd set an American flag on fire and raised it high in the air to shouts of derision and a chorus of Bolivia's national anthem. A group of young anti-communists, several of whom had participated in the morning march, began advancing from about a block away, throwing rocks at the demonstrators. Some of the people on the edges of the crowd moved toward the band of rock throwers and answered with their own barrage of stones. The two sides clashed in a microcosm of what the missile crisis could become: two ideologically opposed groups launching projectiles at each other.

The confrontation quickly devolved into a chaotic riot. Some of the protesters tried to detour toward the US embassy but were deterred by tear gas grenades, and a few others stoned the offices of the conservative Catholic newspaper *Presencia*. Another anti-communist newspaper, *Última Hora*, claimed that Excélsior and another pro-communist trade union radio station had incited workers to spill innocent blood and target the conservative press.[70] The US embassy and local conservative papers painted a dramatic scene of communist demonstrators armed with machine guns, rifles, revolvers, and dynamite clashing with carabineros and Catholic school students, who were outnumbered ten to one and reportedly armed only with tear gas and rocks. The newspaper *El Diario* claimed that the communist groups posted snipers with backpacks of ammunition in strategic locations, and *Presencia* printed photos on its front page of the so-called Assassin in Blue crouching on one knee and firing a rifle at his victims.[71] "Suddenly, as the dull explosion of tear gas bombs was heard, there was the sharp crack of rifle fire, accompanied by the slightly duller sound of revolvers," the first secretary of the US embassy, Melville E. Osborne, recounted. "For the next thirty minutes, battles raged back and forth over several blocks, making it extremely hazardous to be on the streets. Riot-watching was a matter of exposing oneself as a target for the communist snipers."[72] Foreign Minister José Fellman Velarde briefly tried to intervene but had to withdraw when the carabineros' tear gas proved unable to quell the violence. President Víctor Paz Estenssoro finally ordered the army to occupy La Paz about two hours after the riot started; it was the first time the armed forces had been called upon since the Revolution of 1952.[73] By the time that the army restored order, five people had been killed and more than twenty others had been injured.

## Conclusion

On the morning of October 27, CIA director John McCone briefed Kennedy's ExComm on the security situation. "There are reports that anti-US demonstrations have broken out in several Latin American capitals, including Buenos Aires, Caracas, and La Paz," he informed the committee.[74] In the very first meetings of the ExComm, Secretary of State Dean Rusk had warned that the missile crisis could threaten the political stability of countries across Latin America. It appeared that Rusk's words were prophetic: The Cuban Missile Crisis was starting to destabilize the rest of the region. While nuclear war loomed as the greatest threat to world security ever seen, the political fallout of the confrontation over the missiles was already causing bloodshed in Ecuador, Uruguay, Brazil, Argentina, Venezuela, and Bolivia. The violence in these countries was a stark reminder that the Cuban Missile Crisis was about more than just Cuba, more than just missiles. The people fighting and dying in the streets of Latin America were struggling for their own security and their own national and regional sovereignty. Their sacrifices were the ultimate demonstration of solidarity, one that resonated far beyond their countries.

# CHAPTER 9
# CLIMAX

While tensions were rising across Latin America, the atmosphere of calm determination that had prevailed during most of the week in Cuba was starting to crack under the strain. Cuban leaders spent Friday and Saturday, October 26 and 27, in a state of alarm, convinced that the United States was going to attack or invade at any moment. Fidel Castro channeled his anxiety into action, doing everything in his power to seize control of the situation. Castro's frantic efforts, his sense of urgency, and his conviction that war was coming helped push Nikita Khrushchev to the breaking point. Ultimately, both Castro's exhortations and Kennedy's ultimatums caused Khrushchev to back down. The Soviet leader decided that the only way to wrest control back from his increasingly unreliable and unpredictable ally was to strike a deal with his adversary.

## Time Bomb

Like the rest of the world, the Cubans had watched throughout the week as the United States and its Latin American allies established and reinforced a quarantine around their island. Like the rest of the world, they held their breaths as Soviet ships first tested, and then mostly avoided, the quarantine line. But the Cubans had a closer view than the rest of the world, and they had even more to watch than most observers. Residents of Havana could see Cuban warships patrolling the harbor and US ships stationed just three miles beyond, in international waters.[1] People across the island heard and saw US jets flying overhead multiple times a day. Sometimes the reconnaissance planes flew so low it seemed they would skim the palm trees. The roar of their engines was overwhelming, deafening. The supersonic overflights made such an impression that even decades later, Cubans would duck down as they recounted their experiences during those terrifying days. They were convinced that "every plane, every time, was probably the first plane to drop the bombs and begin a war that would end with the total destruction of Cuba."[2] It was impossible to distinguish these unarmed reconnaissance planes from bomber jets, and Cuban leaders correctly noted that one purpose of the overflights was to lull Cubans into a false sense of complacency, into believing that all US planes were unarmed. As Robert McNamara had explained in a meeting of the ExComm on October 25, the low-altitude surveillance pattern "will establish a pattern of operations consistent with an attack, and therefore it will camouflage an attack."[3] When and if an air raid were to come, according to this logic, the Cubans and Soviets would mistake the bombers for the usual reconnaissance planes and be caught by surprise. The Cubans also noted that the number of daily flights was increasing as the week progressed, and they took that as a sign that an attack was imminent.[4]

On Friday, October 26, alarming information from multiple sources began arriving in Havana, further suggesting that time was running out for a peaceful resolution. Intelligence officials working undercover as journalists for the Cuban wire service *Prensa Latina* in New York informed Castro that they had intercepted messages indicating that Kennedy planned to issue an ultimatum to United Nations (UN) secretary-general U Thant demanding a removal of the "offensive weapons."[5] That same morning, João Goulart's government in Brazil had also received word from its ambassador in Washington that the crisis was about to escalate. Ambassador Roberto Campos reported that Kennedy had decided to take military action—an air attack or an invasion—unless work on the missile sites stopped within two days. Foreign Minister Hermes Lima relayed this information to his ambassador in Havana, Luís Bastián Pinto. Lima told the ambassador to contact the Cuban government immediately and beg them to stop work on the launch platforms. If the Cubans and Soviets did not stop within forty-eight hours, Bastián Pinto warned Cuban president Oswaldo Dorticós that evening, "The American Government will take measures that include the utilization of armed force." Dorticós passed the message along to Castro, who took it seriously.[6] The tip from the Brazilians confirmed what the agents from *Prensa Latina* had reported: Time was running out.

UN secretary-general U Thant also sent a message to Castro that day, pleading for urgent action. Thant reported that he had received "fairly encouraging responses" to his appeals to Kennedy and Khrushchev for a negotiated solution, and he asked Castro to "make a significant contribution to the peace of the world at this present critical juncture."[7] He made the same points in this message as he had in his televised appeal to Castro on October 24, reminding the Cuban leader of Oswaldo Dorticós's October 8 speech to the UN General Assembly and asking Castro to suspend work on the missile bases to allow for a period of negotiations. Thant's request closely resembled the reports that Castro was receiving from his *Prensa Latina* agents and the Brazilian ambassador, and its timing seemed to offer further proof that Kennedy was pressuring the UN secretary-general. Thant's message likely confirmed the worrisome message from Castro's other sources that an attack was coming.

Castro concluded that Kennedy had already decided upon military action or was nearly there. After receiving the intelligence reports from *Prensa Latina*, he held a meeting with his general staff on Friday morning, October 26, and told them to ready their forces and raise their alert status to the highest level.[8] Furthermore, if an attack was inevitable, then the Cubans and Soviets no longer needed to continue practicing restraint. On Friday afternoon, Castro issued an additional order that starting on Saturday morning, October 27, Cuban antiaircraft guns could fire on US planes that violated Cuban airspace. There was no reason to allow US aircraft to gather more targeting information or launch a surprise assault. And at the very least, firing on US planes would be good for Cuban morale.[9]

Castro coordinated his defense efforts with the Soviets, trying to convince them to prepare for an attack. The head of Soviet military intelligence in Cuba attended Castro's morning meeting with his general staff and learned of the heightened alerts.[10] That Friday afternoon, Castro visited Soviet military headquarters, located in a former boys' reform school southwest of Havana. There, he met with Gen. Issa Pliyev, the commander of the Soviet troops in Cuba, and a number of Pliyev's subordinates.[11] "We cannot tolerate these low-level overflights because any day at dawn they're going to destroy all these units," Castro warned Pliyev.[12] He told the commander that he had ordered Cuban antiaircraft batteries to start firing on low-level flights, since those posed the greatest immediate threat.[13] Castro also advised Pliyev to relocate some of the missiles to new locations, to reduce the effectiveness of an American first strike, and to turn on the air defense radars to monitor for incoming planes. "You can't stay blind!" Castro exhorted.[14] Pliyev agreed with Castro's recommendations and informed the Cuban leader that all the Soviet forces on the island were ready for combat.

That same afternoon, Castro summoned the Soviet ambassador Aleksandr Alekseev, a trusted friend of the Cuban Revolution, to his command post. The Cuban prime minister, along with President Dorticós, told Alekseev that the *Prensa Latina* reports had led them "to understand the inevitability of an American landing or the bombardment of the objectives in the country." Castro and Dorticós also criticized the performance of the Soviet representative in the UN Security Council on live television the previous day. They believed that Soviet ambassador Valerian Zorin's dogged refusal to answer questions from the US ambassador Adlai Stevenson had hurt their cause and complicated their future actions. Instead of denying the presence of the missiles, the Cubans wanted the Soviets to acknowledge the weapons and announce that they were under Soviet control. Khrushchev needed to make it abundantly clear that this was not just a confrontation between the United States and Cuba—that an attack on the missile bases would cost Soviet lives and risk war with the Soviet Union. Castro and Dorticós returned again and again to the matter of US violations of their airspace and concluded the meeting by asking Alekseev for information about the Soviet government's fears and attitudes.[15] The conversation suggested that the Cubans were running out of patience with diplomacy, especially when their Soviet partners seemed so unwilling to take a strong stand. Castro was about to take matters into his own hands.

While Castro and Dorticós were probing Ambassador Alekseev for information about Soviet attitudes, another Cuban official was tasked with finding information about the likely outcome of a nuclear strike in or near Havana. Carlos Alzugaray Treto, a university student and defense analyst in the foreign ministry's Directorate for Inter-American Affairs, had spent the day digging trenches. When he reported back to the foreign ministry headquarters, he learned that a US attack was expected to take place overnight and that his friends at the ministry wanted to know what to expect. Part of Alzugaray's job at the time was reading Pentagon publications that the foreign ministry had acquired from the US Library of Congress. "Carlos," his friends asked, "you are always reading these books from the Pentagon. Have you come across something about nuclear warfare? What is going to happen tonight?" Alzugaray told his anxious colleagues: "Well, probably they will bomb Havana, they will throw one or two nuclear bombs aimed at the Central Committee, at the Palace of the Revolution. Probably we will see the explosion, a big flash. Then, we will feel a lot of heat. Then the expansion. And then we will be dead!"[16] Alzugaray was even more succinct in a one-sentence report he submitted to his superiors: "In the event that nuclear weapons are used in or near Havana City, it and we shall all be destroyed."[17] Alzugaray later remembered feeling resigned, but not afraid, as he prepared his report. "I don't know if it was because we were too young, or because we were fed up, but we wanted to get it over with," he later recalled. "If it's going to be the annihilation of Cuba, well then let it be."[18] After submitting his bleak report, Alzugaray bunked down for the night with his colleagues at their desks on the fifth floor of the Ministry of Foreign Affairs, ready to respond to an attack at a moment's notice.[19]

That night, Castro decided that his meetings, his military preparations, and his pronouncements were not enough: he had to do more to strengthen Khrushchev's resolve. Castro was convinced that time was up and an attack was coming. He saw no path to peace, no way to avoid war. Frantic, he racked his brain: "What is still to be done? What remains to be done? What can I do? What is the last thing I can do?" In the darkest hours of the night, looking ahead to days of war and bloodshed and sacrifice, Castro decided to write a letter to Khrushchev to provide moral encouragement. Ever the avid student of history, he was afraid that the Soviets would be caught by surprise again, as they had been by the German invasion in World War II.[20] He rushed over to the Soviet embassy in the upscale neighborhood of Vedado a little before 3 a.m. and roused Ambassador Alekseev. Insisting that they take shelter in the bunker under the embassy because the US attack could begin any minute, Castro began dictating his letter. The ambassador and two assistants tried to simultaneously transcribe and translate, as Castro reviewed their work and struggled to find the right wording. As the sun began to rise and Castro rejected yet another draft, Alekseev finally asked him point-blank: "Are you asking Comrade Khrushchev to deliver a nuclear strike on the United States?" After a few moments of silent consideration, the Cuban leader responded, "No, not quite . . . I want to say that the choice is yours, Comrade Nikita: you can destroy the enemy, or you can wait for the enemy to destroy you, after he destroys us." Castro wanted Khrushchev to steel himself for a war that appeared inevitable. After the island was invaded, Khrushchev would have to redeem Cuba's sacrifice by annihilating the United States. "Cuba is ready to martyr itself for the cause of global socialism and the destruction of America's imperial empire," Castro told Alekseev.[21] The shocked ambassador helped Castro write a final draft of the letter and sent it to Moscow as the sun rose over Havana on the morning of Saturday, October 27.

Castro's letter—his suicide note on behalf of the entire Cuban nation—was at once a message of resolve and resignation. He opened with a warning: "I consider that the aggression is almost imminent within the next 24 to 72 hours." He did not expect Kennedy to launch a nuclear first strike directly against the Soviet Union. Instead, he thought it was most likely that the United States would target the missile bases in Cuba in a limited air strike or, somewhat less likely, launch a full-scale invasion of the island. He extolled the extremely high morale of the heroic Cuban people, promising Khrushchev: "You can rest assured that we will firmly and resolutely resist attack, whatever it may be." But Castro wanted to make sure that the Cubans' sacrifices, their martyrdom, would not be in vain. If the United States invaded Cuba, "that would be the moment to eliminate such danger forever through an act of clear legitimate defense, however harsh and terrible the solution would be." Castro was not proposing a nuclear first strike per se; instead, he was trying to prepare Khrushchev to use nuclear weapons as a first response to a US attack or invasion. In Castro's mind, the presence of atomic weapons in Cuba meant that a conventional invasion would inevitably escalate into a nuclear exchange. "The Soviet Union must never allow the circumstances in which the imperialists could launch the first nuclear strike against it," he insisted. Castro closed the letter thanking the Soviet people for their generosity and solidarity and wishing Khrushchev success in his "huge task and serious responsibilities ahead."[22] Castro believed that his own calm contemplation of nuclear war would provide Khrushchev with the moral encouragement that he needed to act, and act quickly, to defend the socialist cause and defeat US imperialism.

As Castro was dictating his fatalistic letter to Khrushchev, a Soviet cruise missile regiment in Oriente province was undertaking final preparations to launch a nuclear attack on the Guantánamo Bay Naval Base. On Friday night, a group of several hundred Soviet soldiers received orders to move their three FKR cruise missile launchers—each of which was armed with a Hiroshima-sized nuclear warhead—to a secret launch position fifteen miles away from the base. The convoy of jeeps, trucks, missiles, and support vehicles slowly traveled ten miles to their new position, an abandoned coffee plantation near the village of Filipinas, under the cover of complete darkness. Suddenly, there was a huge crash followed by screams. The soldiers assumed they were under attack and dove into defensive positions before realizing that the truck carrying the field engineering unit had fallen into a ravine. Two Soviet soldiers were crushed to death under the truck, along with a Cuban bystander. Half a dozen other soldiers were badly injured. After rescue vehicles arrived, the rattled convoy continued.[23] As they approached the launch site, a Cuban post guarding the outer perimeter opened fire on them after a bungled exchange over the password. It took another hour to sort out the confusion and convince the Cubans to let the Soviets pass. Finally, the cruise missiles and launch teams were in place, ready to destroy Guantánamo Bay Naval Base.[24]

## Black Saturday

On Saturday, October 27, the Cuban Missile Crisis reached its climax. That morning, Castro issued a public warning: "Cuba does not accept the vandalistic and piratical privilege of any warplane to violate our airspace, because this essentially affects our security and facilitates the conditions for a surprise attack on our territory. Such legitimate right of defense is inalienable, and therefore, any combat aircraft that invades Cuban airspace does so only at the risk of facing our defensive fire."[25] Cuban soldiers finally had the permission they craved to fire upon the US planes that were terrorizing their country. Antiaircraft gunners took aim through driving rain at two jets that skimmed the trees surrounding the Soviet headquarters near Havana. At a missile base near the town of Sagua la Grande, in central Cuba, angry Soviet soldiers fired pistols at two Navy planes that flew overhead. When jets approached the missile base at San Cristóbal, Cuban soldiers opened fire with rifles and raced across the muddy fields to get to their antiaircraft guns.[26] The jet pilots immediately flew higher and were able to avoid the sudden demonstration of resistance.[27]

At the other end of the island, however, the pilot of a U-2 spy plane was not so lucky. Maj. Rudolf Anderson Jr. had taken off from McCoy Air Force Base outside Orlando, Florida, at 9:09 a.m. local time. It would be his sixth combat mission over Cuba. He had volunteered for the last-minute assignment to photograph Soviet and Cuban deployments around Guantánamo Bay Naval Base and probe the Soviet air defense system.[28] As he entered Cuban airspace, he set off the Soviets' recently activated radar.

By that time, Soviet troops in Cuba were just as convinced as their hosts that war was imminent. A Soviet political officer on the island later recalled that Cuban intelligence services had told them they had obtained information that "the American side was discussing the issues of timing and methods of its invasion of the island."[29] General Pliyev had sent a telegram to Moscow on the evening of October 26, after his meeting with Castro, reporting that "in the opinion of the Cuban friends, the U.S. air strike on our installations in Cuba will occur in the night between October 26 and October 27 or at dawn on October 27." He informed Moscow that, "in the event of a U.S. air attack on our installations, we will employ all available means of air defense."[30] He also sent a message that night to the heads of the missile battalions on the island: "Be prepared for military action, an American intervention is expected."[31] In addition to turning on their radars, the Soviets placed all their surface-to-air missile sites on a six-minute alert. Most of the Soviet officers stayed awake Friday night, waiting for an attack that they expected at any moment.

It was Saturday morning, not Friday night, when Anderson's plane arrived. By that time Pliyev, who was struggling with kidney disease, had taken a break from his headquarters to rest and was out of contact when the radars picked up Anderson's plane. The commanders of the antiaircraft missile (SAM) regiments begged their superiors to allow them to open fire. The jet had flown over the entire eastern half of the island and had almost certainly photographed the latest missile locations, including the cruise missile regiment that was poised to attack the Guantánamo Bay Naval Base. Pliyev's deputy, Lt. Gen. Stepan Grechko, tried repeatedly to reach him, knowing that Soviet troops were prohibited from shooting at US planes without Pliyev's direct orders. Grechko then decided to consult with his own deputies, who were all in favor of shooting down the plane. At the last possible minute, he issued the order to open fire. As Ambassador Alekseev later put it, "The shooting down of the aircraft was an expression of the solidarity of our troops with the Cubans. At the time we were ready to do anything for the Cuban Revolution, and to support

Fidel—all of us who were here."[32] Two hours after Major Anderson had taken off, his jet was shot out of the sky by Soviet troops who had successfully pressured their supervisors to disobey direct orders and take action.[33]

The downing of a US plane set off alarms in Washington. During Secretary of Defense Robert McNamara's visit to the Pentagon on Saturday afternoon, he was informed that a U-2 flight over Cuba was 30–40 minutes overdue on its return to base. When Kennedy's ExComm met shortly thereafter, they learned that the U-2 was still missing and received reports from the pilots returning from the morning's low-level reconnaissance flights over Cuba that gunners had tried to shoot them down.[34] At the 4 p.m. meeting in the White House, the ExComm received further reports that the afternoon group of low-level flights had been fired upon as well. Treasury Secretary C. Douglas Dillon argued that the attacks on US planes cut short the time for decisions. "Well, the way the situation is going in Cuba with this fellow [in the low-level reconnaissance flight] being shot at? We haven't got but one more day," he predicted, and McGeorge Bundy and Robert McNamara agreed.[35]

The new Cuban and Soviet attacks on US planes in Cuban airspace forced Kennedy's hand. Earlier in the week, Kennedy and his advisers had planned to attack any SAM sites that shot down US aircraft.[36] When the news came in on the afternoon of October 27 that low-level reconnaissance flights were taking fire, the ExComm members began discussing a general strike on the island. Then, intelligence arrived that the U-2 plane had been shot down over a SAM site near Banes in eastern Cuba, and that the pilot had been found dead in the wreckage. Kennedy's first reaction was: "This is much [*sic*] of an escalation by them, isn't it?" McNamara was stunned. "How do we interpret this? I don't know how to interpret it," he stammered. Kennedy's assistant secretary for international security affairs, Paul Nitze, was more decisive. "They've fired the first shot," he told the president. Nitze and the chairman of the Joint Chiefs of Staff Gen. Maxwell Taylor recommended immediate retaliation against the SAM site that had brought down Anderson's plane. McNamara recommended waiting until the next morning at dawn, as it was already getting too dark in Cuba to conduct a mission that evening. CIA director John McCone recommended issuing a strong protest to Khrushchev, "demanding that he stop this business and stop it right away, or we're going to take those SAM sites out immediately."[37] This new turn of events suggested that the Cubans and Soviets were preparing for war, and many members of the ExComm unknowingly echoed Castro's sentiments in his letter to Khrushchev when they advised Kennedy that he could not risk being the target of a nuclear first strike.

Kennedy eventually decided to issue stern public and private warnings to Khrushchev that time was running out. That evening, the president sent a telegram to Moscow that he simultaneously released to the press. The message accepted an arrangement that Khrushchev himself had implicitly proposed in a private letter the previous day, that he remove the missiles from Cuba in exchange for a US pledge not to invade the island. Kennedy's message made no mention of the downed U-2, and it did not threaten to attack Soviet SAM sites; but it closed by stressing the urgency of the situation. "The first ingredient, let me emphasize, is the cessation of work on missile sites in Cuba and measures to render such weapons inoperable, under effective international guarantees. The continuation of this threat, or a prolonging of this discussion . . . would lead surely to an intensification of the Cuban crisis and a grave risk to the peace of the world."[38]

At the same time as Kennedy sent his public message, his brother, Robert, met privately with the Soviet ambassador to the United States, Anatoly Dobrynin, for a more forthright line of communication. Robert opened the discussion by informing the ambassador that US officials had learned that their unarmed planes flying over Cuba had been fired upon and that one had been shot down. "I told him this was an extremely serious turn in events," Robert Kennedy reported. "We would have to make certain decisions within the next 12 or possibly 24 hours. There was very little time left. If the Cubans were shooting at our planes, then we were going to shoot back."[39] Robert Kennedy demanded that Khrushchev answer the White House's letter by the next day, warning that otherwise there would be drastic consequences.

Khrushchev was already wavering. In the days since sending the confident letter to Castro on October 23—in which he had denounced Kennedy's "piratical" actions and had informed Castro that Soviet troops in Cuba were ready for combat—Khrushchev had become increasingly convinced that the whole adventure was a mistake and that he had to avoid nuclear war at all costs. On October 25, after receiving another letter from Kennedy and intelligence reports that the US military had elevated its Defensive Condition, or DEFCON, status to level 2—one step short of war—Khrushchev decided that the missiles had to come out of Cuba.[40] By the morning of October 26, alarmed by his morning intelligence briefing, Khrushchev had become desperate to find a political solution. At a meeting of the Presidium, he dictated a letter to Kennedy and ordered it hand-delivered to the US embassy in Moscow. The letter was a sprawling, emotional plea for peace. Khrushchev depicted the situation as one in which he and Kennedy were not enemies but, instead, two world leaders working together to prevent a horrific disaster. Khrushchev denied that the Soviet weapons in Cuba were ever intended to be used in an attack on the United States, arguing that "only lunatics or suicides, who themselves want to perish and before they die destroy the world, could do this." He proposed that if Kennedy would give his assurances that the United States would not attack Cuba and would restrain others from doing so, then there would be no need for Soviet military specialists or weapons in Cuba.[41] Convinced that war was about to break out, Khrushchev spent the night on the couch in his office in the Kremlin, listening half-asleep for the ring of telephones.[42]

The next morning, Khrushchev changed his mind. After the passage of another day without conflict, he wondered whether he might be able to gain more than just a noninvasion pledge in his negotiations with Kennedy. In that morning's intelligence briefing, he learned that many backroom discussions of missile swaps were taking place in Washington and that an influential journalist with White House connections, Walter Lippmann, had proposed just such an arrangement in his *Washington Post* column.[43] Khrushchev instructed his foreign minister to revisit a discarded draft message from the day before, one that had mentioned a Turkey-Cuba missile swap. In addition to proposing a trade, this revived letter also made clear that the Cuban and Turkish governments would have to be included in the agreement and give their permission for inspections.[44] To save time, Khrushchev had his new message released over Radio Moscow; it aired at 5 p.m. in Moscow, 10 a.m. in Washington, 9 a.m. in Havana. Khrushchev was trying to adopt a stronger stance and push Kennedy for more concessions.

By Sunday morning, however, the news had arrived in Moscow that a U-2 plane had been shot down over Cuba; this news, along with Castro's disturbing suicide letter and Kennedy's public and private warnings that time was running out, shattered Khrushchev's newfound resolve. When Khrushchev received Castro's letter, he interpreted it as advocating for a preemptive nuclear first strike on the United States. In his memoirs, Khrushchev described reading the letter and thinking that Castro had "concluded that an attack was unavoidable and that this attack had to be preempted. In other words, we needed to immediately deliver a nuclear missile strike against the United States."[45] Khrushchev, unlike Castro, was adamantly opposed to a nuclear first strike, and he knew enough about Soviet and US nuclear capabilities to predict that the Soviet Union could not win a nuclear war. Soon after receiving Castro's letter, Khrushchev learned from his minister of defense, Rodion Malinovsky, that a US plane had been brought down over Cuba. At first, it was unclear if Khrushchev believed it was the Cubans or the Soviets who were responsible. Khrushchev asked Malinovsky whether the general who had brought down the plane had consulted with anyone before firing. "Did he ask permission to launch?" Malinovsky explained that there was not enough time for consultations and so the general in charge of Soviet surface-to-air missiles had decided to follow Castro's instructions to Cuban antiaircraft forces. That was not what Khrushchev wanted to hear. "Whose army is he in, the Soviet or the Cuban?" he demanded. "If it's the Soviet army, why does he allow himself to obey a foreign commander?"[46] In his letter to Castro the following day, Khrushchev accused the Cuban leader of suddenly escalating tensions: "Yesterday you shot down one of [the US flights], while earlier you didn't shoot them down when they overflew your territory."[47] From his vantage point in Moscow, on the other side of the world, it appeared to Khrushchev that he was quickly losing control over the situation in Cuba.

By the time Khrushchev met with the Presidium at noon in a government dacha in a Moscow suburb, he had decided to beat a hasty retreat. All signs seemed to indicate that the clock on negotiations had run out. If he did not get the missiles out of Cuba soon, his own troops or the Cubans might launch a war without his permission. After all, they had already significantly escalated the situation by shooting down a US plane. Khrushchev provided each member of the Presidium a copy of Castro and Kennedy's latest letters, the suicide note and the ultimatum. He opened the meeting by telling his advisers, "Now we [find] ourselves face to face with the danger of war and of nuclear catastrophe, with the possible result of destroying the human race. In order to save the world, we must retreat."[48] The subsequent discussion was interrupted when the report arrived about Dobrynin's meeting with Robert Kennedy, containing the younger Kennedy brother's desperate warning that time was running out to restrain the war hawks in Washington. According to Dobrynin, Robert Kennedy claimed that there were "many unreasonable heads among the generals, and not only among the generals, 'who are itching for a fight.'"[49] Just as the Presidium agreed with Khrushchev's plan to accept the terms of the White House's proposal—removing the missiles in exchange for a non-invasion pledge—they received another report that President Kennedy was scheduled to give a live, televised speech at 9 a.m. Washington time—that very evening in Moscow. Khrushchev feared that Kennedy was preparing to deliver a dramatic announcement, just as he had done at the beginning of the crisis.[50] Perhaps now, instead of announcing a quarantine, he would announce an invasion of Cuba. Time was up.

## Retreat

Khrushchev revealed his retreat over Radio Moscow. To save time, he had decided to forgo the usually cumbersome diplomatic channels and make his message public. On October 28, at 5 p.m. in Moscow, 9 a.m. in Washington and Havana, an announcer read out Khrushchev's letter to Kennedy: "In order to complete with greater speed the liquidation of the conflict dangerous to the cause of peace, to give confidence to all people longing for peace, and to calm the American people, who, I am certain, want peace as much as the people of the Soviet Union, the Soviet government, in addition to previously issued instructions on the cessation of further work at building sites for the weapons, has issued a new order, on the dismantling of the weapons which you describe as 'offensive,' and their crating and return to the Soviet Union." In exchange for removing the weapons, Khrushchev made clear that he expected Kennedy to honor his part of the bargain that he had proposed in his public offer the previous day: "That no attack will be made on Cuba—that no invasion will take place—not only by the United States, but also by other countries of the Western Hemisphere."[51] The Soviet leader also agreed to allow UN verification of the dismantling of the missile bases, and he made no mention of trading for the removal of US missiles in Turkey. In his rush to forestall any further escalation, Khrushchev ordered Ambassador Dobrynin to meet again with Robert Kennedy before the radio broadcast to tell him that a positive response was forthcoming. He also told Dobrynin to get a pledge that the White House would honor the secret offer that Robert Kennedy had made in their previous meeting, to quietly remove US missiles from Turkey a few months after the crisis in Cuba had passed. Khrushchev sent orders to General Pliyev in Havana to stop the use of all weapons and to begin dismantling the missile sites.[52] Finally, Khruschev sent a message to his ally, Castro, in which he accused him of shooting down the U-2 and asked him not to let himself be provoked by "the militarists in the Pentagon." "I would like to recommend to you now," he cautioned Castro, "at this moment of change in the crisis, not to be carried away by sentiment. . . . I would like to advise you in a friendly manner to show patience, firmness, and even more firmness."[53]

Khrushchev's plea to Castro for patience, delivered via slow diplomatic channels, arrived after the shocking news that the Soviets had capitulated. Castro was meeting with Che Guevara, Celia Sánchez, and other officials around noon on Sunday at his home in Vedado when he received a call from Carlos Franqui, the editor of *Revolución* newspaper. Franqui had just seen the alert come across the Associated Press teletype: "Khrushchev orders the withdrawal of missiles from Cuba." "Fidel, what should we do about this news?" Franqui asked. "What news?" Castro replied. Franqui fell silent, then, upon Castro's insistence, read the news flash over the phone. "Son of a bitch! Bastard! Asshole!" Castro exploded.[54] He slammed the telephone onto the map table, then whirled around and kicked a wall where a huge mirror was hanging. The impact shattered the mirror, and it crashed to the floor in a noisy shower of glass.[55] Silenced momentarily by the destruction, Castro gathered his thoughts and began to take stock of the situation. He explained to Che and the others who were watching him that Khrushchev had betrayed them and struck a deal with Kennedy behind their backs. "We felt that we had become some sort of bargaining chip," he recalled later. "Not only was this a decision taken without consulting us, several steps were taken without informing us . . . we were humiliated."[56]

Stinging from the betrayal and the humiliation, Castro refused to be ignored any longer. He immediately issued his own declaration over the airwaves of Radio Habana and the international newswires of *Prensa Latina*. While addressed to U Thant, it was clearly intended to reach Kennedy, Khrushchev, the Cuban people, and the entire world. In what became known as his Five Points of Dignity declaration, Castro proclaimed:

> The revolutionary government declares that the guarantees of which
> President Kennedy speaks—that there will be no aggression against
> Cuba—will not exist unless, in addition to the elimination of the naval
> blockade he promises, the following measures among others are
> adopted:
> 1. Cessation of the economic blockade and all the measures of
>    commercial and economic pressure which the United States
>    exercises in all parts of the world against our country;
> 2. Cessation of all subversive activities, launching and landing of
>    arms and explosives by air and sea, the organization of mercenary
>    invasions, infiltration of spies and saboteurs, all of which actions are
>    carried out from the territory of the United States and some other
>    accomplice countries;
> 3. Cessation of the pirate attacks which are being carried out from
>    bases existing in the United States and Puerto Rico;
> 4. Cessation of all the violations of our air and naval space by North
>    American war planes and ships;
> 5. Withdrawal of the naval base of Guantánamo and the return of the
>    Cuban territory by the United States.[57]

Castro's Five Points made clear the differences between his perception of the Cuban Missile Crisis and the views of Kennedy and Khrushchev. While the US and Soviet leaders viewed the crisis through the broader lens of their global Cold War confrontation and the threat of a world-ending nuclear war, Castro viewed it through the deeper, narrower lens of US-Cuban relations and his nation's long struggle for sovereignty. For Castro, the crisis was not just about the missiles, and it would not end with their removal. It was a clash not merely between the Eastern and Western camps in the Cold War but also between countries of the Global North and the Global South. The crisis was about guaranteeing Cuba's sovereignty and its military and economic security, and it was about ending the campaign conducted against his government by the United States, Cuban exiles, and other Latin American "accomplice" countries. A simple pledge from Kennedy would not be enough to satisfy Castro.

Other Cuban officials echoed and expanded upon Castro's interpretation of the crisis. Raúl Castro gave a speech later that day in Santiago de Cuba in which he described the missile crisis as Cuba's "climax and the supreme moment." "Now it was no longer a Cuban question," he continued, "now it was no longer a question of the suffering and sacrifice that the Cuban people would have to undergo . . . for us, aggression now entailed a world war, and every country would be enveloped in the flames of an atomic war." Raúl Castro's interpretation bridged those of his brother and Kennedy and Khrushchev; he explained that the Cuban government and public had responded to and participated in the crisis so enthusiastically because it elevated their long struggle for sovereignty. The missiles raised the stakes of the Cuban Revolution and connected Cuba's survival to the survival of the entire world. And, Raúl argued, the people of the world were siding with Cuba, even as their "puppet" governments summoned their armed forces to join the blockade in the Caribbean and attack their own countrymen at home. The audience applauded as Raúl described the protests in Chile, the riots in Bolivia, and the sabotage of the oil fields in Venezuela. Raúl Castro mocked Kennedy's noninvasion pledge—"Our people do not have poor memories, and we remember these same words, spoken very solemnly, just days before the imperialist mercenary aggression of Playa Girón"—and he reiterated his brother's Five Points as the guarantees necessary for a true path to peace. "We demand concrete acts and not words," he insisted.[58]

The Castro brothers were not the only Cubans infuriated by the news of Khrushchev's deal with Kennedy. A hotel worker who had volunteered for militia duty and had been sent to guard a missile base during the crisis was one of the first to learn of Khrushchev's retreat as he watched the missiles being packed up for their return to the Soviet Union. He recalled feeling disappointed and angry. "What a shitty thing they've done!" he thought, "maybe they're cowards. They really screwed us, leaving us unarmed."[59] Other militia members expressed their resentment through insulting chants that spread across the island like a cloud of radiation: "Nikita mariquita—lo que se da no se quita" (Nikita, you little fairy, what is given cannot be taken back).[60] Roving bands of angry young people ripped down pro-Soviet posters and billboards across the island.[61] Carlos Moore, who had been spending nights behind sandbags in a field outside the Ministry of Communications, was bewildered and bitter. "The Russians, we felt, had left Cuba unprotected to save their own skin," he recalled. He remembered thinking, "Those Russian sons-of-bitches are a pack of cowardly traitors."[62] Khrushchev's decision to remove the missiles without consulting Castro drove a clear wedge between the Cubans and their supposed friends and allies.

The Cuban public learned the details of the deal in the pages of *Revolución* on the morning of October 29. The top headline of that day's paper was about Castro's Five Points; just below, were headlines about Khrushchev's decision to remove the missiles and his demands that Kennedy remove the blockade and refrain from invading Cuba. *Revolución* published a detailed timeline of the crisis, along with the text of the declarations and public messages exchanged among Castro, Kennedy, Khrushchev, and Thant. Argentine journalist Adolfo Gilly recalled hearing people all over Havana discussing the news. "Why didn't they consult us since we were the ones who were going to die?" one person remarked. "They betrayed us," concluded another. On street corners, in factories, and at the university, Cubans dissected the published cables line by line and mocked Khrushchev's friendly tone toward Kennedy.[63] *Revolución*'s editor, Carlos Franqui, later reflected that he knew as he went to press that "to publish the news about the missile withdrawal would mean the end of the paper and of me as well. But it was a good story."[64] Franqui recalled that Raúl Castro and others accused him of being anti-Soviet and anti-communist for announcing the Soviet withdrawal so bluntly.

The missiles' removal was a traumatic process for Cubans and Soviet soldiers alike. On the roads of Pinar del Río crowds turned out to stop the trucks that were hauling away the massive weapons. "*Tovarisch*, comrade," they pleaded, "Why are you taking them? Why are you leaving? You have to stay and defend Cuba." Tears ran down the soldiers' face as they explained that they had to follow orders.[65] Other Soviet troops withdrew in the dead of night, under the cover of darkness and shame. "The procedure of withdrawal from Cuba inflicted a deep wound on the souls of our warriors," one Soviet commander recalled. "It was done in secret, and the vehicles were loaded at night, without the usual leave-taking of the Cuban comrades: the ships departed from empty docks. We left Cuba just as if we had been guilty of something, although everyone had honorably and selflessly done his martial duty and carried out the Motherland's command."[66] The sense of humiliation and confusion was palpable.

Amid all the public displays of anger and betrayal, there were also private moments of tenderness. After Che Guevara left the meeting in which he learned that Khrushchev had decided to remove the missiles, he rushed to the home of his ex-wife, Peruvian political organizer Hilda Gadea. Still in his dirty uniform and muddy boots, Che went into his six-year-old daughter Hildita's room, picked her up, and carried her to the living room. The commander and his daughter sat on the floor to avoid dirtying the chairs. Che kissed Hildita and told her, "Dear little daughter, I hardly ever get a chance to see you. We have been through great danger on account of those damn Yankees. When you grow up, you'll know all about it. I had to come first to see you." The babysitter, the soldiers accompanying Che, and the neighbors who had come into the home to watch were in tears. After playing with his daughter and talking with Hilda for a few minutes, Che had to leave. "Forgive me, for coming without getting cleaned up first," he told his ex-wife. "Now I have to go right away. There is much to be done." "Don't worry," she replied. "I understand. I'm glad the danger's past and you're all right."[67] Even for Che Guevara, a man ever ready to sacrifice himself on the altar of revolution, the resolution of the missile crisis brought a profound sense of relief that his daughter would live to see another day. For at least a few minutes, the anger and betrayal could wait.

## Inspections and Sovereignty

Castro also took issue with the promise that Khrushchev had made, behind his back, to allow UN inspections in Cuba. In an open letter to U Thant that he had written on October 27, Castro had expressed readiness to negotiate as long as it was on equal footing and not under the blackmail of a naval blockade. "Cuba can do whatever is asked of it, except undertake to be a victim and to renounce the rights that belong to every sovereign state," he told the secretary-general. He offered to host Thant in an official visit, "with a view to direct discussions on the present crisis."[68] Thant accepted Castro's offer, and the secretary-general's visit was announced on the same day that Cuban newspapers printed Castro's Five Points declaration, perhaps as evidence that Castro was going to play a central role in negotiations.[69] In his message accepting the invitation, Thant appealed to Castro's clearly wounded sense of pride, writing, "It would be my hope that as a result of these discussions, a solution would be reached by which the principle of respect for the sovereignty of Cuba would be assured." In the same message, Thant also reminded Castro that other people and nations had a great deal at stake in the outcome of the crisis. The secretary-general wrote of his hope "that it may also be possible for action to be taken that would reassure other countries that have felt themselves threatened by recent developments in Cuba."[70]

Thant traveled to Havana on Tuesday, October 30, hoping to gain Castro's commitment to negotiations and convince him to allow international inspection of the missiles' removal. At Thant's request, the United States lifted the naval quarantine and halted the overflights during his visit. The secretary-general held two meetings with Cuban leaders, the first on the record and the second in private. In the first meeting, on the afternoon of October 30, he told Prime Minister Castro, President Dorticós, Foreign Minister Raúl Roa, and Cuba's UN representative Carlos Lechuga that he had insisted that any inspections on Cuban territory had to be approved by the Cubans themselves. Thant said that he had informed US and Soviet leadership that "before sending a team to verify [the dismantling of the missile bases], the most important thing is to obtain prior consent from the Cuban government."[71] But Castro adamantly refused to consent to any sort of inspections either on the part of the UN, or, as the Soviets had suggested, on the part of the International Red Cross. He described the very idea as "one more attempt to humiliate our country." Thant recalled that Castro looked very grim during the meeting; Thant's military adviser, Brig. Gen. Indar Jit Rikhye, who was also present, described Castro's mood as "frustrated, intense, psychotic, infuriated." According to Rikhye, Castro spent most of the meeting ranting and screaming that no inspection would be permitted under any circumstances.[72] He demanded to know why Kennedy's noninvasion pledge was considered trustworthy while Khrushchev's promise to remove the missiles required verification. Castro did not appear ready to make concessions to ease the resolution of the crisis.

After his frustrating initial meeting with the Cubans, Secretary General Thant's spirits were lifted when two Soviet officials made a surprise visit to his Havana guest house that evening. The Soviet ambassador to Cuba, Alekseev, arrived looking very nervous, and he brought with him the general in charge of the missile sites, Maj. Gen. Igor Statsenko. Alekseev thanked Thant for his efforts to find a peaceful resolution to the crisis. Thant asked when the dismantling of the missiles would begin and was shocked to learn that the process was already underway and would be concluded within the week. "We started the dismantling on Sunday at 5 p.m.," Statsenko reported. "It will be all over by tomorrow night, or at the latest on Friday . . . the bases no longer exist." Statsenko also told Thant that no Cubans were allowed to observe the dismantling, hinting at the tensions between Cuban and Soviet leadership that the withdrawal had created.[73] The secretary-general thanked the Soviet officials for their visit, which he interpreted as an effort by Moscow to communicate to the UN that Khrushchev was following through with his end of the agreement. After the Soviet ambassador and major general left, Thant's military attaché remarked that this firsthand information from an authentic source had made the trip to Havana "extremely worthwhile."[74]

U Thant's second, private, meeting the next day was slightly more successful, though he still did not manage to convince the Cubans to agree to inspections on the island. Castro started the discussion in a bitter mood. He denounced both Kennedy and Khrushchev for excluding Cuba from the negotiations and told Thant that he was planning to make his displeasure with the Soviets public in his radio broadcast that evening. Castro then reiterated his position from the previous day that his government would strongly oppose any inspections on Cuban territory. But the Cuban leader also offered an alternative. In the earlier meeting, he had responded to the prospect of Red Cross inspections by explaining that he would not allow it in Cuban ports, but "if the Soviet Union permitted the Red Cross to inspect its vessels on the high seas, then that was their business."[75] Castro revisited the idea that he had suggested—of inspections in international waters—and proposed that "the United Nations could inspect anything outside the Cuban territorial waters." He asked Thant to convey this view to both the US and Soviet leaders.[76] Thant tried once again to convince Castro to allow inspections on the island, arguing that the missile crisis was a test case for the efficacy of the UN. "If this problem is not resolved in time," Thant warned, "the United Nations will collapse."

Thant tried to convince Castro that he sympathized with the Cuban point of view. "My colleagues and I are of the opinion—and I let the United States know—that the blockade was illegal," the secretary-general claimed. He told Castro that he had told US officials that their aerial reconnaissance was illegal and had threatened to denounce the United States in the UN Security Council and resign his position as head of the United Nations in protest if Kennedy did anything drastic. "If the United Nations can't stop a great power from attacking a small country, then I don't want to be Secretary General," Thant declared.[77] He also mentioned that he had met with Brazil's ambassador, Luis Bastián Pinto, and Brazil's special envoy to Cuba, Gen. Albino Silva, the previous day; Thant said they all agreed with Castro that the negotiations to end the crisis should address both the immediate problem of the missiles and the long-term problem of US-Cuban relations. When Thant asked for clarification of Castro's position, and whether he insisted that his Five Points be the basis for negotiations, Fidel responded that his points were so reasonable that none of them could be renounced. Castro especially insisted on the return of Guantánamo Bay Naval Base, explaining, "It is very logical, elementary, that, if our friends' weapons leave Cuba, our enemies' weapons shouldn't remain in our territory."[78] Castro pointed out the hypocrisy of the US position on foreign bases in Cuba: If the US base at Guantánamo had been established by a treaty entered into by a Cuban administration, why could another Cuban administration—that is, Castro's—not sign its own treaties to establish other foreign bases? If the Soviet bases had to go, then so too should the US base.

Eventually, after Castro consistently refused to allow inspections, Thant had to admit defeat. He asked whether, if he could not arrange inspections, he could at least leave a UN representative on the island for communications purposes, and Castro rejected this proposal as well. Thant did, however, manage to convince Castro to "practice restraint" and soften the tone of that evening's speech so as "not [to] create more difficulties in finding a just and peaceful solution to the problem."[79] Thant also inquired after the US Air Force pilot, Maj. Rudolf Anderson, who had been shot down on October 27. After denouncing the US overflights as "illegal and intolerable" provocations, Castro agreed to return Anderson's body as a humanitarian gesture of goodwill. Castro ended the meeting much mollified, thanking the secretary-general for his visit to Havana and for his "positive action for the achievement of peace according to the [UN] Charter."[80] "I believe at this moment the United Nations is playing one of the most proper roles of that institution, and that they are playing it successfully," Castro told Thant, "because a collective opinion has been felt in the United Nations in this case; not a bloc opinion, but an institutional opinion."[81] Castro appreciated the fact that the UN secretary-general had used the strength of numbers and his position as a neutral intermediary to help resolve the crisis and to include the Cubans in that resolution.

After his return from Cuba, Thant continued to work to make sure that Kennedy and Khrushchev's agreement could be implemented even without on-the-ground inspections and verification of the missiles' removal. Thant hosted many meetings over the next two months between the US and Soviet negotiating teams at UN headquarters. To address US concerns about verification, Thant raised the possibility of inspections at sea.[82] This was Castro's idea, which he had suggested in his private meeting with the UN secretary-general. But Castro had already publicly committed himself to his intransigent Five Point demands and needed Thant to broach the idea for him in order to avoid looking weak. The UN secretary-general thus served a similar face-saving role for Castro as he did for Kennedy and Khrushchev, using his position as a neutral go-between to officially propose solutions that the three world leaders had privately suggested to him. Eventually, US, Soviet, and Cuban officials tacitly agreed that the United States would be assured of the missiles' removal through a combination of overflights of Cuban territory—which the Cubans and Soviets would not shoot down—and air and naval visual verification of

Soviet ships in international waters. Thanks to the United Nations and its secretary-general, Cuban leaders' suggestions thus became important elements of the resolution of the missile crisis.

## Conclusion

Just as events in and around Cuba caused the missile crisis, events in and around Cuba also helped bring the crisis to a conclusion. Everyone on the island, Cubans and Soviets alike, had been driven to a state of extreme tension, aware that if war broke out, they would be the first casualties. Reports that an invasion was imminent pushed Fidel Castro and his men into action. On the morning of Saturday, October 27, Cuban troops opened fire on US aircraft and encouraged their Soviet comrades to do the same. A brief break in the Soviet chain of command gave Soviet troops an opening, and they shot down a US reconnaissance plane. This clear escalation alarmed and helped prod both Kennedy and Khrushchev out of their stalemate. Neither man wanted to be pulled into a nuclear war over Cuba, but that nightmare scenario was appearing increasingly likely. Khrushchev had additional reason for concern when Castro sent a fatalistic letter that seemed to suggest that he was preparing to sacrifice his entire country to give the communists an advantage in a nuclear war. Kennedy and Khrushchev exchanged desperate messages and offered concessions—some public, others private—to find a peaceful resolution. Khrushchev, fearing that his impetuous ally was about to instigate a war, accepted Kennedy's offers and made the unilateral decision to remove his nuclear weapons. Cuba was saved, and the world was spared a nuclear war. In saving Cuba, however, Khrushchev had also sacrificed some of his ally's sovereignty. UN secretary-general Thant tried to smooth over Castro's wounded pride by including him in the negotiations, but the political fallout of the crisis was just beginning.

# PART III CONSEQUENCES

# CHAPTER 10
# CRISIS AVERTED OR CRISIS PROLONGED?

The Cuban Missile Crisis had both short-term and long-term consequences for Latin American politics and inter-American relations. In the short term, Kennedy, the Organization of American States (OAS), and the United Nations (UN) enjoyed a boost in prestige for the roles they played in resolving the crisis. But the mood of celebration was far from unanimous. Many Latin American officials, especially those in the Caribbean Basin, began to criticize Kennedy almost immediately after the near escape from nuclear Armageddon. They argued that the US president had not done enough to remove the long-term threat of a communist Cuba. They worried that Kennedy had squandered his best opportunity to remove Castro and in so doing had ultimately strengthened Castro's image and his control over Cuba. Sure, the missiles were gone, but Castro's communist regime survived intact and continued to threaten hemispheric security and stability.

## Heroes
The clearest winners in the aftermath of the Cuban Missile Crisis were Kennedy, the OAS, and the UN. The widespread perception that the US president's firm stance had forced the Soviets to back down enhanced Kennedy's image not just in the United States, but across the Americas. Prominent Argentine journalist Jacobo Timerman's magazine *Primera Plana* carried a photograph of Kennedy's triumphant smile on the cover of its first edition in November 1962. An article inside the magazine praised Kennedy effusively: "It was the combination of prudence and firmness, the almost miraculous balance between his strategy and his tactics, that allowed the young American statesman to win the most resounding political victory in the West since the end of the Second World War."[1] In Rio de Janeiro, Brazil, posters appeared all over the city bearing a photograph of the US president with the words "Hail Kennedy, Defender of the Americas!"[2] US diplomats and intelligence officials celebrated the boost in popularity that Kennedy and the United States enjoyed in the wake of the crisis. The US consul in Matamoros, Mexico, reported, "The feeling here with respect to the president's

leadership in this crisis could have been well expressed in the saying that 'Latin America now believes in Kennedy.'"[3] The US ambassador to Chile was no doubt delighted to pass along a description of a meeting with four ex-presidents of the Chilean university federation in which the students claimed, "Castro's surrender of sovereignty and the strong US action leads them to believe that the United States for the first time has a chance to win the Cold War in Latin America."[4] US officials who had watched the missile crisis play out across Latin America concluded afterward that Kennedy's masterful performance had won over previous critics and could, perhaps, be parlayed into an even greater victory in the hemispheric Cold War.

Kennedy received the lion's share of public adulation in the aftermath of the crisis, but attentive observers also praised multilateral organizations for the roles they played. An editorial in *Cuba Nueva*, the Consejo Revolucionario de Cuba's magazine published from exile in Florida, claimed that when the members of the OAS met on October 23 and voted to enact the Rio Pact, they surpassed and replaced the Monroe Doctrine in the regulation of hemispheric affairs. In particular, the editorial praised Kennedy for turning to the OAS instead of acting unilaterally. "Invoking the Monroe Doctrine would have been a step backward," the editorial explained. "This crisis has given the inter-American system the required maturity, a goal that neither men nor institutions reach, except through hard testing periods like the present."[5] An editorial in *El Panamá América* celebrated that "the OAS has shown its faith in democratic principles and, in a categorical warning to enemies inside and outside, has revealed that continental American solidarity exists and is capable of acting vigorously and promptly when the gravity of the situation and the danger so require."[6] The editorialists applauded the fact that the OAS and the Rio Pact had enabled the governments of the region to coordinate their responses to the missile crisis. The OAS's active role in the crisis had strengthened the inter-American security regime under a multilateral, institutional system, which was far preferable to either the unilateral Monroe Doctrine previously imposed by the United States or unilateral, uncoordinated responses on the part of individual countries.

The OAS and UN impressed other observers by defending world peace. An editorial in the Chilean newspaper *El Mercurio* lauded the actions of both multilateral organizations. "Recent world events have most eloquently demonstrated the effectiveness of the action of international organizations . . . if the Organization of American States and the United Nations had not existed, war would have been the natural and logical conclusion of the confrontation," the editorial claimed. "It can be said, without exaggeration, that international organizations have saved the peace."[7] US secretary of state Dean Rusk—one of the earliest and most determined advocates for a multilateral response to the crisis—afterward credited the OAS and the UN with ensuring a peaceful resolution. In his memoirs, he described being "delighted" with the OAS vote, and he attested: "I am convinced that the overwhelming support we received from the international community—and Castro's neighbors in particular—helped persuade Khrushchev to withdraw the missiles." Rusk also praised the UN for facilitating negotiations. "Prolonged discussion lessened the chance that one side would lash out in a spasm and do something foolish," he reflected. "The UN earned its pay for a long time to come just by being there for the missile crisis."[8] Rusk and others recognized that the UN and especially its leader, U Thant, played crucial roles in resolving the missile crisis by slowing the pace of events enough to allow for a peaceful resolution and serving as a mediator between all the parties involved, including Cuba.

Even the those widely regarded as losing the Cuban Missile Crisis—Fidel Castro and Nikita Khrushchev—received praise from some quarters. Castro's most fervent fans tried to look past Cuba's humiliating exclusion from most of the negotiations and the loss of its nuclear arsenal by instead focusing on Castro's Five Points of Dignity declaration. In an editorial written for *Prensa Latina* in Havana, Peruvian writer, humorist, and journalist Luis Felipe Angell, more commonly known by his pseudonym Sofocleto, claimed that "it is not only the sovereignty of Cuba that Commander Fidel Castro defends in the Five Points of his approach, but that of all of Latin America, whose peoples have reiterated their absolute confidence in the decisions of the highest leader." According to Angell, "If there is a clear victory in this crisis, it is to have preserved, complete and resounding, Cuban sovereignty, thanks to the wall of Five Points with which Fidel Castro has made the revolution even greater."[9] Uruguayan writer Eduardo Galeano, who would later become famous worldwide for his anti-imperialist book *The Open Veins of Latin America*, judged that Castro's declaration was motivated by "various just concerns" over the reliability of US promises not to intervene in Cuba, reminding readers about false statements made by US officials before and during the Bay of Pigs invasion. Galeano argued that Castro's Five Points were weapons of defense in a separate war that Cuba was fighting against the United States. While the Soviets were engaged in a Cold War competition between great powers, Cuba was "part of another broader war, harsh and without truce, which constitutes the fundamental event in the world of our time: the revolutionary rise of the subjugated peoples, raised up in a fight that knows no quarter, against their oppressors."[10] According to Angell and Galeano, Castro and other revolutionaries had to keep fighting and could not relax their guard because even when nuclear tensions cooled between the superpowers, the struggle against US imperialism continued.

Castro gained one important benefit from the missile crisis: Kennedy's noninvasion pledge and the end of the joint CIA-Pentagon regime change program known as Operation Mongoose. In his letter to Khrushchev on October 27, at the height of the crisis, Kennedy had proposed that if the missiles were removed under UN observation, then the United States would end the quarantine and "give assurances against an invasion of Cuba."[11] To be sure, Castro's refusal to allow UN inspections gave Kennedy an excuse to avoid cementing his offer with an official, iron-clad pledge, and US efforts to undermine Castro's regime continued in other forms, including supporting exile operations and maintaining the economic embargo. But the fact remained that after the missile crisis, no US president ever sponsored another military invasion of the island, and Operation Mongoose came to an abrupt conclusion.[12] On October 30, Kennedy issued strict orders to halt operations against Cuba: "The activities of Operation Mongoose are to be stopped during the next several days and therefore all prior approvals for sabotage, infiltrations, guerrilla activities, [and] caching of arms are to be temporarily suspended. The direction of Operation Mongoose will be reconsidered after current negotiations are completed."[13] Over the course of the next few months, Kennedy and other US leaders decided to phase out Mongoose and replace it with a more limited program of support for exile operations that—unlike the earlier operation—did not include plans for direct US military intervention. The missile crisis led to an immediate and tangible change in US policy toward Cuba and removed one strategy—direct intervention—from the realm of serious and active consideration.

Even Nikita Khrushchev, who would suffer a great deal of criticism in the months and years to come and who would be stripped of his position as Soviet premier almost exactly two years after the missile crisis, received some praise for his defense of Cuba and world peace. Colombia's communist party newspaper published an editorial titled "The USSR Stopped the War!" The editorial was accompanied by a political cartoon showing a calm Khrushchev restraining a sweating, shaking Kennedy who was reaching for a button labeled "Atomic World War."[14] On October 30, approximately 2,000 people attended a rally in Lima's Plaza San Martín organized by the Peruvian Student Federation and other leftist groups including the National Liberation Front and the Revolutionary Leftist Movement (Movimiento de la Izquierda Revolucionaria). The crowd cheered as one of the speakers proclaimed Khrushchev a candidate for the Nobel Peace Prize.[15] At its national conference in December

A political cartoon by Espártaco that appeared in the Colombian communist party's weekly newspaper. A firm Khrushchev restrains a sweaty, crazed Kennedy from pushing a button labeled "Atomic World War," telling the US president, "No Mr. Kennedy, do not push that button!" *La Voz de la Democracia* (Bogotá), November 2, 1962.

1962, the Partido Comunista Brasileiro passed a resolution that declared, "By removing from Cuban territory the weapons considered 'offensive' by the Kennedy government, the Soviet Union eliminated the pretext used by the imperialist forces for their aggressive action, contributed decisively to safeguarding the country, and met the interests of the brotherly people of Cuba."[16] A few months later, the Communist Party of Argentina held its own national conference. The first speaker, Rodolfo Ghioldi, one of the party's founders, recalled the events of the missile crisis and claimed, "No one ignores that if war was avoided and Cuba was respected without any detriment, it was thanks to the perceptive position of the great Soviet Union, which stopped the aggressor arm and the atomic shot. All the peoples of the earth have seen that the Soviet Union is truly the great standard-bearer of lasting peace among nations."[17] The Argentine communists also reported that they had distributed

100,000 copies of a flyer containing Khrushchev's October 28 Radio Moscow address under the title "The Historic Message of Nikita Khrushchev in Defense of World Peace."[18]

As the world took a collective sigh of relief in the days and weeks after the missile crisis, there was plenty of praise to go around. Kennedy was celebrated for his firm stance during and after the crisis. Since Kennedy's concessions—removing his missiles in Turkey and ending Operation Mongoose—were kept secret, most observers at the time concluded that the US leader's strong declarations and unyielding positions had carried the day. The OAS and the UN were widely applauded for facilitating collective action and peaceful resolutions, while Castro was praised for defending Cuba's sovereignty and Khrushchev was recognized for his dedication to world peace. This chorus of celebration would soon fade, however, as the long-term consequences of the crisis began to set in.

## The Caribbean Basin and the Fight Against Castro

Journalists and politicians throughout the Caribbean Basin spared no time in questioning the terms of the peace. On October 30, just two days after Khrushchev announced that he would remove the missiles from Cuba, Panama City's *La Hora* published an editorial titled "Khrushchev's Retreat." The author argued that the Soviet leader, not Kennedy, had emerged as the victor in the confrontation. In terms of propaganda, Khrushchev could claim to be the primary defender of world peace; and in terms of strategy, well, the Soviets did still have communist allies and military bases in Cuba, even if the nuclear weapons were on the way out. "Only when the communist government that currently reigns in Cuba has been eliminated, only when democracy has fully recovered its validity in the tortured Pearl of the Antilles, [can] freedom and justice be considered to have won the battle in the New World," the editorial claimed. "As long as Russia has the current facilities to install its military bases in Cuba in a matter of a few days, the democracy of our hemisphere will be in danger."[19] This warning, published in a Panamanian paper, soon reached a much wider audience. On November 1, a press attaché from the Voice of America radio network wrote to congratulate the editor of *La Hora* on the article and informed him that his editorial had been broadcast to listeners all across Latin America.[20] The program managers at the Voice of America agreed with the Panamanian journalist that Cuba and the Soviet Union still posed a significant threat.

An editorial in Managua's *La Prensa* also warned readers that the danger had not ended with Khrushchev's withdrawal. "This armistice is not permanent peace! This respite is not a definitive triumph of justice!" the editorial insisted, and then pondered, "What does the future hold for us?" The author contemplated the possibilities that Castro would "continue as director of the communist orchestra" in Latin America, or that the bell would one day ring for the final round of "full-on attack" between the heavyweight boxers of the United States and the Soviet Union. "When? Will they fight with conventional weapons or make use of the new inventions to unleash the horsemen of the apocalypse on Earth?" The editorial, its first half filled with images of uncertainty and doom, transitioned in its second half into a call for action. "Freedom must not die in America," the author urged. Americans from Alaska to Tierra del Fuego needed to join Castro's opponents both on and off the island in their struggle to liberate Cuba. The author predicted that those who were already fighting to liberate Cuba from Castro would be joined by "legionnaires from other brother nations" who shared their dedication to democracy.[21] The editorial concluded on this optimistic note, predicting that people across the continent who had been awakened by the threat of the crisis would continue to act in solidarity and see their fates as intertwined with that of Cuba.

Cuban exiles were among the fiercest critics and opponents of the crisis's peaceful resolution. They had hoped that the missiles would compel Kennedy and other regional leaders to remove Castro once and for all, and they saw those hopes crumble as threats of confrontation turned into drawn-out negotiations. The Mexican delegation of the Revolutionary Student Directorate issued a declaration that was published in papers across the Americas, including in Buenos Aires's *La Razón*, on October 30. The exiled Cuban students declared: "While we applaud the dismantling of the rocket bases in our country . . . we want to state very clearly that this does not solve the problem of Cuba, which will continue to be subjugated by the Soviet Union." They argued that removing the missiles did not remove the ideological threat that communist penetration posed to Cuba and the rest of the hemisphere. Nor did removing the missiles free the Cuban people from the terror and oppression of Castro's government. The exiled students argued that the rest of the Americas should not forget the sense of existential dread that they had experienced during the crisis, because Cubans who were fighting to reclaim their country still faced the daily danger of summary execution by firing squad. "If the rocket bases pointed at the United States and the entire Latin American continent endangered their security," the declaration pointed out, "the people of Cuba lost that same security a long time ago with the infamous *paredón*." The exiles vowed to continue their fight as soon as they had the necessary weapons: "We will destroy their ships in the Antillean seas . . . the Caribbean waters of our oceans will soon be silent witnesses."[22] Even if the governments of the United States and Latin America forgot about Cuba as soon as the missiles had left, the exiles promised that they would never give up. Another exile group, the Miami-based Cuban Revolutionary Council (Consejo Revolucionario Cubano, or Consejo for short), sent an open telegram to UN secretary-general Thant in which they issued similar declarations about continuing the fight against Castro. On the eve of Thant's diplomatic mission to Havana at the end of October, the Consejo's president, José Miró Cardona, warned that any agreements that Thant reached with Castro would be invalid because "Castro's government lacks the sovereignty of the Cuban nation."[23] The Consejo argued that Khrushchev's actions had clearly demonstrated that the Soviets, not Castro, were in charge in Cuba. They declared that they would not consider themselves bound by any invalid agreements made with Cuba's puppet leadership and would continue their armed actions against Castro.

US leaders worried that Cuban exiles' belligerent actions might undermine the US position or endanger the tense negotiations to resolve the crisis. On October 30, the same day that the Consejo issued their warning, the acting director of the US Information Agency (USIA) alerted the White House that Cuban exiles were trying to buy time on US radio stations. "It was expected that if they succeeded," the USIA warned, "they would make inflammatory statements about present U.S. policy toward Cuba." Kennedy authorized the USIA director to speak with the chairman of the Federal Communications Commission to find a way to block the exiles' broadcasts without appearing to be imposing censorship.[24] On October 31, US officials arrested Cuban exiles at sea; they had been heading toward the island. Kennedy instructed his negotiators to inform the Soviet negotiators of the arrests as a demonstration of his good-faith efforts to honor his promise to cease attacks on Castro's government.[25] On November 1, Kennedy decided to cancel a press conference rather than face questions about how his administration was handling Cuban exiles. During the previous week, US law enforcement agencies had quietly kept exile groups "under restraint," as Kennedy's national security adviser, McGeorge Bundy, put it, and Kennedy did not want to have to confirm or deny those restraining efforts.[26]

While US officials were somewhat successful in stifling Cuban exiles' activities, the Cuban opposition's rumor mill posed a greater challenge. Cuban exile groups across the Americas spread the story that the Soviets had not removed all their missiles but instead were secretly hiding them in caves and underground bases.[27] The Chilean embassy in Havana heard from informants within Cuba that the Soviets were lying about removing their atomic weapons. Diplomatic officials passed along reports that the Soviets had buried three rockets in a quarry between the cities of Coliseo and Matanzas, and that some dismantling trucks had been diverted on their way to Havana.[28] The British ambassador in Havana also commented on the cave rumors in one of his reports back to his home office. "Our counter-revolutionary contacts, faced with the realization that the United States marines are now unlikely to be coming to reinstate the old order unless more long-range missiles are reported to be on the island [,] are busy reporting them," he observed. "According to them there are hundreds and hundreds of them in caves." More skeptical than his Chilean colleagues, the British ambassador noted that he had mostly seen evidence of Soviet military equipment leaving the island. He qualified his doubts, however, with the caveat that "one can never be quite sure."[29]

The rumors quickly became so widespread that the White House decided to act. Secretary of State Rusk mentioned them at a meeting of Kennedy's Ex-Comm in early November. "Our problem is how to manage recurrent rumors in the United States and Latin America that the Russians are not moving out their missiles but merely putting them into caves," Rusk told the rest of the group.[30] The secretary of state wanted evidence to counter the stories, and Castro's steadfast refusal to allow inspections made it practically impossible to obtain such evidence. The reconnaissance flights could not reveal the contents of caves and underground shelters and thus were of little use in quelling the reports of subterranean missiles.

Without inspections as a tool to dispel the cave rumors, US and Soviet officials were left to resort to speculation and bluster. On November 20, Khrushchev sent a message to Kennedy in which he addressed the matter. "As for the rumors alleging that the missiles may have been left in Cuba somewhere in the caves, one can say that we do not live in the caveman age," the Soviet leader wrote. In addition to mocking the rumors, Khrushchev also speculated about their possible origins and purposes. "If someone is spreading rumors of this kind," the Soviet leader argued, "he is doing that deliberately to create difficulties in the negotiations."[31] Kennedy's advisers also discussed the source of the rumors but took a more serious view. In a late November meeting of the ExComm, Secretary of Defense McNamara assured his colleagues that US surveillance efforts were sufficient. "There are five types of wicked-looking Soviet defensive missiles," he explained, "and the presence in Cuba of probably 1,000 of such missiles undoubtedly gave rise to some of the refugee reports. These missiles are certainly being stored in warehouses and caves."[32] According to McNamara, the rumors were a result of confusion, not exile trouble-making or Soviet subterfuge. The Soviets and Cubans were storing some, if not many, missiles in caves, but the secretary was confident that the missiles in the caves were short-range defense weapons and that the offensive nuclear weapons whose presence had sparked the crisis were gone.

Faced with the US government's unwillingness to use the missile crisis as a justification for another invasion of Cuba, some exiles concluded that they would have to act independently. US embassy officials in Caracas observed in early December that "glumness" reigned in the Cuban exile community in Venezuela. Local Cuban spokesmen representing the Consejo Revolucionario Cubano and other exile groups criticized the United States' apparent willingness to let Castro remain in power and Kennedy's failure to consult his Latin American counterparts during the negotiations and before concluding the quarantine in late November. Many of the exiles also criticized José Miró Cardona and the Consejo for depending too much on US government approval, logistical support, and policy guidance. According to the embassy observers, the phrase "now we'll have to do it alone," was frequently repeated. The Cuban exiles also proposed looking to their fellow Latin Americans rather than to the United States for support.[33] Kennedy's failure to seize the perfect excuse to invade Cuba and his subsequent efforts to thwart exile activities made it clear that the exiles could not rely on him. The Cuban exiles would have to act independently or cultivate other allies.

Government officials in many Latin American countries shared the exiles' worries that the opportunity to remove Castro was slipping away. Venezuela's foreign minister Marcos Falcón Briceño met with US assistant secretary of state for inter-American affairs Edwin Martin in Washington at the end of November to discuss the Cuba situation. The Venezuelan foreign minister explained that for his country, Cuba was both an immediate and long-term threat. He worried that Castro had suffered "a severe blow to his pride" as a result of the removal of the missiles and might "lash out" against Venezuela, Colombia, or the Dominican Republic in reaction against the loss of face.[34]

Central American politicians also expressed dissatisfaction with the resolution of the crisis. The president of Honduras, Ramón Villeda Morales, told the Voice of America radio program, "For the people and government of Honduras, the Caribbean crisis does not end with the dismantling of the offensive weapons bases in Cuba. . . . The crisis in the Caribbean and America will be permanent as long as there is a regime with a communist structure embedded in the heart of America."[35] Not the typical Central American hawkish dictator, Villeda Morales was a pediatrician by training who was leading his country through a democratic transition with substantial assistance from the Alliance for Progress.[36] His economic reliance on the United States and political similarities with Kennedy—a fellow liberal democratic reformer—did not prevent the Honduran president from issuing pretty severe criticism of how the US president had handled the missile crisis. He condemned Kennedy for promising that Cuba would not be invaded, arguing that this promise guaranteed the stability of a communist regime in the Americas. According to Villeda Morales, Kennedy should not have used the term "invasion" to describe what should by all rights be considered a rescue operation to free the Cuban people from communism. "An invasion is what Russia has carried out in the face of the expectant attitude of America, which with her passivity has established itself as an ally of an invasion," he declared. He swore, "Honduras is ready to support any action aimed at radically eliminating the communist cancer of the crucified island of the Caribbean."[37] Villeda Morales repeated his medical metaphor a few weeks later in his annual address to the Honduran congress, declaring, "Castro-communism is a cancer, and as long as it is not completely excised, the structure of the inter-American system will be in danger of contamination."[38] Castro did not need missiles to pose a threat; his revolutionary ideology itself was contagious.

In late November, President Villeda Morales visited the United States to push for joint action against Castro. He stopped first in Washington, where he met with Kennedy and gave a speech at the OAS. He reiterated his call for collective OAS measures to "rescue Cuba from that horrible state of things."[39] In his private meeting with Kennedy, the Honduran president proposed creating a joint military force in the Caribbean that could fight the spread of communism and act as "a group of firemen ready to answer an alarm." He told Kennedy he had already discussed this idea with the presidents of El Salvador, Guatemala, and Nicaragua and that they were on board. Kennedy encouraged Villeda Morales to continue developing the idea of the joint force and recommended working through the OAS to avoid the "stigma" of US imperialism.

Kennedy also had words of caution for Villeda Morales about the limits of US and Honduran intervention. "The US and Honduras cannot liberate Cuba ... the Cubans must do this for themselves," he insisted. "The US government feels it has a commitment to Cuba, but at the same time the Cuban exiles can and should take up their responsibilities."[40] Villeda Morales then traveled to Miami, where he gave a speech as the guest of honor of the Cuban College of Medicine in Exile. He argued that there had to be unity among all the Cuban exiles and across all the countries of the continent to oust Castro. "The problem of Cuba cannot be isolated by Washington and Havana but must be considered as involving all of Latin America," he declared. "There is no other road than collective action by the Organization of American States to liberate the Cuban people."[41] Everywhere he went, the Honduran president argued that the security of the hemisphere depended upon joint action against Castro. Cuban exiles had to put an end to their fragmented leadership and work together with each other so that the OAS could coordinate collective action against the communist threat.

Like-minded liberal democratic leaders in Costa Rica also shared the Honduran president's desire for joint military action against Castro. Costa Rica's foreign minister, Daniel Oduber Quirós, a longtime partner of Costa Rica's most influential twentieth-century leader, José Figueres, told a *Diario de Costa Rica* reporter that if UN negotiations failed, "there would be no other course than the US destruction of Cuban bases in line with the OAS's decision of October 28 [*sic*] authorizing the use of force."[42] Foreign Minister Oduber expanded upon these remarks when he met privately with US embassy officials in San José in early November.[43] Oduber told the embassy officer that Castro's insulting rejection of observers should have touched off joint OAS military action. In Oduber's view, the OAS had already voted to approve the possibility of military action to remove the missiles, and Castro's refusal of inspections meant that the member countries should follow through with their resolution. A joint military operation was the only way to verify that the nuclear weapons had in fact been removed, especially in light of the rumors about missiles remaining in caves. The Costa Rican foreign minister also recommended that "no commitments against invasion should be made because [they] would weaken [the] present US-OAS position."[44]

The Costa Rican foreign minister worried that if Kennedy reiterated or confirmed his noninvasion pledge it would become more difficult to justify joint military action. Oduber wanted Kennedy to maintain the initiative against Castro; "the US must not appear to back down," he insisted. He recommended that the United States provide full support to "volunteer, irregular troops" for "commando type action" and a heavy sabotage program. "Castro must have what he is giving Venezuela," Oduber argued. He predicted that the OAS would support actions of this type against Castro because, regardless of the elimination of the missile bases, the "base of subversion and aggression must be wiped out if Latin American countries [are] to succeed in resistance against communism."[45] Again and again, Oduber emphasized the need for joint US-OAS military action.

Foreign Minister Oduber and other Costa Rican leaders did not just wait around for the United States to take the lead in continuing the fight against Castro. Oduber and José Figueres—head of the governing National Liberation Party—invited one of the most prominent Cuban exiles, Auténtico Party leader Antonio Santiago Ruiz, to Costa Rica in December 1962 for a series of conferences. Their first step was to issue a joint communiqué "for the purpose of coordinating efforts toward the liberation of the Cuban people and in defense of the democratic institutions of the whole Continent." The Costa Ricans expressed "ample solidarity with the struggle for Cuban liberation" and "repudiation of the communist dictatorship of Fidel Castro."[46] Oduber and Figueres hoped that by working with the Auténtico Party leader, they could coordinate anti-Castro activities among Cuban exile groups and other Latin

Americans who were committed to ousting the Cuban dictator. In a separate meeting with US diplomatic officials, Oduber and his adviser Luis Alberto Monge explained their plan. They wanted to organize political support among seventeen left-wing parties of the hemisphere "to the end that assistance may eventually be given to anti-Castro subversive action."[47] In the shorter term, the Costa Ricans were trying to seize the advantage provided by the missile crisis, before it was forgotten, to organize left-wing propaganda against Castro and the communists. Monge asked the US officials to help distribute their communiqué, since the foreign wire services lacked representatives in Costa Rica. The USIA complied and helped publicize the communiqué about liberating Cuba.

Panamanian officials likewise argued that Cuban exiles needed support in their fight against Castro. Panama's foreign minister, Galileo Solís, warned the US ambassador that even though the atomic threat had been removed, the political threat to Latin American countries was not diminished and would continue until Castro himself was removed. Solís advised against a unilateral US invasion, which he believed would likely inspire widespread criticism and opposition both in Cuba and across Latin America. Instead, Solís argued, the United States and other neighboring countries should provide more equipment and support to guerrilla opposition groups within Cuba. Cuban exiles should also receive more training and equipment as well as assistance in infiltrating back onto the island to join the internal opposition. The Panamanian minister estimated that two-thirds of Castro's militia were forced to participate and would "rapidly melt away if [a] real prospect of Castro's overthrow appeared."[48]

Other Central American leaders were more defiant and outraged by US policy and the lack of progress on the multilateral front, and they vowed to act on their own. Guatemala's president, Gen. Miguel Ydígoras Fuentes, who had been one of the first to warn about nuclear weapons in Cuba, saw Kennedy's noninvasion pledge as an unforgiveable betrayal. Ydígoras made his displeasure clear by sending an open telegram to Republican congressmen Barry Goldwater and Bob Wilson three days before the midterm elections took place in the United States. "Due to the Kennedy-Khrushchev agreement, Latin American countries, especially Central America and particularly Guatemala are anxious to learn if we are going to be abandoned or protected," Ydígoras inquired. He also expressed support for Republicans' efforts to force Kennedy to take a stronger stance on the matter of the remaining Soviet weapons and technicians in the ongoing negotiations.[49] Issuing public statements of solidarity with Kennedy's political rivals on the eve of national elections was a clear provocation.

After Kennedy's party maintained control of both houses of Congress in the midterm elections, Ydígoras decided to stop waiting for US protection and to take the fight to Castro on his own. At a press conference on November 9, the Guatemalan president threatened to recognize and provide asylum and support to a Cuban government-in-exile—led by Julio Garceran—if Castro did not expel former Guatemalan president Jacobo Arbenz, who had taken up residence in Cuba.[50] Guatemala's recognition of Garceran's government-in-exile would have disrupted efforts to unite the inter-American opposition to Castro because Washington and most other countries in the Americas favored other exile organizations like Miró Cardona's Consejo. Dean Rusk instructed the US embassy in Guatemala to dissuade Ydígoras by warning him that recognizing Garceran's government would "stir sharp criticism from most Cuban exile leaders and expose the government of Guatemala to a certain amount of ridicule abroad for having thrown in with an obvious lightweight who is going nowhere." Rusk also predicted that few other countries would follow Guatemala's lead in backing Garceran—the United States certainly would not—and Ydígoras's action "would result in the untimely exposure of hemispheric divisions to the delight of Castro and the Soviets."[51] The thrust of the message was that Ydígoras's efforts threatened to hurt his own reputation, leave his country isolated, and divide the inter-American community. US pressure seemed to work; at the end of December, Ydígoras changed his tune entirely and issued a press release stating that Guatemala was seeking peace in the coming year and was ready to pass the torch of leadership in the fight against Castro. "Guatemala is not throwing in the towel, but it needs peace and tranquility. It has already done its part against Castro," Ydígoras declared. "It is necessary that other countries in Latin America now do their part."[52] As a show of good faith and his desire for improved relations with Cuba, Ydígoras expelled four members of the Consejo and requested reciprocal expulsions from the Cuban government.

Nicaraguan dictator Luis Somoza Debayle, one of the most vocal Latin American advocates of an invasion during the crisis, was more than ready to assume leadership in the efforts against Castro. Somoza wrote Kennedy on October 30, warning of the continued danger that Cuba posed. "The offensive weapons bases are not the whole problem but are the consequence—as are many other existing threats—of the communist regime now in power in Cuba," he insisted. Somoza told Kennedy that he considered the quarantine and other measures taken during the crisis "only the beginning."[53] As it became clearer in the course of the protracted November negotiations that Kennedy was committed to a peaceful resolution, Somoza grew more frustrated. He told reporters in a press conference on November 8, "If the United States does not accompany us in the liquidation of Castro, Latin America will carry that business to its conclusion." Somoza reminded his audience that thousands of his young supporters had asked for weapons during the crisis to help liberate Cuba and were willing to fight for their ideals on Cuban beaches. "Kennedy has not compromised our freedom of action," he proclaimed.[54] In addition to offering Nicaraguan lives, Somoza also pledged to support Cuban exile operations and offered Nicaragua as a base if the United States continued to thwart the actions of Miró Cardona's Consejo.[55] The next day, at a meeting of the OAS, the Nicaraguan representative summed up his government's position. "Cuba with or without rockets will continue to imperil the continent," he declared. "We must dismantle the Cuban government as well."[56]

## Conclusion

While most of the world sighed with relief when the Cuban Missile Crisis came to a peaceful conclusion, the sentiment was by no means universal. Cuban exiles and the leaders of the Caribbean Basin nations had little in common—some were leftist democratic reformers, some were political refugees, others were conservative dictators—but one thing they all shared was a sense of disappointment after the Cuban Missile Crisis. The crisis had raised their hopes that Castro had finally gone too far. When Castro allowed the introduction of Soviet nuclear missiles in the hemisphere, the Cuban Revolution had escalated from posing a political and ideological threat to posing an existential one. Leaders and Cuban exiles throughout the Caribbean Basin had been trying to topple Castro's government ever since he came into power and were thrilled when it appeared that the entire continent was finally ready to act together to eliminate the communist menace. But hemispheric solidarity lasted only as long as the missiles remained in Cuba; as soon as Khrushchev announced that he would remove them, divisions quickly appeared.

Kennedy's promise not to invade Cuba outraged Caribbean Basin leaders and Cuban exiles. They hated to see the opportunity to oust Castro come to an end and tried to extend and expand the crisis; they argued that it was not just about the missiles but about the threat that Castro and the Cuban Revolution in general posed to hemispheric security. Some tried to convince Kennedy to continue supporting efforts to unseat Castro, while others declared that they did not need US support or permission. Some continued working through the OAS to isolate Castro, and others supported Cuban exiles who conducted attacks on the Cuban government. To a certain extent, Kennedy and his successors participated in these multilateral efforts to isolate Castro and destabilize his government. But Kennedy also refused to let Cuban exiles and their

Caribbean Basin collaborators goad him into another invasion. The missile crisis marked the apex of inter-American cooperation against Castro, but that unity of action was temporary. Once the crisis ended, Castro's opponents in the Caribbean Basin lacked the coordination and US support necessary to mount a significant challenge to his rule. In this sense, then, Castro emerged from the Cuban Missile Crisis more secure than ever.

# CHAPTER 11
# REALIGNMENTS

The Cuban Missile Crisis had a profound impact on international relations between the United States and some of Latin America's largest and most influential countries: Mexico, Bolivia, Argentina, and Brazil. In the years and months leading up to the missile crisis, these four countries had been some of the most resistant to cooperation with US and multilateral efforts to oust Castro. President Kennedy and others in Washington interpreted Mexican, Bolivian, Brazilian, and Argentine leaders' responses to the crisis as a sort of litmus test of their loyalties to the United States. Those who passed the test and demonstrated solidarity with the United States were able to heal the rifts in their relations with Washington or build new ties, but those who failed never recovered US support.

## Healing Rifts

Mexico and Bolivia, two nations with their own revolutionary legacies, were some of the most prominent defenders of the Cuban Revolution in the years before the missile crisis. Both countries defended the Cuban Revolution by refusing to cut diplomatic ties with Cuba and abstaining from the January 1962 vote that expelled the nation from the Organization of American States (OAS). And in both countries, national leaders used their solidarity with Cuba to burnish their own revolutionary legitimacy and to curry favor among leftist groups that were considering splitting from the governing parties. Mexico and Bolivia's ties to Cuba threatened to unsettle their relations with the United States on the eve of the missile crisis.

In Mexico, Kennedy and other US officials had tried on numerous occasions before the missile crisis to convince President Adolfo López Mateos to cut ties with Cuba and to take a stronger stance on communism. US leaders had even resorted to diplomatic and economic pressure in their efforts to change Mexico's policy toward Cuba, with little success. Thomas Mann, the US ambassador to Mexico from 1961 to 1963, led these efforts and spent much of his time in Mexico testing different tactics to pressure his hosts to change their foreign policy. On the eve of the January 1962 OAS meeting in Punta del

Este, Ambassador Mann recommended that Washington use its political and economic leverage to influence Mexico's vote on expelling Cuba and applying sanctions. He proposed that the US government delay action on any loans and encourage international lending institutions to do the same. To send the message that the United States did not approve of its neighbor's independent foreign policy, Mann also suggested indefinitely postponing a state visit that Kennedy had planned to make to Mexico.[1]

A more powerful official than the ambassador—President Kennedy—had also tried to influence Mexico's policy toward Cuba in the months leading up to the missile crisis. In June 1962, Kennedy and his wife, Jacqueline, made a state visit to Mexico, and the US president took the opportunity to press his Mexican counterpart on the issues of Cuba and communism. In his first private meeting with President López Mateos, Kennedy asked: "What does Mexico think should be done to prevent the spread of Communism in other American Republics?"[2] López Mateos replied that economic growth was the best way to combat the communist threat and pointed to the Alliance for Progress as a promising initiative. In another private meeting at the end of Kennedy's visit, López Mateos tried to convince Kennedy to accept Mexico's position on Cuba. He explained that he recognized that his relations with Castro had created doubts "in some parts of United States' opinion" about Mexico's loyalties, but he told Kennedy that he wished to reassure him and his people that "in case any conflict should arise, Mexico would be glad to guard the United States' rear with its 35 million people."[3] The Mexican president was not willing to cut relations with Cuba, but he vowed that his country's fundamental ties and loyalties were with the United States.

The Cuban Missile Crisis offered López Mateos the opportunity to live up to his promise to Kennedy. Mexican representatives in the OAS, who had conspicuously abstained from voting to expel Cuba in January 1962, changed their tune and voted to approve the quarantine. The Mexican army deployed troops to protect the country's valuable oil installations, and the navy sent ten small ships to patrol the Yucatan Channel between Mexico and Cuba.[4] Intelligence agents and other security officials closely monitored the actions of all political organizations and prominent individuals. When leftist groups tried to hold a large pro-Cuba demonstration at a workers' union building in Mexico City on the morning of November 4, riot police showed up two hours before the event and ordered the organizers to tear down their protest banners and vacate the premises.[5]

US officials took note. Ambassador Mann celebrated the fact that no violent pro-Castro activities took place in Mexico, and he attributed the peaceful public response to the "firm control maintained by national and local police and military forces."[6] A year and a half after the crisis, President Lyndon B. Johnson told President López Mateos that he trusted that "when the chips were down, Mexico would be on the side of the United States."[7] Half a year later, López Mateos's successor, Gustavo Díaz Ordaz, used the same turn of phrase when he reminded Johnson of Mexico's position during the missile crisis. He explained that it was proof that "the United States could be absolutely sure that when the chips were really down, Mexico would be unequivocally by its side."[8]

Mexican support for the United States during the missile crisis led to a subtle but important shift in the relationship between the two countries. Before October 1962, Mann, Kennedy, and other US officials had worried that the Mexicans were not taking the communist threat seriously, and they had tried to use diplomatic and economic pressure to compel Mexico to break relations with Cuba. However, when Kennedy presented the world with indisputable proof of Soviet nuclear warheads in the Caribbean, the Mexican government had to choose a side. By supporting the United States and voting in the OAS to approve the quarantine in that crucial moment, López Mateos demonstrated where his true loyalties lay and gained the United States' acceptance of his foreign policy toward Cuba. US officials stopped pressuring the Mexican government to cut relations with Cuba and instead started embracing Mexico's unique position in the hemisphere. US trust in Mexico's loyalties helped smooth the way for Mexican leaders to stake out a prominent role in inter-American politics, especially in their pursuit of international peace.

The Cuban Missile Crisis also helped heal a rift in Bolivia's relations with the United States. At the time of the crisis, Bolivia's government was headed by Víctor Paz Estenssoro, a political chameleon—or perhaps, more fittingly, a spider—who climbed and clung to power by building intricate webs of domestic and international relations. Under Paz's leadership, Bolivia's moderate-left, middle-class Revolutionary Nationalist Movement (Movimiento Nacionalista Revolucionario [MNR]) had seized power in April 1952 by forming an alliance with the powerful miners' federation, arming the public, and overthrowing the military and traditional political parties. Paz then began the process of overseeing—and taming—one of Latin America's most significant social and economic revolutions of the twentieth century. Like the government that emerged from the Mexican Revolution, Paz's MNR pursued a program of resource nationalism, agrarian reform, and modernization that became significantly less revolutionary the longer the governing party stayed in power.[9]

Amid this tumultuous revolution, Paz needed foreign investment and aid to keep the national economy afloat. To avoid completely alienating foreign investors or the US government, Paz compensated the former owners of nationalized tin mines and left other mines intact. As a further way to signal that the MNR was not a communist movement, Bolivia's leaders opened their state-owned petroleum industry to foreign investment in 1955 and accepted an extremely austere IMF-designed monetary stabilization plan a year later. The IMF plan marked the beginning of the end of the Bolivian Revolution, closing the era of radical reforms and opening the spigot of ever-greater amounts of foreign aid.[10] By the end of the 1950s, Bolivia had become the single largest recipient of US economic assistance in Latin America and the second-largest per capita recipient of US aid in the world. This aid, hundreds of millions of dollars, constituted 40 percent of Bolivia's entire national budget and 20 percent of its GDP by the 1960s, making the country extremely dependent on US largesse.[11] The United States also poured weapons, ammunition, and other forms of military aid into Bolivia, working with President Paz to strengthen the Bolivian military against the threat of workers' militias.[12]

Paz was able to gain so much US support for his revolutionary government by manipulating US leaders' Cold War anxieties. Paz used an independent foreign policy to gain US backing for his government. He unsettled US leaders by "playing the Soviet card," entertaining generous offers of assistance from the Soviet bloc to gain attention and aid from the United States.[13] He invited leaders of the Non-Aligned Movement to visit Bolivia, including Indonesian president Sukarno and Yugoslav prime minister Josip Broz Tito, and sent a delegation to observe the inaugural meeting of the movement in Yugoslavia in September 1961.[14] As a journalist for the MNR newspaper, *La Nación*, put it, President Paz "wanted to be a Latin American Tito, to play both sides of the Cold War."[15] Paz also maintained relations with Castro's Cuba, even after most Latin American countries had cut ties and expelled Cuba from the OAS, and he even allowed the Cuban embassy to operate in La Paz with almost total impunity.[16]

In October 1962, US-Bolivian relations were experiencing their own crisis. That July, the State Department had announced that the US Treasury would begin unloading thousands of tons of tin every week from the nation's strategic stockpile. Tin was Bolivia's main export; and the sell-off depressed already-declining world market prices and threatened Bolivia's economy. Paz retaliated by postponing a visit to Washington and by temporarily pulling Bolivia out of the OAS.[17] Both chambers of the Bolivian congress passed unanimous resolutions condemning the US tin sales and demanding compensation for damage to the Bolivian economy.[18] Leftist senators pressured President Paz to move forward on Soviet aid offers, including an agreement that a parliamentary delegation had signed in June with the Czechoslovakian government to provide Bolivia with its own long-desired antimony smelter.[19]

Assistant Secretary of State Edwin Martin warned that President Paz was facing the prospect of a "complete takeover by the MNR Left Sector, accompanied by large-scale Soviet aid."[20] Paz's intricate web of domestic and international relations was on the verge of unraveling.

As soon as news broke of the missiles in Cuba, however, US and local officials in Bolivia put aside their differences and jumped into action. US ambassador Ben Stephansky called on President Paz and Foreign Minister José Fellman Velarde shortly before Kennedy's speech on the evening of October 22. Paz praised Kennedy's actions as responsible and intelligent, pointing out that the US president showed great restraint by resisting the temptation to invade Cuba. He also promised to fulfill Bolivia's international obligations under the Rio Treaty and comply with any OAS decisions. The three men discussed how to manage Bolivia's reentry into the OAS considering the urgent crisis.[21] By the next morning, Bolivia's OAS representative was at the meeting, declaring that "Bolivia is present, at this moment of such extraordinary gravity, to express its absolute and categorical solidarity with the people and governments of our hemisphere and its intense concern regarding the aggressive intervention of international communism in our continent."[22] Bolivia had thus officially rejoined the hemispheric community firmly on the side of the United States.

After the conclusion of the missile crisis, President Paz seized the opportunity to repair his partnership with the United States. On October 31, he sent a letter to Kennedy in which he explained: "My country, in line with its traditions, has wanted to demonstrate its hemispheric solidarity by acting jointly with all the nations of the Hemisphere . . . and it has so acted, despite the limitations caused by its internal order." This was a reference, of course, to the violent riots in La Paz on October 26. The pro-Castro participants in the riots argued that they were showing solidarity with Cuba, and President Paz used the same term—solidarity—to describe his decision to rejoin the OAS and vote to approve the quarantine. The Bolivian president closed the letter expressing his "sincere happiness" that his country's stance had been appreciated by the government of the United States, "to which we are bound by so many close ties."[23] Ambassador Stephansky celebrated the fact that the missile crisis had prompted Paz to reaffirm his connections with the United States at a time when US tin dumping had endangered the relationship and provoked a leftward turn in Bolivian policy.[24]

Paz Estenssoro's decision to use the missile crisis to gain further US backing for the Bolivian regime smoothed over the rocky relations between the two countries. The crisis also marked the end of the Bolivian president's attempts to feign neutrality and play the Soviet Union and United States off each other.

The Bolivian government, now firmly in the US camp, stopped courting the Soviets and broke relations with Cuba in 1964.[25]

## New Alliances

The Cuban Missile Crisis marked an even greater watershed in US-Argentine relations. Argentina's military, the real power behind the country's nominally civilian government, undertook the hemisphere's greatest shift in strategy in response to the crisis. Previously, Argentina's military had closer ties with France than with the United States and was primarily concerned with internecine competition and the fight against Peronism.[26] The experience of participating in the Inter-American Quarantine Force demonstrated the benefits of coordinating its strategies with the United States in pursuing both local and international goals. Argentine military leaders and their civilian allies, especially those among the *azules* faction in power at the time, were quick to seize this opportunity. No longer touting their traditional independence, they shifted their strategy to cooperate more fully with their US counterparts.

As one of the Latin American countries most directly involved in the quarantine, Argentina took a proactive position in coordinating the hemispheric response during the missile crisis. In addition to being the first country to offer its participation and one of the few to contribute functional warships, Argentina also worked through the inter-American system to make sure that all the participants in the quarantine were cooperating and communicating. On November 2, the Argentine ambassador to the OAS called for an emergency meeting in order to discuss how to implement the October 23 resolutions and synchronize hemispheric efforts.[27] When the member countries met the following week, they unanimously approved the Argentine proposal to coordinate inter-American military actions in the quarantine by improving direct communications among all participants.[28] Far from its previous independent foreign policy, Argentina's policy during the missile crisis emphasized cooperation and its new ambitions of hemispheric leadership.

After the crisis, Argentina's civilian leaders moved quickly to consolidate their new policy. At the end of November, Minister of Defense José Manuel Astigueta met with the deputy chief of mission of the US embassy, Henry A. Hoyt, to discuss Cuba. Astigueta told Hoyt, "The recent Argentine attitude with respect to the Cuban issue represented a distinct and important change in Argentina's traditional posture." The minister argued that the armed forces were responsible for this shift in national policy. "The armed forces and the military of Argentina had become convinced that an open stand in favor of the West, rather than a fence-straddling or neutral position, was the proper posture for

Argentina to assume," he explained.[29] Astigueta's colleague, Foreign Minister Carlos Muñiz, also worked to solidify Argentina's newfound partnership with the United States and its new leadership role in hemispheric affairs. In January 1963, Muñiz visited Washington, where he met with President Kennedy and Secretary of State Dean Rusk and gave a speech to the OAS. Kennedy thanked Muñiz for Argentina's prompt participation in the quarantine, explaining that it had been particularly helpful because it "encouraged other Latin American countries to come in and thus gave convincing proof that the nations of the Western Hemisphere were united in preventing communist infiltration and aggression."[30] Argentina's response to the crisis promised to establish it as a leader in the region, and helped reinforce the message that the quarantine was a multilateral hemispheric operation, not a unilateral US act of war.

Argentina's military leaders took their own steps to formalize the new partnership with the United States. On November 20, Argentine secretary of war Gen. Benjamin Rattenbach handed US ambassador Robert McClintock a formal proposal, approved by Foreign Minister Muñiz, for military cooperation and training. The proposal explained that Argentina's economic challenges were limiting its military's modernization, and that the missile crisis had "hastened in the Argentine Army the necessity of bringing it into line with the requirements of modern organization and training." During the crisis, the army had cooperated with the US military mission in Argentina to organize an experimental 3,000-man brigade to be sent to the Caribbean if necessary. Now, the Argentine military proposed that the brigade be sent instead to the United States for training. "This training of Argentine troops outside country will contribute much in overcoming, among graduates, old resistance to inter-American military cooperation," the proposal argued. Rattenbach told McClintock that an additional goal was to "bring the Argentine Army to a higher standard of professionalism in order to channel attention and energies of the Officer Corps away from politics."[31] Instead of attacking each other or interfering with their government's civilian leadership, Argentina's armed forces should be equipped to focus on hemispheric defense, Rattenbach argued. He made a compelling case that military cooperation with the United States could benefit Argentina's domestic political situation and its international relations.

Ambassador McClintock was convinced and worked to gain US support for Argentina's new policy. In his message to Washington about the Argentine proposal, he wrote, "Our long experience with the proud Argentine Army and its reluctance even to contemplate hemispheric cooperation shows what a decisive turn in attitude of mind is revealed in General Rattenbach's paper." The ambassador believed that a change could benefit not just Argentina but the

United States as well. "We have a unique opportunity not only to consolidate new lines of cooperation with the Argentine Army but [also] to accomplish the strategic and policy objectives which form our basic military guidance to CINCARIB [Commander in Chief, Caribbean] and his sub-ordinate commanders."[32] Cooperation with Argentina would be good for relations with their influential military and could help the United States achieve its objectives in other parts of the region, especially the Caribbean. Ambassador McClintock recommended that Washington agree to train Argentina's elite brigade and establish direct contact among army commanders in both countries.

Financial and logistic limitations prevented Argentina's entire brigade from getting trained in the United States, but some elements of the proposed co-operation did go into effect. The chief of the US Army mission in Argentina and Ambassador McClintock identified Juan Carlos Onganía, the Argentine army commander in chief, as the most influential man in the army and recommended inviting him and a few of his officers to the United States for training.[33] Secretary of State Dean Rusk approved the idea of inviting Onganía, as long as his visit came after the visit of Foreign Minister Muñiz. It was important for Washington to demonstrate support for civilian rule in Argentina by not appearing to favor connections with its military leaders, Rusk argued.[34] The invitation eventually came, and over the following years, Onganía and other Argentine military leaders would grow ever closer with their counterparts in the Pentagon and civilians in Washington.[35]

Kennedy was quite vocal about his gratitude for the role that Argentina's armed forces played in the missile crisis. In March 1963, a group of staff and students from the Argentine War College visited the United States and received a warm welcome from the president. In a speech in the White House Rose Garden, Kennedy told the visitors:

> We are very grateful to you for your support during the difficulties which we had in October in the Caribbean with Cuba, the fact that the Argentine immediately not only supported the effort in the OAS but also sent air and naval forces to assist in the quarantine was important. Not only because of the forces involved, but also because it indicated that symbolically that though the Argentine was far away and many thousands of miles and the communications were long, it indicated a sense of solidarity which was very valuable to us not only in this hemisphere but I think in maintaining our posture throughout the world. And this is particularly appreciated because several Argentine soldiers lost their lives as a result of the air crash which was tied to the activities of that operation. We've got a good deal of unfinished

business in this hemisphere, and I think that it's important that in the days to come as we attempt to protect this hemisphere from foreign subversion and foreign activities directed against the liberties of this hemisphere that the Argentine and the United States stay closely together.[36]

Kennedy expressed his government's appreciation for Argentina's diplomatic and military leadership, especially because it showed that even countries far from the epicenter of the crisis felt the need to eliminate both the immediate threat of the missiles and the longer-term threat of foreign subversion. In honoring the memory of the Argentine soldiers who had died during the missile crisis, Kennedy also acknowledged the sacrifices that members of Argentina's military had made for the sake of hemispheric security. And most crucially, he portrayed the crisis as a turning point in US relations with Argentina, the beginning of a partnership in which both countries would work together to defend the hemisphere.

To facilitate this partnership, the United States substantially increased financial support for Argentina's military in the years after the missile crisis. In January 1963, the United States and Argentina began negotiating a new military assistance agreement under the auspices of the US Military Assistance Program (MAP). In the initial proposal for funds sent to Ambassador McClintock in Argentina, the US Army proposed providing $16 million in 1964 and an additional $35 million over the following four years. The memorandum attached to the proposal recognized that the missile crisis had brought about a change in the Argentine military's appetite for cooperation and explained that "the current unanimous desire of all three Argentine Armed Forces for a U.S.-Argentine bilateral agreement presents an opportunity for the U.S. to influence positively the establishment and maintenance of political stability in Argentina as well as to enhance the effectiveness of the Argentine Armed Forces."[37] It took over a year to hammer out the details of the agreement, but on May 10, 1964, Argentina became the last country in the Americas to join the United States' Military Assistance Program. For US officials, the MAP agreement signaled that they had finally succeeded in integrating all the countries in the Americas—with the obvious exception of Cuba—into a united anti-communist front.[38] The final agreement cited the Rio Treaty as justification for military cooperation, in addition to the resolutions passed at the emergency OAS meeting in October 1962 about hemispheric security measures.[39]

In addition to initiating closer military ties with the United States, Argentina's stance in the missile crisis also garnered the country significant economic support to prop up its struggling civilian government. Jacobo Timerman's magazine, *Primera Plana*, noted widespread public speculation about the possible economic benefits of participation in the quarantine. In an article in mid-November titled "Argentina Abandons Its Neutral Tradition," the author quoted a man reading newspapers on the Avenida de Mayo who argued, "If nuclear war had broken out, we would all be at the dance, with or without [President] Guido's declaration. If there is no war, our ships in the Caribbean may mean more financial support from the United States before we all go down the drain." The man, a self-described realist, made the convincing point that a nuclear war would have had no winners, but being on the winning side in a negotiated resolution could benefit Argentina. And sure enough, a few days after the Argentine destroyers set sail, the International Monetary Fund (IMF) reportedly announced in Buenos Aires to delegates of the Industrial Union that the fund was considering adopting a more flexible policy toward the country.[40] The IMF's harsh austerity measures, imposed under prior president Arturo Frondizi's economic liberalization program, remained extremely unpopular and many Argentines were desperately hoping that their military's enthusiastic participation in the missile crisis might buy them some relief.

Discussion of financial matters dominated Foreign Minister Muñiz's meetings during his visit to Washington in January 1963. The foreign minister told President Kennedy that Argentina was in a "period of deep crisis" and remarked that it was "nothing short of a miracle that the working class had remained calm in the face of increasing adversity." "The masses still believe in democracy but there is a limit to their patience," he warned. Muñiz claimed that President Guido and his team of economic ministers were desperately trying to resist public and military pressure to abandon their free enterprise economy in favor of a directed one. Guido was also worried that economic turmoil could endanger the elections that had been scheduled for later that year. Muñiz confided in a later meeting with Ambassador McClintock that the military chiefs, including Onganía, had threatened that President Guido's team of liberal economic ministers had until the end of January to solve the immediate economic emergency or they would install a new team of ministers who would impose a directed economy. The foreign minister's efforts to secure aid bore fruit; on March 28, the State Department announced that Argentina would receive an additional $75 million in loans and $92 million in debt refinancing.[41] It was enough to hold off the public and the military, at least in the short term.

Argentina's civilian government survived the missile crisis and weathered the storms of public protests and internal conflict that the crisis had generated, but it could not withstand the greater threat posed by its own armed forces. The attacks on US businesses and property during the crisis and the outraged words used in the pamphlets littering the streets of Buenos Aires illustrated a rising tide of economic nationalism that the next president, Arturo Illia, rode into office in July 1963. Almost exactly a year after the missile crisis, on November 16, 1963, Illia caved to public pressure and honored his campaign promise to cancel private contracts held by transnational oil companies. US officials, infuriated and worried that Argentina's economic nationalism might spread, responded by cutting assistance and foreign aid to Argentina's civilian government. One of those US officials who felt most betrayed by the cancellation of oil contracts, Ambassador McClintock, still pressed for a military assistance agreement, however. He wrote to Washington that the "most effective single step would be to quietly negotiate a MAP agreement without publicity." Such an agreement would "show General Onganía that we had faith in him."[42]

Onganía, the golden boy of the United States, would go on to consolidate his control over Argentina's government. In a speech at West Point in August 1964, Onganía warned that Argentina's military owed obedience only to the country's constitution and laws, not to the authorities who happened to be in power. The military, he argued, had the right to replace an abusive or despotic government.[43] Then, in June 1966, Argentina's armed forces ousted President Illia and installed Onganía as the head of a military junta. The coup ushered in an era of increasingly violent, US-backed military dictatorships that would dominate Argentine politics for the next two decades.

## Irreconcilable Differences

In Brazil, President João Goulart's actions during the missile crisis drove a permanent wedge between his administration and Washington. Brazilian officials' statements defending Cuba's national sovereignty and Goulart's failure to follow the US plan for the secret diplomatic mission to Havana led US officials to question their support for Goulart's government.

Brazil's response to the missile crisis was the topic of much talk and speculation in Washington. Argentina's ambassador reported that State Department officials were "perplexed" by Brazil's stance. "Even though in the recent crisis it was possible to obtain their support, with certain limitations, in the OAS, the declarations of senior government officials and even the attitude of the delegation in the United Nations constitute contradictions that are inexplicable," he noted.[44] The Brazilian ambassador to the United States, Roberto Campos, observed that while some members of the public and the Kennedy administration appreciated Brazil's efforts in the OAS and the United Nations (UN) to find a peaceful resolution to the crisis, other sectors of the press and some Latin American diplomats were more critical. There were murmurs that the Brazilians did not understand the difference between homegrown communism and communist infiltration at the service of Soviet foreign policy, that Brazil was too distant from Cuba to appreciate the ways that a nuclear-armed Castro would upset the balance of power in the hemisphere, and that Brazilians did not realize that Castro was too entangled with the communists to allow for the prospect of peaceful coexistence as long as he remained in power.[45]

Ambassador Campos recommended that his country join the Inter-American Quarantine to smooth over Brazil's relations with the United States and the rest of the hemisphere. At the end of October, he reported receiving information that the chief of Brazil's delegation to the Inter-American Defense Board and the military aides of Brazil's embassy in Washington were suggesting to Brazil's joint chiefs of staff and the military chiefs of some of the larger states that the Brazilian government offer elements of their armed forces for participation in the quarantine. Campos said that although he had not received any pressure or formal request from the US State Department for participation, he had "sensed the desire of responsible elements that the Brazilian government do so and a certain disappointment for not having done so until now." It would be ideal for an offer of participation to come as soon as possible, he said, to get ahead of diplomatic and public pressure and to avoid the appearance of caving to those pressures. The ambassador also argued that a gesture of cooperation would help counterbalance criticism of Brazil's posture in the US Congress, where implementation of the new Hickenlooper amendment to the Foreign Assistance Act was being debated. He also pointed out that the majority of other Latin American countries had offered to assist with or participate in the quarantine, and that Brazil had, after all, voted in the OAS to approve the quarantine. Furthermore, Campos observed, even leaders of the Brazilian left, such as Governor Leonel Brizola, had made declarations indicating that the missile crisis had given them a new understanding of the Cuban problem. If radical Brazilian leftists were criticizing Cuba, how could Goulart justify to the US public and government his continued refusal to participate in the quarantine? Finally, Ambassador Campos argued, any Brazilian offer at this point, now that Khrushchev had already agreed to remove the missiles, would be "a limited gesture of solidarity" and probably would not actually require implementation.[46] The ambassador built a compelling case for Brazil to join the Inter-American Quarantine Force, but his advice went unheeded, and Brazil remained outside the military coalition.

Ambassador Campos was right: US officials were indeed very displeased with Brazil's stance. In a three-hour-long meeting in early November with Brazil's prime minister and foreign minister, Hermes Lima, US ambassador Lincoln Gordon delivered what he considered an "extensive . . . polite but firm" lecture about the many deficiencies in Brazil's response to the crisis. Gordon chastised Lima for the confusion in the Brazilian press about the country's OAS vote and questioned whether the Brazilian representative had violated his instructions; Gordon also noted the "petulant" tone of Goulart's letter to Kennedy on October 25 and some of Lima's own statements to protesting workers and students that had implied support for Castro's government. Regarding Gen. Albino Silva's mission to Havana to negotiate with Castro, Ambassador Gordon worried that the publicity surrounding what had been designed to be a secret visit could "add to Castro's prestige and perhaps fortify his intransigence." Furthermore, Gordon pointed out, the Brazilian government had been one of the most vocal proponents of the idea of UN inspections but had failed to publicly criticize Castro's refusal to accept them. Hermes Lima sat quietly, patient and uncomfortable, as he listened to the litany of his government's errors. Gordon left the meeting thoroughly unimpressed with Lima, describing him as "not overly intelligent." In Gordon's mind, Lima was an overly romantic, "old fashioned academic" socialist who was ignorant of the realities of the Cold War and the nature of Castro's regime.[47] Gordon's conclusions echoed much of the criticism that Roberto Campos had noticed in the US press and among Latin American ambassadors: The Brazilians were unable or unwilling to recognize the true threat that Castro posed to hemispheric security.

Higher-ups in the State Department shared Gordon's concerns about Brazil's leadership. In mid-November, Assistant Secretary of State Edwin Martin, with Dean Rusk's approval, instructed Gordon to press President Goulart and his advisers to change what observers in Washington perceived as a "trend on the part of the Government of Brazil away from hemispheric solidarity internationally and liberal representative democracy internally." The State Department viewed these issues as even more worrisome than Brazil's financial plight and wanted Gordon to warn Goulart that "such a trend would limit our ability to help Brazil and Brazil's ability to help herself." Martin denounced the increasing "extreme leftist" influence on Goulart and specifically pointed to Brazil's response to the missile crisis as evidence of excessive leftist influence. "The Government of Brazil's support for the hemispheric and US position on the Cuban issue has been lukewarm and equivocal. It has offered no, repeat *no*, military or even moral support to the quarantine which its representatives approved," Martin complained. Like Gordon, he was particularly incensed by Hermes Lima's behavior. "Prime Minister [Lima] found it desirable and appropriate, apparently for domestic political reasons, to address personally and reassure a few hundred noisy pro-Castroites—this at a time when all governments in the Western Hemisphere were confronting the critical danger of the Communist military buildup in Cuba." Martin and Rusk were unsure whom Gordon should approach with his "arguments designed to modify the position of the Brazilian government in our favor," and they left the decision to the ambassador's discretion.[48]

Ambassador Gordon agreed that President Goulart's political stances, especially during the missile crisis, were causing significant damage to Brazil's relations with Washington. He also agreed that the Brazilian government's political orientation was an even greater concern than its financial struggles. In response to Martin's instructions to pressure Goulart, Gordon predicted, "We may be dangerously close to irreparable political degeneration." He reported that he and friendly allies among the northeastern governors in Brazil "have noted signs, partly in reaction to our success on Cuban missiles, by communist and allied forces to commit Brazil to a course fundamentally hostile to us."[49] According to the US ambassador, President Goulart himself was not opposed to the United States but was allied with and dependent upon internal groups who were.

João Goulart did not respond well to US pressure tactics. In a meeting with Ambassador Gordon on November 16, the president issued a series of warnings that Gordon believed came close to political blackmail. President Goulart reportedly threatened that if Washington did not help Brazil "on its own terms," he would denounce the United States, the Alliance for Progress, and the IMF. Furthermore, he would launch a "program of socialization" and would encourage the rest of Latin America to join. According to Gordon, Goulart denied having plans to seek massive Soviet help in his hemispheric program of socialization but could "almost be paraphrased" as threatening that "the alternative to support for the Government of Brazil on his terms was a second Yugoslavia at best and a second Cuba at worst."[50] Instead of working to repair his relationship with the United States after the missile crisis, Goulart had apparently decided to resort to threats.

US officials did not appreciate Goulart's thinly concealed attempts at blackmail and decided it was time for more drastic action. The Brazilian affairs specialists in the State Department prepared a secret set of recommendations at the end of November that Assistant Secretary Martin approved. The memorandum accompanying the recommendations referred repeatedly to Goulart's dissatisfactory actions during the missile crisis and compared them to those of other sectors of the Brazilian population. "We have had various positive gestures of stronger support for the U.S. from the Brazilian military than from the Brazilian government during the recent Cuban crisis" the authors observed. The military and various state governors appeared to be much more inclined to cooperate with the United States than with Goulart, an opportunity and an internal division that US officials could exploit. "The chief problem appears to be Goulart himself," the memorandum argued. It described the president as inadequate and inconsistent, "distrusted, weak, and unrespected [*sic*]." The State Department's suggested guidelines for a course of action included making it clear to the Brazilians in all official contacts "that the US opposes the recent Brazilian policy line on (a) the role of the OAS in relation to Cuba and (b) on Cuba itself." US officials should also refuse to succumb to Brazilian blackmail and threats about closer ties with the communist bloc. If those warnings failed, the State Department recommended promoting "the mobilization of a strong, widespread resistance within Brazil" that would "force the Goulart administration either along lines conducive to more harmonious Brazil-US relations *or out of power*." Either Goulart would start cooperating with the United States, or US officials would actively work to strengthen his domestic enemies. "Our influence can contribute but cannot be decisive . . . the foregoing alternative results [of Goulart's removal] cannot be brought about principally by US actions but must be generated within Brazil by the Brazilians,"[51] the recommendations cautioned. The preference was to work with Goulart to change his stance, but the State Department was also open to collaborating with the president's opponents if he proved unwilling to adopt policies more friendly to US interests.

President Kennedy agreed that firm measures were needed to redirect Goulart's political drift. In early December, Kennedy discussed the State Department's policy paper with the rest of his National Security Council. He accepted their recommendations that the best course of action was "to seek to change the political and economic orientation of Brazilian president Goulart and his government."[52] The president immediately dispatched his pugnacious younger brother, Attorney General Robert Kennedy, on a special mission to Brazil to press Goulart to accept political and economic policies more in line with US interests. During their three-hour meeting, Kennedy confronted Goulart about his tolerant attitude toward communists and insisted that the Brazilian president demonstrate a more cooperative attitude on international issues and the Alliance for Progress. Goulart left the meeting angry with US "presumptuousness," and Robert Kennedy concluded that Goulart was an irresponsible leader who could not be trusted.[53] The emergency mission backfired; instead of bringing Goulart more in line with US policy, it cemented hostilities between Brazilian and US authorities.

Thereafter, US officials aggressively pushed to change the political orientation of Goulart and his government while also working along a parallel path to strengthen his domestic opponents. Ambassador Gordon recommended in early 1963 that the United States provide economic aid to Brazil "on a 'short-leash' basis permitting periodic review and making possible the withdrawal of support on either economic or political grounds."[54] Through the Alliance for Progress, Washington tried first to pressure Goulart to align with US positions, and when relations failed to improve, instead channeled funding to and cultivated connections with the Brazilian military and opposition. US officials, led by Ambassador Gordon, worked with anti-communist and anti-Goulart state governors like Carlos Lacerda in an "islands of administrative sanity" approach to funnel assistance to state governments friendly to the United States and away from the federal government.[55] The US Information Agency (USIA) and State Department contributed tens of millions of dollars to anti-communist propaganda campaigns in Brazil; in 1963 alone, the USIA distributed more than 1,700 films to the Brazilian military, reaching an audience of around 180,000 officers and soldiers.[56]

Col. Vernon Walters, whom Gordon had summoned to Brazil to be the US connection to the Brazilian military during the missile crisis, took the lead on cultivating relations with the armed forces. Walters had fought alongside members of Brazil's military in Italy during World War II and became particularly close to one individual, Humberto de Alencar Castelo Branco. Walters stayed on in Brazil as the US military attaché after the missile crisis. He listened to his old friends in the Brazilian military "pour out their worry at seeing their country drifting toward what so many called 'another Cuba.'"[57] Walters's confidants worried that Goulart was seeding the military with communists and leftist extremists and would refuse to give up power, as Fidel Castro had done in Cuba. Walters followed his instructions and kept Ambassador Gordon and other US officials informed on developments within Brazil's military. By the end of 1963, Ambassador Gordon was urging Washington to consider providing logistic and military assistance for a possible coup, a contingency plan that eventually became known as Operation Brother Sam and that involved providing light weapons to the Brazilian military and deploying a US fleet off the Brazilian coast.[58] In March 1964, conservative military officers led by General Castelo Branco overthrew Goulart in a largely bloodless coup. Brazil cut relations with Cuba that May.

The Brazilian government's reaction to the Cuban Missile Crisis had convinced US officials that Goulart and his closest advisers were clueless and unreliable at best and directly opposed to the United States at worst. Goulart's response to the crisis was certainly not the only reason for his declining relations with the United States, but it confirmed US officials' worst suspicions about him and helped solidify their determination to reform or remove him. When Goulart proved unresponsive to US pressure, Kennedy,

Gordon, Walters, and other US officials took advantage of the deep divisions in Brazil's political landscape and threw their support behind Goulart's civilian and military opposition. The United States did not overthrow Goulart or orchestrate the coup against him, but it did work in numerous ways to aid and encourage those who did. As Vernon Walters later put it, "A regime basically unfriendly to the United States had been replaced by another one much more friendly."[59] The 1964 coup ushered in two decades of military rule in Brazil and marked the beginning of a wave of similar right-wing military coups and dictatorships across Latin America.

## Conclusion

The Cuban Missile Crisis caused significant changes in relations between Washington and four of Latin America's most influential nations: Mexico, Bolivia, Argentina, and Brazil. Mexico and Bolivia's response to the crisis smoothed over rough patches in their relations with the United States. Mexican leaders' demonstration of solidarity by approving the quarantine in the OAS showed that Mexico could be counted upon in times of crisis. US diplomats and presidents stopped pressuring Mexico to break relations with Cuba and started respecting Mexico's sovereign right to determine its own foreign policy. Bolivian leaders used the missile crisis as an opportunity to rejoin the OAS and show solidarity with hemispheric security efforts. Their decision healed the rift with the United States caused by tin dumping and marked the end of Bolivian efforts to court assistance from the Soviet Union. In Argentina, civilian and military leaders' quick and enthusiastic support of US policy and participation in the Inter-American Quarantine helped strengthen ties with the United States. The missile crisis paved the way for a new alliance between US and Argentine officials—especially among the two countries' armed forces. Brazilian president João Goulart's equivocal stance during the crisis, meanwhile, caused numerous US observers to doubt his reliability and his loyalties. Less than a month after the end of the missile crisis, US officials concluded that Goulart had to change his political orientation or be removed from power.

Decisions that civilian and military leaders in Argentina and Brazil made during the Cuban Missile Crisis regarding solidarity and alignment with the United States intensified preexisting divisions within these countries. In both countries, military leaders solidified their institutional ties with the United States, while civilians saw their own ties dissolve. In the years following the missile crisis, military officials took advantage of their closer connections with the United States to seize power in both South American nations. These coups helped bring about one of the most oppressive and violent eras of the hemispheric Cold War.

# CHAPTER 12
# FALLOUT

The Cuban Missile Crisis had perhaps its greatest fallout in its effects on international leftist solidarity and Cuba's relations with the Soviet Union. Some Latin Americans who had previously celebrated Fidel Castro's nationalism now condemned and even mocked him for entrusting his country's security and sovereignty to the Soviets. Nikita Khrushchev's decision to abandon his Cuban ally also planted doubt among other leftists in Latin America who had hoped that the Soviets might lend them a hand in their own political ambitions. The sudden, unilateral Soviet retreat damaged the Soviet Union's standing in the Americas and caused a significant rift between Cuba and the Soviet Union.

## Divisions on the Left

The Cuban Missile Crisis played into and exacerbated divisions among Latin America's fractious left wing. Some of Castro's most vocal defenders expressed dismay and disillusionment after the crisis. One of the most prominent was Brazilian Leonel Brizola, governor of the state of Rio Grande do Sul and brother-in-law to President João Goulart. Brizola had given a long speech at the beginning of the missile crisis denouncing Brazil's representative to the Organization of American States (OAS) for not voting with Cuba. But on October 30, Brizola issued a statement that Khrushchev's admission that he had indeed placed nuclear missiles in Cuba showed that the Soviet Union was taking advantage of the Cuban people's fight for liberation to make its own gains in the Cold War. He also criticized Castro's judgment for allowing his country to be used in such a manner. "This fact—the existence of Russian bases in Cuba—now surprisingly confirmed, is profoundly saddening for all of us, Brazilians and Latin Americans. The Cuban Revolution and its leaders have seriously compromised themselves by permitting the installation of Russian military bases on their own national territory."[1]

Brizola was outraged that Castro had sold out the Cuban Revolution and betrayed not only his own countrymen but also those from other parts of the Americas who had aided them. "When we supported the Cuban people in their fight for freedom from plunder and social injustice, intolerance, oppression, and domination by economic groups and by the government of the powerful United States, we never accepted and will never accept that Cuba become transformed into a satellite of the Soviet Union," he declared. Brizola demanded that there should be no foreign militaries, whether from the Soviet Union or the United States, in Cuban territory. His criticism manifested the profound disappointment that Latin American nationalists felt in seeing hard proof that their hero had relinquished control over his country's security to an imperialist power. Before the missile crisis, Castro had been seen as the chief champion of Cuban sovereignty; now, Latin Americans who wanted to continue defending Cuban sovereignty faced the difficult question of whether supporting Castro was the best strategy.

Brizola's denunciation was a major blow. A charismatic populist and influential career politician, he had close personal and political ties to the former president and dictator Getúlio Vargas and to the current president João Goulart; Brizola had helped both presidents consolidate their positions.[2] The *New York Times* correspondent in Brazil considered Brizola "the leader of the radical nationalist Left."[3] Just weeks before the missile crisis, Brizola had been elected to Brazil's Chamber of Deputies in the National Congress from the new state of Guanabara (home to Rio de Janeiro) with the most votes ever received by any candidate, and in April 1963 he was elected deputy majority leader in the National Congress.[4] Brizola's declarations made headlines in newspapers across the hemisphere; Managua's *La Prensa* reported that the Brazilian politician had denounced Soviet colonialism, while the *New York Times* claimed that Brizola's statement "has had a powerful effect on the Brazilian Left."[5]

Brazil's ambassador in Havana, Luís Bastián Pinto, reported that Brizola's criticism had caught the attention of the Cubans as well. In early November 1962, the ambassador claimed that a reliable source who was observing Castro's negotiations with the Soviet envoy Anastas Mikoyan told him that "the declarations of Governor Brizola profoundly impressed the Cuban leaders and Fidel Castro." According to the ambassador, Castro was using Brizola's criticism "to explain to Mikoyan the necessity of the Cuban government maintaining a minimum of its own demands as a signal of its independence in relation to the Soviet Union."[6] Ambassador Bastián Pinto speculated that the reaction of Brizola and other independent Latin American leaders had hardened Castro's position in insisting on his Five Points of Dignity declaration as a basis for negotiations. The ambassador argued that, whereas the Soviets were more concerned with the politics of peace, in Latin America, pacifist movements were practically nonexistent, and public opinion was focused on issues of national sovereignty and independence.

Brizola's denunciation was indicative of a wider pattern; leftists who were not members of Soviet-line communist parties were dismayed by both the confirmation of Soviet missiles in Cuba and by Khrushchev's unilateral decision to remove them. In the first issue of its magazine *Izquierda Nacional*, Argentina's Socialist Party of the National Left (Partido Socialista de Izquierda Nacional) published an article condemning Khrushchev's treatment of Cuba. "Similar to Stalin's times, the Kremlin is willing to sacrifice any revolution that does not affect its strategic area in exchange for any diplomatic advantage in its zones of influence," the authors wrote. "The Soviet Union has ended up negotiating over Castro's head . . . to Kennedy's old accusations that Cuba was a Russian satellite, at the time of the crisis Khrushchev has proceeded as if it were so." The article also described how the events were being perceived in Argentina: "The grandiose cynicism of these acts has left the working class outraged and the sepoy left parties mute."[7] Argentina's Trotskyists also denounced the Soviets for betraying Cuba. They issued a manifesto that argued that the Kremlin "should be criticized for having maneuvered without having previously agreed with Fidel Castro, for having accepted the unilateral sending of UN [United Nations] 'inspectors' to Cuba without the consent of the Cuban government." The Argentine Trotskyists portrayed Khrushchev as an unreliable and gullible ally, who should have consulted with the Cubans instead of trusting Kennedy's promises not to try another invasion. "In this way, the Soviet bureaucracy, always pursuing the chimera of a 'global compromise' with Washington, has lulled the vigilance of the world masses at the precise moment when the danger weighing on Cuba is greater than ever."[8] Uruguay's leading leftist newspaper, *Marcha*, published a front-page editorial titled "Neither Yankee nor Soviet Bases" that summed up the main lessons from the missile crisis: "Do not trust others. Trust only in ourselves. Do not tie ourselves to the interests of others . . . the hand that is extended to give also imprisons." It is likely that the clever author of the piece intentionally echoed Kennedy's choice of words, as the US president had only days before referred to Cuba as an "imprisoned island" in his broadcast announcing the presence of Soviet missiles. The editorial condemned Castro for "trusting with childish candor in the generosity of a new ally" and for linking Cuba's destiny to that of another, stronger country. "Behind the back of the weak one, without his agreement, without even consulting him, the strong one decides, when he believes it necessary or convenient, what should be done."[9] The common theme in all these condemnations was that Soviet leaders were not reliable and would readily abandon and ignore their allies. Critiquing the Soviet Union was not new among the noncommunist left in Latin America, but the implied criticism of Castro—that he had been a fool to trust the Soviets—was rarer and thus more shocking.

US officials avoided boastful public statements that might upset the tenuous peace, but their classified reports gleefully celebrated the damage that the missile crisis had done to Castro's and Khrushchev's standing among leftists. In Guadalajara, Mexico, the US consul described a failed effort among left-wing students to organize a demonstration against the United States at the state university on the morning of October 30. Some 100 students gathered around a microphone that was set up in front of the law school between classes, but no one spoke. According to the consul, "One person present stated that even the communists were embarrassed for words because they could not discuss Cuba without criticizing the Soviet 'betrayal' of Fidel Castro and could not praise Soviet action without disparaging Castro."[10] Khrushchev's abandonment of Castro had left supporters in Mexico speechless: The clear divisions between the two leaders put their followers in the unenviable position of having to choose sides or remain silent. The US ambassador in Ecuador reported that Cuba's public image had suffered its greatest blow since Castro had revealed his communist convictions. According to the ambassador, the crisis had its most profound effects on the left wing of the political spectrum. "It was the cherished conception of Cuba and the Soviet Union in the minds of the adherents of the extreme left that suffered most," he claimed. "Most of them were shocked at the Soviet retreat and apparent abandonment of Cuba to whatever fate awaited it, and the conclusion of just how much support a Communist Ecuador could expect in a pinch was not lost on the leaders." The ambassador also passed along the blunt assessment of a leader of Ecuador's Revolutionary Socialist Party, who reportedly said that the missile crisis had "set back the Communist revolution in Latin America a hundred years."[11]

Observers in the CIA and US Information Agency (USIA) were equally celebratory in their assessments of the effects of the missile crisis on leftist movements. In early November, the CIA reported, "Usually reliable sources in the Communist parties of Chile and Uruguay report continuing evidence of a decline in Soviet and Cuban prestige among Latin American Communists and other pro-Castro groups as a result of the events of the past week."[12] Six months later, intelligence officials provided an even more sweeping analysis of the impact of the crisis. "In virtually every country of Latin America, Castro's prestige, which had begun to decline well before the missile crisis, remains low. His image has been most seriously damaged in the eyes of non-Communists, particularly among labor groups and leftist intellectuals and politicians who had sympathized with his anti-U.S. position," the CIA claimed. Revolutionary leftists who had before sought alliances with Moscow-oriented communists and *fidelistas* were responding by shifting toward Indigenous, nationalist revolutions.[13] The USIA compiled an assessment of the impact of

"Castro-Communist" propaganda efforts in Latin America in spring 1963 in which they claimed, "As a result of the October crisis[,] the general population in the hemisphere saw Cuba as a victim of international communism and as a contradiction of the people's basic belief in nonintervention and self-determination." Even among leftists and communists, "Castroism appeared to have lost most of its general appeal for purposes of proselytizing." Leftist propaganda began emphasizing "local themes in lieu of earlier emphasis on Castro-Cuban themes."[14] The missile crisis had left Khrushchev looking untrustworthy and Castro looking weak: Latin American revolutionaries would have to rely on themselves and focus on their own national conditions.

Other leftists who had not yet given up on foreign alliances pivoted toward China after the missile crisis. The Communist Party of Brazil, an extreme leftist revolutionary offshoot of the main Brazilian communist party, began embracing Maoism in the years after the missile crisis. The party went from praising the Soviet Union in its February 1962 manifesto to denouncing Khrushchev's "antisocialist character" and celebrating the Chinese support for national liberation movements in a 1963 publication.[15] In Ecuador, the US ambassador reported that "among leftists generally the Cuban crisis led to a tendency to look more favorably toward Communist China."[16] A year later, the CIA echoed the ambassador's conclusions about the growing influence of the Chinese among Ecuadorean communists and noted similar patterns in Venezuela and Peru as well. According to the CIA, Venezuelan Communist Youth members reacted extremely negatively to Khrushchev's retreat, which aggravated preexisting differences within the Venezuelan Communist Party between leaders sympathetic to Moscow and those sympathetic to Beijing. In Peru, the CIA claimed, "although the central party leadership is reported to have strongly supported Khrushchev's actions, the dissidents are said to have echoed Chinese charges that he had shown weakness in the face of imperialism."[17]

Among the Maoist dissidents in the Peruvian Communist Party at the time of the missile crisis was a young philosophy professor named Abimael Guzmán Reynoso. Guzmán was the chair of the small Ayachucho regional communist committee before he founded a clandestine pro-China Red Faction (within the Peruvian Communist Party) that gained influence in the San Cristóbal de Huamanga University throughout the 1960s. He was arrested in 1969 and expelled from the Peruvian Communist Party; the next year, his Red Faction formed a new party called Sendero Luminoso, or Shining Path.[18] Guzmán's party, which would become the most violent and influential Maoist-inspired guerrilla group in Latin American history in the 1980s, thus originated in the years that Peruvian communists were choosing sides between the Soviets and Chinese. The Cuban Missile Crisis provided fodder for the Maoist

Peruvians, including Guzmán, who were criticizing Soviet pacifism and advocating for a violent path to power.

The Chinese alternative may have been especially appealing for Cubans; the population had already started adjusting to communism and, after all, the Cubans were the ones who had been most directly affected by Khrushchev's retreat. Even before the missile crisis, many of Cuba's revolutionary leaders—especially Che Guevara—had been more ideologically aligned with the Maoist embrace of armed struggle than with the gradualist approach of the Soviet Union.[19] The word on the streets of Havana after the crisis was that "Fidel's head is with Moscow but his heart is with Peking."[20] Argentine Trotskyist Adolfo Gilly, who was still in Cuba in the days following the crisis, noted that average Cubans were even more demonstrative than their country's leaders in showing their disdain for the Soviets. "With the withdrawal of the missiles, Khrushchev's prestige with the Cuban people fell sharply," he recounted. "Not a single portrait of Khrushchev is hung anywhere in Cuba except on the initiative of the apparatus, and the portraits of Mao Tse-tung that appeared everywhere were certainly not the apparatus's idea."[21] Swapping one foreign leader's portrait for another was a safe way for everyday Cubans to display their disgust with Khrushchev and their search for alterative allies.

While Cubans, Brazilians, Ecuadoreans, Venezuelans, Peruvians, and other Latin Americans were looking west across the Pacific Ocean at China, the Chinese communists were also eyeing Latin America with heightened interest. According to one scholar of the Sino-Soviet competition, "the Cuban Missile Crisis played a decisive role in turning the Sino-Soviet relationship in the developing world into an outright battle for influence."[22] In the years after the missile crisis, the Chinese started providing training and millions of dollars to a Peruvian revolutionary party called the Movement of the Revolutionary Left (Movimiento de la Izquierda Revolucionaria) that had split from Víctor Raúl Haya de la Torre's APRA (American Popular Revolutionary Alliance; Alianza Popular Revolucionaria Americana).[23] In 1963, the Chinese gave Ecuadorean communists thousands of dollars to publish anti-Soviet pamphlets, and a Chinese trade delegation offered Mexican communists financial aid if they agreed to support the Chinese Communist Party against the Soviets.[24] Also in 1963, the People's Republic of China bought more than $6 million in surplus Mexican agricultural goods and sponsored a trade fair in Mexico City. This was the first trade fair the Chinese had ever held in Latin America outside of Cuba, and it was much larger than the ones in Havana.[25] In the wake of the missile crisis, Chinese communists deployed economic weapons to gain advantages in a part of the world where the Soviet communists had disgraced themselves.

The Chinese paired this increased investment and involvement in Latin America after the missile crisis with an extensive propaganda campaign. The CIA composed a detailed report on the ramifications of the Sino-Soviet struggle in Latin America a year after the missile crisis and concluded that the Chinese made "an extreme effort" to use the crisis to injure their Soviet competitors' standing in Cuba and around the world. According to the CIA, "The Chinese accused Khrushchev of having committed both the error of 'adventurism' for putting the missiles into Cuba and the error of 'capitulationism' for taking them out." The Chinese especially tried to win Castro over to their side by promoting his Five Points of Dignity declaration and printing posters of Castro with the title "Cuban Sovereignty Is Inviolable!" The Chinese flooded Cuba with a "torrent of editorials, broadcasts, speeches, and editorial notes" in which they implied that Khrushchev was an appeaser and should not have been intimidated by the paper tiger of US imperialism.[26] Chinese officials in Cuba made similar arguments. On December 1, 1962, the Chinese ambassador to Cuba, Shen Jian, meet with Che Guevara and told the frustrated revolutionary that he could not trust Moscow. The Chinese diplomat observed that the Soviets tended to treat their Marxist-Leninist friends poorly while accommodating their imperialist enemies.[27] The resolution of the missile crisis was the perfect evidence for the argument that the Chinese had been making for years: that the Soviets were timid and unreliable allies for Third World revolutionaries.

In order to answer Chinese criticism and retain some of their lost influence in the wake of the missile crisis, the Soviet Union became more open to the Cuban policy of providing support to Latin American communist parties who opted for armed struggle. The pro-Soviet leader of the Ecuadorean communists reportedly traveled to Moscow in November 1962 and received instructions to adopt a more militant posture "to undercut the appeal of . . . the pro-Chinese forces in the party."[28] In 1963, the CIA claimed that the Soviets had doubled financial support and training for Venezuelan revolutionaries. CIA analysts commented that "the Soviets seem embarked on a course of vigorously competing with the Chinese for the affections of the Communist Party of Venezuela (Partido Comunista de Venezuela [PCV]) by aiding the violent PCV efforts more actively than ever before."[29] Soviet documents confirm the CIA's assessment that financing for the Venezuelan Communist Party doubled between 1962 and 1963, and it continued to increase yearly until peaking in 1965.[30] In December 1962, the Soviets also began a joint operation with Cuba and Czechoslovakia called Operation Manuel, in which the Soviets and Czechs helped Latin American combatants travel to and from Cuba via Prague for guerrilla training.[31] Increased support for revolution in Latin

Chinese poster proclaiming support for Castro with the caption: "Cuban Sovereignty Is Inviolable!" (Courtesy of the Propaganda Poster Art Centre. Used by permission.)

America was no minor change in policy for Moscow; it directly contradicted their previous approach of gradual political organizing and endangered their simultaneous efforts to pursue a limited détente with the United States. Supporting violent revolution in Latin American was thus a significant concession to the Cubans—who had been encouraging armed struggle in the region since 1959—and a desperate attempt to retain influence among disillusioned Latin American communists.

## Alienated Allies

Cuba's leaders certainly were disillusioned—to put it mildly—with the way their foremost ally had treated them. Khrushchev immediately sent his closest adviser and second-in-command, Anastas Mikoyan, to Cuba to repair relations. Mikoyan had already visited the island back in 1960, and the Soviets hoped that he would be able to use his significant diplomatic skills and previous rapport with Castro to mollify the Cuban leader. Mikoyan later recalled that "Khrushchev made me clean up his mess yet again!"[32]

The Soviet envoy did his best to start the negotiations with the Cubans on a positive note. Even before setting foot on Cuban soil, he issued a declaration of support for Castro's Five Points of Dignity demands.[33] Mikoyan and his small retinue, including his son Sergo, landed in Havana at twilight on

Cubans waiting to greet Soviet envoy Anastas Mikoyan at the Havana airport. (Photograph by Carlos Nuñez. Courtesy of Prensa Latina. Used by permission.)

the evening of November 2. Crowds of Cuban officials and members of the public gathered at the Havana airport to greet Mikoyan and his entourage. They brought bouquets of flowers and stood below signs declaring their adherence to Castro's Five Points declaration. Sergo noted the contrast from their previous visit. "Havana looked nothing like the city I remembered . . . Twin-barreled antiaircraft guns and artillery crews in olive-colored fatigues were found everywhere from public squares to rooftops . . . all that remained was an atmosphere of anxiety that, unwittingly, even conveyed itself to me."[34] Cuban leaders had gone to great lengths to keep the public's spirits high and maintain an appearance of unity and defiance, but foreign observers noticed the strain.

Mikoyan spent most of November 1962 in Cuba, a tense month of declarations, debates, and decisions. The stalwart diplomat remained even when his wife died of heart failure back in the Soviet Union. During the first of many meetings, Castro told Mikoyan that Khrushchev's concessions had produced a sense of "oppressiveness" in Cuba. "A feeling of deep disappointment, bitterness, and pain has appeared, as if we were deprived of not only the missiles, but of the very symbol of solidarity," he explained. According to Castro, the confusion caused by the sudden retreat could undermine Cubans' resolve and their faith in the revolution. "We were afraid that these decisions could provoke a breach in the people's unity, undermine the prestige of the revolution in the eyes of Latin American peoples, in the eyes of the whole world."[35] Castro kept talking about the moral and political implications of the crisis, suggesting that he was concerned with the symbolism of the missiles as much or more than with their strategic or military value.

In their second conversation, Castro gave Mikoyan a lesson in Cuban history to explain the egregious offense that Khrushchev had committed when he unilaterally made decisions about Cuba's fate. "It is important to take into account the special delicacy of our people which has been created as a result of several historical developments," Castro explained. "The Platt Amendment, imposed by the Americans upon Cuba, played a particular role in this regard. Using the Platt Amendment, the United States of America prohibited the Cuban government from deciding by itself questions of foreign policy." Khrushchev's behavior was so appalling, such a betrayal, because it resembled that of the US imperialists who had treated Cuba as a colony, instead of a sovereign, independent country. "During the current crisis there was also an impression that important issues, concerning all of us, were discussed and resolved in the absence of Cuban representatives, without consultations with the Cuban government,"[36] Castro continued. Khrushchev's sudden retreat, his lack of consultation, and his offer to allow inspections in Cuban territory made the Cubans look and feel like a colony yet again. "What do you think we are?" Castro asked Mikoyan at one point. "A zero on the left, a dirty rag."[37] In one of his reports back to the Soviet Union, Mikoyan noted that Castro's pride had been wounded; "Castro takes it hard when he reads the statements of reactionary agencies in which he is called a 'puppet of the USSR.'"[38] Castro's criticism of his Soviet ally echoed many of the accusations that had been printed in the US and Latin American press, that the resolution of the crisis suggested that Khrushchev was acting like Cuba's new imperial master.

Throughout the November meetings with Mikoyan, Castro and other Cuban leaders repeatedly emphasized the moral, psychological, and political damage wrought by the crisis. Che Guevara was especially aggrieved by the harm done to the prospects for revolution in Latin America, telling Mikoyan that the crisis had created an "extremely complicated situation." "Many communists who represent other Latin American parties, and also revolutionary divisions like the Front for People's Action in Chile [a left-wing coalition of parties led by Salvador Allende], are wavering. They are dismayed by the actions of the Soviet Union," he reported. Che described the damage done to leftist solidarity and cooperation. "A number of divisions have broken up. New groups are springing up, factions are springing up . . . we can now expect the decline of the revolutionary movement in Latin America, which in the recent period had been greatly strengthened." Che then summed up the injuries inflicted upon Cuba and the revolutionary movement by quoting Castro, who had absented himself from that particular meeting with Mikoyan. According to Che, Castro had concluded that "the USA wanted to destroy us physically, but the Soviet Union with Khrushchev's letter destroyed us legally."[39] In backing down, Khrushchev had validated the US violation of international law and allowed the United States to coerce another country into giving up its right to offer bases to an ally. Khrushchev's hasty concessions had done lasting damage to the international legal regime, one of the most important tools that the Latin American countries had built to protect their security and sovereignty.[40]

Mikoyan at times lost his composure as he listened to the barrage of criticism. In response to Guevara's accusations, Mikoyan reminded the famously idealistic revolutionary of the harsh geopolitical realities of the situation. Mikoyan admitted point-blank that the Soviets were not willing to sacrifice themselves or risk the fate of the world. "We have at our disposal global rockets. Using them would lead to nuclear war," he told Che. "What do you say to this? Shall we die heroically?" Mikoyan answered his own rhetorical question: "That is romance. . . . To die heroically, that's not enough. To live in shame is not permitted, but nor is it permitted to give to the enemy your own destruction." Soviet solidarity had its limits. Mikoyan was not impressed by Castro or Che's bravado or their dreams of martyrdom. He had read Castro's desperate letter to Khrushchev in which the Cuban leader had claimed that Cuba was ready to sacrifice itself for the cause of global socialism. Like Khrushchev, the Soviet Union's second-in-command was horrified by Castro's offer. "We do not want to die beautifully," he repeated. "Socialism must live." The Soviet Union had already invested a great deal militarily, economically, and politically in Cuba, and wanted to see the only communist government in the Americas survive. "We did everything so that Cuba would not be destroyed," Mikoyan insisted.[41]

By the end of his stay in Havana, Mikoyan decided that Cuba's leaders were unreliable allies and made another unilateral decision on behalf of the Soviet Union. Mikoyan told Castro in a four-hour meeting on November 22 that the Soviets were going to withdraw the Luna missiles—tactical weapons with nuclear warheads—that were still secretly in Cuba, in addition to the missiles and IL-28 bombers that had been part of the agreements with Washington. Kennedy did not know that the Soviets had also brought tactical nuclear weapons, and throughout November the Soviet leadership had not yet decided whether to leave the Luna missiles in Cuba. But after spending a month with the Cubans and hearing over and over about their determination to defend their revolution at all costs, Mikoyan began to have doubts about the wisdom of providing them with nuclear weapons. He had also watched in horror when, in mid-November, Castro issued orders to his soldiers to open fire on low-flying US reconnaissance planes in the middle of tense negotiations. Finally, on November 20, Castro risked revealing the presence of the tactical weapons by instructing his UN representative to try to use references to them to gain advantage in the negotiations.

Mikoyan had seen enough. He cabled the Soviet Party Presidium in Moscow and told them that he thought that he should inform Castro that the tactical nuclear weapons would be removed and not left on the island. The rest of the Soviet Presidium back in Moscow had already started considering Castro's position as "unreasonable [and] loud" and were more than ready to wrap up negotiations, concluding, "We have come to a turning point: Either [the Cubans] will cooperate or we will remove our people."[42] During his meeting with Castro on November 22, Mikoyan, to justify the removal of the tactical weapons, made up an excuse that the Soviets had a law prohibiting the transfer of any nuclear weapons—including tactical—to anyone.[43] "The Americans are not aware that the tactical nuclear weapons are here, and we are taking [them] out not because of the American demands, as you would think, but of our own will," he explained.[44] His negotiations concluded, Mikoyan departed on November 26, and one month later—Christmas Day—the Soviets sailed away from Cuba with the last of their nuclear weapons.[45]

As they had from the beginning, Cuban actions shaped the outcome of the crisis by influencing Soviet decisions. Mikoyan's last-minute change in policy and his determination to remove the final nuclear arms from Cuba was not based on US actions or pressure; as he made clear to Castro, Washington did not even know about the tactical missiles. It was not based on Soviet law; despite what he told Castro, such a law prohibiting the transfer of weapons did not exist. Mikoyan's decision was a response to Cuban actions. It was the Cuban leadership's intransigence and unpredictability that pushed the Soviet envoy to doubt the wisdom of entrusting unreliable allies with powerful weapons. In yet another way, then, Cuban actions shaped the Cuban Missile Crisis.

Castro had to accept his Soviet allies' decisions because Cuba was dependent upon the Soviet Union. He walked a tightrope in the months after the crisis, nursing his countrymen's wounded pride while protecting his relations with the Soviets. Throughout November, Castro made multiple impromptu late-night visits to the University of Havana, where he gathered groups of students to discuss the situation. The British ambassador to Cuba discounted rumors that Castro spent these sessions ranting against the Soviets in general and Mikoyan in particular. "The most reliable evidence I have," the ambassador noted, "is that he has not hidden his disagreement with the Russians on their present or long-term policy, but that he specifically called for solidarity with [the] USSR as an essential to [the] survival of the revolution."[46] In requesting solidarity with the Soviet Union, Castro was perhaps trying to portray Cuba's relationship with the USSR as one of equality rather than dependence. According to another account of these meetings, Castro "refrained from slamming the door in Russia's face." He told the students, "We shall not break with the Russians."[47] After Cuban newspaper editor Carlos Franqui published in *Revolución* a series of articles that were critical of the Soviet Union, Castro made a call to the journalist. "Lay off the Soviets, ok?" he told Franqui. "Eleven articles is more than enough."[48] In Castro's last meeting with Anastas Mikoyan at the end of November 1962, when the Soviet envoy asked what final message Castro wanted conveyed to Khrushchev, the Cuban leader replied: "Tell him we were sad, distressed, but firmly united with the Soviet Union."[49] Castro's words perfectly described the difficult situation in which he found himself at the end of the crisis: Khrushchev's actions had caused significant damage to relations between the two allies, but ultimately Castro still needed the Soviets.

To appease Castro and to heal the rift in the alliance caused by the missile crisis, the Soviets made additional economic concessions and diplomatic overtures. In February 1963, the Soviet Union and Cuba finally concluded lengthy negotiations for an updated trade agreement, which included a new long-term credit to Cuba. The Cubans, in return, agreed to greater oversight of their economy by Soviet "technicians." In the Soviet May Day slogans of 1963, for the first time, Cuba was included among the list of countries in the socialist bloc.[50] Khrushchev invited Castro to visit the Soviet Union, and the Cuban leader spent over a month there from late April until the end of May. During his stay, the Soviets pulled out all the stops: Castro enjoyed parades, parties, tours, and awards galore. According to the CIA, "Soviet propaganda attention to this visit far exceeded the welcome ever extended to any other foreign visitor."[51] Castro and Soviet leaders made effusive speeches. During a reception on the nuclear-powered icebreaker *Lenin*, Castro told the Soviet sailors assembled to honor him, "Here we deeply felt how great is the solidarity of the Soviet people with Cuba, how great is the friendship of the Soviet Union with Cuba."[52] In a farewell toast at a gala marking the end of the visit, Khrushchev reiterated his promises of protection. "Any attack on Cuba we will consider as an attack on the Soviet Union," he swore.[53] The missiles might be out, but Cuba still remained under the Soviet Union's nuclear umbrella. In private conversations, Khrushchev tried to convince Castro that the missile crisis had ended in victory. "We won, we are the winners," Khrushchev insisted. The Soviet leader also warned Castro not to trust the Chinese because they wanted to split the socialist camp. "Instead of concentrating our revolutionary efforts against the enemy, they opened fire against us," he complained. "Who benefitted from it? The revolutionary forces? No, it was the imperialist forces who benefitted [*sic*] from the disintegration and fragmentation of the revolutionary forces."[54] Apparently mollified, Castro returned to Cuba and gave a press conference about his trip in which he rewrote the history of the missile crisis. Castro referred to himself as the victor in the confrontation, swearing, "We won't budge an inch from the Socialist camp." He also described Khrushchev as "a daring politician, a great leader, and a formidable adversary of imperialism."[55] Cuba's rift with the Soviet Union appeared to have been mended.

But just because Cuba's leaders publicly forgave the Soviets did not mean that they forgot the betrayal. Che Guevara—hardly a fan of the communist old guard or the Soviet policy of peaceful coexistence before the missile crisis—took the outcome as confirmation that Latin American and other Third World revolutionaries had to chart their own path. In February 1963, Guevara summoned his longtime friend and confidant Ricardo Rojo to Havana. In the first of their many long conversations during Rojo's stay, the two men discussed the crisis. Guevara recounted the moments when he and Castro had first learned—from news reports, not Khrushchev himself—that the Soviet leader had decided to withdraw the missiles. "The Russians had decided a Cuban problem without consulting us," Guevara recalled bitterly. Rojo tried to get his friend to look at the situation from another perspective. Perhaps, by creating the artificial problem of the missile crisis, Khrushchev had actually succeeded in distracting Kennedy from the real issue: the survival of Cuba's revolutionary government. The Soviets had let US leaders feel victorious by removing the missiles, but in the long term they had guaranteed the security of Castro's regime. According to this logic, Rojo suggested, the Soviets had lost the battle for the missile bases but won the war for Cuba's survival.

But Che remained focused on the issue of sovereignty, not security. "The real question is," he insisted, "must Cuba give up its sovereignty to the Russians?" The Soviet Union should have respected Cuba's history of imperial exploitation and its long fight for independence, he argued. "If there is no understanding of national particularities within international socialism," Che confided to his friend, "we might as well give up."[56] Over the course of the next few years, the icon of revolutionary internationalism became increasingly disillusioned with the Soviet Union's failures to provide significant support for other armed liberation movements, adding to his determination to chart an independent course.

Guevara's disappointment with the Soviets remained foremost in his mind as he prepared to launch himself into new revolutionary struggles. In a February 1965 speech delivered in Algiers, he was extremely critical of the Soviet Union for failing to provide generous aid to liberation movements in Asia and Africa. Shortly after his controversial speech, Che returned to Cuba and accepted Castro's invitation to lead Cuba's revolutionary expedition to Zaire.[57] In his farewell letter to Castro, written on the eve of his departure in April 1965, Guevara wrote: "I have lived magnificent days, and I felt at your side the pride of belonging to our people in the luminous and sad days of the Caribbean crisis." Those fraught hours were some of Che's most treasured memories from his time in Cuba, but he recalled them with a mixture of joy and bitterness. He praised Castro's performance—"rarely has any statesman shone more brilliantly than you did in those days"—but had nothing to say anywhere in the letter about Khrushchev or the Soviets.[58] Perhaps he was showing restraint, anticipating correctly that Castro would make the letter public.

A few weeks earlier, Che had spoken more candidly about his feelings about the Soviets in a late-night farewell conversation with one of the veterans of the 26th of July Movement who had become a close friend, José Luis Llovio-Menéndez. Che, by then in hiding, summoned Llovio to a dusty, dimly lit, abandoned cabin at the end of a dirt road. Sometimes perched on a wooden stool, sharing mate from his thermos, sometimes pacing the small room, the restless revolutionary unburdened himself to his friend. Clearly struggling to reconcile gratitude with resentment, Che reflected that the Soviets had been good to Cuba: "They gave us weapons so we could defend ourselves, and that's what we've done." Not all the weapons were given freely, however, and not all of them were given permanently. "But we don't need their rockets!" he exclaimed. "Like cowards, they gave them to us only to take them back again the first time the Yanquis let out a yelp." He bemoaned the change in Soviet foreign policy since the missile crisis and the Soviet refusal to provide the same amount of military support to other revolutionaries as they had provided to the Cubans. According to Guevara, the Soviets had gone on the defensive and stopped helping other revolutionary movements. "But we won't back down!" Che declared, "We'll go on helping all the liberation movements."[59]

Che also continued to be consumed with the issue of Cuba's sovereignty, which Khrushchev had so callously overlooked in the resolution to the missile crisis. "Cuba can't be a mere pawn," he insisted to Llovio-Menéndez. "It won't yield to either side . . . Cuba will not be anybody's satellite." He worried especially about Cuba's continued dependence on the Soviets. "Soviet aid becomes more and more dangerous for Cuba," he fretted. "Whoever keeps you wants to rule you. . . . I no longer have confidence in the USSR."[60] As dawn approached,

Che bid a final farewell to his friend and swore him to silence, worried that his words of doubt might harm the revolution that he had worked so hard to build. After their conversation, Llovio-Menéndez looked back through his notes from more than five years of intermittent discussions and concluded that Che had gradually lost faith in the Soviets after the missile crisis, to the point where he became an obstacle in relations between Cuba and the Soviet Union. According to Llovio-Menéndez, this was why Che was leaving Cuba.

Three years later, in January 1968, Fidel Castro voiced his own lingering frustration with his Soviet allies to a much larger audience. By that point, Cuban-Soviet relations were once again on the decline, thanks in large part to ongoing differences over the question of support for global revolution and armed struggle. In 1967, one of the Soviet Union's top men in Cuba, old-line communist party leader Aníbal Escalante, had begun trying to reassert control over the party in Cuba and was promoting pro-Soviet views. Over the course of two days in January, Castro responded by calling the first plenary meeting of the Cuban Communist Party's Central Committee in order to oust Escalante and his supporters. Castro gave a secret, twelve-hour speech to the 100 members who had gathered to decide the direction of Cuban policy.[61] Much of the speech was devoted to recounting the missile crisis to show the dangers of relying on the Soviet Union. Castro called the Soviet draft of the agreement to install the missiles "one of the shoddiest things ever written"; he described the "preposterous lack of foresight" as the Soviets failed to conceal the missile sites; he condemned Khrushchev's "weakness" and "capitulation" for trying to hide the bases in the first place instead of insisting on the Cuban government's right to defend itself; he called Khrushchev's letter to Castro on October 28 in which he tried to justify his retreat "dreadful"; and he blasted Khrushchev's "lies" and his "ostrich-like, rights-abdicating defense policy."[62] Castro remained particularly incensed by Khrushchev's offer to allow inspections in Cuba, describing it as "that gross, insolent, arbitrary measure, contrary to all principles, of taking upon themselves the faculty of deciding matters under our jurisdiction."[63]

But Castro was, above all, a pragmatist. He then recounted how a new, tense phase unfolded in Cuban-Soviet relations in the wake of the missile crisis. "We had to dissemble, contain, hold back our indignation, our outrage and prevent any sustained deterioration in those relations from affecting our primary problem: fighting imperialism." According to Castro, he withheld all his criticism for the sake of Cuba's economic and military security, but he had lost confidence in the Soviet Union's leaders. Castro's faith was further shaken when, during his visit to the Soviet Union in 1963, Khrushchev accidentally let slip that Kennedy had secretly removed US missiles from Turkey and Italy as part of the agreement to end the crisis. "It reveals that in the middle of this whole affair was an agreement that must have been a great satisfaction to him over there, a compensation," Castro observed bitterly. Anyone in Castro's position would have been resentful upon learning that their ally had been making secret deals for their own gain. Cuba and the Soviet Union had not lost the crisis together; it turned out that Khrushchev had quietly benefited. "I am sincerely convinced that the Soviet Party bears great responsibility in what happened and acted in a totally disloyal manner in its relations with us," Castro continued. The damage done by the Soviet treachery extended beyond Cuba, according to Castro. "That episode was an evident defeat for the socialist community and for the revolutionary movement."[64] Khrushchev's decision to back down showed that the superpower would not risk its own security for the sake of global revolution, and his dealings behind Castro's back revealed that the Soviets would not treat their allies as equals or respect their sovereignty. Castro's speech perfectly captured the lasting scars that the crisis had left on Cuban-Soviet relations.

Decades after the missile crisis, Castro still harbored resentment about the way Khrushchev and Kennedy had resolved the crisis behind his back. In an interview with his "autobiographer" Ignacio Ramonet, Castro bitterly described Kennedy and Khrushchev's negotiations as a "love affair that emerged during those difficult days, hot love in the middle of a cold war."[65] The crisis had brought the two superpowers closer together on issues of geopolitical security while causing numerous fractures in the communist world. The strategic and economic alliance between Cuba and the Soviet Union had survived, but the psychological wounds never fully healed. Castro argued that Cubans had to be careful to never again hand over their sovereignty or security to the Soviets.

## Conclusion

The missile crisis caused significant damage to leftist solidarity efforts and alliances throughout the Americas and around the world. Cuba's revolutionary leaders, who had inspired so many national liberation movements across the hemisphere, came out of the crisis looking weak and dependent. Khrushchev, who had sworn to defend Cuba against all its aggressors, had broken his promises and deserted the island at its moment of greatest need. Many, though not all, Latin American leftist organizers drew the logical conclusion that they could not expect much support from either Cuba or the Soviet Union and instead had to look inward or to China. While the latter option had its appeal, the fact was that China had significantly fewer resources than the Soviet Union and had, relative to Cuba, no geographical advantage or shared cultural heritage. Latin America's would-be liberators were left on their own.

The bonds that Cuban and Soviet leaders had built before the crisis were stretched almost to the breaking point. Castro, Che, and the Cuban public felt betrayed and abandoned by their Soviet allies. Khrushchev, Mikoyan, and other members of the Soviet Presidium, meanwhile, were dismayed by the Cubans' bravado and recklessness. The two sides managed to come to a tense peace, but the idea that they were partners in leading the global communist revolution died in October 1962; it was one of the chief casualties of the crisis. A senior member of Cuba's Communist Party commented thirty years after the missile crisis, "History has yet to record whether Cuba has suffered more from U.S. imperialism or Soviet friendship."[66] The Cubans learned a hard lesson, that Soviet solidarity had its limits. They continued to work with and rely upon the Soviet Union, but they would never again entrust their fate so completely to another country.

# Epilogue

The Cuban Missile Crisis—and especially its fallout—brought a great deal of death and destruction to Latin America, but it also had one extremely positive consequence. The close brush with Armageddon prompted Latin American governments to work together to create the world's first nuclear weapons–free zone, established in 1967 through the Treaty of Tlatelolco.

During the crisis, on October 29, 1962, Brazil presented a draft resolution in the United Nations (UN) that Latin America be declared a nuclear weapons–free zone. It generated significant discussion and garnered press attention across the Americas, and the governments of Chile, Bolivia, and Ecuador signed on as cosponsors.[1] A reporter for the Televisora Nacional network in Panama City expressed enthusiastic support for Brazil's proposal, explaining, "The fear and anguish experienced by the Panamanian people during the past week, due to the world crisis and the threat of war, led us to appraise the initiative Brazil broached in the United Nations, as it is an issue of the utmost importance." The reporter insisted that supporting a nuclear-free zone in Latin America was not the same as declaring neutrality in the Cold War. The intent, rather, was "to make it known to the whole world that Panama is not a battlefield." Panama, like many countries in Latin America, was a "small, defenseless nation" that could not afford minimum security, much less advanced weaponry. The Panamanian broadcaster pointed out that if any part of Latin America were to be converted into a nuclear missile base, Panama would become "a first-class military objective in the event an international emergency arises."[2] For Panamanians, whose canal had been identified as a prime target during the missile crisis, and whose government could not afford to compete in a nuclear arms race, it was imperative to prevent nuclear proliferation in the region. The Cuban Missile Crisis showed people across the hemisphere how terrifying it was to be a potential battlefield in a nuclear war. For the Cubans, stronger weapons had promised greater security, but for the rest of Latin America the opposite was true.

But the Panamanian broadcaster and others would have to wait; Brazil's attempts to work through the UN to establish a nuclear weapons–free zone in the Americas proved unsuccessful. Cuban opposition played a significant role in scuttling Brazil's efforts. Cuban foreign minister Raúl Roa withheld support unless the Brazilians included Puerto Rico and the Panama Canal Zone in their proposal, and they required the elimination of foreign military bases in Latin America, which would include the US base at Guantánamo Bay.[3] These were amendments that the US government would reject, and the Cubans knew it. As Roa confessed in a secret telegram to his representative in the UN, "To be honest, it is not in our interests to support the Brazilian proposal."[4] US officials publicly endorsed creating a nuclear weapons–free zone in Latin America but avoided giving any impetus to the measures needed to create one.[5] Furthermore, US diplomats "were not inclined" to encourage their Latin American counterparts to pursue Brazil's proposal without Cuban participation.[6] One of the leading US arms control negotiators called the Cubans' demands "frivolous" and claimed they showed that the Cubans would not cooperate in nonproliferation efforts.[7]

Many Latin American governments also had their own concerns about Brazil's proposal. At a meeting of Latin American ambassadors to the UN, Argentina's representative wondered whether countries that agreed to join a nuclear weapons–free zone would tie their hands from developing defensive nuclear capacities in the future.[8] Argentina's government was deeply invested in its own independent nuclear energy program and protested that Brazil's proposal would infringe on its national sovereignty and technological advancement.[9] When Latin American ambassadors to the White House and the Organization of American States (OAS) met with Assistant Secretary of State Edwin Martin to discuss the missile crisis and Brazil's denuclearization proposal, they engaged in what Mexico's OAS representative described as "a marathon of senselessness and lack of dignity." The representative from the Dominican Republic insisted that his government would not agree to denuclearization "because Castro still has atomic bombs in Cuba and for other reasons." Brazil's ambassador to the United States tried to explain that the denuclearization proposal was not meant to reintegrate Castro into the OAS or to repair relations between Washington and Havana but was instead squarely focused on preventing nuclear proliferation in Latin America.[10] By mid-November, the Brazilians had concluded that they did not have enough support from the White House, Cuba, or fellow Latin American governments to see their denuclearization proposal succeed in the UN. They indefinitely postponed the vote.

Mexico's government stepped into the breach. Mexico was perhaps better positioned than Brazil to lead the inter-American community, having emerged unscathed from the missile crisis with newfound US support for its independent foreign policy. Unlike Brazilian president João Goulart, Mexican president Adolfo López Mateos had consistently fought for peace during the crisis and had avoided alienating the United States, Cuba, or any other country in the region. Mexico's ambassador to Brazil at the time of the missile crisis, Alfonso García Robles, had become familiar with Brazil's nonproliferation efforts during his stay in Rio.[11] García Robles and other Mexican officials took advantage of their country's hemispheric leadership role to push for nuclear nonproliferation while memories of the crisis were still fresh.

Over the course of the next four years, Mexican officials orchestrated a series of declarations and conferences. President López Mateos began by sending letters to the presidents of Brazil, Bolivia, Chile, and Ecuador in March 1963 to gauge their interest in jointly pursuing hemispheric nuclear nonproliferation.[12] A month later, those five countries signed a declaration announcing their plans to establish a nuclear weapons–free zone. López Mateos celebrated Mexico's unique position in the Cold War when he presented the declaration over radio and television. "In the current Cold War situation, in which the major power groups confront each other, minute by minute, from their respective positions of strength, it is up to our country to carry out an essentially moderating function." Mexico and the other nations of Latin America had an opportunity to push the rest of the world toward a more peaceful future, the president continued. "The pacifist vocation of the Mexican people also demand[s] that Mexico combine its efforts with those of other similarly willing States, to urge with their example the Great Powers not to stop for a single moment in the search for formulas that could lead to universal and complete disarmament."[13] In November 1963, shortly after the first anniversary of the missile crisis, the UN General Assembly approved a resolution that expressed full support for the Latin American denuclearization project. Mexico's representative, Alfonso García Robles, told the UN assembly that the effort to establish a nuclear weapons–free zone in Latin America was a "testimony that Latin America has now come of age and knows how to correctly perceive the authentic designs of its people . . . we know what we want and we know how to make it happen."[14] The denuclearization effort was a demonstration of Latin American sovereignty and maturity, its ability to define and establish security on its own terms.

With Mexico at the helm, the push for Latin American denuclearization had the necessary momentum and direction. Formal negotiations began in 1964, with Mexico's undersecretary of foreign affairs, Alfonso García Robles, acting as president and host of the conferences. Over the course of the next couple years, delegates from twenty-one Latin America nations and observers from the United States, Europe, the Middle East, and Asia worked together to find a way to protect hemispheric security while balancing demands from countries like Argentina and Brazil that they had the sovereign right to develop peaceful independent nuclear energy programs.[15] On February 14, 1967, leaders of fourteen Latin American countries gathered in Mexico City to sign the Treaty of Tlatelolco, voluntarily agreeing to ban the testing, use, production, storage, installation, or deployment of nuclear weapons within their territories. The nuclear weapons–free zone went into effect in 1969, when enough countries ratified the treaty. Latin America became the first nuclear weapons–free zone in the world, and the Treaty of Tlatelolco served as a model—or, as García Robles put it, "a gadfly and inspiration"—for the 1968 Treaty on the Non-Proliferation of Nuclear Weapons and the creation of other nuclear weapons–free zones around the globe.[16] Alfonso García Robles was awarded the Nobel Peace Prize in 1982 for his role in promoting regional and global nuclear nonproliferation. The Treaty of Tlatelolco remains in effect to this day, and all the nations of Latin America and the Caribbean have become members, including Cuba.

At the beginning of this book, I promised a new history of the Cuban Missile Crisis. By widening the scope of the story to include all the people and governments of the Americas, this new history changes how we think about the who, what, when, where, why, and "so what" of the Cuban Missile Crisis.

The history of the Cuban Missile Crisis has long been told as a story of US confrontation with the Soviet Union. However, looking at this event through a wider lens reveals that the crisis was not caused or resolved by John F. Kennedy and Nikita Khrushchev alone, and it did not affect just the two superpowers. The Cubans, whose revolution wrested national sovereignty from the United States and who turned to the Soviet Union for security and solidarity, caused the crisis. Latin Americans, who embraced and defended the Cuban Revolution and who sought to spread it to their own countries, caused the crisis. Other Latin Americans, who threatened the security of Fidel Castro's regime through attacks and isolation, caused the crisis. People and governments across the Americas also participated in the crisis and shaped its outcome. Latin American leaders joined together in the OAS to establish the quarantine and threatened to take even stronger measures. Those who sought a peaceful resolution worked through the UN to slow the pace of the confrontation. News of the missiles in Cuba inspired thousands of people to take up rifles and bombs, write poems and pamphlets, and debate questions of war and peace. Castro's supporters and detractors across the hemisphere committed acts of sabotage and participated in bloody riots. Reports of rising tensions in neighboring countries and the increasingly strained atmosphere on the island drove Castro to take control of the situation. Castro's actions, combined with Kennedy's increasingly dire warnings, convinced Khrushchev that the world was only moments away from nuclear war. People and governments across the Americas were thus critical participants in every phase of the Cuban Missile Crisis, from its origins to its resolution.

Widening our lens reveals that the Cuban Missile Crisis was not only a close call that ended in peace but also a dangerous reckoning of the price of security, sovereignty, and solidarity. Just as the Cold War appears less cold when we recenter our focus from the United States and Soviet Union to consider other parts of the world including Latin America, the Cuban Missile Crisis also transforms from a story of a tense standoff to a story of violence and turmoil. Yes, the missile crisis—like the rest of the hemispheric Cold War—was a confrontation between capitalism and communism, but it was also much more than that. It was a confrontation between different ways of understanding and pursuing security: a collision between individual and collective security, security pursued through advanced weaponry pitted against security pursued through arms control. It was a trial of the limits of national sovereignty: Opening Cuban territory to Soviet bases was interpreted as both the ultimate expression and the ultimate sacrifice of Cuban sovereignty. The missile crisis was also a test of solidarity: In the end, Castro and other Latin Americans proved more willing to sacrifice their lives and even world peace for the sake of geopolitical and ideological commitments than either Kennedy or Khrushchev. The Cuban Missile Crisis was a violent, destructive event because global battles over capitalism and communism collided with locally salient struggles over the values of security, sovereignty, and solidarity.

This book has also widened the chronological and geographic scope of the history of the Cuban Missile Crisis. The crisis did not last just thirteen days; it was years in the making and its consequences influenced the course of Latin American history and inter-American relations for decades after the missiles had been removed. The Cuban Missile Crisis also did not just take place in Havana, or Washington, or Moscow, but in Buenos Aires, Panama City, Bogotá, Rio de Janeiro, and La Paz, as well. This was a truly hemispheric crisis that resulted from the actions of people across the Americas and affected the lives of millions.

That leaves our final questions: Why, and So What? Why did the Cuban Missile Crisis happen and why did it end the way it did? Why did the missile crisis matter? By widening the chronological and geographic scope of the story, and including more participants, this book offers new answers to these questions.

Why did the crisis happen? I argue that hemispheric reactions to the Cuban Revolution laid the foundations for the missile crisis. Enthusiasm for and fear of the revolution spread across the Americas, driving some people and governments to defend Castro's regime while others attacked it. Fidel Castro's efforts to defend Cuba's sovereignty and security by encouraging, supporting, and showing solidarity with fellow Latin American revolutionaries drove ever more Latin American and US officials to conclude that his destabilizing influence was unacceptable. Their many attempts to remove Castro and isolate Cuba convinced Castro and Khrushchev that they would have to take drastic measures to protect Cuba's revolutionary government. Castro pressured his ally for traditional weaponry, and Khrushchev responded with an offer of nuclear missiles. Khrushchev offered the missiles, and Castro accepted them because people and governments across the Americas had clearly demonstrated that the Cuban Revolution was under attack.

Why did the crisis end without a nuclear war? I argue that Kennedy and Khrushchev grew desperate for a peaceful resolution because they realized that their control over the situation was tenuous at best and becoming weaker by the day. Kennedy watched as violence exploded across the Americas and people took to the streets to demonstrate solidarity with Cuba and demand change at home. He strained to hold back war-hungry hawks in the Pentagon, the Caribbean Basin, and the Cuban exile community who were pushing for a final solution to the Cuban question. At the same time, Khrushchev was also straining to contain his own ally, an increasingly frantic Castro who was convincing Soviet troops to shoot down US airplanes and proposing nuclear first strikes. The actions of Latin Americans and what was happening in Latin America pushed Kennedy and Khrushchev to find a hasty resolution. Ironically, the Cuban Missile Crisis ended peacefully because the situation in Latin America was spinning out of control and becoming increasingly violent.

Why did the Cuban Missile Crisis matter? Most histories conclude that the crisis mattered because it was the closest the world has ever come to nuclear war . . . and that is true. But it is not the whole story.

The Cuban Missile Crisis mattered because it forced people and governments across the Americas to confront the Cold War and their role in it. It inspired them to question their understandings of security, sovereignty, and solidarity. The threat of nuclear war pushed questions of security to the forefront of national leaders' concerns, and they unanimously agreed to sacrifice Cuba' sovereignty when they voted to establish the quarantine. The Inter-American Quarantine Force marked the zenith, the ultimate height of inter-American cooperation, as Latin American governments came together in defense of hemispheric security. The crisis also caused deep divisions, both between and within the nations of the Americas. It left Castro even more isolated but safe from the prospect of another invasion. The crisis strengthened ties between the United States and the governments of Mexico, Bolivia, and Argentina; but it deepened the rift between Washington and João Goulart's administration in Brazil. At the same time, thousands of Latin American citizens challenged their governments' decisions to prioritize hemispheric security over Cuban sovereignty. They accused their leaders of bowing to US pressure and sacrificing their own national sovereignty. These critics showed solidarity with Castro through their pamphlets, demonstrations, and acts of sabotage. The crisis thus posed a double threat: it could escalate into a nuclear war, but it could also intensify the latent violence that had been building up across the region into a continental wave of death and destruction.

Finally, the Cuban Missile Crisis mattered because it forced people across the Americas to recognize that their fates were connected. That Bolivian ambassador, sitting at his desk in Bogotá compiling newspaper clippings about the threat that the nuclear missiles posed to Colombia, knew that what happened in Cuba would affect him and everyone around him. Diplomats, presidents, military officers, senators, journalists, poets, workers, housewives, students . . . people across Latin America were confronted with the ties that bound them, and they used those ties to protect themselves, their families, their countries, their hemisphere, and the entire world. Latin Americans' cooperative efforts in defense of security, sovereignty, and solidarity shaped the course and consequences of the Cuban Missile Crisis and the hemispheric Cold War.

# Notes

## Abbreviations

AMREB    Archivo del Ministerio de Relaciones Exteriores de Bolivia, La Paz

CDF    Central Decimal File

CIA-FOIA    CIA Freedom of Information Act Electronic Reading Room, www.cia .gov/readingroom/

CPM    Comisión Provincial por la Memoria, Fondo DIPPBA División Central de Documentación, Registro, y Archivo, "Asunto Cuba," Mesa C, Carpeta Varios, Legajo 207, La Plata, Argentina

DIPPBA    Dirección de Inteligencia de la Policía de la Provincia de Buenos Aires, La Plata, Argentina

DNSA    Digital National Security Archive, https://nsarchive.gwu.edu/dnsa

JFK    John F. Kennedy Presidential Library, Boston, MA

MINRELACIONES Chile    Archivo General Histórico del Ministerio de Relaciones Exteriores de Chile, Santiago

NARA    National Archives and Records Administration, College Park, MD

RG    Record Group

UN    UN Archive, New York City

## Introduction

1. "Bogotá bajo la amenaza nuclear," *El Espectador* (Bogotá), October 23, 1962; "Una tesis tranquilizadora sobre el peligro" *El Espectador*, October 27, 1962; "Una bomba en Panamá nos traería una muerte lenta," *El Espectador*, October 24, 1962; "Efectos mortales en Colombia tendría una 'guerra nuclear,'" *La República* (Bogotá), October 25, 1962; César Garrido, "Y habría sobrevivientes?," *La República*, October 26, 1962, sec. Editorial. All articles found in Embajada de Bolivia en Bogotá, 1962, AMREB.

2. While historians of the crisis have extended their perspectives from the original US-centric approach to include the Soviet Union and, more recently, Cuba, the work that goes beyond those three countries remains limited. The first wave of missile crisis histories were triumphalist accounts and analyses of the crisis that focused on President John F. Kennedy and US actions and perspectives. See Sorensen, *Kennedy*; Schlesinger, *Thousand Days*; Kennedy, *Thirteen Days*; Allison, *Essence of Decision*. A second wave emerged in the 1980s and 1990s as the Soviet Union began to collapse and a series of critical oral history conferences brought together US, Soviet, and Cuban participants and scholars. This wave incorporated the Soviet Union and Cuba. See Blight, *On the Brink*; Blight, Allyn, and Welch, *Cuba on the Brink*; Fursenko and Naftali, *One Hell of a Gamble*; Dobbs, *One Minute to Midnight*; Mikoyan, *Soviet Cuban Missile Crisis*; Plokhy, *Nuclear Folly*; Spenser, "The Caribbean Crisis"; Bayard de Volo, "Masculinity and the Cuban Missile Crisis"; Laffey and Weldes, "Decolonizing the Cuban Missile Crisis"; Diez Acosta, *Octubre de 1962*; Diez Acosta, *Peligros y*

*principios*. A third wave has begun to broaden the scope of analysis to include the global repercussions of the crisis and the actions of everyday people. See Hershberg and Ostermann, "Global Cuban Missile Crisis at 50"; Getchell, *Cuban Missile Crisis*; Hershberg, "United States, Brazil, and the Cuban Missile Crisis, 1962 (Part 1)"; Hershberg, "United States, Brazil, and the Cuban Missile Crisis (Part 2)"; George, *Awaiting Armageddon*; Campus, "Missiles Have No Colour." Recently, Latin American historians have started uncovering the impact of the crisis within individual countries of the region and the effects of the crisis on bilateral relations between Cuba and some of its neighbors. See Moniz Bandeira, *De Martí a Fidel*; Morgenfeld, "Argentina, Estados Unidos y el sistema interamericano"; Míguez and Morgenfeld, "Las relaciones entre Argentina y Cuba"; Hermosilla, "La cuestión cubana en 'risas' chilenas"; García Ferreira and Girona, "Una 'inmensa potencia explosiva.'"

3. On transnational and international history, see C. A. Bayly et al., "AHR Conversation"; Chamberlin et al., "On Transnational and International History." On microhistory, see Magnússon and Szijártó, *What Is Microhistory?* On combining historical scales, see Putnam, "To Study the Fragments/Whole"; Trivellato, "Is There a Future?"; Aslanian et al., "AHR Conversation."

4. For reasons of space, I decided to exclude Canada and most of the other English-, French-, and Dutch-speaking parts of the mainland and Caribbean.

5. On this point, see Grandin, *Last Colonial Massacre*; Grandin and Joseph, *Century of Revolution*; Harmer, *Allende's Chile*; McPherson, "Afterword"; Loaeza, "Estados Unidos y la contención del comunismo"; Harmer, "Cold War in Latin America"; Booth, "Rethinking Latin America's Cold War."

6. On the historiography of Latin America's Cold War, see Marchesi, "Escribiendo la Guerra Fría latinoamericana"; Pettiná, *Historia mínima*; Joseph, "Border Crossings"; Casals, "Which Borders"; Rostica and Sala, "La guerra fría en América Latina." There are, of course, exceptions to these trends. For examples of other works that transcend national boundaries, decenter the United States, or integrate moderate actors, see García Ferreira, *Bajo vigilancia*; Harmer, *Beatriz Allende*; Field Jr., Krepp, and Pettiná, *Latin America and the Global Cold War*; Rojas, *El árbol de las revoluciones*; Lessa, *Condor Trials*; Wells, *Latin America's Democratic Crusade*; van Ommen, *Nicaragua Must Survive*; Brown, *Weak and the Powerful*; Jarquín, *Sandinista Revolution*.

7. During Latin America's Cold War, military authorities in Argentina, Brazil, and elsewhere developed and operated under an ideology they called National Security Doctrine, which focused on internal threats and justified sacrificing their own citizens' personal security—or human rights—for the sake of national security. On National Security Doctrine, see Finchelstein, *Ideological Origins*, 2–3; Chirio, *Politics in Uniform*, 22–29; Sala, "La doctrina de seguridad nacional;" Osuna and Pontoriero, "El impacto de la doctrina."

8. On the history of sovereignty, see Philpott, *Revolutions in Sovereignty*. On the various kinds of sovereignty, see Krasner, *Sovereignty*.

9. On solidarity, see Featherstone, *Solidarity*; Stites Mor, *Human Rights and Transnational Solidarity*.

10. Gaddis, *Strategies of Containment*; Leffler, *A Preponderance of Power*; Moyn, *Last Utopia*; Snyder, *Human Rights Activism*.

11. Westad, *Global Cold War*. See also McMahon, *Cold War in the Third World*; Chamberlin, *Cold War's Killing Fields*.

12. See Prashad, *Darker Nations*; Mahler, *From the Tricontinental*; Parrott and Lawrence, *Tricontinental Revolution*.

## Chapter 1

1. Cushion, *Hidden History*, 14.

2. Castro, *La historia me absolverá*.

3. Guerra, *Heroes, Martyrs, and Political Messiahs*, ch. 5. Cuba's communist party, the Partido Comunista Cubano, founded in 1925, renamed itself the Partido Socialista Popular in 1944.

4. Cushion, *Hidden History*, 36, 106.

5. Chase, "The Trials," 168–70.

6. Herbert L. Matthews, "Cuban Rebel Is Visited in Hideout: Castro Is Still Alive and Still Fighting in Mountains," *New York Times*, February 24, 1957.

7. Keller, *Mexico's Cold War*, 50.

8. Zimmermann, *Sandinista*, 50.

9. Brown, *Cuba's Revolutionary World*, 225; Velasco, *Barrio Rising*, 87–88.

10. Salcedo Ávila, *Venezuela, campo de batalla*, 105.

11. Velasco, *Barrio Rising*, 4–7.

12. My thanks to Gustavo for sharing his grandmother's memories. Gustavo Salcedo Ávila, email exchange with Renata Keller, November 20, 2023.

13. Luis Báez, "Crónica de un testigo sobre la visita de Fidel a Venezuela hace 50 Años," *Cubadebate*, January 22, 2009, www.cubadebate.cu/opinion/2009/01/22 /cronica-de-un-testigo-sobre-la-visita-de-fidel-a-venezuela-hace-50-anos/.

14. Neruda, *Confieso*, 438.

15. Báez, "Crónica de un testigo"; Wells, *Latin America's Democratic Crusade*, 475.

16. Schlesinger, *Letters of Arthur Schlesinger, Jr.*, 104.

17. Neruda, *Confieso*, 438–39.

18. Alexander, *Rómulo Betancourt*, 541–42.

19. Brown, *Cuba's Revolutionary World*, 226.

20. Reeves, "Extracting the Eagle's Talons."

21. Only Mexico, Uruguay, and Argentina maintained consistent diplomatic relations with the Soviet Union. Blasier, *Giant's Rival*, 23; Pettiná, "Mexican-Soviet Encounters," 84.

22. Cerdas Cruz, *La hoz y el machete*.

23. "Inter-American Treaty of Reciprocal Assistance," Multilateral Treaties, *Department of International Law, OAS*, accessed October 25, 2021, www.oas.org /juridico/english/treaties/b-29.html.

24. Guerra, *Visions of Power*, 65.

25. Andrew and Mitrokhin, *World Was Going Our Way*, 34.

26. Andrew and Mitrokhin, *World Was Going Our Way*, 28.

27. Getchell, *Cuban Missile Crisis*, 37.

28. Fursenko and Naftali, *One Hell of a Gamble*, 11. Lillian Guerra claims that the Soviet training program in Cuba started as early as March 1959. Guerra, *Visions of Power*, 79.

29. Fursenko and Naftali, *One Hell of a Gamble*, 12.

30. Andrew and Mitrokhin, *World Was Going Our Way*, 35.

31. Boughton, "Soviet-Cuban Relations, 1956–1960," 447–51. On the Soviet exhibit and Mikoyan's visit to Mexico, see Zolov, *Last Good Neighbor*, ch. 2.

32. On Perón's foreign policy, see Semán, *Ambassadors of the Working Class*.

33. Salas, *Uturuncos*, 69.

34. Brown, *Cuba's Revolutionary World*, 380–82. On the Uturuncos, see Nicanoff and Castellano, *Las primeras experiencias guerrilleras*.

35. James, *Resistance and Integration*, 149.

36. McPherson, *The Invaded*.

37. On Borge's encounter with Castro, see Zimmermann, *Sandinista*, 43.

38. Hodges, *Intellectual Foundations*, 164.

39. Fonseca, *Long Live Sandino*, 8.

40. Zimmermann, *Sandinista*, 59–61.

41. Zimmermann, *Sandinista*, 9.

42. Brown, *Cuba's Revolutionary World*, 57–63. On the June 1959 attempted invasion, see also Zimmermann, *Sandinista*, 53–56.

43. Robbins, *Cuban Threat*, 9. For a more positive take on Cubans' "export of revolutionary aid," see Randall, *Exporting Revolution*.

44. "Entrainement de Latino-Americains," February 11, 1963, Dossier "Reserve 27-7-1," Numéro 51, sous Série "Cuba," Série "B, Amérique, 1952–1963," Centre des Archives diplomatiques du ministère des Affaires étrangères, La Courneuve, France. My thanks to Aaron Coy Moulton for sharing this document. The CIA reported the same number of trainees in 1962. See Director of Central Intelligence, "Situation and Prospects in Cuba: National Intelligence Estimate 85-63," June 14, 1963, National Security Files, National Intelligence Estimates, Box 9, Lyndon B. Johnson Presidential Library.

45. Guerra, *Visions of Power*, 112.

46. On debates over the original nature of the Cuban Revolution, see Bustamante, *Cuban Memory Wars*.

47. Chase, "Confronting the Youngest Revolution," 8, 10–11.

48. Chase, "Confronting the Youngest Revolution," 11–12.

49. On Cuban immigration to the United States after the Cuban Revolution, see Masud-Piloto, *From Welcomed Exiles*.

50. Pérez, *Cuba and the United States*. A smaller, but still significant, number also emigrated to Union City, New Jersey and to other countries in the hemisphere.

51. Eckstein, *Immigrant Divide*, 45.

52. Salinas Price, *Mis años con Elektra*, 122; Pensado, "'To Assault,'" 498; Herrán Ávila, "Las guerrillas blancas," 20.

53. Jean F. Nougués, "Radioscopia subversiva," *Revista de La Escuela Superior de Guerra*, March 1962. My thanks to James Shrader for sharing this article.

## Chapter 2

1. Despite their public defense of the Cuban Revolution, Mexican government leaders and intelligence officials secretly cooperated with US anti-Castro efforts. Keller, *Mexico's Cold War*, 70–71. Brazilian officials, especially Brazil's ambassador to Cuba, Vasco Tristão Leitão da Cunha, often expressed concerns about Castro's

government in private conversations, and he eventually started collaborating with Cuban exiles. Hershberg, " 'Friend of the Revolution.'"

2. Zolov, *Last Good Neighbor.*

3. *Los Presidentes de México,* 82.

4. "Memorandum estríctamente confidencial para el Señor Presidente de la República," May 19, 1961, SPR-400-9, Archivo Histórico Genaro Estrada, Secretaría de Relaciones Exteriores, Mexico City, Mexico.

5. "Punta del Este," *Política* (Mexico City), February 1, 1962.

6. Marques Bezerra, *Da revolução ao reatamento,* 62. On Cuban support for the Ligas Camponesas, see Moniz Bandeira, *De Martí a Fidel,* 304–5.

7. Brown, *Cuba's Revolutionary World,* 239.

8. John W. F. Dulles contends that Guevara requested the meeting with Quadros, while Jonathan Brown claims that Quadros initiated the visit. See Dulles, *Unrest in Brazil,* 125; Brown, *Cuba's Revolutionary World,* 242–43.

9. On Lacerda as the destroyer of presidents, see Skidmore, *Politics in Brazil,* 200.

10. Quadros, "Brazil's New Foreign Policy," 24.

11. Skidmore, *Politics in Brazil,* 206.

12. "Havana Prensa Latina in Spanish to Latin America," August 29, 1961, Tad Szulc, Box 61, Folder: "Legal Materials: CIA Documents," Department of Special Collections, Howard Gotlieb Archival Research Center, Boston University.

13. On Castro's 1959 resignation, see Thomas, *Cuban Revolution,* 454–55. On Quadros's presidency and resignation, see Moniz Bandeira, *O 24 de agôsto*; Chaia, *A liderança.*

14. Hershberg, "United States, Brazil, and the Cuban Missile Crisis, 1962 (Part 1)," 9.

15. Bobadilla González, *México y la OEA,* 122.

16. Brown, *Cuba's Revolutionary World,* 52. On Trujillo's support of Batista and Cuban exiles, see also Rabe, "Caribbean Triangle," 60.

17. Ropp, *Panamanian Politics,* ch. 2. On Panama as an oligarchy, see Soler, *Panamá.*

18. Conniff, *Panama and the United States,* 111–12.

19. Castillero R., *Historia de Panamá,* 217–18; Conniff, *Panama and the United States,* 112.

20. Guevara Mann, *Panamanian Militarism,* 103.

21. Brown, *Cuba's Revolutionary World,* 53–57. While Brown argues that Castro likely knew about and supported the Panamanian adventure, other historians such as Dirk Kruijt contend that it was more likely a private initiative by Cuban revolutionary veterans. Kruijt, *Cuba and Revolutionary Latin America,* 94.

22. Between 1959 and 1961, thirteen member countries of the Organization of the American States broke diplomatic and commercial relations with Cuba. Bobadilla González, *México y la OEA,* 254.

23. Bobadilla González, *México y la OEA,* 74–75.

24. Galileo Solís, "Memorias del Ministerio de Relaciones Exteriores: Informe, parte expositiva," October 1, 1962, 591.005.14 Caja 20, Acervo Histórico Diplomático de Panamá, Panama City.

25. "Guatemala Talks of War on Cuba as Rebels' Ally," *Chicago Daily Tribune,* November 17, 1960.

26. "Cuba Charged with Threat to Panama Canal," *Los Angeles Times*, November 16, 1960.

27. "U.S. Warships Speed to Patrol Caribbean," *Los Angeles Times*, November 18, 1960.

28. R. Hart Phillips, "300,000 Rally to Back Castro," *New York Times*, October 27, 1959.

29. Bonsal, *Cuba, Castro, and the United States*, 108.

30. Schoultz, *That Infernal Little Cuban Republic*, 104–5.

31. Bolender, *Voices*, 184.

32. Bolender, *Voices*, ch. 10.

33. Guerra, *Visions of Power*, 125.

34. Kornbluh, *Bay of Pigs Declassified*, 24.

35. Kornbluh, *Bay of Pigs Declassified*, 28–29.

36. Cuba Revolutionary Armed Forces, "Informe general sobre la brigada mercenaria 2506, que invadío Playa Larga y Playa Girón el 17 de abril de 1961," September 18, 1961, Cuban Missile Crisis Revisited, DNSA.

37. CIA History Staff, "Official History of the Bay of Pigs Operation: Volume III— Evolution of CIA's Anti-Castro Policies, 1959–January 1961," December 1979, Bay of Pigs Release, CIA-FOIA, www.cia.gov/readingroom/docs/bop-vol3.pdf; Kornbluh, *Bay of Pigs Declassified*, 32.

38. Draper, *Castro's Revolution*, 95. On the difficulty of maintaining secrecy in Guatemala, see Kornbluh, *Bay of Pigs Declassified*, 97.

39. "Denies Fleet in Guatemala to Invade Cuba," *Chicago Daily Tribune*, October 29, 1960.

40. Kornbluh, *Bay of Pigs Declassified*, 55.

41. On this shift, see Gleijeses, "Ships in the Night."

42. Rasenberger, *Brilliant Disaster*, 109.

43. Rasenberger, *Brilliant Disaster*, 117–20.

44. McGeorge Bundy, "Memorandum of Discussion on Cuba," January 28, 1961, in *Foreign Relations*, 10:61–62.

45. Somoza and Cox, *Nicaragua traicionada*, 212–13.

46. García Marquez, "Recuerdos de periodista," April 18, 2023, *Prensa Latina*, www.prensa-latina.cu/2023/04/18/recuerdos-de-periodista. My thanks to Osvaldo Rodríguez Martínez for sharing this article.

47. Salcedo Ávila, *Venezuela, campo de batalla*, 176.

48. Cuba Revolutionary Armed Forces, "Información sobre preparativos de barcos de guerra norteamericanos y del traslado de mercenarios y esbirros por via aerea hacia Panamá," March 17, 1961, Cuban Missile Crisis Revisited, DNSA.

49. Brown, *Cuba's Revolutionary World*, 117.

50. Ferrer, *Cuba: An American Story*, 365–67; Rasenberger, *Brilliant Disaster*, 170–71; 214–15.

51. "Palabras de Fidel en el sepelio de las víctimas del ataque yanqui," *Noticias de Hoy* (Havana), April 18, 1961.

52. Rasenberger, *Brilliant Disaster*, 323.

53. Daniel M. Braddock, "Political-Economic Relations Between Cuba and the Sino-Soviet Bloc," November 23, 1960, RG 59, CDF 1960–1963, Box 1329, Decimal Folder 637.60/1–760, NARA.

54. Hershberg and Ostermann, "Global Cuban Missile Crisis at 50," 781. See also Brown, *Cuba's Revolutionary World*, 86–87.

55. "A los pueblos de América y del mundo," *Che* 1, no. 12 (April 20, 1961) and *Bohemia* 53, no. 17 (April 23, 1961).

56. Corvalán, *De lo vivido*, 79.

57. C. E. Bartch, "Cuba Series: Invasion of Cuba Prompts Castro-Communists to Demonstrate against the United States," April 26, 1961, RG 59, CDF 1960–1963, Box 1553, Decimal Folder 723.00/1–560, NARA.

58. Field, "Ideology as Strategy," 162.

59. "Fidel Backers Demonstrate in Americas," *Chicago Daily Tribune*, April 18, 1961.

60. "Red-Led Mobs Protest 'U.S. Role' in Cuban War," *Washington Post*, April 20, 1961.

61. Vrana, *This City Belongs to You*, 113.

62. Robert C. Albright, "Kennedy Takes Blame for U.S. Role in Cuba Invasion," *Washington Post*, April 25, 1961.

63. "Demonstration in Montevideo Is Nation's Largest in Recent Years," *New York Times*, April 23, 1961.

64. Somoza and Cox, *Nicaragua traicionada*, 216.

65. "Prisoners Face Death, Castro Says," *Los Angeles Times,* April 24, 1961; Rasenberger, *Brilliant Disaster*, 323.

66. "Confirman los mercenaries: Armados e instruidos por EE.UU," *Noticias de Hoy* (Havana), April 22, 1961.

67. Leogrande and Kornbluh, *Back Channel to Cuba*, 45.

68. "Memorandum from President Kennedy," November 30, 1961, in *Foreign Relations*, 10:688–89. On Operation Mongoose, see Fursenko and Naftali, *One Hell of a Gamble*, ch. 7; Blight and Kornbluh, *Politics of Illusion*, ch. 5.

69. Talbott, *Khrushchev Remembers*, 492.

70. "Text of Kennedy Speech on U.S. Latin Aid," *New York Times*, March 14, 1961.

71. On Kubitschek's foundational role in the Alliance for Progress, see Darnton, "Asymmetry and Agenda-Setting." On the Alliance for Progress more generally, see Taffet, *Foreign Aid*; Kirkendall, *Hemispheric Alliances*.

72. On military aspects of the Alliance for Progress, see Schmidli, *Fate of Freedom Elsewhere*, ch. 1; Field, *From Development*.

73. On the embargo, see Schoultz, *That Infernal Little Cuban Republic*, 200–208.

74. Karl, "Reading the Cuban Revolution from Bogotá," 344.

75. Roldán, *Blood and Fire*.

76. On Alberto Lleras Camargo and Colombia's mid-century politics, see Karl, *Forgotten Peace*, ch. 1.

77. On development efforts in mid-century Colombia, see Offner, *Sorting Out*.

78. Romero Sánchez, "El miedo a la revolución," 160–61.

79. Wells, "Telegram from the Embassy in Colombia to the Department of State," May 6, 1961, in *Foreign Relations*, 12:251–53.

80. Chester Bowles, "Telegram from the Department of State to the Embassy in Venezuela," May 19, 1961, in *Foreign Relations*, vol. 12, doc. 113, https://history.state.gov/historicaldocuments/frus1961-63v12/d113.

81. Latham, *Modernization as Ideology*, 82–83.

82. Taffet, *Foreign Aid*, 149; Offner, *Sorting Out*, 6.

83. Taffet, *Foreign Aid*, 154; Romero Sánchez, "El miedo a la revolución," 147.

84. Fair Play for Cuba Committee, "Fidel Castro Speaks on Marxism-Leninism," December 2, 1961, PRISM collection, University of Central Florida Digital Library, https://ucf.digital.flvc.org/islandora/object/ucf%3A5073.

85. Romero Sánchez, "El miedo a la revolución," 154–55.

86. Karl, "Reading the Cuban Revolution," 355–56; Schoultz, *That Infernal Little Cuban Republic*, 173–74.

87. Bobadilla González, *México y la OEA*, 125–26.

88. Dean Rusk, "Telegram from Secretary of State Rusk to the Department of State," January 31, 1962, in *Foreign Relations*, 12:307–8. On negotiations during the meeting of foreign ministers, see Harmer, " 'Cuban Question,'" 133–36.

## Chapter 3

1. Diez Acosta, *Octubre de 1962*, 85–86.

2. Talbott, *Khrushchev Remembers*, 493. At the time of the missile crisis, the Soviets had only a few dozen relatively inaccurate long-range intercontinental missiles (ICBMs) capable of reaching targets in the United States, whereas the United States had recently installed nuclear missiles in Turkey that could easily reach Moscow. Khrushchev was probably also motivated to send the missiles to strengthen Soviet-Cuban ties in the wake of the Escalante affair (the expulsion of one of Cuba's top communist leaders) and signals that the Cubans might be moving closer to the Chinese communists. See Fursenko and Naftali, *One Hell of a Gamble*, 160–72. For some of the first detailed discussions of Khrushchev's motives in offering the missiles that took the "protection of Cuba" idea seriously, under "The Cuban Missile Crisis Reconsidered," in *Diplomatic History* 14, no. 2 (1990); see, especially, Greiner, "Soviet View."

3. Paterson, "Commentary: The Defense-of-Cuba Theme," 252.

4. Fursenko and Naftali, *One Hell of a Gamble*, 134–37; Hershberg, "New Russian Evidence."

5. Blight, Allyn, and Welch, *Cuba on the Brink*, 197.

6. Plokhy, *Nuclear Folly*, 68.

7. Castro Ruz and Ramonet, *Fidel Castro*, 272.

8. On Cuba's relations with the Non-Aligned Movement, see Getchell, "Cuba, the USSR, and the Non-Aligned Movement."

9. Fursenko and Naftali, *One Hell of a Gamble*, 179.

10. Plokhy, *Nuclear Folly*, 69. See also Diez Acosta, *Octubre de 1962*, 96–97; Lechuga, *In the Eye of the Storm*, 34–35.

11. Diez Acosta, *Octubre de 1962*, 97. Soviet first deputy premier Anastas Mikoyan had expressed similar doubts about maintaining secrecy during the initial meetings in the Kremlin about the missile operation. Plokhy, *Nuclear Folly*, 59–60.

12. Castro Ruz, "Documento 3," 3.

13. Blight, Allyn, and Welch, *Cuba on the Brink*, 351: Lechuga, *In the Eye of the Storm*, 44.

14. Fursenko and Naftali, *One Hell of a Gamble*, 188. Before Kennedy announced the quarantine, the Soviets managed to get the medium-range missiles operational in six sites across the island. The installations for the intermediate range missiles were ready, but the warheads for those missiles never made it to the island. Diez Acosta, *Octubre de 1962*, 118–20.

15. Plokhy, *Nuclear Folly*, 84.

16. Blight, Allyn, and Welch, *Cuba on the Brink*, 60–61; Diez Acosta, *Octubre de 1962*, 115.

17. Blight and Lang, *Dark Beyond Darkness*, 32.

18. Fursenko and Naftali, *One Hell of a Gamble*, 191; Gribkov and Smith, *Operation Anadyr*, 15.

19. Plokhy, *Nuclear Folly*, 85–96.

20. Kalfon, *Che Ernesto Guevara*, 378–80.

21. Franqui, *Family Portrait*, 188.

22. Blight, Allyn, and Welch, *Cuba on the Brink*, 207.

23. Blight and Brenner, *Sad and Luminous Days*, 40.

24. Blight, Allyn, and Welch, *Cuba on the Brink*, 207.

25. Franqui, *Family Portrait*, 189.

26. Blight, Allyn, and Welch, *Cuba on the Brink*, 206; Burström et al., "Memories of a World Crisis," 307–9.

27. Burström et al., "Memories of a World Crisis," 307–9.

28. "Cuba Periling Latin Nations, Refugee Says," *Chicago Daily Tribune*, August 13, 1962.

29. Joseph A. Loftus, "Russians Step Up Flow of Arms Aid to Castro Regime," *New York Times*, August 25, 1962.

30. "Cuba, base soviética?," *El Tiempo* (Bogotá), August 25, 1962.

31. Arthur J. Olsen, "Kennedy Pledges Any Steps to Bar Cuban Aggression," *New York Times,* September 5, 1962.

32. "Una revolución pacífica evita una revolución cruenta: ALM," *Excélsior* (Mexico City), October 4, 1962. On López Mateos's distinction between offensive and defensive weapons, see also Carlos Denegri, "Nueva actitud si Cuba tiene poder ofensivo," *Excélsior* (Mexico City), October 23, 1962.

33. Francis L. McCarthy, "Presidentes de centroamérica y Panamá señalan el peligro comunista de Cuba," *El Panamá América* (Panama City), October 1, 1962.

34. Memorandum, Gilberto Arias to George A. Smathers, Re: Cuban Crisis, September 17, 1962, RG 59, CDF 1960–1963, Box 1625, Decimal Folder 737.00/9–1362, NARA.

35. "People of the Week: Anti-Castro Campaigner Gilberto Arias of Panama," *El Panamá América* (Panama City), October 4, 1962.

36. Galileo Solís, "Memorias del Ministerio de Relaciones Exteriores: Informe, Parte Expositiva," October 1, 1962, 591.005.14 Caja 20, Acervo Histórico Diplomático de Panamá.

37. "Discussion of Cuban Situation," August 31, 1962, RG 59, CDF 1960–1963, Box 1330, Decimal Folder 637.61/8–362, NARA.

38. CIA Office of Current Intelligence, "Current Intelligence Weekly Summary," September 14, 1962, CIA Reading Room, https://www.cia.gov/readingroom/docs /CIA-RDP79-00927A003700120001-0.pdf.

39. Alexander, *Venezuela's Voice for Democracy*, 77. See also Salcedo Ávila, *Venezuela, campo de batalla*, ch. 5.

40. Consejo de la Organización de los Estados Americanos, "Acta de la sesión ordinaria celebrada el 9 de octubre de 1962," appendix C.

41. Telegram, Department of State to All ARA Diplomatic Posts, October 4, 1962, RG 59, CDF 1960–1963, Box 1330, Decimal Folder 637.61/8–362, NARA.

42. Chang and Kornbluh, *Cuban Missile Crisis, 1962*, 359–411.

43. Naftali, May, and Zelikow, *Presidential Recordings*, 2:405–7, timestamp October 16, 1962, 11:50 a.m.–1:00 p.m.

44. Naftali, May, and Zelikow, *Presidential Recordings*, 2:434, timestamp October 16, 1962, 6:30–8 p.m.

45. Naftali, May, and Zelikow, *Presidential Recordings*, 2:442, timestamp October 16, 1962, 6:30 p.m.

46. John A. McCone, "Memorandum Concerning Actions against the Soviet-Cuban Military Threat," October 19, 1962, General CIA Records, CIA-FOIA, www.cia.gov /readingroom/docs/CIA-RDP80B01676R001700130003-9.pdf.

47. Drew Pearson, "Weak Leadership Hampers the OAS," *Washington Post*, September 23, 1962.

48. Naftali, May, and Zelikow, *Presidential Recordings*, 2:415, timestamp October 16, 1962, 11:50 a.m.–1:00 p.m.

49. Naftali, May, and Zelikow, *Presidential Recordings*, 2:422, timestamp October 16, 1962, 11:50 a.m.

50. Naftali, May, and Zelikow, *Presidential Recordings*, 2:524, timestamp October 18, 1962, 11:10 a.m.–1:15 p.m.

51. Naftali, May, and Zelikow, *Presidential Recordings*, 2:542, timestamp October 18, 1962, 11:10 a.m.–1:15 p.m.

52. Naftali, May, and Zelikow, *Presidential Recordings*, 2:543–44, timestamp October 18, 1962, 11:10 a.m.–1:15 p.m.

53. Naftali, May, and Zelikow, *Presidential Recordings*, 2:577, timestamp October 18, near midnight.

54. Naftali, May, and Zelikow, *Presidential Recordings*, 2:600, timestamp October 19, 1962. For further elaboration of the OAS's role in authorizing the blockade, see Abram Chayes, "An Interpretation by Department of State Legal Adviser Abram Chayes on US Legal Position, November 3, 1962," in Larson, *"The Cuban Crisis,"* 244–48; Colman, "Toward 'World Support.'"

55. Wilson, "International Law."

56. "Minutes of the 506th Meeting of the National Security Council," October 21, 1962, in *Foreign Relations*, 11:143.

57. Naftali, May, and Zelikow, *Presidential Recordings*, 2:529, timestamp October 18, 1962, 11:10 a.m.

58. Naftali, May, and Zelikow, *Presidential Recordings*, 2:600, timestamp October 19, 1962.

59. Naftali, May, and Zelikow, *Presidential Recordings*, 2:606, timestamp October 20, 3:30–5:10 p.m.

60. May and Zelikow, *Kennedy Tapes*, 178.

61. Dean Rusk, "Eyes Only Ambassador from Secretary," October 21, 1962, RG 59, CDF 1960–1963, Box 1625, Decimal Folder 737.00/10-1262, NARA.

62. For the full transcript of Kennedy's speech, see Chang and Kornbluh, *Cuban Missile Crisis*, 160–64.

## Chapter 4

1. "Guerra mundial por um fio!," *Última Hora* (Rio de Janeiro), October 23, 1962.

2. "Lima, dentro de la zona amagada por los proyectiles de alcance intermedio instalados por rusos," *El Comercio* (Lima), October 23, 1962.

3. "La primera bomba puede caer en Panamá," *La Hora* (Panama City), October 23, 1962.

4. "Batiendo palmas," *El Diario* (La Paz), October 24, 1962.

5. Orlando Mattos, "[Political cartoon of Kennedy and Krushchev playing chess with missiles]," *Folha de São Paulo*, October 26, 1962.

6. Hernando Turriago Riaño (Chapete), "En tierras de América," *El Tiempo* (Bogotá), October 24, 1962.

7. "Solidaridad ante la provocación evidente," *El Tiempo* (Bogotá), October 23, 1962.

8. "Con Cuba contra el crimen," *Época* (Montevideo), October 23, 1962.

9. "Como en la Europa de 1939," *El Tiempo* (Bogotá), October 24, 1962.

10. "Responsabilidad de los grandes," *El Diario* (La Paz), October 25, 1962.

11. Francisco de Alvarez, "Sicosis de guerra en México," *Última Hora* (La Paz), October 23, 1962.

12. 'Al fin y al cabo,' *Bohemia Libre* (Caracas), November 11, 1962.

13. The first part of the proposal was a formality. According to OAS procedures, member states must hold a vote to invoke the Rio Treaty and to approve meeting as an "Organ of Consultation" in order to consider urgent problems.

14. Consejo de la Organización de los Estados Americanos, "Acta de la sesión extraordinaria celebrada el 23 de octubre de 1962."

15. Article 6 of the Rio Treaty states: "If the inviolability or the integrity of the territory or the sovereignty or political independence of any American State should be affected by an aggression which is not an armed attack or by an extra-continental or intra-continental conflict, or by any other fact or situation might endanger the peace of America, the Organ of Consultation shall meet immediately in order to agree on the measures which must be taken in case of aggression to assist the victim of the aggression or, in any case, the measures which should be taken for the common defense and for the maintenance of the peace and security of the Continent." Article 8 of the treaty states: "For the purposes of this Treaty, the measures on which the Organ of Consultation may agree will comprise one or more of the following: recall of chiefs of diplomatic missions; breaking of diplomatic relations; breaking of consular relations; partial or complete interruption of economic relations or of rail, sea, air, postal, telegraphic, telephonic, and radiotelephonic or radiotelegraphic communications; and use of armed force." See "Inter-American Treaty of Reciprocal

Assistance," Multilateral Treaties, *Department of International Law, OAS*, accessed October 25, 2021, www.oas.org/juridico/english/treaties/b-29.html. Emphasis added.

16. When broken into specifics about the actual measures, the section establishing the quarantine to prevent Cuba from receiving further offensive weapons passed with 16 votes in favor and 3 abstentions; and the section on the use of armed force to prevent weapons already on the island from being converted into an active threat passed with 16 votes in favor and 4 abstentions. Mexico, Uruguay, and Bolivia abstained on the establishment of the quarantine; they were joined by Brazil in abstaining on the use of force to disarm the weapons already in Cuba. "Hubo una abstención absoluta y varias parciales sobre la resolución de la O.E.A.," *La Nación* (La Paz), October 24, 1962. Brazil, Mexico, and Bolivia inserted a note into the final record of the meeting stating that their support for the resolution as a whole should not be interpreted as support for an armed attack against Cuba. Bobadilla González, *México y la OEA*, 155.

17. Naftali, May, and Zelikow, *Presidential Recordings*, 2:130–31, timestamp October 23, 1962, 10:00–11:03 a.m.

18. Chang and Kornbluh, *Cuban Missile Crisis*, 172.

19. Naftali, May, and Zelikow, *Presidential Recordings*, 2:177, timestamp October 23, 1962, 7:10–7:20 p.m.

20. Kennedy, *Thirteen Days*, 40.

21. B. Ochoteco, "Cuarentena impuesta por U.S.A. a los barcos destinados a Cuba," October 31, 1962, Fondo Legaciones y Embajadas, Embajada de Uruguay en Estados Unidos, Caja 29, Carpeta 5, Archivo del Ministerio de Relaciones Exteriores de Uruguay. My thanks to Roberto García Ferreira for sharing this document.

22. Ministerio de Relaciones Exteriores y Culto, "Boletín de la Dirección General de Política," November 1962, AH/0118, Serie 80-OEA y ONU, Expediente Boletines de la Dirección General de Política 1962, Archivo de Cancillería Argentina. UN secretary-general U Thant told the US permanent representative to the UN, Adlai Stevenson, that the African and Asian countries were putting a great deal of pressure on the Soviets to accept negotiations. "Telegram from the Foreign Mission to the United Nations to the Department of State," October 25, 1962, in *Foreign Relations*, 11:203–4.

23. José A. Mora, Secretary-General, Organization of American States, to U Thant, Secretary-General, United Nations, October 23, 1962, S-0873 Box 1 File 4, UN. Thant was appointed acting secretary-general in November 1961 following the death of Dag Hammarskjöld; he was then appointed secretary-general on November 30, 1962, with the title retroactively applied to his entire time in office.

24. "Chapter 8: Questions Relating to the Americas," in "Section 1: Political and Security Questions," *Yearbook of the United Nations 1962*, 106.

25. Thant, *View from the UN*, 160.

26. Thant, *View from the UN*, 173. Emphasis in original.

27. Thant, *View from the UN*, 168.

28. Thant, *View from the UN*, 155.

29. Thant, *View from the UN*, 161–62; Rickey Rosenthal, "50 Smaller UN Nations Forced War Compromise," *Panama Tribune*, October 27, 1962; Thomas J. Hamilton, 'Stevenson Charges in U.N. Cuba Is Soviet Bridgehead,' *New York Times*, October

24, 1962. On responses to the missile crisis from other non-aligned countries, see Elbahtimy and Hershberg, "Egypt and the Cuban Missile Crisis." On the Non-Aligned Movement's dedication to nuclear nonproliferation, see Lüthi, "The Non-Aligned Movement."

30. Thant, *View from the UN*, part III, appendix A, 460. See also Lechuga, *In the Eye of the Storm*, 121.

31. "Statement Made by Acting Secretary-General U Thant before Security Council," October 24, 1962, S-0872, Box 2, File 6, UN. See also Nassif, *U Thant in New York*, 27–29.

32. Thant, *View from the UN*, 165.

33. Thant, *View from the UN*, appendices C and D, 461–62. On Thant's role in setting up negotiations, see Dorn and Pauk, "Unsung Mediator." On the UN's role in slowing the pace of events in the Cuban Missile Crisis, see Sayward, *United Nations*, 43.

34. Carlos Denegri, "Nueva actitud si Cuba tiene poder ofensivo," *Excélsior* (Mexico City), October 23, 1962.

35. López Mateos, "Message from Mexican President Adolfo López Mateos to Cuban President Osvaldo Dorticós," October 23, 1962, Legajo III, Expediente 5664-1, Archivo Histórico Genaro Estrada, Secretaría de Relaciones Exteriores, Mexico City, Mexico.

36. Secretaría de Relaciones Exteriores, "Declaración mexicana sobre Cuba y las armas atómicas," *Política* (Mexico City), November 1, 1962.

37. *Presencia internacional*, 1:398–99.

38. Lincoln Gordon, briefing of Brazilian president Goulart on Soviet missiles in Cuba, October 22, 1962, CU00565, Cuban Missile Crisis Revisited, DNSA; Walters, *Silent Missions*, 375.

39. "Brasil não apóia medidas de intervenção em Cuba," *Correio da Manhã* (Rio de Janeiro), October 24, 1962; Edísio Gomes de Matos, "Delegado do Brasil na OEA não seguia a linha do govêrno brasileiro," *Jornal do Brasil* (Rio de Janeiro), October 25, 1962.

40. "Brizola acusa Marinho de desobedecer o govêrno ao votar contra Cuba na OEA," *Jornal do Brasil* (Rio de Janeiro), October 25, 1962.

41. "Definição do Brasil no caso Cuba-EUA; Nota oficial," *Folha de São Paulo*, October 24, 1962.

42. Campos, *A lanterna na popa*, 496.

43. Hershberg and Ostermann, "Global Cuban Missile Crisis at 50," 237.

44. James Hershberg comes to a similar conclusion about Pena Marinho's instructions, noting that Brazil's Foreign Ministry archive contains no evidence to suggest that the OAS representative deviated from his orders. Hershberg, "Soviet-Brazilian Relations," 192.

45. Hershberg, "Soviet-Brazilian Relations," 193. The Soviet Union had an acting ambassador in Brazil during the missile crisis because their formally appointed ambassador, Ilya S. Chernyshev, drowned while swimming in heavy surf near Rio de Janeiro on October 21, 1962. "Report about Death of Soviet Ambassador to Brazil," October 24, 1962, Embajada de Bolivia en Rio de Janeiro, 1962, AMREB.

46. José Luis Salcedo-Bastardo, "Brasil y el bloqueo a Cuba," October 26, 1962, DPI, 1962, EE.UU., Exp 355 (Crisis de los Misiles Cuba–USA), Archivo Ministerio del Poder

Popular para Relaciones Exteriores de la República Bolivariana de Venezuela. My thanks to Gustavo Salcedo for sharing this document.

47. "Presidente e Congresso: Apêlo á paz com independência," *Última Hora* (Rio de Janeiro), October 25, 1962; "Coexistência é imperativo da paz, diz Presidente Goulart," *Jornal do Brasil* (Rio de Janeiro), October 25, 1962.

48. Codacci-Pisanilli, "Text of Letter and Resolution Addressed to the President by Mr. Codacci-Pisanilli, President of the Inter-Parliamentary Council," October 26, 1962, National Security Files, Countries, Box 13, JFK.

49. Hershberg, "United States, Brazil, and the Cuban Missile Crisis (Part 2)," 15–17.

50. Serrano, *Common Security*, 8.

51. Mateos and Suárez-Díaz, "Atoms for Peace."

52. Dawood and Herz, "Nuclear Governance."

53. Hunt, "Mexican Nuclear Diplomacy," 180.

54. Melo Franco, *Planalto*, 202.

55. Serrano, *Common Security*, 18. On Mexican and Brazil efforts at nuclear nonproliferation, see Sotomayor, "Brazil and Mexico."

56. Hershberg and Ostermann, "Global Cuban Missile Crisis at 50," 238.

57. Hershberg and Ostermann, "Global Cuban Missile Crisis at 50," 239.

58. Hershberg, "Soviet-Brazilian Relations," 188.

59. "Proposta brasileira poderá solucionar a crise," *Jornal do Brasil* (Rio de Janeiro), October 26, 1962.

60. "Summary Record of the Fifth Meeting of the Executive Committee of the National Security Council," October 25, 1962, in *Foreign Relations*, 11:205.

61. "Summary Record," 207.

62. Hershberg, "United States, Brazil, and the Cuban Missile Crisis (Part 2)," 7–8.

63. "Telegram from the Department of State to the Embassy in Brazil," October 26, 1962, in *Foreign Relations*, 11:228.

64. "Telegram," October 26, 1962, 11:228–29.

65. Hershberg, "United States, Brazil, and the Cuban Missile Crisis, 1962 (Part 1)," 11–20.

66. Goulart had his dates a little confused, as he meant to refer to Dantas's proposals for negotiation at the January—not February—OAS meeting.

67. João Goulart, letter to Kennedy, October 25, 1962, President's Office Files, Countries Brazil Box 112 Folder 16, JFK.

68. Lima discusses his role in recommending Gen. Albino Silva in his memoirs. See Lima, *Travessia*, 268.

69. CIA, "Central Intelligence Bulletin: Brazil," October 30, 1962, General CIA Records, CIA-FOIA, www.cia.gov/readingroom/docs/CIA-RDP79T00975A006600510001-2.pdf.

70. "Goulart envia um emissário a Havana," *Jornal Do Brasil* (Rio de Janeiro), October 30, 1962; "H. Lima: O Brasil inicia ação mais efetiva na crise," *Folha de São Paulo*, October 31, 1962.

71. "'Brasil foi vitorioso na sua missão,' diz. General Albino Silva," *Diario Carioca* (Rio de Janeiro), November 1, 1962.

72. "Albino voltou confiante no êxito de sua missão em Cuba," *Jornal do Brasil* (Rio de Janeiro), November 2, 1962.

## Chapter 5

1. "Informes de los gobiernos sobre las medidas adoptadas de acuerdo con el párrafo segundo de la resolución aprobada por el Consejo de la Organización de los Estados Americanos, actuando provisionalmente como órgano de consulta, en la sesión celebrada el 23 de octubre de 1962," October 1962, S-0872 Box 2 File 5, UN.

2. Maurice M. Bernbaum, "Cuban Situation," November 2, 1962, RG 59, CDF 1960–1963, Box 1626, Decimal Folder 737.00/11–1662, NARA.

3. Naval History and Heritage Command, "The Naval Quarantine of Cuba, 1962: Abeyance and Negotiation, 31 October–13 November," accessed January 24, 2025, www.history.navy.mil/research/library/online-reading-room/title-list-alphabetically/c/cuban-missile-crisis/abeyance-and-negotiation.html. Trinidad and Tobago gained independence on August 31, 1962, and joined the Organization of American States in 1967. Stoetzer, *Organization of American States*, 56–57.

4. Forrest R. Johns, "United We Stood," *U.S. Naval Institute Proceedings*, January 1985, www.usni.org/magazines/proceedings/1985/january/united-we-stood. My thanks to Gustavo Salcedo Ávila for calling my attention to the geographic location of the deployment. Salcedo Ávila, "Venezuela ante la crisis".

5. Martin, *Overtaken by Events*, 240.

6. John Bartlow Martin, "Joint Weeka No. 43," October 28, 1962, RG 59, CDF 1960–1963, Box 1642, Decimal Folder 739.00 (W)/10–2862, NARA; John Bartlow Martin, "Joint Weeka No. 45," November 11, 1962, RG 59, CDF 1960–1963, Decimal Folder 739.00 (W)/11–1162, NARA.

7. Martin, *Overtaken by Events*, 242.

8. John Bartlow Martin, "Joint Weeka No. 46," November 18, 1962, RG 59, CDF 1960–1963, Decimal Folder 739.00 (W)/11–1862, NARA.

9. Martin, *Overtaken by Events*, 242. See also Gleijeses, *Dominican Crisis,* 70.

10. Gleijeses, *Shattered Hope,* 155–64.

11. Harms, "'God Doesn't Like the Revolution'"; Gleijeses, *Shattered Hope*, 208–22; Grandin, *Last Colonial Massacre*, 78–86. On counterrevolutionary and anticommunist ideology within Guatemala, see Vela Castañeda, "Guatemala, 1954."

12. Moulton, "Building Their Own Cold War."

13. Schlesinger and Kinzer, *Bitter Fruit*, 88.

14. Perutka, "Arms for Arbenz"; Getchell, "Revisiting the 1954 Coup."

15. On Ydígoras's rise to power, see Gleijeses, *Shattered Hope*, 75, 83–84, 217; Ruano Najarro, "El golpe de estado de 1963," 84–108.

16. Fernández Ordóñez, *Anatomía del enfrentamiento*, 5–6.

17. Figueroa Ibarra, Paz Cárcamo, and Taracena Arriola, "El primer ciclo de la insurgencia," 46–49.

18. "Relaciones con Cuba suspensas: Maquinaciones castristas contra la paz de Guatemala se revelan," *El Imparcial* (Guatemala City), April 29, 1960; "Guatemala Talks of War on Cuba as Rebels' Ally." *Chicago Daily Tribune,* November 17, 1960. For Ydígoras's interpretation of the uprising, see Ydígoras Fuentes, *My War with Communism,* 159–70.

19. On right-wing guerrilla groups, see Grandin, *Last Colonial Massacre*, 87. On student protests in March 1962, see Vrana, *This City Belongs to You*, 112–24.

20. On the impact of the Cuban Revolution in Guatemala, see Figueroa Ibarra, Paz Cárcamo, and Taracena Arriola, "El primer ciclo de la insurgencia," 44–46.

21. Figueroa Ibarra, "Violencia y revolución en Guatemala," 196. Another Guatemalan that Guevara befriended during his time in Guatemala in 1954 became one of the founding members of the Rebel Armed Forces (Fuerzas Armadas Rebeldes) guerrilla group. See *Construyendo caminos*, 14–15.

22. Figueroa Ibarra, "Violencia y revolución en Guatemala," 198–99.

23. Central Intelligence Agency, "The Communist Insurgency Movement in Guatemala," September 20, 1968, National Security Files, Latin America—El Salvador and Guatemala, Box 54, Lyndon B. Johnson Presidential Library.

24. Figueroa Ibarra, "Violencia y revolución en Guatemala," 281.

25. Silva, "Telegram from Mexican Embassy, Guatemala City," October 23, 1962, in *Cold War International History Project Bulletin*, no. 17/18 (2012): 195–96, www.wilsoncenter.org/publication/bulletin-no-1718-fall-2012; "Posición de gobiernos americanos," *Época* (Montevideo), October 24, 1962.

26. Naval History and Heritage Command, "The Naval Quarantine of Cuba, 1962: Stand Down and Conclusion," accessed January 24, 2025, www.history.navy.mil/research/library/online-reading-room/title-list-alphabetically/c/cuban-missile-crisis/stand-down-and-conclusion.html. Ultimately, the repairs to the *Burrunida* were not completed in time for the ship to join the quarantine force. Johns, "United We Stood."

27. Letter, Guatemalan OAS Delegation to OAS President, October 25, 1962, S-0872 Box 2 File 5, UN; Ydígoras Fuentes, *My War with Communism*, 222; Arnaldo Otero, "Ydígoras seis días antes del bloqueo a Cuba había informado sobre las bases de teledirigidos en la isla," *El Imparcial* (Guatemala City), October 26, 1962. The photograph of the warships from *El Imparcial* can be found in the archives of the Centro de Investigaciones Regionales de Mesoamérica (CIRMA). This book does not represent the opinions of CIRMA. The responsibility for the contents and the execution belong to the author.

28. "Gobierno de Nicaragua alabó tono firme del discurso de J. Kennedy," *Novedades* (Managua), October 23, 1962.

29. Federico Schneegans, "Con Kennedy por la libertad del mundo," *Novedades* (Managua), October 24, 1962.

30. Julio H. Riethmüller Spoerer, "Informe sobre la política internacional," October 31, 1962, Fondo Paises, NIC 3 (1962), MINRELACIONES Chile.

31. "Obrerismo libre nicaragüense respaldó con mitin el bloqueo de Cuba ordenado por Kennedy," *Novedades* (Managua), October 25, 1962.

32. Alexander, *Communist Party of Venezuela*, 60.

33. León, "Un modelo cubano en Venezuela."

34. Salcedo Ávila, *Venezuela, campo de batalla*, 209–10.

35. Wickham-Crowley, *Guerrillas and Revolution*, 38–39.

36. CIA, "Current Intelligence Weekly Summary," October 12, 1962, General CIA Records, CIA-FOIA, www.cia.gov/readingroom/docs/CIA-RDP79-00927A003800040001-8.pdf

37. Gott, *Guerrilla Movements*, 111.

38. Blanco Muñoz, *La lucha armada: Hablan*, 349.

39. Blanco Muñoz, *La lucha armada: La izquierda*, 234.

40. Rabe, *Most Dangerous Area in the World*, 106; Brown, *Cuba's Revolutionary World*, 257.

41. For example, see Fair Play for Cuba Committee, "Fidel Castro Speaks on Marxism-Leninism," December 2, 1961, PRISM collection, University of Central Florida Digital Library, https://ucf.digital.flvc.org/islandora/object/ucf%3A5073.

42. "Charles Allan Stewart Oral History Interview," October 23, 1967, 26, https://archive1.jfklibrary.org/JFKOH/Stewart,%20C(harles)%20Allan/JFKOH-CAS-01/JFKOH-CAS-01-TR.pdf.

43. Levine, *Conflict and Political Change*, 47.

44. CIA, "Central Intelligence Bulletin," October 11, 1962, General CIA Records, CIA-FOIA, www.cia.gov/readingroom/docs/CIA-RDP79T00975A006600430001-1.pdf.

45. Gastón Aráoz, untitled report about Venezuela's internal politics, October 24, 1962, Embajada de Bolivia en Caracas, 1961–1964, AMREB.

46. CIA, "Current Intelligence Weekly Summary," October 19, 1962, General CIA Records, CIA-FOIA, www.cia.gov/readingroom/docs/CIA-RDP79-00927A003800050001-7.pdf.

47. Telegram, Charles Allan Stewart, Caracas, to Secretary of State, October 19, 1962, RG 59, CDF 1960–1963, Box 1569, Decimal Folder 731.00/8-162, NARA.

48. Redfield Peattie, *View from the Barrio*, 112.

49. Gastón Aráoz, untitled report about Venezuelan reaction to Cuban Missile Crisis, October 29, 1962, Embajada de Bolivia en Caracas, 1961–1964, AMREB.

50. Comité Nacional de COPEI, "Venezuela está amenazada por la agresión comunista," *El Nacional* (Caracas), October 23, 1962.

51. "Movilización de las fuerzas armadas con determinación de zonas de operaciones," *El Nacional* (Caracas), October 28, 1962.

52. "The Naval Quarantine of Cuba, 1962: Abeyance and Negotiation, 31 October–13 November," Naval History and Heritage Command, accessed March 28, 2025, www.history.navy.mil/research/library/online-reading-room/title-list-alphabetically/c/cuban-missile-crisis/abeyance-and-negotiation.html.

53. Rómulo Betancourt, "Venezuela supo dar el ejémplo," *Life en Español*, December 28, 1964.

54. Edward T. Long, "Weeka No. 47," November 23, 1962, RG 59, CDF 1960–1963, Box 1571, Decimal Folder 731.00 (W)/7-772, NARA.

55. Letter, Dean Rusk to Marcos Falcón Briceño, December 10, 1962, DPI, 1962, EE.UU., Exp 355 (Crisis de los Misiles Cuba–USA), Archivo Ministerio del Poder Popular para Relaciones Exteriores de la República Bolivariana de Venezuela. My thanks to Gustavo Salcedo for providing a copy of this letter.

56. "Zonas de operaciones militares," *El Nacional* (Caracas), October 29, 1962.

57. Aráoz, untitled report.

58. Long, "Weeka No. 47."

59. "Caracas ocupada por fuerzas del ejército y de la policía," *Revolución* (Havana), November 1, 1962.

60. Sikkink, *Ideas and Institutions*, 89–104; Walcher, "Petroleum Pitfalls."

61. Szusterman, *Frondizi*, epilogue.

62. Sikkink, *Ideas and Institutions*, 111–12.

63. Brown, *Cuba's Revolutionary World*, 236; telegram, Henry A. Hoyt, Buenos Aires, to Secretary of State, January 22, 1962, RG 59, CDF 1960–1963, Box 1597, Decimal 735.5/1-460, NARA.

64. Telegram, Henry A. Hoyt, Buenos Aires, to Secretary of State, February 1, 1962, RG 59, CDF 1960–1963, Box 1597, Decimal 735.00/2-162, NARA.

65. Potash, *Army and Politics*, vol. 2, ch. 9; Robben, *Political Violence*, 34.

66. Telegram, unnamed sender, Buenos Aires, to Secretary of State, March 30, 1962, RG 59, CDF 1960–1963, Box 1596, Decimal 735.11/2-762, NARA.

67. Sheinin, *Argentina and the United States*, 125. On divisions between the *azules* and *colorados*, see also Míguez, "¿Anticomunistas, antiestatistas, antiperonistas?"

68. Robert McClintock, [Telegram from Buenos Aires to Secretary of State], October 10, 1962, RG 59, CDF 1960–1963, Box 1597, Decimal 635.00/10-1062, NARA.

69. Robert McClintock, untitled memo on Argentinean support for US position in Cuban Missile Crisis, October 22, 1962, CU00564, Cuban Missile Crisis Revisited, DNSA.

70. "La Argentina se alineó primera," *Clarín* (Buenos Aires), September 14, 1997.

71. Robert McClintock, "Joint Weeka No. 43," October 27, 1962, RG 59, CDF 1960–1963, Box 1596, Decimal 735.00 (W)/10-2762, NARA.

72. "La Argentina apoyará la convocatoria," *La Nación* (Buenos Aires), October 23, 1962.

73. "La decisión argentina: La marina prestará la cooperación que se le solicita," *El Litoral* (Santa Fe), October 24, 1962.

74. "La flota argentina en defensa del continente," *La Nación* (Buenos Aires), October 24, 1962.

75. "El jefe del estado despidió las naves que van al Caribe," *La Nación* (Buenos Aires), October 28, 1962.

76. "Van hacia el caribe barcos de guerra de la Armada Nacional," *La Nación* (Buenos Aires), October 29, 1962.

77. "Rápida decisión en nuestra conducta internacional," *Clarín* (Buenos Aires), October 25, 1962.

78. Telegram, Robert McClintock, Buenos Aires, to Secretary of State, October 24, 1962, RG 59, CDF 1960–1963, Box 1625, Decimal Folder 737.00/10-1262, NARA.

79. "Se adoptarán nuevas medidas para apoyar la defensa del continente americano," *La Razón* (Buenos Aires), October 25, 1962.

80. Telegram, Robert McClintock, Buenos Aires, to Secretary of State, October 24, 1962, RG 59, CDF 1960–1963, Box 1597, Decimal 735.5/1-460, NARA.

81. Telegram, Robert McClintock, Buenos Aires, to Secretary of State, November 2, 1962, RG 59, CDF 1960–1963, Box 1597, Decimal 611.3722/11-262, NARA.

82. Telegram, Robert McClintock, Buenos Aires, to Secretary of State, November 5, 1962, National Security Files, Countries, Box 7, JFK.

83. Telegram, Robert McClintock, Buenos Aires, to Secretary of State, November 5, 1962, RG 59, CDF 1960–1963, Box 1597, Decimal 611.3755/11-562, NARA.

84. Robert McClintock, "Joint Weeka No. 45," November 10, 1962, 45, RG 59, CDF 1960–1963, Box 1596, Decimal 735.00 (W)/11-1062, NARA.

85. Telegram, Dean Rusk to Robert McClintock, Buenos Aires, November 17, 1962, National Security Files, Countries, Box 7, JFK.

86. Letter, John F. Kennedy to José María Guido, December 26, 1962, President's Office Files Countries Argentina Box 111 Folder 13, JFK.

87. Blight, Allyn, and Welch, *Cuba on the Brink*, 186.

## Chapter 6

1. Lechuga, *In the Eye of the Storm*, 66–67.

2. Dobbs, *One Minute to Midnight*, 48.

3. Castro Ruz and Ramonet, *Fidel Castro*, 275–76.

4. "Preparativos de agresión yanqui," *Revolución* (Havana), October 22, 1962.

5. Dobbs, *One Minute to Midnight*, 39.

6. Lechuga, *In the Eye of the Storm*, 63; Valle Jimenez, *Un pueblo invencible*, 19; Diez Acosta, *Peligros y principios*, 229.

7. Dobbs, *One Minute to Midnight*, 48, 80–82.

8. Dobbs, *One Minute to Midnight*, 50.

9. US Foreign Broadcast Information Service, "Daily Report . . . No. 207."

10. Gilly, *Inside the Cuban Revolution*, 48; "Clima bélico en la isla cubana," *Clarín* (Buenos Aires), October 25, 1962; Bermúdez, *La imagen constante*, 157.

11. Luis Hernández Serrano, "Cincuenta octubres de un cartel," *Juventud Rebelde* (Havana), October 23, 2012, www.juventudrebelde.cu/cuba/2012-10-23 /cincuenta-octubres-de-un-cartel.

12. Blight, Allyn, and Welch, *Cuba on the Brink*, 212–13.

13. US Foreign Broadcast Information Service, "Daily Report . . . No. 208."

14. Sergio Pineda, "Cuba frente a la agresión," *Marcha* (Montevideo), October 26, 1962.

15. Dobbs, *One Minute to Midnight*, 75.

16. Gilly, *Inside the Cuban Revolution*, 48–49. On the Posadist party and Gilly's participation, see Gittlitz, *I Want to Believe*.

17. Halperin, *Rise and Decline*, 190–91; Lewis, Lewis, and Rigdon, *Four Men*, 539–40; Lewis, Lewis, and Rigdon, *Four Women*, 85.

18. Gilly, *Inside the Cuban Revolution*, 51.

19. Dobbs, *One Minute to Midnight*, 48.

20. Blight, Allyn, and Welch, *Cuba on the Brink*, 21.

21. "Movilización general en Cuba," *Crítica* (Panama City), October 25, 1962.

22. Moore, *Pichón*, 243–45.

23. "Los medios modernos de agresión y destrucción," *Bohemia* (Havana), October 26, 1962.

24. "Dona sangre la dirección nacional de la FMC," *Noticias de Hoy* (Havana), October 25, 1962.

25. "Con gran fervor patriótico nuestro pueblo dona sangre," *Noticias de Hoy* (Havana), October 26, 1962.

26. Jaime Gravalosa, "'Yo he venido aquí a sustituir a mi hijo,'" *Noticias de Hoy* (Havana), October 27, 1962.

27. El Indio Naborí, "Al son de la historia: Piratas y patriotas," *Noticias de Hoy* (Havana), October 25, 1962.

28. Blight and Brenner, *Sad and Luminous Days*, 49.

29. "El taller de la UNEAC," *Noticias de Hoy* (Havana), October 26, 1962.

30. "Colombianos en una brigada de combate en Cuba, se informa," *El Espectador* (Bogotá), October 26, 1962.

31. Zimmermann, *Sandinista*, 77–78; Blandón, *Entre Sandino y Fonseca*, 667–68.

32. Mariblanca Sabas Alomá, "Nuestros fieles hermanos," *Bohemia* (Havana), November 2, 1962.

33. Bustos, *El Che quiere verte*, 112–13.

34. "Apoyada Cuba por la solidaridad del mundo entero," *Revolución* (Havana), October 24, 1962; "Aumenta en el mundo la repulsa a la provocación de los yanquis," *Revolución* (Havana), October 24, 1962.

35. "From Havana to Foreign Office," October 24, 1962, in Priestland, *British Archives*, 169.

36. Brown, *Cuba's Revolutionary World*, 38.

37. Matos, *Cómo llegó la noche*, 411–12.

38. Edmundo Desnoes email to Renata Keller, November 7, 2017.

39. Dobbs, *One Minute to Midnight*, 161.

40. On the semi-autobiographical nature of the novel, see Luis and Desnoes, "America Revisited," 11.

41. Desnoes, *Memories of Underdevelopment*, 82.

42. Edmundo Desnoes, email to Renata Keller, November 7, 2017.

43. Desnoes, *Memories of Underdevelopment*, 83–87.

44. Donoghue, *Borderland on the Isthmus*, 176–77.

45. "De 'claro y preciso' califica el Canciller Solís el discurso del presidente de los Estados Unidos," *La Estrella de Panamá* (Panama City), October 23, 1962.

46. "Panamá adoptará cualquier medida para el fortalecimiento de la defensa del hemisferio occidental—Roberto F. Chiari," *La Estrella de Panamá* (Panama City), October 24, 1962.

47. Donoghue, *Borderland on the Isthmus*, 161.

48. Teófilo Reyes C., "Cable de Panamá a Santiago," November 6, 1962, Fondo Paises, PAN 2 (1962), MINRELACIONES Chile.

49. Telegram, Joseph Simpson Farland, Panama City, to Secretary of State, October 22, 1962, Cuban Missile Crisis Revisited, DNSA.

50. "Mayor vigilancia e inspección habrá para barcos soviéticos que tengan que cruzar el Canal," *La Estrella de Panamá* (Panama City), October 27, 1962.

51. US Foreign Broadcast Information Service, "Daily Report . . . No. 209."

52. "Adoptarán medidas para la defensa de los civiles," *El Panamá América* (Panama City), October 25, 1962.

53. Comisión Nacional de Defensa Civil, "Boletín de Instrucciones," *La Estrella de Panamá* (Panama City), October 26, 1962.

54. "Civil Defense Pamphlets Put Out for Public," *Panama Star and Herald* (Panama City), October 27, 1962.

55. "Al Paredón," *Crítica* (Panama City), October 30, 1962.

56. "La Zona debe responsabilizarse por la defensa civil de Panamá," *El Panamá América* (Panama City), October 26, 1962.

57. "El Ministerio de Gob. y Justicia toma medidas para la población civil," *La Estrella de Panamá* (Panama City), October 26, 1962.

58. Untitled report on Panamanian reactions to Cuban Missile Crisis, October 1962, RG 59, CDF 1960–1963, Box 1535, Decimal Folder 719.00/10–562, NARA.

59. "Robles Reiterates Firm Stand against Pro-Red Activity," *Panama Star and Herald* (Panama City), October 26, 1962; "Govt Warnings Dampen RP Pro-Castro Students," *Panama Tribune* (Panama City), October 27, 1962.

60. King, *El problema de la soberanía*, 153–54.

61. Del Vasto, *História del Partido del Pueblo*, 82; "Thelma King, la líder más controversial de los 60," *La Estrella de Panamá* (Panama City), www.laestrella.com.pa/nacional/190127/king-lider-thelma-controversial.

62. US Foreign Broadcast Information Service, "Daily Report . . . No. 210."

63. Taffet, *Foreign Aid*, 158.

64. Romero Sánchez, "El miedo a la revolución," 252.

65. Untitled report on reactions in Colombia to missile crisis, October 23, 1962, Embajada de Bolivia en Bogotá, 1962, AMREB.

66. Romero Sánchez, "El miedo a la revolución," 251–52.

67. Karl, *Forgotten Peace*, 173.

68. "Colombia reitera adhesión al Pacto de Rio de Janeiro," *El Tiempo* (Bogotá), October 23, 1962.

69. Jaime Villamil León, "Las fuerzas militares de Colombia atenderán llamamiento de la OEA," *El Siglo* (Bogotá), October 25, 1962.

70. CIA, "The Crisis USSR/Cuba: Information As of 0600, 28 October 1962," October 28, 1962, Cuban Missile Crisis Revisited, DNSA.

71. "Colombia prestará apoyo moral y material en acción colectiva contra Fidel Castro," *El Siglo* (Bogotá), October 28, 1962.

72. "Una bomba en Panamá nos traería una muerte lenta," *El Espectador* (Bogotá), October 24, 1962.

73. "Bomba atómica en Panamá no afectaría a Colombia," *El Tiempo* (Bogotá), October 24, 1962.

74. "Compaña masiva para defensa de los civiles: Proteja su familia, construya su casa con refugio para emergencias," *El Espectador* (Bogotá), October 24, 1962.

75. Luis A. Santacruz, "En atomos volando," *El Tiempo* (Bogotá), October 25, 1962.

76. "Otra encuesta de El Tiempo: divididas las opiniones sobre crisis mundial," *El Tiempo* (Bogotá), October 24, 1962.

77. "Ante la amenaza atómica no hay motivo de alarma en el país," *El Tiempo* (Bogotá), October 25, 1962.

78. "'Terrorismo atómico'?," *El Espectador* (Bogotá), October 26, 1962.

79. César Garrido, "Y habría sobrevivientes?," *La República* (Bogotá), October 26, 1962.

80. For example, in July 1959, *La República* published an editorial that compared violence in Colombia with the Mau Mau insurgency in Kenya. Karl, *Forgotten Peace*, 102–3.

81. "Julio abril," *El Siglo* (Bogotá), October 27, 1962.

82. "Por la paz de Colombia y del mundo pidió el nuncio de S.S.," *El Tiempo* (Bogotá), October 29, 1962.

83. "Injustificada ola de pánico surgió ayer," *El Tiempo* (Bogotá), October 25, 1962.

84. "En algunas capitales latinoamericanas hubo nerviosidad y hasta se informó que 'llovían bombas sobre Cuba,'" *El Mundo* (Buenos Aires), October 24, 1962.

85. "Sicosis de peligro nuclear," *El Siglo* (Bogotá), October 24, 1962.

86. "Siete días de inquietud nacional," *El Tiempo* (Bogotá), October 28, 1962.

87. Crayón, "Sicosis de pánico," *El Siglo* (Bogotá), October 29, 1962.

88. Gilberto Vieira, "Intervención yanqui en el país con ocasión del bloqueo a Cuba," *La Voz de la Democracia* (Bogotá), November 2, 1962.

## Chapter 7

1. Harmer, *Allende's Chile*, 31. On the Cuban stance toward Allende and the "vía chilena," see Pedemonte, "La Revolución Cubana." On the Chilean road to socialism, see Furci, *El Partido Comunista de Chile*; Casals Araya, *El alba de una revolución*.

2. The other Latin American countries that maintained relations with Cuba in October 1962 were Mexico, Brazil, Bolivia, and Uruguay.

3. "Armamentismo de Cuba pone en grave peligro la paz de América," *El Mercurio* (Santiago), October 24, 1962.

4. Consejo de la Organización de los Estados Americanos, "Acta de la sesión extraordinaria celebrada el 23 de octubre de 1962."

5. "Schweitzer exhortó a Cuba que acepte una inspección de observadores de la NU," *El Mercurio* (Santiago), October 25, 1962.

6. "Senado: Versión extratada oficial," *El Mercurio* (Santiago), October 24–26, 1962.

7. "Senado: Versión extratada oficial," *El Mercurio* (Santiago), October 26, 1962.

8. "Senado: Versión extratada oficial," *El Mercurio* (Santiago), October 27 and 29, 1962.

9. "Venezuela está legalmente comprometida a una acción multilateral americana," *El Nacional* (Caracas), October 27, 1962.

10. León, "Un modelo cubano en Venezuela," 9.

11. On Lugo Rojas's arrest, see Estep, *Latin American Nations*, 271.

12. "Venezuela está legalmente comprometida a una acción multilateral americana," *El Nacional* (Caracas), October 27, 1962.

13. "Neruda izó la bandera cubana en su residencia," *El Panamá América* (Panama City), October 30, 1962; "Contratiempo para Neruda," *La Razón* (Buenos Aires), October 30, 1962.

14. "Intelectuais manisfestam solidariedade a Cuba," *Última Hora* (Rio de Janeiro), October 27, 1962.

15. "Sandinistas con Cuba," *Revolución* (Havana), October 30, 1962.

16. Luís Edgar de Andrade, "Lacerda telegrafou a Kennedy," *Jornal do Brasil* (Rio de Janeiro), October 25, 1962.

17. Raymond Telles, "Joint Weeka No. 46," November 16, 1962, RG 59, CDF 1960–1963, Box 1532, Decimal Folder 718.00 (W)/10-462, NARA.

18. On the National Liberation Front (Frente de Liberación Nacional [FLN]), see Bolo Hidalgo, *Cristianismo y liberación nacional*; Frente de Liberación Nacional (Peru), *El FLN*; Heilman, "Yellows against Reds," 158.

19. "Communist Protest Effort against United States' Cuba Stand Fails Miserably," November 1, 1962, RG 59, CDF 1960–1963, Box 1555, Decimal Folder 723.00/11-162, NARA.

20. "Peace Corps in Arequipa May Come under Increasing Communist Attack," November 28, 1962, RG 59, CDF 1960-1963, Box 1555, Decimal Folder 723.00/10-362, NARA. Emphasis in original.

21. Comite Pro-Frente Nacional de Defensa de Cuba, "Llamado en defensa de Cuba: Todo el pueblo unido contra la agresión Yanqui," no date, RG 59, CDF 1960-1963, Box 1626, Decimal Folder 737.00/10-2562, NARA.

22. El Comite de auspicio al II Congreso Americano de Mujeres, "A las mujeres de Bolivia," October 23, 1962, RG 59, CDF 1960-1963, Box 1561, Decimal Folder 724.00 /10-162, NARA.

23. "J. Kennedy quiere quemar el mundo," and "¡Morirían 750 millones de hombres!," *El Pueblo* (La Paz), October 24, 1962.

24. Comisión Política del Comité Central del Partido Comunista de Bolivia, "Decreta estado de emergencia y movilización de todos sus militantes," October 1962, RG 59, CDF 1960-1963, Box 1626, Decimal Folder 737.00/10-2562, NARA.

25. Juventud Comunista, "Fidel . . . seguro a los yanquis dales duro!," no date, RG 59, CDF 1960-1963, Box 1561, Decimal Folder 724.00/10-162, NARA.

26. Anonymous, pink fliers, RG 59, CDF 1960-1963, Box 1561, Decimal Folder 724.00/10-162, NARA.

27. Comité Regional de la Juventud del Sector de Izquierda del MNR de La Paz, "Manifiesto al pueblo boliviano," October 23, 1962, RG 59, CDF 1960-1963, Box 1626, Decimal Folder 737.00/10-2562, NARA.

28. Comité Regional del Partido Obrero Revolucionario (Trotskista) de La Paz, "¡¡¡Viva el Estado Obrero Cubano!!!," October 26, 1962, RG 59, CDF 1960-1963, Box 1561, Decimal Folder 724.00/10-162, NARA.

29. National Executive Committee of the Central Obrera Boliviana, "English Translation of Bolivian Labor Central Revolution" [typo in original, should read "resolution"], October 23 1962, RG 59, CDF 1960-1963, Box 1626, Decimal Folder 737.00/10-2562, NARA.

30. "La Conferencia Minera aprobó resolución en favor de Cuba," *El Diario* (La Paz), October 24, 1962.

31. "El Frente Boliviano de defensa de la libertad," *El Diario* (La Paz), October 25, 1962; "El Frente Boliviano de defensa de la libertad," *Presencia* (La Paz), October 25, 1962.

32. Frente de Agrupaciones Juveniles Anticomunistas de Bolivia, "A la opinión pública en general," no date, RG 59, CDF 1960-1963, Box 1626, Decimal Folder 737.00/10-2562, NARA.

33. Frente Juvenil Anticomunista Boliviano, "A los católicos del pueblo paceño," October 26, 1962, RG 59, CDF 1960-1963, Box 1561, Decimal Folder 724.00/10-162, NARA.

34. Juan José, "Solución original contra la guerra mundial," *La Nación* (La Paz), October 25, 1962.

35. "El pueblo de Colombia respalda a Cuba," *La Voz de la Democracia* (Bogotá), November 2, 1962.

36. Agents of the Intelligence Department of the Police of Buenos Aires Province (Dirección de Inteligencia de la Policía de la Provincia de Buenos Aires, or DIPPBA) collected copies of more than forty different pro-Cuban and anti-Cuban pamphlets in

October and November 1962 and preserved them, along with reports about where and how the pamphlets were distributed, in their archives. All the pamphlets and reports discussed here can be found in CPM. Lightning protest meetings are quick meetings that are designed to end before the authorities can intervene.

37. Comisión de Solidaridad con Cuba de San Nicolás, "Peligra la paz mundial," October 23, 1962, CPM.

38. Partido Comunista Comite Villa Ballester, "El pueblo argentino contra la pirateria guerrerista yanky," October 25, 1962, CPM.

39. Comisión Nacional de Solidaridad con la Revolución Cubana, "¡Unidos para defender a Cuba!" October 1962, CPM.

40. Partido Comunista de Junín, "Pueblo de Junín," October 1962, CPM; Sector Universitario de la Federación Juvenil Comunista, "Cuba piensa invadir a los EE.UU.?," no date, CPM.

41. Partido Comunista Comité Local Morón, "El imperialismo pirateril yanqui amenaza la paz del mundo al pretender atacar a Cuba," October 24, 1962, CPM.

42. Sector Universitario de la Federación Juvenil Comunista, "Cuba piensa invadir a los EE.UU.?"; [Movimiento de Unidad y Coordinación Sindical], "La agresión a CUBA es la guerra mundial," no date, CPM. On the Movimiento de Unidad y Coordinación Sindical, see Murmis, "El sindicalismo comunista."

43. Comisión Directiva Nacional del Consejo Argentino de la Paz, "Ante la inminencia de la guerra," October 23, 1962, CPM. On the World Peace Council, see Iber, *Neither Peace nor Freedom*.

44. Partido Comunista Floresta Norte, "Argentinos!," October 25, 1962, CPM.

45. Comité Local del Partido Comunista de Mar del Plata, "El pueblo argentino está con Cuba!," October 26, 1962, CPM.

46. Partido Comunista Centro Liniers, "Salud a la actitud del gobierno soviético en defensa de la paz mundial," October 29, 1962, CPM.

47. The US ambassador to Argentina, Robert McClintock, estimated that in June 1962 the Communist Party of Argentina had about 50,000 members; but he warned that "its limited numerical strength is counteracted by its cohesive and disciplined organization." Robert McClintock, "Assessment of Communism in Argentina," June 7, 1962, RG 59, CDF 1960–1963, Box 1596, Decimal 735.001/2–860, NARA.

48. Unión de Mujeres de la Argentina Filial Mar del Plata, "¡Alerta madres argentinas! La paz del mundo está amenazada," no date, CPM.

49. Brigadas Juveniles de Apoyo a la Revolución Cubana, Centro Socialista Argentino de Vanguardia San Nicolás, Comisión de Solidaridad con Cuba San Nicolás, Federación Juvenil Comunista San Nicolás, Juventud Socialista Argentina de Vanguardia San Nicolás, and Partido Comunista San Nicolás, "A los soldados y suboficiales del Batallón de Ingenieros de San Nicolás," November 14, 1962, CPM.

50. Partido Comunista Comité Local San Martín, "Fuera las garras Yanquis de Cuba," October 24, 1962, CPM.

51. Partido Comunista Comité de la Capital Federal, "¡Salgamos a la calle para defender a CUBA y la PAZ MUNDIAL!," no date, CPM.

52. Partido Comunista Centro Liniers, "El pueblo argentino no será verdugo de los hermanos cubanos," October 25, 1962, CPM.

53. Comisión Nacional de Solidaridad con la Revolución Cubana, "¡Unidos para defender a Cuba!"

54. Comisión de Solidaridad con Cuba de San Nicolás, "Peligra la paz mundial."

55. Osvaldo J. J. de Baldrich, Departmento "C" Delegación del SIPBA de San Martín, "Comunicar campana de acción psicológica," October 25, 1962, CPM.

56. Centro Juvenil Anticomunista de San Martín, "¡Colaboremos a sacar al comunismo de América!," October 25, 1962, CPM.

57. Centro Juvenil Anticomunista de San Martín, "Los comunistas son hombres sin patria y sin Dios," October 25, 1962, CPM.

58. Centro Juvenil Anticomunista de San Martín, "¡Antes que sea tarde!," October 25, 1962, CPM; Centro Estudiantil de Juventud Anticomunista, "La juventud argentina está al lado . . . ," October 25, 1962, CPM; Centro Juvenil Anticomunista de San Martín, "!Para que mañana nadie nos lo reproche!," October 25, 1962, CPM.

59. Centro Juvenil Anticomunista de San Martín, "Para que el infierno rojo no llegue a nosotros," October 25, 1962, CPM.

60. Osvaldo J. J. de Baldrich, "Comunicar campana de acción psicológica."

61. Report about volante, November 22, 1962, CPM.

## Chapter 8

1. "Rogando por la paz," *Crítica* (Panama City), October 29, 1962.

2. "Mitin rojo en la Universidad de León, ayer," *Novedades* (Managua), October 26, 1962.

3. "Estudiantes costarricenses piden acción inmediata contra Cuba," *Crítica* (Panama City), October 27, 1962; Raymond Telles, "Joint Weeka No. 44," November 2, 1962, 44, RG 59, CDF 1960–1963, Box 1532, Decimal Folder 718.00(W)/10–462, NARA.

4. "Incidentes hubo despues de concentración efectuada en Alameda Bernardo O'Higgins," *El Mercurio* (Santiago), October 26, 1962; telegram, Charles Cole, Santiago, to Secretary of State," October 26, 1962, RG 59, CDF 1960–1963, Box 1565, Decimal Folder 725.00/9–362, NARA. The US embassy estimated that 3,500 people attended the demonstration, while the Cuban magazine *Bohemia* put the number at 20,000. "El mundo contra ellos," *Bohemia* (Havana), November 2, 1962.

5. "Indígenas en manifestación ayer en el Capitolio," *El Espectador* (Bogotá), October 27, 1962; "Delegado indígena habla para VOZ," *La Voz de la Demócracia* (Bogotá), November 2, 1962.

6. "El pueblo de Colombia respalda a Cuba," *La Voz de la Democracia* (Bogotá), November 2, 1962.

7. "Prohibidas manifestaciones anti-americanas en el país," *El Comercio* (Quito), October 25, 1962.

8. "Quito estuvo expectante alrededor del diferendo ruso-americano, por Cuba," *El Comercio* (Quito), October 25, 1962.

9. "Izquierdistas provocaron disturbios en Guayaquil," *El Comercio* (Quito), October 26, 1962.

10. "Cinco muertos y 26 heridos en motines ayer en La Paz," *El Tiempo* (Bogotá), October 27, 1962.

11. On the telegrams and letters, see García Ferreira, "Cuban Embassy in Uruguay," 8. On Castro's speech, see García Ferreira and Girona, "Una 'Inmensa potencia explosiva,'" 119–20.

12. On Che's visit and the popularity of the Cuban Revolution in Uruguay, see Brown, *Cuba's Revolutionary World*, 230–35.

13. Nercesian, *La política en armas*, 156.

14. Aparicio, García Ferreira, and Terra, *Espionaje y política*, 192.

15. "Resolución unánime: El ejecutivo apoya a Estados Unidos," *Época* (Montevideo), October 25, 1962.

16. Ralph S. Collin, "Weeka No. 43," October 27, 1962, RG 59, CDF 1960–1963, Box 1587, Decimal Folder 733.00 (W)/1–562, NARA.

17. "Acto y manifestación: El pueblo en la calle, 'Cuba, Sí,'" *Época* (Montevideo), October 25, 1962. A report from the Chilean embassy estimated the size of the crowd at 20,000; a report from the Cuban embassy in Montevideo put it at 18,000; while a report from the US embassy claimed that 7,000 people attended. Sergio Labarca, "El bloqueo de Cuba y la posición de Uruguay," October 28, 1962, Fondo Paises, URU 7 (1962), MINRELACIONES Chile. See also García Ferreira and Girona, "Una 'Inmensa potencia explosiva,'" 127–28; Collin, "Weeka 43," October 27, 1962.

18. Collin, "Weeka No. 43," October 27, 1962.

19. "Castro Terror Order!: U.S. Tips Off Latins After Oil Sabotage," *Chicago Daily Tribune*, October 29, 1962.

20. "Bayonetas para una adhesión estudiantil," *Época* (Montevideo), October 30, 1962. On collaboration between Uruguayan police and anti-communist student groups, see Aparicio, García Ferreira, and Terra, *Espionaje y política*.

21. Fernández Huidobro, *Historia de los Tupamaros*, 54. On the Tupamaros, see Gatto, *El cielo por asalto*.

22. "En Brasil hubo manifestaciones de trabajadores," *El Diario* (La Paz), October 24, 1962.

23. "Hermes Lima: 'Confiem na política externa do Brasil,'" *Jornal do Comercio* (Rio de Janeiro), October 24, 1962.

24. "Trabalhadores protestam contra bloqueio de Cuba e 'premier' explica a posição do govêrno," *Correio da Manhã* (Rio de Janeiro), October 24, 1962; José Luis Salcedo-Bastardo, "Brasil y el bloqueo a Cuba," October 26, 1962, DPI, 1962, EE.UU., Exp 355 (Crisis de los Misiles Cuba–USA), Archivo Ministerio del Poder Popular para Relaciones Exteriores de la República Bolivariana de Venezuela.

25. Telegram, Frank Micelotta, AmEmbassy Rio de Janeiro, to Secretary of State, October 26, 1962, RG 59, CDF 1960–1963, Box 1626, Decimal Folder 737.00/10–2562, NARA.

26. "Reverso: Protesta contra a posição da Chancelaria leva Itamarati á agitação," *Correio da Manhã* (Rio de Janeiro), October 25, 1962. On the Brazilian Women's Campaign for Democracy (Campanha da Mulher pela Democracia), see Chirio, *Politics in Uniform*, 25–26; Martins Cordeiro, *Direitas em Movimento*.

27. "'Premier' (apupado por mulheres) diz que o Brasil apóia bloqueio, mas é contra invasão," *Jornal do Brasil* (Rio de Janeiro), October 25, 1962.

28. "Aumenta en el mundo la repulsa a la provocación de los Yanquis," *Revolución* (Havana), October 25, 1962.

29. "PM dissolveu no Recife comício contra EUA pelo bloqueio a Cuba," *Jornal do Brasil* (Rio de Janeiro), October 25, 1962.

30. "Recife: Violências da polícia contra manisfestantes pró-Cuba," *Última Hora* (Rio de Janeiro), October 25, 1962.

31. Eugene Delgado-Arias, "Weeka No. 18," November 1, 1962, RG 59, CDF 1960–1963, Box 1580, Decimal Folder 732.00/11–162, NARA.

32. "Povo nas ruas da Guanabara enfrenta a polícia e protesta contra bloqueio," *Última Hora* (Rio de Janeiro), October 26, 1962; "Polícia dissolve com gas e "Brucutu" passeata de duas mil pessoas pró-Cuba," *Jornal do Brasil* (Rio de Janeiro), October 26, 1962; John Keppel, "Weeka No. 43," October 30, 1962, RG 59, CDF 1960–1963, Box 1582, Decimal Folder 732.00 (W)/10–262, NARA.

33. "Atacó a balazos a la Policía un grupo de Castristas," *La Prensa* (Buenos Aires), October 24, 1962.

34. "Cometióse una agresión contra EL DIA," *El Día* (La Plata), October 24, 1962, Comisión Provincial por la Memoria, Fondo DIPPBA División Central de Documentación, Registro y Archivo, Mesa Ds, Carpeta Daños, Legajo 1690, La Plata, Argentina.

35. Telegram, Robert McClintock, Buenos Aires, to Department of State, October 25, 1962, RG 59, CDF 1960–1963, Box 1594, Decimal 735.00/10–2562, NARA.

36. "Bombas contra la muestra 'Aliados para el Progreso,'" *La Prensa* (Buenos Aires), October 25, 1962; "Hubo atentados perpetrados por los comunistas," *El Litoral* (Santa Fe), October 25, 1962; "Cometiéronse diversos atentados," *La Prensa* (Buenos Aires), October 26, 1962.

37. Pascual Amendola, "Asunto: comunicar novedades," October 26, 1962, CPM; "Atentado y 'daño,'" October 25, 1962, Comisión Provincial por la Memoria, Fondo DIPPBA División Central de Documentación, Registro y Archivo, Mesa Ds, Carpeta Daños, Legajo 1671, La Plata, Argentina; "Autores ignorados arrojaron bomba 'Molotov' en agencia diario 'Clarín' ubicada en Galeria Nueve de julio y 29 de septiembre originando daños en vidriera," October 24, 1962, Comisión Provincial por la Memoria, Fondo DIPPBA División Central de Documentación, Registro y Archivo, Mesa Ds, Carpeta Daños, Legajo 1689, La Plata, Argentina; "Más atentados se han cometido en Buenos Aires," *El Litoral* (Santa Fe), October 26, 1962.

38. Telegram, Robert McClintock, Buenos Aires, to Secretary of State, October 26, 1962, RG 59, CDF 1960–1963, Box 1594, Decimal 735.00/10–2562, NARA.

39. "Bombas Molotov," *Clarín* (Buenos Aires), October 29, 1962.

40. "Produjéronse disturbios y atentados: Varios detenidos," *Clarín* (Buenos Aires), October 27, 1962; "Adictos a Castro causaron incidentes en Buenos Aires," *El Plata* (La Plata), October 27, 1962; "Cometiéronse diversos atentados con bombas en la Capital Federal," *El Día* (La Plata), October 27, 1962; "Cometiéronse atentados contra varios locales," *La Prensa* (Buenos Aires), October 27, 1962; telegram, Robert McClintock, Buenos Aires, to Secretary of State, October 27, 1962, RG 59, CDF 1960–1963, Box 1594, Decimal 735.00/10–2562, NARA.

41. "HOY función extraordinaria de trasnoche," *La Razón* (Buenos Aires), October 27, 1962.

42. "Terrorismo," *La Razón* (Buenos Aires), October 28, 1962; "Atentados comunistas," *El Mundo* (Buenos Aires), October 29, 1962.

43. Telegram, Robert McClintock, Buenos Aires, to Secretary of State, October 29, 1962, RG 59, CDF 1960–1963, Box 1594, Decimal 735.00/10–2562, NARA.

44. Telegram, Robert McClintock, Buenos Aires, to Secretary of State, October 31, 1962, RG 59, CDF 1960–1963, Box 1594, Decimal 735.00/10–2562, NARA.

45. On the Mothers of the Plaza de Mayo, see Guzman Bouvard, *Revolutionizing Motherhood;* Kelly, *Sovereign Emergencies*, ch. 6.

46. Movimiento Nacionalista Tacuara, "Número extraordinario, órgano oficial del Departamento de Formación del Movimiento Nacionalista Tacuara," No. 11, El Topo Blindado, November 1962, https://eltopoblindado.com/nacionalismo-derecha /decada-1960-nacionalismo-derecha/tacuara/ofensiva-no-11/.

47. Robert McClintock, "Weeka No. 47," November 24, 1962, RG 59, CDF 1960–1963, Box 1596, Decimal 735.00 (W)/11–1762, NARA. On the history of the Tacuara, see Gutman, *Tacuara*, 152–53; Finchelstein, *Ideological Origins*.

48. C. Allan Stewart, "Internal Situation," October 23, 1962, National Security Files, Countries, Box 192, JFK.

49. Gastón Aráoz, untitled report on Venezuelan reaction to Cuban Missile Crisis, October 29, 1962, Embajada de Bolivia en Caracas, 1961–1964, AMREB; "El mundo contra ellos," *Bohemia* (Havana), November 2, 1962.

50. Telegram, C. Allan Stewart, Caracas, to Secretary of State, October 25, 1962, RG 59, CDF 1960–1963, Box 1569, Decimal Folder 731.00/8–162, NARA.

51. Edward T. Long, "Weeka No. 44," November 3, 1962, RG 59, CDF 1960–1963, Box 1571, Decimal Folder 731.00 (W)/7–772, NARA.

52. Telegram, Hernandez, Caracas, to Ministro de Relaciones Exteriores, October 30, 1962, Fondo Paises, VEN 4 (1962), MINRELACIONES Chile; Aráoz, untitled report on Venezuelan reaction to Cuban Missile Crisis, October 29, 1962; "Pánico en Caracas," *Revolución* (Havana), October 27, 1962.

53. Telegram, C. Allan Stewart, Caracas, to Secretary of State, October 27, 1962, RG 59, CDF 1960–1963, Box 1569, Decimal Folder 731.00/8–162, NARA.

54. "No tengo por que negar que es dificil y riesgosa la situación de hoy," *El Nacional* (Caracas), October 28, 1962.

55. CIA, "Amendment to the US Oil Import Program and Venezuelan Petroleum," December 13, 1962, National Security Files, Countries, Box 192, JFK.

56. Long, "Weeka No. 44," November 3, 1962.

57. "Caracas Guards Oil after 4 Red Blasts," *New York Times*, October 29, 1962.

58. "El mundo contra ellos."

59. "Castro dió instrucciones a los comunistas venezolanos para el saboteo de campos petroleros," *La Estrella de Panamá* (Panama City), October 29, 1962; "Castro Orders for Terrorism Intercepted: Link with Oil Fields Sabotage in Venezuela," *The Times* (London), October 30, 1962.

60. "La industria petrolífera venezolana sufre otro acto de sabotaje en la región Oriental," *El Diario* (La Paz), November 4, 1962.

61. "Venezuela pedirá reunión de emergencia de la OEA," *El Nacional* (Caracas), November 6, 1962; "Venezuela denunció ante la OEA a Cuba como responsable de los sabotajes en Maracaibo," *El Nacional* (Caracas), November 10, 1962.

62. "Otra farsa de los lacayos yanquis: Conjura de Venezuela y la OEA contra Cuba," *Revolución* (Havana), November 6, 1962.

63. "Dinamitan instalaciones petroleras en Venezuela: Más de 1 millón de dólares diarios en pérdidas," *Revolución* (Havana), October 29, 1962.

64. Samuel H. Young, "Maracaibo Political Summary: October 23–November 6, 1962," November 8, 1962, RG 59, CDF 1960–1963, Box 1569, Decimal Folder 731.00 /8-162, NARA.

65. "Más de un millón de dólares perdidos en sabotaje a la Creole en Tía Juana," *El Nacional* (Caracas), November 2, 1962.

66. "Frustrado intento de paralizar la industria petrolera," *El Nacional* (Caracas), October 29, 1962; Long, "Weeka No. 44," November 3, 1962.

67. El Directorio de la Federación Departamental de Trabajadores Fabriles de La Paz, "¡Gran manifestación!" October 25, 1962, RG 59, CDF 1960–1963, Box 1561, Decimal Folder 724.00/10-162, NARA.

68. Melville E. Osborne, "Events of October 26," October 30, 1962, 26, RG 59, CDF 1960–1963, Box 1561, Decimal Folder 724.00/10-162, NARA; "Comunicado oficial da cuenta que hubo un saldo de cinco muertos y 24 heridos ayer," *El Diario* (La Paz), October 27, 1962.

69. "Comunistas ensangrentaron la capital," *Presencia* (La Paz), October 27, 1962; Osborne, "Events of October 26." On Escobar and Pimentel, see Field, *From Development to Dictatorship*.

70. "Bandas comunistas y dos radioemisoras cumplieron su propósito de ensangrentar ayer las calles de la ciudad de La Paz," *Última Hora* (La Paz), October 27, 1962.

71. "Sangrienta lucha libraron castristas y anticomunistas: Hubo francotiradores apostados en la Av. Santa Cruz," *El Diario* (La Paz), October 27, 1962; "Comunistas ensangrentaron la Capital."

72. Osborne, "Events of October 26."

73. Telegram, Ben Stephansky, La Paz, to Secretary of State, October 26, 1962, RG 59, CDF 1960–1963, Box 1561, Decimal Folder 724.00/10-162, NARA.

74. Naftali, May, and Zelikow, *Presidential Recordings*, 3:357, timestamp October 27, 1962, 10:05–11:55 a.m.

### Chapter 9

1. Emilio Edwards Bello, report from Chilean embassy in Havana, October 23, 1962, Fondo Paises, CUB 4 (1962), MINRELACIONES Chile; Lewis, Lewis, and Rigdon, *Four Men*, 539. On US warships' visible presence, see Thant, *View from the UN*, 181.

2. Blight and Lang, *Armageddon Letters*, 113.

3. Naftali, May, and Zelikow, *Presidential Recordings*, 3:241, timestamp October 25, 1962, 10:00–11:10 a.m.

4. Diez Acosta, *Octubre de 1962*, 175.

5. Fursenko and Naftali, *One Hell of a Gamble*, 268.

6. Hershberg, "United States, Brazil, and the Cuban Missile Crisis (Part 2)," 33–35.

7. Thant, *View from the UN*, 464.

8. Diez Acosta, *Octubre de 1962*, 175; Fursenko and Naftali, *One Hell of a Gamble*, 268.

9. Blight and Lang, *Armageddon Letters*, 116.

10. Fursenko and Naftali, *One Hell of a Gamble*, 268.

11. Plokhy, *Nuclear Folly*, 203; Blight and Lang, *Armageddon Letters*, 115.

12. Fursenko and Naftali, *One Hell of a Gamble*, 269.

13. Blight, Allyn, and Welch, *Cuba on the Brink*, 107.

14. Dobbs, *One Minute to Midnight*, 159–60; Diez Acosta, *Octubre de 1962*, 176.

15. Soviet Union Embassy in Cuba, "Likelihood of U.S. Invasion of Cuba; Attachment Not Included", October 26, 1962, Cuban Missile Crisis: 50th Anniversary Update, DNSA.

16. Carlos Alzugaray Treto, interview by Renata Keller, July 20, 2022.

17. Blight, Allyn, and Welch, *Cuba on the Brink*, 248–49.

18. Carlos Alzugaray Treto, interview by Renata Keller.

19. Dobbs, *One Minute to Midnight*, 182–83.

20. Blight, Allyn, and Welch, *Cuba on the Brink*, 109.

21. Blight and Lang, *The Armageddon Letters*, 116.

22. Chang and Kornbluh, *The Cuban Missile Crisis*, 199.

23. Dobbs, *One Minute to Midnight*, 178–81.

24. Dobbs, *One Minute to Midnight*, 205–6.

25. Del Valle Jimenez, *Un pueblo invencible*, 55.

26. Dobbs, *One Minute to Midnight*, 238–39.

27. Blight, Allyn, and Welch, *Cuba on the Brink*, 107.

28. Dobbs, *One Minute to Midnight*, 219.

29. Mikoyan, *Soviet Cuban Missile Crisis*, 143.

30. Fursenko and Naftali, *One Hell of a Gamble*, 271.

31. Plokhy, *Nuclear Folly*, 236.

32. Blight, Allyn, and Welch, *Cuba on the Brink*, 119.

33. Plokhy, *Nuclear Folly*, 240–45; Dobbs, *One Minute to Midnight*, 232–33, 236–37; Blight, Allyn, and Welch, *Cuba on the Brink*, 104–5.

34. Naftali, May, and Zelikow, *Presidential Recordings*, 3:388–89, timestamp October 27, 1962.

35. Naftali, May, and Zelikow, *Presidential Recordings*, 3:405, timestamp October 27, 1962, 4:00–7:45 p.m.

36. Naftali, May, and Zelikow, *Presidential Recordings*, 3:115, timestamp October 23, 1962, 10:00–11:03 a.m.

37. Naftali, May, and Zelikow, *Presidential Recordings*, 3:446–47, 461, timestamp October 27, 1962, 4:00–7:45 p.m.

38. Chang and Kornbluh, *Cuban Missile Crisis*, 233–35.

39. Naftali, May, and Zelikow, *Presidential Recordings*, 3:486, timestamp October 27, 1962, 8 p.m.; Robert Kennedy to Dean Rusk, October 30, 1962, President's Office Files, JFK.

40. Plokhy, *Nuclear Folly*, 194.

41. Chang and Kornbluh, *Cuban Missile Crisis*, 195–98.

42. Khrushchev, *Nikita Khrushchev*, 590–91.

43. Walter Lippmann, "Today and Tomorrow," *Washington Post*, October 25, 1962.

44. Chang and Kornbluh, *Cuban Missile Crisis*, 207–9.

45. Blight, Allyn, and Welch, *Cuba on the Brink*, 362. It is unclear exactly when Khrushchev read Castro's letter. Michael Dobbs writes that Khrushchev's aides read him Castro's letter over the phone at 1am Sunday morning. Dobbs, *One Minute to*

*Midnight*, 295. Aleksandr Fursenko and Timothy Naftali claim that even though the reports about the U-2 and Castro's letter arrived at the Kremlin overnight, Khrushchev didn't learn of them until he woke up on Sunday morning. Fursenko and Naftali, *One Hell of a Gamble*, 283. Oleg Troyanovsky, Khrushchev's special assistant, recalls "The letter was received, I think, very early in the morning of the 28th. There was, subsequently, a meeting of the Presidium in the morning of the 28th, immediately after that. They were familiar with that letter already at the meeting." Blight, Allyn, and Welch, *Cuba on the Brink*, 115. James G. Blight and janet M. Lang, along with Nikita Khrushchev's son Sergei, say that Khrushchev learned of Castro's letter during his meeting with the Presidium but before he had drafted his letter to Kennedy. Blight and Lang, *Armageddon Letters*, 121; Khrushchev, *Nikita Khrushchev*, 625–26. Serhii Plokhy says that Khrushchev did not read it until Sunday afternoon, after he had already dictated his radio statement accepting Kennedy's deal. Plokhy, *Nuclear Folly*, 285.

46. Khrushchev, *Nikita Khrushchev*, 608.

47. Blight, Allyn, and Welch, *Cuba on the Brink*, appendix 2, 482–83.

48. Fursenko and Naftali, *One Hell of a Gamble*, 284.

49. Dobrynin, "Dobrynin's Cable."

50. On Khrushchev's meeting with the Presidium, see Dobbs, *One Minute to Midnight*, 321–23. Kennedy never planned to give a television address on Sunday morning; the Soviet report about it had mistaken a re-broadcast of his October 22 speech for a new speech. Plokhy, *Nuclear Folly*, 287–88.

51. Chang and Kornbluh, *Cuban Missile Crisis*, 236–39. On October 28, Washington and Havana were observing the same time, as the United States set its clocks back one hour at 2 a.m. on the morning of October 28. Cuba did not change its clocks for Daylight Saving Time in 1962.

52. Fursenko and Naftali, *One Hell of a Gamble*, 285–87.

53. Blight and Lang, *The Armageddon Letters*, 122.

54. Franqui, *Family Portrait*, 194.

55. Rojo, *My Friend Che*, 134; Bustos, *El Che quiere verte*, 113.

56. Blight, Allyn, and Welch, *Cuba on the Brink*, 214.

57. "Castro Statement," October 28, 1962, General CIA Records, CIA-FOIA, www.cia .gov/readingroom/docs/CIA-RDP79T00428A000200040036-3.pdf; del Valle Jimenez, *Un pueblo invencible*, 65.

58. "Kennedy garantiza que no invadirá a Cuba y bien recordamos Girón; estamos mas alerta que nunca," *Revolución* (Havana), October 29, 1962.

59. Lewis, Lewis, and Rigdon, *Four Men*, 539–40.

60. Karol, *Guerrillas in Power*, 272.

61. Blight and Brenner, *Sad and Luminous Days*, 25.

62. Moore, *Pichón*, 246.

63. Gilly, *Inside the Cuban Revolution*, 54–55.

64. Franqui, *Family Portrait*, 195.

65. Gilly, *Inside the Cuban Revolution*, 57.

66. Plokhy, *Nuclear Folly*, 328.

67. Gadea, *Ernesto*, 226.

68. Message from Acting Secretary-General U Thant to Premier Fidel Castro and Castro's reply, October 26, 1962, S-0872 Box 2 File 7, UN.

69. "Viene U Thant con funcionarios de la ONU; garantia a la soberania de Cuba," *Revolución* (Havana), October 29, 1962.

70. Letter, Acting Secretary-General U Thant to Premier Fidel Castro, October 28, S-0872, Box 2, File 6, UN.

71. "Boletín de Prensa Latina," *Prensa Latina* (Havana), November 2, 1962, José Revueltas Papers Box 96, Folder 3, Nettie Lee Benson Latin American Collection, University of Texas Libraries, Austin, TX.

72. Thant, *View from the UN*, 182; "Memorandum of a Telephone Conversation between Secretary of State Rusk and the Permanent Representative to the United Nations," October 31, 1962, in *Foreign Relations*, 11:324.

73. "Memorandum of a Telephone Conversation," October 31, 1962, 323.

74. Thant, *View from the UN*, 186.

75. Thant, *View from the UN*, 185.

76. Nassif, *U Thant*, 38–48, 39.

77. Del Valle Jimenez, *Un pueblo invencible*, 91–92.

78. Lechuga, *In the Eye of the Storm*, 131.

79. Nassif, *U Thant*, 41.

80. Nassif, *U Thant*, 45 and 47.

81. Del Valle Jimenez, *Un pueblo invencible*, 99.

82. Dorn and Pauk, "Unsung Mediator," 288.

## Chapter 10

1. "Desafío y negociación: fórmula del triunfo de USA en el Caribe," *Primera Plana* (Buenos Aires), November 13, 1962.

2. John Keppel, "Brasilia Weeka 44," November 6, 1962. RG 59, CDF 1960–1963, Box 1582, Decimal Folder 732.00 (W)/10-262, NARA. Keppel described the posters as "blooming" and did not identify the source of the posters.

3. Eberhardt, Matamoros consular report to the State Department, November 5, 1962, RG 59, CDF 1960–1963, Box 1511, Decimal Folder 712.00/10-362, NARA.

4. Telegram, Charles Cole, Santiago, to Secretary of State, November 16, 1962, RG 59, CDF 1960–1963, Box 1626, Decimal Folder 737.00/11-1662, NARA.

5. "¿Por qué el Presidente Kennedy no invocó la Doctrina Monroe?," *Cuba Nueva* (Coral Gables), November 15, 1962.

6. Artemio Diaz Gomez, "Problema de toda América," *El Panamá América* (Panama City), October 30, 1962.

7. "Los organismos internacionales en el último conflicto," *El Mercurio* (Santiago), October 30, 1962.

8. Rusk, *As I Saw It*, 236.

9. Luis Felipe Angell, "Con Cuba, con Fidel, con América Latina," *Boletín de Prensa Latina* (Havana), November 1, 1962.

10. Eduardo H. Galeano, "Cuba, una apuesta contra la muerte," *Marcha* (Montevideo), November 3, 1962.

11. "Day 12, Oct. 27," *13 Days in October*, John F. Kennedy Presidential Library and Museum, accessed January 25, 2025, https://microsites.jfklibrary.org/cmc /oct27/.

12. *Kennedy and Cuba: Operation Mongoose*, National Security Archive, October 3, 2019, https://nsarchive.gwu.edu/briefing-book/cuba/2019-10-03/kennedy-cuba-operation-mongoose.

13. "CIA, Director John McCone, Memorandum for General Marshall S. Carter, 'Urgent,' October 30, 1962," in *Kennedy and Cuba: Operation Mongoose*, National Security Archive, https://nsarchive.gwu.edu/document/19631-national-security-archive-doc-20-cia-director.

14. "La URSS detuvó la guerra!" *La Voz de la Democracia* (Bogotá), November 2, 1962.

15. Douglas Henderson, [Peruvian Reactions to the Cuban Missile Crisis], Lima, October 31, RG 59, CDF 1960–1963, Box 1555, Decimal Folder 723.00/10–362, NARA.

16. Partido Comunista Brasileiro, "Resolução política dos comunistas," *Novos Rumos* (Rio de Janeiro), December 14, 1962.

17. Partido Comunista de la Argentina, *XII Congreso del Partido Comunista de la Argentina*, 6.

18. Partido Comunista de la Capital Federal, "El histórico mensaje de Nikita Khrushchev en defensa de la paz mundial," Fondo Colección 2: Volantes, Carpeta 30: Partido Comunista, Centro de Documentación e Investigación de la Cultura de Izquierdas, Buenos Aires.

19. "La retirada de Kruschev," *La Hora* (Panama City), October 30, 1962.

20. "La Hora en la Voz de América," *La Hora* (Panama City), November 2, 1962.

21. Ricardo Duarte Moncada, "América no puede darle las espaldas a Cuba en este momento," *La Prensa* (Managua), November 1, 1962.

22. "Declaración de los exiliados," *La Razón* (Buenos Aires), October 30, 1962.

23. "El C. Revolucionario Cubano no tomará en consideración los acuerdos de Thant y F. Castro," *La Estrella de Panamá* (Panama City), October 31, 1962.

24. "Summary Record of the 13th Meeting of the Executive Committee of the National Security Council," October 30, 1962, in *Foreign Relations*, 11:303–4.

25. "Summary Record of the 15th Meeting of the Executive Committee of the National Security Council," October 31, 1962, in *Foreign Relations*, 11:333–34.

26. "Daily White House Staff Meeting," October 31, 1962, in *Foreign Relations*, 11:319–20.

27. "Cuba: Primera base militar rusa en América," *Combate* (Santiago), November 1962; Joint Week No. 46, San José, Costa Rica, November 16, 1962, RG 59, CDF 1960–1963, Box 1532, Decimal Folder 718.00(W)/10–462, NARA.

28. Telegram, Emilio Edwards Bello, Chilean embassy, Havana, to Santiago, Chile, November 11, 1962, Fondo Paises, CUB 4 (1962), MINRELACIONES Chile.

29. Priestland, *British Archives on the Cuban Missile Crisis*, 661; Herbert Marchant, report from Havana embassy to British Foreign Office, November 30, 1962.

30. "Summary Record of the 22nd Meeting of the Executive Committee of the National Security Council," November 7, 1962, in *Foreign Relations*, 11:406.

31. "Message from Chairman Khrushchev to President Kennedy," November 20, 1962, in *Foreign Relations*, 11:499.

32. "Summary Record of the 31st Meeting of the Executive Committee of the National Security Council," November 29, 1962, in *Foreign Relations*, 11:542.

33. Amembassy Caracas, "Current Cuban Exile Attitudes in Venezuela," December 5, 1962, RG 59, CDF 1960–1963, Box 1626, Decimal Folder 737.00/12–562, NARA.

34. Edwin Martin, memorandum of conversation with Marcos Falcón Briceño, November 20, 1962, RG 59, CDF 1960–1963, Box 1626, Decimal Folder 737.00/11–2062, NARA.

35. "Declaración del Presidente de la República a 'La Voz de Estados Unidos,'" November 12, 1962, RG 59, CDF 1960–1963, Box 1626, Decimal Folder 737.00/11–1662, NARA.

36. Argueta, *Ramón Villeda Morales*, 200; Bruneau, "Ramón Villeda Morales."

37. "Declaración del Presidente de la República a 'La Voz de Estados Unidos.'"

38. *Informe*, 22.

39. Dan Kurzman, "Honduras Urges Stepup in Oust-Castro Efforts," *Washington Post*, December 1, 1962.

40. "Memorandum of Conversation: Communism, Cuba, and Caribbean Security," November 30, 1962, US State Department Central Files, 1960–1969, Europe and Latin America: Country Files, Honduras 12/62–9/63 Reference Box 105, ProQuest History Vault.

41. Jules Dubois, "Exiles Urged to Unify, Help OAS Free Cuba: President of Honduras Outlines Program," *Chicago Daily Tribune*, December 3, 1962.

42. Edward T. Long, "Joint Weeka No. 44," November 2, 1962, San Jose, Costa Rica, RG 59, CDF 1960–1963, Box 1532, Decimal Folder 718.00(W)/11–262, NARA.

43. On Oduber, see "Costa Rica's Man in the Shadow: Daniel Oduber Quirós," *New York Times*, February 8, 1974.

44. Telegram, Raymond Telles, San Jose, to Secretary of State, November 6, 1962, RG 59, CDF 1960–1963, Box 1626, Decimal Folder 737.00/11–662, NARA.

45. Telegram, Raymond Telles, San Jose, to Secretary of State, November 6, 1962.

46. "Comunicado de la Secretaría General del Partido Liberación Nacional a las fuerzas democráticas del continente Americano," *La Nación* (San José), December 8, 1962.

47. Telegram, Raymond Telles, AmEmbassy San Jose, to Department of State, December 10, 1962, RG 59, CDF 1960–1963, Box 1626, Decimal Folder 737.00/12–1062, NARA.

48. Telegram, Wallace Stuart, Panama City, to Secretary of State, January 7, 1963, RG 59, CDF 1960–1963, Box 1626, Decimal Folder 737.00/1–263, NARA.

49. "Tells Anxiety for Future of Latin America," *Chicago Daily Tribune*, November 4, 1962.

50. Horacio Suárez, "Repercusión crisis cubana," November 12, 1962, Fondo Paises, GUA 2 (1962), MINRELACIONES Chile.

51. Telegram, Department of State to AmEmbassy Guatemala, November 14, 1962, RG 59, CDF 1960–1963, Box 1626, Decimal Folder 737.00/11–1462, NARA.

52. Telegram, John O. Bell, Guatemala City, to Secretary of State," December 28, 1962, RG 59, CDF 1960–1963, Box 1626, Decimal Folder 737.00/12–2862, NARA.

53. Letter, President Somoza to President Kennedy, October 30, 1962, RG 59, CDF 1960–1963, Box 1626, Decimal Folder 737.00/10–3062, NARA.

54. "'Los liberales no toleramos a ningún dictador': L. Somoza," *Novedades* (Managua), November 8, 1962.

55. "Nicaraguan Is for Invasion of Cuba Despite U.S. View," *New York Times*, November 9, 1962.

56. Cabell Phillips, "Venezuelan Links Cuba to Sabotage: Offers O.A.S. Documentary Proof," *New York Times*, November 10, 1962.

## Chapter 11

1. Telegram 1634, Thomas Mann to Secretary of State, December 6, 1961, Papers of Arthur M. Schlesinger, Jr., White House Files, Classified Subject File, WH-41, JFK.

2. "Communism in Latin America," June 29, 1962, NSF, Trips and Conferences, Box 236, JFK.

3. "Salinity and Other Problems," June 30, 1962, NSF, Trips and Conferences, Box 236, JFK.

4. "La Armada de México hace patrullaje," *El Diario* (La Paz), October 28, 1962.

5. Manuel Rangel Escamilla, "Movimiento de Liberación Nacional," November 4, 1962, Dirección Federal de Seguridad, Expediente 11-6-62, Legajo. 9, Hoja 47, Archivo General de la Nación, Mexico City.

6. Telegram, Thomas Mann, Mexico City, to Department of State, November 7, 1962, RG 59, CDF 1960–1963, Box 1512, Decimal Folder 712.001/1–262, NARA.

7. "Meeting between President Johnson and President López Mateos," February 21, 1964, NSF, Mexico, Box 61, Folder 2, Document 34b, Lyndon B. Johnson Presidential Library.

8. "Mexican-Cuban Relations," November 12, 1964, NSF, Mexico, Box 61, Folder 5, Document 39b, Lyndon B. Johnson Presidential Library.

9. On resource nationalism in the Bolivian Revolution, see Young, *Blood of the Earth;* Hines, *Water for All*, ch. 3. On agrarian reform, see Soliz, *Fields of Revolution*. On modernization in Bolivia, see Field, *From Development to Dictatorship*.

10. Wilkie, *Bolivian Revolution*, 43.

11. Field, *From Development to Dictatorship*, 3n9.

12. Field, *From Development to Dictatorship*, ch. 1.

13. Siekmeier, *Bolivian Revolution*, 97–98.

14. Field, *From Development to Dictatorship*, 11; Field, "Bolivia between Washington, Prague, and Havana," 54.

15. Field, "Ideology as Strategy," 153.

16. Field, "Bolivia between Washington, Prague, and Havana," 54.

17. Field, *From Development to Dictatorship*, 63.

18. Melville E. Osborne, "1962 Bolivian Congressional Activities," September 18, 1962, RG 59, CDF 1960–1963, Box 1563, Decimal 724.5/3–460, NARA.

19. Young, *Blood of the Earth*, 85; Field, "Bolivia between Washington, Prague, and Havana," 58–60.

20. Field, *From Development to Dictatorship*, 65.

21. Osborne, Melville E., "Bolivia and the United States Actions Against Cuba," October 30, 1962, RG 59, CDF 1960–1963, Box 1626, Decimal Folder 737.00/10–2562, NARA.

22. Consejo de la Organización de los Estados Americanos, "Acta de la sesión extraordinaria celebrada el 23 de octubre de 1962."

23. Letter, Victor Paz Estenssoro to John F. Kennedy, October 31, 1962, President's Office Files Countries Bolivia Box 112 Folder 2, JFK.

24. Field, "Conflict on High," 132–33.

25. Siekmeier, *Bolivian Revolution*, 98.

26. Schmidli, *Fate of Freedom Elsewhere*, 29–30.

27. Arnaldo Otero, "Una reunión de emergencia de la OEA pide Argentina," *La Prensa* (Buenos Aires), November 3, 1962.

28. "Se aprobó en la OEA la moción argentina," *La Prensa* (Buenos Aires), November 6, 1962.

29. Robert McClintock, "Argentine Posture with Respect to Cuba," November 24, 1962, RG 59, CDF 1960–1963, Box 1626, Decimal Folder 737.00/11–1662, NARA.

30. "Memorandum of Conversation, Call of Argentine Foreign Minister (Carlos Manuel Muniz) on President Kennedy," January 22, 1963, in *Foreign Relations*, 12:406.

31. Robert McClintock, memo on Argentine army training, November 20, 1962, National Security Files, Countries, Box 7, JFK.

32. Telegram about military proposal, Robert McClintock, Buenos Aires, to Secretary of State, November 20, 1962, RG 59, CDF 1960–1963, Box 1597, Decimal 735.5/11–2062, NARA.

33. Telegram about inviting Onganía, Robert McClintock, Buenos Aires, to Secretary of State, November 30, 1962, RG 59, CDF 1960–1963, Box 1597, Decimal 735.5/11–3062, NARA.

34. Telegram, Dean Rusk, Department of State, to AmEmbassy Buenos Aires, December 31, 1962, RG 59, CDF 1960–1963, Box 1597, Decimal 735.5/12–3162, NARA.

35. Míguez and Morgenfeld, "Las relaciones entre Argentina y Cuba," 177; Schmidli, *Fate of Freedom Elsewhere*, 37–38.

36. "Remarks to a Group of Staff Members and Students of the Argentine War College, 1 March 1963," Archives, John F. Kennedy Presidential Library and Museum, accessed January 25, 2025, www.jfklibrary.org/Asset-Viewer/Archives/JFKWHA-168-003.aspx.

37. David O. Byars Jr., "Forces Suggested for Support Under Proposed U.S.-Argentina Bilateral Agreement," January 14, 1963, RG 59, CDF 1960–1963, Box 1597, Decimal 735.5/1–1463, NARA.

38. Schmidli, *Fate of Freedom Elsewhere*, 39.

39. "Ayuda militar EE.UU.-Argentina, memorandum de entendimiento," May 10, 1964, AH/0019, Ministerio de RREE, Fecha 1951/1957/1964, Serie 41-Fondo E, Expediente Ayuda Militar EEUU-Argentina, Archivo de Cancillería Argentina.

40. "Argentina abandona su tradición neutral," *Primera Plana* (Buenos Aires), November 13, 1962.

41. "Memorandum of Conversation, Call of Argentine Foreign Minister," January 22, 1963, 406.

42. Walcher, "Petroleum Pitfalls," 54.

43. Potash, *Army and Politics*, 3:132–33.

44. Ministerio de Relaciones Exteriores y Culto, "Boletín de la Dirección General de Política." AH/0118, Serie 80-OEA y ONU, Expediente Boletines de la Dirección General de Política 1962, Archivo de Cancillería Argentina.

45. Roberto Campos, "SITUAÇÃO POLITICA—CUBA de novembro a dezembro de 1962," November 1, 1962, in *Cold War International History Project Bulletin*, no. 17/18 (2012): 255–61, www.wilsoncenter.org/publication/bulletin-no-1718-fall-2012.

46. Roberto Oliveira Campos, "Telegram from the Brazilian Embassy in Washington," October 31, 1962, in *Cold War International History Project Bulletin*, no. 17/18 (2012): 255, www.wilsoncenter.org/publication/bulletin-no-1718-fall-2012.

47. Telegram about missile crisis, Lincoln Gordon, Rio de Janeiro, to Secretary of State, November 5, 1962, RG 59, CDF 1960–1963, Box 1580, Decimal Folder 732.00/11-162, NARA.

48. Edwin M. Martin, "Brazilian Political Orientation," November 15, 1962, President's Office Files Countries Brazil Box 112 Folder 16, JFK.

49. Lincoln Gordon, report on Brazilian financial situation and political orientation, November 19, 1962, President's Office Files Countries Brazil Box 112 Folder 16, JFK.

50. Gordon, report on Brazilian financial situation.

51. Wellman, "U.S. Government Posture in Existing Political Situation in Brazil," November 30, 1962, RG 59, CDF 1960–1963, Box 1580, Decimal Folder 732.00/11-1962, NARA. Emphasis added.

52. McGeorge Bundy, "NSC Executive Committee Meeting, December 11, 1962, 10:00 a.m., Meeting No. 35," December 11, 1962, CC02728, Cuban Missile Crisis, DNSA.

53. Taffet, *Foreign Aid*, 105; Rabe, *Most Dangerous Area in the World*, 69.

54. Lincoln Gordon, "Memorandum from the Ambassador to Brazil (Gordon) to President Kennedy," undated, in *Foreign Relations*, 12:495–99.

55. Loureiro, "Making the Alliance for Progress," 171. See also Loureiro, *A aliança para o progresso*. On Gordon's leadership in these efforts, see Taffet, *Foreign Aid*, 110.

56. Chirio, *Politics in Uniform*, 25.

57. Walters, *Silent Missions*, 377.

58. Chirio, *Politics in Uniform*, 25, 35. For a detailed analysis of Operation Brother Sam, including scans of U.S. plans, see Fico, *O grande irmão*.

59. Walters, *Silent Missions*, 389.

## Chapter 12

1. "Leonel Brizola acusa: URSS usou Cuba como instrumento da 'Guerra Fria,'" *Última Hora* (Rio de Janeiro), October 30, 1962.

2. "Leonel de Moura Brizola," CPDOC—Centro de Pesquisa e Documentação de História Contemporânea do Brasil, accessed January 25, 2025, www18.fgv.br/CPDOC /acervo/dicionarios/verbete-biografico/leonel-de-moura-brizola.

3. Juan de Onis, "Cuban Bases Jar Brazil's Leftists: Brizola Says Soviet Used Castro Regime to Serve Own Ends in Cold War," *New York Times*, October 31, 1962.

4. "Leonel de Moura Brizola."

5. "Inesperada declaración: Denuncia brasileña al colonialismo soviético," *La Prensa* (Managua), November 1, 1961; de Onis, "Cuba Bases Jar Brazil's Leftists."

6. Luiz Leivas Bastian Pinto, "Telegram from the Brazilian Embassy in Havana about Negotiations," November 9, 1962, in *Cold War International History Project Bulletin*, no. 17/18 (2012): 268, www.wilsoncenter.org/publication/bulletin-no-1718-fall-2012.

7. "Cuba: Traicionada por Khrushchev y estrangulada por Kennedy," *Izquierda Nacional* (Buenos Aires), November 1962. "Cipayo," or sepoy, is a derogatory term used to describe a local person who serves foreign interests. On *Izquierda Nacional* and the missile crisis, see Ribadero, *Tiempo de profetas*, 229-39.

8. "Manifiesto de la IV Internacional sobre la amenaza imperialista al estado obrero cubano," *Boletín Trotskista* (Buenos Aires), November 1962.

9. "Ni bases yankis ni soviéticas," *Marcha* (Montevideo), November 3, 1962.

10. Kneeland, report from Guadalajara to Department of State, October 31, 1962, RG 59, CDF 1960-1963, Box 1511, Decimal Folder 712.00/10-362, NARA.

11. Maurice M. Bernbaum, "Cuba Series, June-December 1962," December 14, 1962, RG 59, CDF 1960-1963, Box 1626, Decimal Folder 737.00/11-1662, NARA.

12. CIA, "The Crisis USSR/Cuba: Information as of 0600, 2 November 1962," CU00993, Cuban Missile Crisis Revisited, DNSA.

13. Director of Central Intelligence, "Situation and Prospects in Cuba: National Intelligence Estimate 85-63," June 14, 1963, National Security Files, National Intelligence Estimates, Box 9, Lyndon B. Johnson Presidential Library.

14. US Information Agency, "Informal Assessment of Extent and Impact of Castro-Communist Propaganda Efforts in Latin America," March 27, 1963, CC03020, Cuban Missile Crisis, DNSA.

15. Nercesian, *La política en armas*, 132.

16. Bernbaum, "Cuba Series, June-December 1962." On the effects of the Sino-Soviet split in Ecuador, see Becker, *CIA in Ecuador*, 248.

17. CIA Directorate of Intelligence, "The Sino-Soviet Struggle in Cuba and the Latin American Communist Movement," November 1, 1963, CAESAR, POLO, and ESAU Papers, CIA-FOIA, www.cia.gov/readingroom/docs/esau-22.pdf.

18. Degregori, "Return to the Past," 34-35.

19. Anderson, *Che Guevara*, 548.

20. Quirk, *Fidel Castro*, 449.

21. Gilly, *Inside the Cuban Revolution*, 57.

22. Friedman, *Shadow Cold War*, 93.

23. Brown, *Cuba's Revolutionary World*, 319.

24. CIA Directorate of Intelligence, "Sino-Soviet Struggle in Cuba."

25. González, *Paisanos Chinos*, 121-32; Zolov, *Last Good Neighbor*, 227-28.

26. CIA Directorate of Intelligence, "Sino-Soviet Struggle in Cuba." On Chinese efforts to use the missile crisis for propaganda gains in Africa and Asia, see Friedman, *Shadow Cold War*, 96-97; Brown, *Cuba's Revolutionary World*, 90-91.

27. Fardella, "Mao Zedong and the 1962 Cuban Missile Crisis," 83.

28. CIA Directorate of Intelligence, "Sino-Soviet Struggle in Cuba."

29. CIA Directorate of Intelligence, "Sino-Soviet Struggle in Cuba."

30. Spenser, "Caribbean Crisis," 100.

31. Spenser, "Operation Manuel."

32. Mikoyan, *Soviet Cuban Missile Crisis*, 156.

33. Mikoyan, *Soviet Cuban Missile Crisis*, 162.

34. Mikoyan, *Soviet Cuban Missile Crisis*, 173.

35. "Mikoyan's Mission to Havana," 93-94

36. "Mikoyan's Mission to Havana," 94-101.

37. "Memorandum of A. I. Mikoyan's Conversation with Comrades F. Castro, O. Dorticós, E. Guevara, E. Aragonés, and C.R. Rodriguez," November 22, 1962. National Security Archive, https://nsarchive2.gwu.edu/NSAEBB/NSAEBB393/docs /Mikoyan%20Castro%20memcon%2011%2022%2062.pdf.

38. "New Book Shows Crisis Unresolved until November 22, 1962," book release announcement for Sergo Mikoyan's *The Soviet Cuban Missile Crisis: Castro, Mikoyan, Kennedy, Khruschev, and the Missiles of November,* edited by Svetlana Savranskaya, "50 Years: Cuban Missile Crisis," October 10, 2012, National Security Archive, https://nsarchive2.gwu.edu/NSAEBB/NSAEBB393/.

39. "Mikoyan's Mission to Havana," 105–9.

40. On Latin Americans' use of international law, see Lorca, *Mestizo International Law*; Scarfi, *The Hidden History*.

41. "Mikoyan's Mission to Havana," 105–9.

42. Mikoyan, *Soviet Cuban Missile Crisis,* 218.

43. "New Book Shows Crisis Unresolved."

44. "Memorandum of A. I. Mikoyan's Conversation with Comrades F. Castro, O. Dorticós, E. Guevara, E. Aragonés, and C. R. Rodriguez," November 22, 1962, National Security Archive, https://nsarchive2.gwu.edu/NSAEBB/NSAEBB393/docs /Mikoyan%20Castro%20memcon%2011%2022%2062.pdf.

45. Fursenko and Naftali, *One Hell of a Gamble,* 315.

46. "From Havana to the Foreign Office," November 24, 1962, in Priestland, *British Archives,* 532–33.

47. Karol, *Guerrillas in Power,* 273–74.

48. Franqui, *Family Portrait,* 197.

49. Mikoyan, *Soviet Cuban Missile Crisis,* 515.

50. CIA Directorate of Intelligence, "The Sino-Soviet Struggle in Cuba and the Latin American Communist Movement."

51. CIA Directorate of Intelligence, "The Sino-Soviet Struggle in Cuba and the Latin American Communist Movement."

52. "Speech by F. Castro at the Cocktail Party on April 28," in Svetlana Savranskaya, "Fidel Castro's Victory Tour: New Evidence from Russian Archives," Briefing Book #859, National Security Archive, April 29, 2024, https://nsarchive .gwu.edu/briefing-book/russia-programs/2024-04-29/fidel-castros-victory-tour-new -evidence-russian-archives.

53. "Nikita Hurls New War Threat: Blow at Cuba Is Attack on Us, He Warns," *Chicago Tribune,* May 24, 1963.

54. "Record on Conversation between N. S. Khrushchev and F. Castro," May 26, 1963, in Savranskaya, "Fidel Castro's Victory Tour"; "Stenographic Record of Session of Presidium of the CC CPSU on Agenda Item I, II 'N. S. Khrushchev Report on Conversations with F. Castro during Visit in the South of the Country and the Trip to Yaroslavl,'" June 7, 1963, in Savranskaya, "Fidel Castro's Victory Tour."

55. George Arfeld, "Soviet Arms Supreme, Castro Tells Cuba," *Washington Post,* June 6, 1963.

56. Rojo, *My Friend Che,* 134.

57. On Guevara's speech in Algiers and the decision to go to Zaire, see Gleijeses, *Conflicting Missions,* 104–5.

58. Blight and Brenner, *Sad and Luminous Days*, xvi.

59. Llovio-Menéndez, *Insider*, 112–13.

60. Llovio-Menéndez, *Insider*, 112–16.

61. Blight and Brenner, *Sad and Luminous Days*, xxi–xxiv.

62. Blight and Brenner, *Sad and Luminous Days*, 36, 45, 41, 42, 49, 53.

63. Blight and Brenner, *Sad and Luminous Days*, 58.

64. Blight and Brenner, *Sad and Luminous Days*, 61–67.

65. Castro Ruz and Ramonet, *Fidel Castro*, 287.

66. Blight and Brenner, *Sad and Luminous Days*, 93.

## Epilogue

1. Donald Johnston, "Brasil pide que América Latina sea zona libre de armas atómicas," *El Panamá América* (Panama City), October 30, 1962; "Brasil pide medidas urgentes para hacer de Latinoamérica una zona desnuclearizada," *El Nacional* (Caracas), November 9, 1962; William N. Oatis, "Plan for Latin Nuclear-Free Zone Shelved in UN at Brazil's Request: Postponement Unopposed Seek to Cut Tension," *Washington Post*, November 20, 1962.

2. "The Road to Survival," Panama City Televisora Nacional (in Spanish), October 31, 1962, in US Foreign Broadcast Information Service, "Daily Report . . . No. 213." On the ideals behind the push to create a nuclear weapons–free zone in Latin America, see Musto, "'Desire So Close,'"160–74.

3. Luiz Leivas Bastian Pinto, "Telegram from the Brazilian Embassy in Havana," November 14, 1962, in *Cold War International History Project Bulletin*, no. 17/18 (2012): 273 www.wilsoncenter.org/publication/bulletin-no-1718-fall-2012.

4. Raúl Roa to Cuban UN Mission, "Cable cifrado número 748 de Raúl Roa al embajador Carlos Lechuga," November 20, 1962, in *Conferencia internacional "La Crisis de Octubre: Una visión política 40 años después" Documentos de los archivos cubanos*, 2a Carpeta, Centro Fidel Castro Ruz, Havana, Cuba.

5. Dean Rusk, "Brazilian Proposal for Latin American Denuclearized Zone," November 10, 1962, President's Office Files Countries Brazil Box 112 Folder 16, JFK.

6. "Memorandum para el Doctor Anibal Dao, Encargado del Ministerio de Relaciones Exteriores," November 16, 1962, DPI, 1962, EE.UU., Exp 355 (Crisis de los Misiles Cuba–USA), Archivo Ministerio del Poder Popular para Relaciones Exteriores de la República Bolivariana de Venezuela. My thanks to Gustavo Salcedo for sharing this document.

7. Oatis, "Plan for Latin Nuclear-Free Zone Shelved."

8. Afonso Arinos de Melo Franco, "Telegram from the Brazilian Delegation at the United Nations," November 2, 1962, in *Cold War International History Project Bulletin*, no. 17/18 (2012): 262, www.wilsoncenter.org/publication/bulletin-no-1718-fall-2012.

9. On Argentina's nuclear ambitions, see Dunlap, "Parallel Power Play."

10. Vicente Sánchez Gavito, "Letter from Mexican Ambassador to the Organization of American States to Mexican Foreign Minister," November 14, 1962, in *Cold War International History Project Bulletin*, no. 17/18 (2012): 210–12, www.wilsoncenter.org/publication/bulletin-no-1718-fall-2012.

11. Hunt, *The Nuclear Club*, 178.

12. Mateos and Suárez-Díaz, "'We Are Not a Rich Country,'" 251.

13. Alfonso García Robles, "La desnuclearización de la América Latina," 323.

14. Robles, "La desnuclearización de la América Latina," 326.

15. Robles, "La desnuclearización de la América Latina," 329–30. Dawood and Herz, "Nuclear Governance in Latin America." On Brazil's nuclear ambitions, see Spektor, "Evolution of Brazil's Nuclear Intentions," 639; Patti, *Brazil in the Global Nuclear Order*.

16. Hunt, *Nuclear Club*, 250; J. Luis Rodriguez, "Mexican Leadership in Addressing Nuclear Risks, 1962–1968," *Sources and Methods: Wilson Center History and Public Policy Program* (blog), January 10, 2023, www.wilsoncenter.org/blog-post/mexican -leadership-addressing-nuclear-risks-1962-1968; Serrano, *Common Security*.

# Bibliography

**PRIMARY SOURCES**
**Archives and Libraries**

ARGENTINA

Archivo Histórico de la Cancillería Argentina, Buenos Aires
    AH/0256 Departamento de América del Sur, 1962/1966
    AH/0118 Serie 80-OEA y ONU
Archivo Intermedio del Archivo General de la Nación, Buenos Aires
    Inspección General de Justicia, Registro de Asociaciones Civiles
    Consejo Supremo de las Fuerzas Armadas Archivo Judicial Militar
Biblioteca del Congreso Nacional, Buenos Aires
    Hemeroteca
Biblioteca Nacional Mariano Moreno, Buenos Aires
    Fondo Alicia Eguren-John William Cooke
    Fondo Rogelio Garcia Lupo
    Fondo Fernando Nadra
Centro de Documentación e Investigación de la Cultura de Izquierdas, Buenos Aires
    Fondo Max Sztrum
    Fondo Roberto Baschetti
    Fondo Colección 2 Volantes
Comisión Provincial por la Memoria, División Central de Documentación, Registro
    y Archivo, Mar del Plata
    Fondo DIPPBA
    Mesa Ds, Carpeta Daños, Legajo 1671
    Mesa Ds, Carpeta Varios, Legajo 1689
    Mesa Ds, Carpeta Varios, Legajo 1690
    Mesa C, Carpeta Varios, Legajo 207

BOLIVIA

Archivo y Biblioteca Nacional, Sucre
    Revistas Bolivianas
    Fondo Walter Guevara Arze
    Fondo Presidencia de la República
Archivo del Ministerio de Relaciones Exteriores de Bolivia, La Paz
    Embajada de Bolivia en Bogotá, 1962
    Embajada de Bolivia en Rio de Janeiro, 1962
    Embajada de Bolivia en Ecuador, 1961-1965
    Embajada de Bolivia en Argentina, 1962
    Embajada de Bolivia en Caracas, 1961-1964
    Embajada de Bolivia en Estados Unidos, 1962
Biblioteca del Congreso, La Paz
    Hemeroteca

CHILE
Archivo General Histórico del Ministerio de Relaciones Exteriores de Chile, Santiago
    Fondo Países, BRA
    Fondo Países, CUB
    Fondo Países, ECU
    Fondo Países, GUA
    Fondo Países, HON
    Fondo Países, MEX
    Fondo Países, NIC
    Fondo Países, PAN
    Fondo Países, PAR
    Fondo Países, URU
    Fondo Países, VEN
Biblioteca Nacional, Santiago
    Hemeroteca

COLOMBIA
Biblioteca Nacional, Bogotá
    Hemeroteca
Biblioteca del Banco de la República, Bogotá
    Hemeroteca

CUBA
Biblioteca de la Casa de las Américas, Havana
    Hemeroteca
Centro Fidel Castro Ruz, Biblioteca Sierra Maestra, Havana
Instituto de Historia de Cuba, Havana
    Fondo Crisis de Octubre
Prensa Latina, Havana
    Fototeca

FRANCE
Centre des Archives diplomatiques du ministère des Affaires étrangères, La Courneuve

GUATEMALA
Centro de Investigaciones Regionales de Mesoamérica, Antigua
    Fondo *El Imparcial*

MEXICO
Archivo General de la Nación, Mexico City
    Grupo Documental Dirección Federal de Seguridad
Archivo Histórico Genaro Estrada, Secretaría de Relaciones Exteriores, Mexico City
Biblioteca Lerdo de Tejada, Mexico City
    Hemeroteca

PANAMA
Acervo Histórico Diplomático de Panamá, Panama City
Biblioteca Nacional, Panama City

Hemeroteca
Biblioteca de la Autoridad del Canal de Panamá, Panama City
   Hemeroteca
Biblioteca Simón Bolívar, Universidad de Panamá, Panama City
   Hemeroteca

UNITED STATES
Howard Gotlieb Archival Research Center, Boston University
   Department of Special Collections, Tad Szulc
John F. Kennedy Presidential Library, Boston
   Papers of Arthur M. Schlesinger, Jr., White House Files
   National Security Files, Countries
   President's Office Files, Countries
Latin American Library, Tulane University, New Orleans
   deLesseps S. Morrison Collection
Lyndon B. Johnson Presidential Library, Austin
   National Security Files, Countries
   National Security Files, National Intelligence Estimates
Organization of American States Columbus Memorial Library, Washington DC
United Nations Archive, New York City
University of Texas Libraries, Austin, Texas
   Nettie Lee Benson Latin American Collection
US National Archives, College Park, Maryland
   Record Group 59: General Records of the Department of State
   Record Group 306: United States Information Agency

URUGUAY
Archivo del Ministerio de Relaciones Exteriores de Uruguay

VENEZUELA
Archivo del Ministerio del Poder Popular para Relaciones Exteriores de la República
   Bolivariana de Venezuela

## Interviews by the Author
Carlos Alzugaray Treto (via Zoom), July 20, 2022
Edmundo Desnoes (via email), November 7, 2017
Gustavo Salcedo (via email), November 20, 2023

## Online Primary Source Collections
Biblioteca Nacional de Brazil, Hemeroteca Digital, https://bndigital.bn.gov.br
   /hemeroteca-digital/
CIA Freedom of Information Act Electronic Reading Room, www.cia.gov/readingroom
   Bay of Pigs Release, www.cia.gov/readingroom/collection/bay-pigs-release
   CAESAR, POLO, and ESAU Papers, www.cia.gov/readingroom/collection
      /caesar-polo-and-esau-papers
   General CIA Records, www.cia.gov/readingroom/collection/general-cia-records
Centro de Pesquisa e Documentação de História Contemporânea do Brasil

Dicionários Histórico-Biográficos, https://cpdoc.fgv.br/acervo/dicionarios
Digital Library of the Caribbean, www.dloc.com/
    Caribbean Newspapers Collection, www.dloc.com/collections/cndl
Digital National Security Archive, https://nsarchive.gwu.edu/dnsa
    Cuban Missile Crisis: 50th Anniversary Update
    The Cuban Missile Crisis, 1962
    The Cuban Missile Crisis Revisited: An International Collection of Documents,
        from the Bay of Pigs to the Brink of Nuclear War
University of Central Florida Digital Library
    PRISM: Political and Rights Issues and Social Movements,
        https://stars.library.ucf.edu/prism/
Wilson Center Digital Archive, https://digitalarchive.wilsoncenter.org/

## Periodicals

*Bohemia* (Havana)
*Chicago Tribune*
*Chicago Daily Tribune*
*Clarín* (Buenos Aires)
*Combate* (Santiago)
*El Comercio* (Quito)
*Correio da Manhã* (Rio de Janeiro)
*Crítica* (San José)
*Cuba Nueva* (Coral Gables)
*El Día* (La Plata)
*El Diario* (La Paz)
*Época* (Montevideo)
*El Espectador* (Bogotá)
*La Estrella de Panamá* (Panama City)
*Excélsior* (Mexico City)
*Folha de São Paulo*
*Foreign Affairs* (New York City)
*La Hora* (Panama City)
*El Imparcial* (Guatemala City)
*Izquierda Nacional* (Buenos Aires)
*Jornal do Brasil* (Rio de Janeiro)
*Jornal do Comércio* (Rio de Janeiro)
*Life en Español*
*El Litoral* (Santa Fe)
*Los Angeles Times*
*Marcha* (Montevideo)
*El Mercurio* (Santiago)
*El Mundo* (Buenos Aires)

*La Nación* (Buenos Aires)
*La Nación* (La Paz)
*El Nacional* (Caracas)
*The New York Times*
*Noticias de Hoy* (Havana)
*Novedades* (Managua)
*Novos Rumos* (Rio de Janeiro)
*El Panamá America* (Panama City)
*Panama Star and Herald* (Panama City)
*Panama Tribune* (Panama City)
*Política* (Mexico City)
*La Prensa* (Buenos Aires)
*La Prensa* (Managua)
*Presencia* (La Paz)
*Primera Plana* (Buenos Aires)
*La Razón* (Buenos Aires)
*La República* (Bogotá)
*Revista de La Escuela Superior de Guerra*
    (Buenos Aires)
*Revolución* (Havana)
*El Siglo* (Bogotá)
*El Tiempo* (Bogotá)
*Última Hora* (La Paz)
*Última Hora* (Rio de Janeiro)
*U.S. Naval Institute Proceedings*
    (Annapolis)
*La Voz de la Democracia* (Bogotá)
*The Washington Post*

## Published Primary Sources

Andrew, Christopher, and Vasili Mitrokhin. *The World Was Going Our Way: The KGB
    and the Battle for the Third World.* New York: Basic Books, 2005.

Blanco Muñoz, Agustín. *La Lucha armada: Hablan seis comandantes.* Testimonios
violentos no. 3. Caracas: Universidad Central de Venezuela, 1981.
———. *La Lucha armada: La izquierda revolucionaria insurge.* Testimonios
violentos no. 5. Caracas: Universidad Central de Venezuela, 1981.
Bolender, Keith. *Voices from the Other Side: An Oral History of Terrorism against
Cuba.* London: Pluto Press, 2010.
Bustos, Ciro. *El Che quiere verte: La historia jamás contada del Che en Bolivia.*
Buenos Aires: Javier Vergara Editores, 2007.
Campos, Roberto. *A lanterna na popa.* Rio de Janeiro: Topbook, 1994.
Castro, Fidel. *La historia me absolverá.* Havana: Editora Política, 1964.
Castro Ruz, Fidel. "Documento 3: Fragmentos de la intervención del Comandante
en Jefe Fidel Castro en el Pleno del Comité Central del Partido Comunista de
Cuba, 25-26 de enero de 1968." In *La crisis de Octubre,* edited by Yahima Rosaenz
León, 114-33. Havana: Alejandro Ediciones, 2022.
Castro Ruz, Fidel, and Ignacio Ramonet. *Fidel Castro: My Life, A Spoken
Autobiography.* Translated by Andrew Hurley. New York: Scribner, 2006.
Chang, Laurence, and Peter Kornbluh, eds. *The Cuban Missile Crisis, 1962: A
National Security Archive Documents Reader.* Rev. ed. New York: The New Press,
1998.
Consejo de la Organización de los Estados Americanos. "Acta de la sesión
extraordinaria celebrada el 23 de octubre de 1962." *Actas de las sesiones* 42 (1962):
iii-33.
———. "Acta de la sesión ordinaria celebrada el 9 de octubre de 1962." *Actas de las
sesiones* 42 (1962): ii-119.
*Construyendo caminos: Tres documentos históricos de la guerrilla guatemalteca.*
Guatemala City: Centro Rolando Morán, 2008.
Corvalán, Luis. *De lo vivido y lo peleado: Memorias.* Santiago: LOM ediciones, 1997.
Desnoes, Edmundo. *Memories of Underdevelopment: A Novel from Cuba.* Translated
by Al Schaller. Pittsburgh: Latin American Literary Review Press, 2004.
Fonseca, Carlos. *Long Live Sandino.* Managua: Department of Propaganda and
Political Education of the FSLN, 1984.
*Foreign Relations of the United States, 1961-1963.* Vol. 10, *Cuba, January 1961-
September 1962,* edited by Louis J. Smith. Washington, DC: US Government
Printing Office, 1997.
*Foreign Relations of the United States, 1961-1963.* Vol. 11, *Cuban Missile Crisis and
Aftermath,* edited by Edward C. Keefer, Charles S. Sampson, and Louis J. Smith.
Washington, DC: US Government Printing Office, 1996.
*Foreign Relations of the United States, 1961-1963.* Vol. 12, *American Republics,*
edited by Edward C. Keefer, Harriet Dashiell Schwar, and W. Taylor Fain III.
Washington, DC: US Government Printing Office, 1996.
Franqui, Carlos. *Family Portrait with Fidel.* Translated by Alfred MacAdam. New
York: Random House, 1984.
Frente de Liberación Nacional (Peru). *El FLN, el PCP y la revolución peruana.* Lima:
Ediciones "Liberación Nacional," 1964.
Gadea, Hilda. *Ernesto: A Memoir of Che Guevara.* Translated by Carmen Molina and
Walter I. Bradbury. New York: Doubleday, 1972.

Gilly, Adolfo. *Inside the Cuban Revolution*. Translated by Felix Gutierrez. New York: Monthly Review Press, 1964.

Hershberg, James G., and Christian F. Ostermann, eds. "The Global Cuban Missile Crisis at 50." Special issue, *Cold War International History Project Bulletin* 17/18 (Fall 2012). www.wilsoncenter.org/publication/bulletin-no-1718-fall-2012.

*Informe que el excelentísimo Señor Doctor Ramón Villeda Morales, presidente constitucional de la república, presenta al soberano Congreso Nacional.* Tegucigalpa, Honduras: [Ministerio de la Presidencia, Oficina de Información], 1962.

Kennedy, Robert F. *Thirteen Days: A Memoir of the Cuban Missile Crisis*. 2nd ed. New York: W. W. Norton, 1999.

Khrushchev, Sergei N. *Nikita Khrushchev and the Creation of a Superpower*. Translated by Shirley Benson. University Park: Pennsylvania State University Press, 2000.

King H., Thelma. *El problema de la soberanía en las relaciones entre Panamá y los Estados Unidos de América*. Panama: Ministerio de Educación de Panamá, 1961.

Kornbluh, Peter, ed. *Bay of Pigs Declassified: The Secret CIA Report on the Invasion of Cuba*. New York: New Press, 1998.

Larson, David. L., ed. *"The Cuban Crisis" of 1962: Selected Documents and Chronology*. Boston: Houghton Mifflin, 1963.

Lechuga, Carlos. *In the Eye of the Storm: Castro, Khrushchev, Kennedy, and the Missile Crisis*. Melbourne: Ocean Press, 1995.

Lima, Hermes. *Travessia (Memórias)*. Rio de Janeiro: Jose Olympio Editora, 1974.

Llovio-Menéndez, José Luis. *Insider: My Hidden Life as a Revolutionary in Cuba*. Toronto: Bantam Books, 1988.

*Los presidentes de México: Discursos políticos 1910–1988*. Vol. 4. Mexico City: El Colegio de México, 1988.

Martin, John Bartlow. *Overtaken by Events: The Dominican Crisis from the Fall of Trujillo to the Civil War*. New York: Doubleday, 1966.

Matos, Huber. *Cómo llegó la noche: Memorias*. Barcelona: Tusquets Editores, 2002.

May, Ernest, and Philip D. Zelikow, eds. *The Kennedy Tapes: Inside the White House During the Cuban Missile Crisis*. New York: W. W. Norton, 2002.

Melo Franco, Afonso Arinas. *Planalto*. Rio de Janeiro: Jose Olympio Editora, 1968.

Mikoyan, Sergo. *The Soviet Cuban Missile Crisis: Castro, Mikoyan, Kennedy, Khrushchev, and the Missiles of November*. Edited by Svetlana Savranskaya. Washington, D.C. and Stanford: Woodrow Wilson Center Press and Stanford University Press, 2012.

"Mikoyan's Mission to Havana: Cuban-Soviet Negotiations, November 1962." *Cold War International History Project Bulletin* 5 (Spring 1995): 93–109. www.wilsoncenter.org/publication/bulletin-no-5-spring-1995.

Moore, Carlos. *Pichón: Race and Revolution in Castro's Cuba: A Memoir*. Chicago: Lawrence Hill Books, 2008.

Naftali, Timothy, Ernest R. May, and Philip Zelikow, eds. *The Presidential Recordings: John F. Kennedy; The Great Crises*. Vol. 2, *1 September 1962–21 October 1962*, edited by Timothy Naftali and Philip Zelikow. New York: W. W. Norton, 2001.

———, eds. *The Presidential Recordings: John F. Kennedy; The Great Crises*. Vol. 3, 22 *October 1962–28 October 1962*, edited by Philip Zelikow and Ernest R. May. New York: W. W. Norton, 2001.

Nassif, Ramses. *U Thant in New York, 1961–1971: A Portrait of the Third UN Secretary General*. New York: St. Martin's Press, 1988.

Neruda, Pablo. *Confieso que he vivido: Memorias*. Barcelona: Editorial Seix Barral, 1974.

Partido Comunista de la Argentina. *XII Congreso del Partido Comunista de la Argentina*. Buenos Aires: Editorial Anteo, 1963.

*Presencia internacional de Adolfo López Mateos*. Volume 1. Mexico City: Talleres Gráficos de la Nación, 1963.

Priestland, Jane, ed. *British Archives on the Cuban Missile Crisis 1962*. London: Archival Publications International Limited, 2001.

Quadros, Jânio. "Brazil's New Foreign Policy," *Foreign Affairs* 40, no. 1 (October 1961): 19–27.

Robles, Alfonso García. "La desnuclearización de la América Latina." *Foro Internacional* 6, no. 2/3 (22–23) (1965): 323–40.

Rojo, Ricardo. *My Friend Ché*. Translated by Julian Casart. New York: Dial Press, 1968.

Rusk, Dean. *As I Saw It*. New York: W. W. Norton, 1990.

Salinas Price, Hugo. *Mis años con Elektra: Memorias*. Mexico City: Editorial Diana, 2000.

Schlesinger, Arthur. *The Letters of Arthur Schlesinger, Jr.* Edited by Andrew Schlesinger, Stephen C. Schlesinger, and Arthur Schlesinger. New York: Random House, 2013.

Somoza, Anastasio, and Jack Cox. *Nicaragua traicionada: Según fue relatado personalmente por el expresidente SOMOZA a Jack Cox*. Belmont: Western Islands Publishers, 1980.

Talbott, Strobe, ed. *Khrushchev Remembers*. Boston: Little, Brown, 1970.

Thant, U. *View from the UN*. Garden City, NY: Doubleday, 1978.

United Nations. *Yearbook of the United Nations 1962*. New York: United Nations Office of Public Information, 1964.

US Foreign Broadcast Information Service. "Daily Report: Foreign Radio Broadcasts. No. 207." October 23, 1962. Google Books.

———. "Daily Report: Foreign Radio Broadcasts, No. 208." October 24, 1962. Google Books.

———. "Daily Report: Foreign Radio Broadcasts, No. 209." October 25, 1962. Google Books.

———. "Daily Report: Foreign Radio Broadcasts, No. 210." October 26, 1962. Google Books.

———. "Daily Report: Foreign Radio Broadcasts, No. 213." October 31, 1962. Google Books.

Walters, Vernon A. *Silent Missions*. Garden City, NY: Doubleday, 1978.

Ydígoras Fuentes, Miguel. *My War with Communism, as Told to Mario Rosenthal*. Englewood Cliffs, NJ: Prentice-Hall, 1963.

## SECONDARY SOURCES

Alexander, Robert J. *Rómulo Betancourt and the Transformation of Venezuela*. New Brunswick, NJ: Transaction Books, 1982.

———. *The Communist Party of Venezuela*. Stanford: Hoover Institution Press, 1969.

———. *Venezuela's Voice for Democracy: Conversations and Correspondence with Rómulo Betancourt*. New York: Praeger, 1990.

Allison, Graham T. *Essence of Decision: Explaining the Cuban Missile Crisis*. Boston: Little, Brown, 1971.

Anderson, Jon Lee. *Che Guevara: A Revolutionary Life*. New York: Grove Press, 1997.

Aparicio, Fernando, Roberto García Ferreira, and Mercedes Terra. *Espionaje y política: Guerra fría, inteligencia policial y anticomunismo en el sur de América Latina, 1947–1961*. Montevideo: Ediciones B, 2013.

Argueta, Mario R. *Ramón Villeda Morales: Luces y sombras de una primavera política*. Tegucigalpa: Editorial Guaymuras, 2009.

Aslanian, Sebouh David, Joyce E. Chaplin, Ann McGrath, and Kristin Mann. "AHR Conversation: How Size Matters: The Question of Scale in History." *American Historical Review* 118, no. 5 (2013): 1431–72.

Báez, Luis. "Crónica de un testigo sobre la visita de Fidel a Venezuela hace 50 Años." *Cubadebate*, January 22, 2009. www.cubadebate.cu/opinion/2009/01/22 /cronica-de-un-testigo-sobre-la-visita-de-fidel-a-venezuela-hace-50-anos/.

Bayard de Volo, Lorraine. "Masculinity and the Cuban Missile Crisis: Gender as Pre-Emptive Deterrent." *International Affairs* 98, no. 4 (2022): 1211–29.

Bayly, C. A., Sven Beckert, Matthew Connelly, Isabel Hofmeyr, Wendy Kozol, and Patricia Seed. "AHR Conversation: On Transnational History." *American Historical Review* 111, no. 5 (December 2006): 1441–64.

Becker Lorca, Arnulf. *Mestizo International Law: A Global Intellectual History 1842–1933*. Cambridge: University Press, 2014.

Becker, Marc. *The CIA in Ecuador*. Durham, NC: Duke University Press, 2020.

Bermúdez, Jorge R. *La imagen constante: El cartel cubano del Siglo XX*. Havana: CITMATEL and Cubaliteraria, 2019.

Blanco Muñoz, Agustín. *La lucha armada: La izquierda revolucionaria insurge*. Vol. 5. Caracas: Universidad Central de Venezuela, 1981.

Blandón, Jesús Miguel. *Entre Sandino y Fonseca*. 2nd ed. Managua: Segovia Ediciones Latinoamericanos, 2008.

Blasier, Cole. *The Giant's Rival: The USSR and Latin America*. Pittsburgh: University of Pittsburgh Press, 1983.

Blight, James G. *On the Brink: Americans and Soviets Reexamine the Cuban Missile Crisis*. New York: Hill and Wang, 1989.

Blight, James G., Bruce J. Allyn, and David A. Welch. *Cuba on the Brink: Castro, the Missile Crisis, and the Soviet Collapse*. New York: Pantheon Books, 1993.

Blight, James G., and Philip Brenner. *Sad and Luminous Days: Cuba's Struggle with the Superpowers after the Missile Crisis*. Lanham: Rowman and Littlefield, 2002.

Blight, James G., and Peter Kornbluh, eds. *Politics of Illusion: The Bay of Pigs Invasion Reexamined*. Boulder: Lynne Rienner, 1998.

Blight, James G., and Lang, janet M. *Dark Beyond Darkness: The Cuban Missile Crisis as History, Warning, and Catalyst.* Lanham: Rowman and Littlefield, 2018.

———. *The Armageddon Letters: Kennedy/Khrushchev/Castro in the Cuban Missile Crisis.* Lanham, MD: Rowman and Littlefield, 2012.

Bobadilla González, Leticia. *México y la OEA: Los debates diplomáticos, 1959–1964.* Mexico City: Secretaria de Relaciones Exteriores, 2006.

Bolo Hidalgo, Salomón. *Cristianismo y liberación nacional.* Lima: Ediciones Liberación, 1962.

Bonsal, Philip W. *Cuba, Castro, and the United States.* Pittsburgh: University of Pittsburgh Press, 1971.

Booth, William A. "Rethinking Latin America's Cold War." *Historical Journal* 64, no. 4 (2021): 1128–50.

Boughton, George J. "Soviet-Cuban Relations, 1956–1960." *Journal of Interamerican Studies and World Affairs* 16, no. 4 (1974): 436–53.

Brown, Jonathan C. *Cuba's Revolutionary World.* Cambridge: Harvard University Press, 2017.

———. *The Weak and the Powerful: Omar Torrijos, Panama, and the Non-Aligned Movement in the World.* Pittsburgh: University of Pittsburgh Press, 2024.

Bruneau, Mylene. "Ramón Villeda Morales: The 'Little Bird' Who Brought Big Changes and Honor to Honduras." Council on Hemispheric Affairs, May 8, 2009. https://coha.org/ramon-villeda-morales-the-little-bird-who-brought-big -changes-and-honor-to-honduras/.

Burström, Mats, Tomás Diez Acosta, Estrella González Noriega, Anders Gustafsson, Ismael Hernández, Håkan Karlsson, Jesús M. Pajón, Jesús Rafael Robaina Jaramillo, and Bengt Westergaard. "Memories of a World Crisis: The Archaeology of a Former Soviet Nuclear Missile Site in Cuba." *Journal of Social Archaeology* 9, no. 3 (October 1, 2009): 295–318.

Bustamante, Michael J. *Cuban Memory Wars: Retrospective Politics in Revolution and Exile.* Chapel Hill: University of North Carolina Press, 2021.

Campus, Leonardo. "Missiles Have No Colour: African Americans' Reactions to the Cuban Missile Crisis." *Cold War History* 15, no. 1 (February 2015): 49–72.

Casals Araya, Marcelo. *El alba de una revolución: La izquierda y el proceso de construcción estratégica de la "vía chilena al socialismo," 1956–1970.* Santiago de Chile: LOM Ediciones, 2010.

Casals, Marcelo. "Which Borders Have Not Yet Been Crossed? A Supplement to Gilbert Joseph's Historiographical Balance of the Latin American Cold War." *Cold War History* 20, no. 3 (2020): 367–72.

Castillero R., Ernesto J. *Historia de Panamá.* Panama City: Impresora Panamá, 1962.

Cerdas Cruz, Rodolfo. *La hoz y el machete: La Internacional Comunista, América Latina, y la revolución en Centroamérica.* San José: Editorial Universidad Estatal a Distancia, 1986.

Chaia, Vera Lúcia Michalany. *A liderança política de Jânio Quadros, 1947–1990.* Ibitinga: Humanidades, 1991.

Chamberlin, Paul Thomas. *The Cold War's Killing Fields: Rethinking the Long Peace.* New York: HarperCollins Publishers, 2018.

Chamberlin, Paul Thomas, Kaysha Corinealdi, Cindy Ewing, Hussein Fancy, Arunabh Ghosh, Rebecca Herman, Raevin Jimenez, et al. "On Transnational and International History." *American Historical Review* 128, no. 1 (March 2023): 255–332.

Chase, Michelle. "Confronting the Youngest Revolution: Cuban Anti-Communists and the Global Politics of Youth in the Early 1960s." *Journal of Latin American Studies* 53, no. 4 (2021): 643–66. https://doi.org/10.1017/S0022216X2100050X.

———. "The Trials: Violence and Justice in the Aftermath of the Cuban Revolution." In *A Century of Revolution: Insurgent and Counterinsurgent Violence during Latin America's Long Cold War*, edited by Greg Grandin, and Gilbert M. Joseph, 163–98. Durham, NC: Duke University Press, 2010.

Chirio, Maud. *Politics in Uniform: Military Officers and Dictatorship in Brazil, 1960–1980*. Pittsburgh: University of Pittsburgh Press, 2018.

Colman, Jonathan. "Toward 'World Support' and 'The Ultimate Judgment of History': The U.S. Legal Case for the Blockade of Cuba during the Missile Crisis, October–November 1962." *Journal of Cold War Studies* 21, no. 2 (2019): 150–73.

Conniff, Michael L. *Panama and the United States: The End of the Alliance*. Athens: University of Georgia Press, 2012.

Cushion, Stephen. *A Hidden History of the Cuban Revolution: How the Working Class Shaped the Guerillas' Victory*. New York: Monthly Review Press, 2016.

Darnton, Christopher. "Asymmetry and Agenda-Setting in U.S.-Latin American Relations: Rethinking the Origins of the Alliance for Progress." *Journal of Cold War Studies* 14, no. 4 (2012): 55–92.

Dawood, Layla, and Mônica Herz. "Nuclear Governance in Latin America." *Contexto Internacional* 35, no. 2 (2013): 497–535.

Degregori, Carlos Iván. "Return to the Past." In *The Shining Path of Peru*, edited by David Scott Palmer, 33–44. New York: St. Martin's Press, 1992.

Del Vasto, César. *Historia del Partido del Pueblo, 1943–1968*. Panama City: Editorial Universitaria "Carlos Manuel Gasteazoro," 1999.

Diez Acosta, Tomás. *Octubre de 1962: A un paso del holocausto*. Havana: Editora Política, 2002.

———. *Peligros y principios*. 2nd ed. Havana: Casa Editorial Verde Olivo, 2012.

Dobbs, Michael. *One Minute to Midnight: Kennedy, Khrushchev, and Castro on the Brink of Nuclear War*. New York: Knopf, 2008.

Dobrynin, Anatoly. "Dobrynin's Cable to the Soviet Foreign Ministry, October 27, 1962." *Cold War International History Project Bulletin* 5 (1995): 79–80.

Donoghue, Michael. *Borderland on the Isthmus: Race, Culture, and the Struggle for the Canal Zone*. Durham, NC: Duke University Press, 2014.

Dorn, A. Walter, and Robert Pauk. "Unsung Mediator: U Thant and the Cuban Missile Crisis." *Diplomatic History* 33, no. 2 (April 2009): 262–92.

Draper, Theodore. *Castro's Revolution: Myths and Realities*. New York: Frederick A. Praeger, 1962.

Dulles, John W. F. *Unrest in Brazil: Political-Military Crises 1955–1964*. Austin: University of Texas Press, 1970.

Dunlap, Christopher Thomas. "Parallel Power Play: Nuclear Technology and Diplomacy in Argentina and Brazil, 1945-1995." PhD diss., University of Chicago, 2017.

Eckstein, Susan Eva. *The Immigrant Divide: How Cuban Americans Changed the US and Their Homeland*. New York: Routledge, 2009.

Elbahtimy, Hassan, and James G. Hershberg. "Egypt and the Cuban Missile Crisis." Working Paper No. 17. Nuclear Proliferation International History Project, Wilson Center, May 2021. www.wilsoncenter.org/publication/egypt-and-cuban-missile-crisis.

Estep, Raymond. *The Latin American Nations Today: A Study of Political Developments Since World War II*. Maxwell Air Force Base, AL: Documentary Research Division, Aerospace Studies Institute, Air University, 1964.

Fardella, Enrico Maria. "Mao Zedong and the 1962 Cuban Missile Crisis." *Cold War History* 15, no. 1 (2015): 73-88.

Featherstone, David. *Solidarity: Hidden Histories and Geographies of Internationalism*. London: Bloomsbury Press, 2012.

Fernández Huidobro, Eleuterio. *Historia de los Tupamaros*. Montevideo: Tupac Amaru Editories, 1986.

Fernández Ordóñez, Rodrigo. *Anatomía del enfrentamiento armado interno: Orígenes de la Guatemala contemporánea*. Las Vegas: Wartime Books, 2024.

Ferrer, Ada. *Cuba: An American Story*. New York: Scribner, 2021.

Fico, Carlos. *O grande irmão: Da Operação Brother Sam aos anos de chumbo*. Rio de Janeiro: Civilazação Brasileira, 2008.

Field, Thomas C., Jr. "Bolivia between Washington, Prague, and Havana: The Limits of Nationalism, 1960-1964." In *Latin America and the Global Cold War*, edited by Thomas C. Field Jr., Stella Krepp, and Vanni Pettiná, 44-72. Chapel Hill: University of North Carolina Press, 2020.

———. "Conflict on High: The Bolivian Revolution and the United States, 1961-1964." PhD diss., London School of Economics and Political Science, 2010.

———. *From Development to Dictatorship: Bolivia and the Alliance for Progress in the Kennedy Era*. Ithaca, NY: Cornell University Press, 2014.

———. "Ideology as Strategy: Military-Led Modernization and the Origins of the Alliance for Progress in Bolivia." *Diplomatic History* 36, no. 1 (2012): 147-83.

Field, Thomas C., Jr., Stella Krepp, and Vanni Pettiná, eds. *Latin America and the Global Cold War*. Chapel Hill: University of North Carolina Press, 2020.

Figueroa Ibarra, Carlos. "Violencia y revolución en Guatemala: 1954-1972." PhD diss., Universidad Nacional Autónoma de México, 2000.

Figueroa Ibarra, Carlos, Guillermo Paz Cárcamo, and Arturo Taracena Arriola. "El primer ciclo de la insurgencia revolucionaria en Guatemala (1954-1972)." In *Guatemala: Historia reciente (1954-1996)*, vol. 2, *La dimensión revolucionaria*, edited by Virgilio Álvarez Aragón, 29-120. Guatemala City: FLACSO Guatemala, 2013.

Finchelstein, Federico. *The Ideological Origins of the Dirty War: Fascism, Populism, and Dictatorship in Twentieth Century Argentina*. New York: Oxford University Press, 2014.

Friedman, Jeremy. *Shadow Cold War: The Sino-Soviet Competition for the Third World*. Chapel Hill: University of North Carolina Press, 2015.

Furci, Carmelo. *El Partido Comunista de Chile y la vía al socialismo*. Santiago de Chile: Ariadna Ediciones, 2008.

Fursenko, Aleksandr, and Timothy Naftali. *One Hell of a Gamble: Khrushchev, Castro, and Kennedy, 1958-1964: The Secret History of the Cuban Missile Crisis*. New York: W. W. Norton, 1998.

Gaddis, John Lewis. *Strategies of Containment: A Critical Appraisal of Postwar American National Security Policy*. New York: Oxford University Press, 1982.

García Ferreira, Roberto. *Bajo vigilancia: La CIA, la policía uruguaya y el exilio de Arbenz (1957-60)*. Guatemala City: Centro de Estudios Urbanos y Regionales, Universidad de San Carlos de Guatemala, 2013.

———. "The Cuban Embassy in Uruguay, 1959-1964." In *Oxford Research Encyclopedia of Latin American History*, February 26, 2018. https://10.1093/acrefore/9780199366439.013.476.

García Ferreira, Roberto, and Mario Ayala. "Solidaridad democrática en Guerra Fría: El caso de la política de asilo diplomático de Uruguay en Cuba durante la dictadura de Fulgencio Batista (1957-1958)." *Cuadernos de Historia: Serie Economía y Sociedad*, no. 29 (2022): 144-72.

García Ferreira, Roberto, and Martín Girona. "Una 'inmensa potencia explosiva': Uruguay y la ruptura de relaciones con Cuba en 1964." In *Los condicionantes internos de la política exterior: Entramados de las relaciones internacionales y transnacionales*, edited by María Cecilia Míguez and Leandro Morgenfeld, 109-40. Buenos Aires: Teseo Press, 2020.

Gatto, Hebert. *El cielo por asalto: El Movimiento de Liberación Nacional (Tupamaros) y la izquierda uruguaya (1963-1972)*. Montevideo: Ediciones Santillana, 2004.

George, Alice L. *Awaiting Armageddon: How Americans Faced the Cuban Missile Crisis*. Chapel Hill: University of North Carolina Press, 2003.

Getchell, Michelle. "Cuba, the USSR, and the Non-Aligned Movement: Negotiating Non-Alignment." In *Latin America and the Global Cold War*, edited by Thomas C. Field Jr., Stella Krepp, and Vanni Pettiná, 148-73. Chapel Hill: University of North Carolina Press, 2020.

———. *The Cuban Missile Crisis and the Cold War: A Short History with Documents*. Cambridge, MA: Hackett Publishing Company, 2018.

———. "Revisiting the 1954 Coup in Guatemala: The Soviet Union, the United Nations, and 'Hemispheric Solidarity.'" *Journal of Cold War Studies* 17, no. 2 (2015): 73-102.

Gittlitz, A. M. *I Want to Believe: Posadism, UFOs, and Apocalypse Communism*. London: Pluto Press, 2020.

Gleijeses, Piero. *Conflicting Missions: Havana, Washington, and Africa, 1959-1976*. Chapel Hill: University of North Carolina Press, 2002.

———. *The Dominican Crisis: 1965 Constitutionalist Revolt and American Intervention*. Baltimore, MD: Johns Hopkins University Press, 1978.

———. *Shattered Hope: The Guatemalan Revolution and the United States, 1944-1954*. Princeton, NJ: Princeton University Press, 1991.

————. "Ships in the Night: The CIA, the White House and the Bay of Pigs." *Journal of Latin American Studies* 27, no. 1 (1995): 1–42.

Gleijeses, Piero, Melvyn P. Leffler, and Odd Arne Westad. "Cuba and the Cold War, 1959–1980." In *The Cambridge History of the Cold War*, vol. 2, *Crises and Détente*, edited by Melvyn P. Leffler and Odd Arne Westad, 327–48. Cambridge: Cambridge University Press, 2010.

González, Fredy. *Paisanos Chinos: Transpacific Politics Among Chinese Immigrants in Mexico*. Berkeley: University of California Press, 2017.

Gott, Richard. *Guerrilla Movements in Latin America*. Garden City, N.Y: Doubleday, 1971.

Grandin, Greg. *The Last Colonial Massacre: Latin America in the Cold War*. Chicago: University of Chicago Press, 2004.

Grandin, Greg, and Gilbert Joseph, eds. *A Century of Revolution: Insurgent and Counterinsurgent Violence during Latin America's Long Cold War*. Durham, NC: Duke University Press, 2010.

Greiner, Bernd. "The Soviet View: An Interview with Sergo Mikoyan." *Diplomatic History* 14, no. 2 (1990): 205–22.

Gribkov, General Anatoli I., and General William Y. Smith. *Operation Anadyr: U.S. and Soviet Generals Recount the Cuban Missile Crisis*. Edited by Alfred Friendly Jr. Chicago: Edition q, 1994.

Guerra, Lillian. *Heroes, Martyrs, and Political Messiahs in Revolutionary Cuba, 1946–1958*. New Haven, CT: Yale University Press, 2018.

————. *Visions of Power in Cuba: Revolution, Redemption, and Resistance, 1959–1971*. Chapel Hill: University of North Carolina Press, 2012.

Guevara Mann, Carlos. *Panamanian Militarism: A Historical Interpretation*. Athens: Ohio University Center for International Studies, 1996.

Gutman, Daniel. *Tacuara: Historia de la primera guerrilla urbana argentina*. Buenos Aires: Ediciones B Argentina, 2003.

Guzman Bouvard, Marguerite. *Revolutionizing Motherhood: The Mothers of the Plaza de Mayo*. Lanham: Rowman and Littlefield, 1994.

Halperin, Maurice. *The Rise and Decline of Fidel Castro*. Berkeley: University of California Press, 1972.

Harmer, Tanya. *Allende's Chile and the Inter-American Cold War*. Chapel Hill: University of North Carolina Press, 2011.

————. *Beatriz Allende: A Revolutionary Life in Cold War Latin America*. Chapel Hill: University of North Carolina Press, 2020.

————. "The Cold War in Latin America." In *The Routledge Handbook of the Cold War*, edited by Artemy M. Kalinovsky, and Craig Daigle, 133–48. New York: Routledge, 2016.

————. "The 'Cuban Question' and the Cold War in Latin America, 1959–1964." *Journal of Cold War Studies* 21, no. 3 (2019): 114–51.

Harms, Patricia. "'God Doesn't Like the Revolution': The Archbishop, the Market Women, and the Economy of Gender in Guatemala, 1944–1954." *Frontiers (Boulder)* 32, no. 2 (2011): 111–39.

Heilman, Jaymie Patricia. "Yellows against Reds: Campesino Anticommunism in 1960s Ayacucho, Peru." *Latin American Research Review* 50, no. 2 (2015): 154–75.

Hermosilla, Matías. "La cuestión cubana en 'risas' chilenas: El triunfo de la revolución cubana (1959) y la crisis de los misiles (1962) en la revista Topaze." *Revista de la Red Intercátedras de Historia de América Latina Contemporánea*, no. 7 (2017): 104–19.

Herrán Ávila, Luis Alberto. "Las guerrillas blancas: Anticomunismo transnacional e imaginarios de derechas en Argentina y México, 1954–1972." *Quinto Sol* 19, no. 1 (2015): 1–26.

Hershberg, James G. "The Cuban Missile Crisis." In *The Cambridge History of the Cold War*, vol. 2, *Crises and Détente*, edited by Melvyn P. Leffler and Odd Arne Westad, 65–87. Cambridge: Cambridge University Press, 2010.

——. "A 'Friend of the Revolution' or a 'Traitor'? Vasco Tristão Leitão da Cunha, Fidel Castro (and His Sister), and Brazilian-Cuban Relations, 1956–1964." Paper presented at the International Studies Association conference, Buenos Aires, July 23, 2014. https://paperzz.com/doc/9159406/vasco-trist%C3%A3o -leit%C3%A3o-da-cunha--fidel-castro.

——. "The Global Cuban Missile Crisis: Surfing the Third Wave of Missile Crisis Scholarship." *Cold War International History Project Bulletin*, no. 17/18 (2012). www.wilsoncenter.org/publication/bulletin-no-1718-fall-2012.

——. "New Russian Evidence on Soviet-Cuban Relations, 1960–61." Working Paper No. 90. Cold War International History Project, Wilson Center, February 6, 2019. www.wilsoncenter.org/publication/new-russian-evidence-soviet-cuban -relations-1960-61-when-nikita-met-fidel-the-bay-pigs.

——. "Soviet-Brazilian Relations and the Cuban Missile Crisis." *Journal of Cold War Studies* 22, no. 1 (2020): 175–209.

——. "The United States, Brazil, and the Cuban Missile Crisis, 1962 (Part 1)." *Journal of Cold War Studies* 6, no. 2 (2004): 3–20.

——. "The United States, Brazil, and the Cuban Missile Crisis (Part 2)." *Journal of Cold War Studies* 6, no. 3 (2004): 5–67.

Hines, Sarah T. *Water for All: Community, Property, and Revolution in Modern Bolivia*. Oakland: University of California Press, 2022.

Hodges, Donald. *Intellectual Foundations of the Nicaraguan Revolution*. Austin: University of Texas Press, 1986.

Hunt, Jonathan R. "Mexican Nuclear Diplomacy, the Latin American Nuclear-Weapon-Free Zone, and the NPT Bargain, 1962–1968." In *Negotiating the Nuclear Non-Proliferation Treaty*, edited by Roland Popp, Liviu Horovitz, and Andreas Wenger, 178–202. New York: Routledge, 2017.

——. *The Nuclear Club: How America and the World Policed the Atom from Hiroshima to Vietnam*. Stanford, CA: Stanford University Press, 2022.

Iber, Patrick. *Neither Peace nor Freedom: The Cultural Cold War in Latin America*. Cambridge, MA: Harvard University Press, 2015.

James, Daniel. *Resistance and Integration: Peronism and the Argentine Working Class, 1946–1976*. Cambridge: Cambridge University Press, 1993.

Jarquín, Mateo. *The Sandinista Revolution: A Global Latin American History*. Chapel Hill: University of North Carolina Press, 2024.

Joseph, Gilbert M. "Border Crossings and the Remaking of Latin American Cold War Studies." *Cold War History* 19, no. 1 (2019): 141–70.

Kalfon, Pierre. *Che Ernesto Guevara: Una leyenda de nuestro siglo*. Barcelona: Plaza and Janés, 1997.

Karl, Robert A. *Forgotten Peace: Reform, Violence, and the Making of Contemporary Colombia*. Oakland: University of California Press, 2017.

———. "Reading the Cuban Revolution from Bogotá, 1957-1962." *Cold War History* 16, no. 4 (2016): 337-58.

Karol, K. S. *Guerrillas in Power: The Course of the Cuban Revolution*. New York: Hill and Wang, 1970.

Keller, Renata. "The Latin American Missile Crisis." *Diplomatic History* 39, no. 2 (2015): 195-222.

———. *Mexico's Cold War: Cuba, the United States, and the Legacy of the Mexican Revolution*. New York: Cambridge University Press, 2015.

———. "Research Note: The Cuban Missile Crisis and a War of Words in Argentina." *Journal of Cold War History* 22, no. 4 (2022): 521-28. www.tandfonline.com.

———. "Responsibility of the Great Ones: How the Organization of American States and the United Nations Helped Resolve the Cuban Missile Crisis." *Journal of Latin American Studies* 51, no. 4 (2019): 883-904.

———. "Rockets Here, in Our Pretty Little Cuba: The View from the Epicenter of the Cuban Missile Crisis." *History Today* 72, no. 10 (2022): 28-41.

Kelly, Patrick William. *Sovereign Emergencies: Latin America and the Making of Global Human Rights Politics*. New York: Cambridge University Press, 2018.

Kirkendall, Andrew J. *Hemispheric Alliances: Liberal Democrats and Cold War Latin America*. Chapel Hill: University of North Carolina Press, 2022.

Krasner, Stephen D. *Sovereignty: Organized Hypocrisy*. Princeton, NJ: Princeton University Press, 1999.

Kruijt, Dirk. *Cuba and Revolutionary Latin America: An Oral History*. London: Zed Books, 2017.

Laffey, Mark, and Jutta Weldes. "Decolonizing the Cuban Missile Crisis." *International Studies Quarterly* 52, no. 3 (2008): 555-77.

Latham, Michael E. *Modernization as Ideology: American Social Science and "Nation Building" in the Kennedy Era*. Chapel Hill: University of North Carolina Press, 2000.

Leffler, Melvyn P. *A Preponderance of Power: National Security, the Truman Administration, and the Cold War*. Stanford, CA: Stanford University Press, 1992.

Leogrande, William M., and Kornbluh, Peter. *Back Channel to Cuba: The Hidden History of Negotiations between Washington and Havana*. Chapel Hill: University of North Carolina Press, 2014.

León, Ángel Dámaso Luis. "Un modelo cubano en Venezuela: El Movimiento de Izquierda Revolucionaria." *Izquierdas*, no. 50 (2021): 1-21.

Lessa, Francesca. *The Condor Trials: Transnational Repression and Human Rights in South America*. New Haven, CT: Yale University Press, 2022.

Levine, Daniel H. *Conflict and Political Change in Venezuela*. Princeton, NJ: Princeton University Press, 1973.

Lewis, Oscar, Ruth M. Lewis, and Susan M. Rigdon. *Four Men: Living the Revolution; an Oral History of Contemporary Cuba*. Urbana: University of Illinois Press, 1977.

———. *Four Women: Living the Revolution; an Oral History of Contemporary Cuba.* Urbana: University of Illinois Press, 1977.

Loaeza, Soledad. "Estados Unidos y la contención del comunismo en América Latina y en México." *Foro Internacional* 53, no. 1 (211) (2013): 5–56.

Loureiro, Felipe P. *A aliança para o progresso e o governo João Goulart (1961–1964): Ajuda econômica norte-americana a estados brasileiros e a desestabilização da democracia no Brasil pós-guerra.* São Paulo: Editora UNESP, 2020.

———. "Making the Alliance for Progress Serve the Few: U.S. Economic Aid to Cold War Brazil (1961–1964)." *Journal of Cold War Studies* 25, no. 1 (2023): 168–207.

Loveman, Brian. *For La Patria: Politics and the Armed Forces in Latin America.* Wilmington, DE: Scholarly Resources, 1999.

Luis, William, and Edmund Desnoes. "America Revisited: An Interview with Edmund Desnoes." *Latin American Literary Review* 11, no. 21 (1982): 7–20.

Lüthi, Lorenz M. "The Non-Aligned Movement and the Cold War, 1961–1973." *Journal of Cold War Studies* 18, no. 4 (2016): 98–147.

Magnússon, Sigurður Gylfi, and István M. Szijártó. *What Is Microhistory?: Theory and Practice.* New York: Routledge, 2013.

Mahler, Anne Garland. *From the Tricontinental to the Global South: Race, Radicalism, and Transnational Solidarity.* Durham, NC: Duke University Press, 2018.

Marchesi, Aldo. "Escribiendo la Guerra Fría latinoamericana: Entre el Sur 'local' y el Norte 'global.'" *Estudos Históricos* 30, no. 60 (2017): 187–202.

Marques Bezerra, Gustavo Henrique. *Da revolução ao reatamento: A política externa brasileiro e a questão cubana (1959–1986).* Brasília: Fundação Alexander de Busmõ, 2012.

Martins Cordeiro, Janaina. *Direitas em movimento: Campanha da Mulher pela Democracia e a ditadura no Brasil.* Rio de Janeiro: Editora FGV, 2009.

Masud-Piloto, Felix Roberto. *From Welcomed Exiles to Illegal Immigrants: Cuban Migration to the U.S., 1959–1995.* Lanham, MD: Rowman and Littlefield, 1996.

Mateos, Gisela, and Edna Suárez-Díaz. "Atoms for Peace in Latin America." *Oxford Research Encyclopedia of Latin American History*, April 5, 2016. https://doi.org /10.1093/acrefore/9780199366439.013.317.

———. "'We Are Not a Rich Country to Waste Our Resources on Expensive Toys': Mexico's Version of Atoms for Peace." *History and Technology* 31, no. 3 (2015): 243–58.

McMahon, Robert J., ed. *The Cold War in the Third World.* New York: Oxford University Press, 2013.

McPherson, Alan. *The Invaded: How Latin Americans and Their Allies Fought and Ended U.S. Occupations.* New York: Oxford University Press, 2014.

———. "Afterword: The Paradox of Latin American Cold War Studies." In *Beyond the Eagle's Shadow: New Histories of Latin America's Cold War*, edited by Virginia Garrard, Mark Lawrence, and Julio Moreno, 307–19. Albuquerque: University of New Mexico Press, 2013.

Míguez, María Cecilia. "¿Anticomunistas, antiestatistas, antiperonistas? La 'nacionalización' de la doctrina de seguridad nacional en la Argentina y la legitimación del golpe de Estado de 1966." *Revista de la Sociedad Argentina de Análisis Político* 7, no. 1 (2013): 65-95.

Míguez, María Cecilia, and Morgenfeld, Leandro. "Las relaciones entre Argentina y Cuba y su impacto en el sistema interamericano en los años 60." In *Historia oral de la política exterior argentina (1930-1966)*, edited by Mario Rapoport, 159-200. Buenos Aires: Editorial Octubre Editorial, 2015.

Moniz Bandeira, Luiz Alberto. *De Martí a Fidel: A revolução cubana e a América Latina*. Rio de Janeiro: Civilização Brasileira, 1998.

———. *O 24 de agôsto de Jânio Quadros*. Rio de Janeiro: Editora Melso, 1961.

Morgenfeld, Leandro Ariel. "Argentina, Estados Unidos y el sistema interamericano durante la crisis de los misiles (1962)." *Historia: Debates e Tendencias* 12, no. 2 (2012): 326-44.

Moulton, Aaron Coy. "Building Their Own Cold War in Their Own Backyard: The Transnational, International Conflicts in the Greater Caribbean Basin, 1944-1954." *Cold War History* 15, no. 2 (2015): 135-54.

Moyn, Samuel. *The Last Utopia: Human Rights in History*. Cambridge, MA: Belknap Press of Harvard University Press, 2010.

Murmis, Ezequiel P. "El sindicalismo comunista en la reorganización del movimiento obrero: hacia la formación del Movimiento de Unidad y Coordinación Sindical (MUCS) en 1958-1959." *e-l@tina: Revista Electrónica de Estudios Latinoamericanos* 18, no. 72 (2020): 1-21.

Musto, Ryan A. "'A Desire So Close to the Hearts of All Latin Americans': Utopian Ideals and Imperfections behind Latin America's Nuclear Weapon Free Zone." *Bulletin of Latin American Research* 37, no. 2 (2018): 160-74.

Nercesian, Inés. *La política en armas y las armas de la política: Brasil, Chile, y Uruguay, 1950-1970*. Buenos Aires: CLACSO, 2013.

Nicanoff, Sergio M., and Axel Castellano. *Las primeras experiencias guerrilleras en la Argentina: La historia del "Vasco" Bengochea y las Fuerza Armadas de la Revolución Nacional*. Buenos Aires: Ediciones del Centro Cultural Floreal Gorini, 2006.

Offner, Amy C. *Sorting Out the Mixed Economy: The Rise and Fall of Welfare and Developmental States in the Americas*. Princeton, NJ: Princeton University Press, 2019.

Osuna, María Florencia, and Esteban Pontoriero. "El impacto de la doctrina 'de la seguridad nacional' en la Argentina durante la guerra fría, (1955-1983)." *Izquierdas* 49 (2020): 352-64.

Parrott, R. Joseph, and Mark Atwood Lawrence, eds. *The Tricontinental Revolution: Third World Radicalism and the Cold War*. New York: Cambridge University Press, 2022.

Paterson, Thomas G. "Commentary: The Defense-of-Cuba Theme and the Missile Crisis." *Diplomatic History* 14, no. 2 (1990): 249-56.

Patti, Carlo. *Brazil in the Global Nuclear Order, 1945-2018*. Baltimore, MD: Johns Hopkins University Press, 2021.

Pedemonte, Rafael. "La Revolución Cubana de cara al desafío ideológico de la 'Vía chilena al socialismo' (1959-1973)." *Revista de Indias* 82, no. 286 (2022): 859-92.

Pensado, Jaime. "'To Assault with the Truth': The Revitalization of Conservative Militancy in Mexico during the Global Sixties." *The Americas* 70, no. 3 (2014): 489–521.

Pérez, Louis A. *Cuba and the United States: Ties of Singular Intimacy*. Athens: University of Georgia Press, 1990.

Perutka, Lukás. "Arms for Arbenz: Czechoslovakia's Involvement in the Cold War in Latin America." *Central European Journal of International and Security Studies* 3 (2013): 98–114.

Pettiná, Vanni. *Historia mínima de la Guerra Fría en América Latina*. Mexico City: El Colegio de México, 2018.

———. "Mexican-Soviet Encounters in the Early 1960s: Tractors of Discord." In *Latin America and the Global Cold War*, edited by Thomas C. Field Jr., Stella Krepp, and Vanni Pettiná, 73–99. Chapel Hill: University of North Carolina Press, 2020.

Philpott, Daniel. *Revolutions in Sovereignty: How Ideas Shaped Modern International Relations*. Princeton, NJ: Princeton University Press, 2001.

Plokhy, Serhii. *Nuclear Folly: A History of the Cuban Missile Crisis*. New York: W. W. Norton, 2021.

Potash, Robert A. *The Army and Politics in Argentina, 1945–1962*. Vol. 2, *Perón to Frondizi*. Stanford, CA: Stanford University Press, 1980.

———. *The Army and Politics in Argentina, 1962–1973*. Vol. 3, *From Frondizi's Fall to the Peronist Restoration*. Stanford, CA: Stanford University Press, 1996.

Prashad, Vijay. *The Darker Nations: A People's History of the Third World*. New York: New Press, 2008.

Putnam, Lara. "To Study the Fragments/Whole: Microhistory and the Atlantic World." *Journal of Social History* 39, no. 3 (2006): 615–30. https://doi.org /10.2307/3790281.

Quirk, Robert E. *Fidel Castro*. New York: Norton, 1995.

Rabe, Stephen G. "The Caribbean Triangle: Betancourt, Castro, and Trujillo and U.S. Foreign Policy, 1958–1963." *Diplomatic History* 20, no. 1 (1996): 55–78.

———. *The Most Dangerous Area in the World: John F. Kennedy Confronts Communist Revolution in Latin America*. Chapel Hill: University of North Carolina Press, 1999.

Randall, Margaret. *Exporting Revolution: Cuba's Global Solidarity*. Durham, NC: Duke University Press, 2017.

Rasenberger, Jim. *The Brilliant Disaster: JFK, Castro, and America's Doomed Invasion of Cuba's Bay of Pigs*. New York: Scribner, 2011.

Redfield Peattie, Lisa. *The View from the Barrio*. 2nd ed. Ann Arbor: University of Michigan Press, 1972.

Reeves, Michelle Denise. "Extracting the Eagle's Talons: The Soviet Union in Cold War Latin America." PhD diss., University of Texas at Austin, 2014.

Ribadero, Martín. *Tiempo de profetas: Ideas, debates y labor cultural de la izquierda nacional de Jorge Adelardo Ramos (1945–1962)*. Bernal: Universidad Nacional de Quilmes Editorial, 2017.

Robben, Antonius C. G. M. *Political Violence and Trauma in Argentina*. Philadelphia: University of Pennsylvania Press, 2011.

Robbins, Carla Anne. *The Cuban Threat*. New York: McGraw-Hill, 1983.

Rojas, Rafael. *El árbol de las revoluciones: Ideas y poder en América Latina*. Mexico City: Turner, 2021.

Roldán, Mary. *Blood and Fire: La Violencia in Antioquia, Colombia, 1946–1953*. Durham, NC: Duke University Press, 2002.

Romero Sánchez, Susana. "El miedo a la revolución: Interamericanismo y anticomunismo en Colombia, 1958–1965." MA thesis, Universidad Nacional de Colombia, 2007.

Ropp, Steven C. *Panamanian Politics: From Guarded Nation to National Guard*. Stanford, CA: Hoover Institution Press, 1982.

Rostica, Julieta, and Sala, Laura. "La Guerra Fría en América Latina y los estudios transnacionales: Introducción." *Secuencia* 111 (2021): 1–7.

Ruano Najarro, Edgar. "El golpe de estado de 1963." In *Guatemala: Historia Reciente (1954–1996)*, vol. 1, *Proceso político y antagonismo social*, edited by Virgilio Álvarez Aragón, Carlos Figueroa Ibarra, Arturo Taracena Arriola, Sergio Tischler Visquerra, and Edmundo Urrutia Garcí, 77–167. Guatemala City: FLACSO Guatemala, 2012.

Sala, Laura Yanina. "La doctrina de seguridad nacional en América Latina. Un repaso por los estudios clásicos y sus críticos." *e-l@tina: Revista Electrónica de Estudios Latinoamericanos* 20, no. 80 (2022): 1–24.

Salas, Ernesto. *Uturuncos: El origen de la guerrilla peronista*. Buenos Aires: Editorial Biblos, 2003.

Salcedo Ávila, Gustavo Enrique. "Venezuela ante la crisis de los Misiles." CEL-UNSAM (Centro de Estudios Latinoamericanos de la Universidad Nacional de San Martín en Argentina) y UDEAR (Universidad de la República en Uruguay), 2022. Unpublished, in the author's possession.

———. *Venezuela, campo de batalla de la guerra fría: Los Estados Unidos y la era de Rómulo Betancourt (1958–1964)*. Caracas: Ediciones Nueve 12, 2018.

Sayward, Amy L. *The United Nations in International History*. London: Bloomsbury Academic Press, 2017.

Scarfi, Juan Pablo. *The Hidden History of International Law in the Americas: Empire and Legal Networks*. New York: Oxford University Press, 2017.

Schlesinger, Arthur M. *A Thousand Days: John F. Kennedy in the White House*. Boston: Houghton Mifflin, 1965.

Schlesinger, Stephen C, and Stephen Kinzer. *Bitter Fruit: The Story of the American Coup in Guatemala*. Rev. and expanded ed. Cambridge, MA: Harvard University, David Rockefeller Center for Latin American Studies, 2005.

Schmidli, William Michael. *The Fate of Freedom Elsewhere: Human Rights and U.S. Cold War Policy Toward Argentina*. Ithaca, NY: Cornell University Press, 2013.

Schoultz, Lars. *That Infernal Little Cuban Republic: The United States and the Cuban Revolution*. Chapel Hill: University of North Carolina Press, 2009.

Semán, Ernesto. *Ambassadors of the Working Class: Argentina's International Labor Activists and Cold War Democracy in the Americas*. Durham, NC: Duke University Press, 2017.

Senkman, Leonardo. "The Right and Civilian Regimes, 1955–1976." In *The Argentine Right: Its History and Intellectual Origins, 1910 to the Present*, edited by Sandra McGee Deutsch and Ronald H. Dolkart, 119–46. Lanham: Scholarly Resources, 1993.

Serrano, Mónica. *Common Security in Latin America: The 1967 Treaty of Tlatelolco.* London: University of London Institute of Latin American Studies, 1992.

Sheinin, David. *Argentina and the United States: An Alliance Contained.* Athens: University of Georgia Press, 2006.

Siekmeier, James F. *The Bolivian Revolution and the United States, 1952 to Present.* University Park: Pennsylvania State University Press, 2011.

Sikkink, Kathryn. *Ideas and Institutions: Developmentalism in Brazil and Argentina.* Ithaca, NY: Cornell University Press, 1991.

Skidmore, Thomas E. *Politics in Brazil, 1930–1964: An Experiment in Democracy.* New York: Oxford University Press, 1967.

Snyder, Sarah B. *Human Rights Activism and the End of the Cold War: A Transnational History of the Helsinki Network.* Cambridge: Cambridge University Press, 2011.

Soler, Ricuarte. *Panamá: Nación y oligarquía, 1925–1975.* Panama City: Ediciones Tareas, 1976.

Soliz, Carmen. *Fields of Revolution: Agrarian Reform and Rural State Formation in Bolivia, 1935–1964.* Pittsburgh: University of Pittsburgh Press, 2021.

Sorensen, Theodore C. *Kennedy.* New York: Harper and Row, 1965.

Sotomayor, Arturo C. "Brazil and Mexico in the Nonproliferation Regime." *Nonproliferation Review* 20, no. 1 (2013): 81–105. https://doi.org/10.1080/10736700.2013.769377.

Spektor, Matias. "The Evolution of Brazil's Nuclear Intentions." *Nonproliferation Review* 23, nos. 5–6 (2017): 635–52.

Spenser, Daniela. "Operation Manuel: Czechoslovakia and Cuba." Working Paper e-Dossier No. 7. Cold War International History Project, Wilson Center, July 7, 2011. www.wilsoncenter.org/publication/operation-manuel-czechoslovakia -and-cuba.

——. "The Caribbean Crisis: Catalyst for Soviet Projection in Latin America." In *In from the Cold: Latin America's New Encounter with the Cold War*, edited by Gilbert M. Joseph and Daniela Spenser, 77–111. Durham, NC: Duke University Press, 2008.

Stites Mor, Jessica, ed. *Human Rights and Transnational Solidarity in Cold War Latin America.* Madison: University of Wisconsin Press, 2013.

Stoetzer, O. Carlos. *The Organization of American States.* 2nd ed. Westport: Praeger, 1993.

Szusterman, Celia. *Frondizi and the Politics of Developmentalism in Argentina, 1955–62.* London: Macmillan, 1993.

Taffet, Jeffrey F. *Foreign Aid as Foreign Policy: The Alliance for Progress in Latin America.* New York: Routledge, 2007.

Thomas, Hugh. *The Cuban Revolution.* New York: Harper Torchbooks, 1971.

Trivellato, Francesca. "Is There a Future for Italian Microhistory in the Age of Global History?" *California Italian Studies* 2, no. 1 (January 1, 2011). http://escholarship .org/uc/item/0z94n9hq.

Valle Jimenez, Sergio, del. *Un pueblo invencible.* Havana: Editorial Jose Marti, 1991.

van Ommen, Eline. *Nicaragua Must Survive: Sandinista Revolutionary Diplomacy in the Global Cold War.* Berkeley: University of California Press, 2024.

Vaughan, Mary Kay. *Cultural Politics in Revolution: Teachers, Peasants, and Schools in Mexico, 1930–1940*. Tucson: University of Arizona Press, 1997.

Vela Castañeda, Manolo E. "Guatemala, 1954: Las ideas de la contrarrevolución." *Foro Internacional* 45, no. 1 (2005): 89–114.

Velasco, Alejandro. *Barrio Rising: Urban Popular Politics and the Making of Modern Venezuela*. Oakland: University of California Press, 2015.

Vrana, Heather. *This City Belongs to You: A History of Student Activism in Guatemala, 1944–1996*. Oakland: University of California Press, 2017.

Walcher, Dustin. "Petroleum Pitfalls: The United States, Argentine Nationalism, and the 1963 Oil Crisis." *Diplomatic History* 37, no. 1 (2013): 24–57.

Wells, Allen. *Latin America's Democratic Crusade: The Transnational Struggle Against Dictatorship, 1920s–1960s*. New Haven, CT: Yale University Press, 2023.

Westad, Odd Arne. *The Global Cold War*. Cambridge: Cambridge University Press, 2007.

Wickham-Crowley, Timothy P. *Guerrillas and Revolution in Latin America: A Comparative Study of Insurgents and Regimes Since 1956*. Princeton, NJ: Princeton University Press, 1992.

Wilkie, James W. *The Bolivian Revolution and U.S. Aid since 1952: Financial Background and Context of Political Decisions*. Los Angeles: University of California Press, 1969.

Wilson, Larman C. "International Law and the United States Cuban Quarantine of 1962." *Journal of Inter-American Studies* 7, no. 4 (1965): 485–92.

Young, Kevin A. *Blood of the Earth: Resource Nationalism, Revolution, and Empire in Bolivia*. Austin: University of Texas Press, 2017.

Zimmermann, Matilde. *Sandinista: Carlos Fonseca and the Nicaraguan Revolution*. Durham, NC: Duke University Press, 2000.

Zolov, Eric. *The Last Good Neighbor: Mexico in the Global Sixties*. Durham, NC: Duke University Press, 2020.

# Index

Central Intelligence Agency (CIA), 21–22, 28, 32, 52, 81–82, 114, 217–18, 220, 226

Chaguaramas Naval Base, 79

Chapultepec Conference, 38

Chiari, Roberto, 108

Chile, 1, 41, 54, 63, 74, 122–28, 143, 232, 234

China, 117–18, 218–21

Chinese Communist Party, 219

Christian Democratic youth group (Costa Rica), 129

Christian Democrat party (Venezuela), 87–88

CIA Program of Covert Action (Cuba, 1960), 32

Civil Defense Corps, Bogotá, 115–17

*Clarín* (Buenos Aires), 91–92, 150

Colegio Ayacucho, 156

collective security, 38, 40, 127

Colombia, 30, 37–40, 50–52, 79, 81, 104, 113–21, 134–35, 144

Comando Geral dos Trabalhadores, 147

Comité de Organización Política Electoral Independiente (Venezuela), 87–88

Committees for the Defense of the Revolution (Cuba), 34

communism, 14–17, 38–41, 64–65, 186–95, 197–201, 208, 219

Communist Party of Argentina, 135–38, 185–86

Communist Party of Brazil, 218

Communist Party of Venezuela, 85–87, 154, 220

Constitution of 1917 (Mexico), 26

*convivencia* agreement (Colombia), 38, 113

COPEI (Comité de Organización Política Electoral Independiente), 87–88

Corvalán, Luis, 35, 124–26, 143

Costa Rica, 1, 51, 79, 81, 104, 129, 191–93

*La Coubre* (ship), 31–32

Council of the Organization of American States (COAS), 63–67, 90

counterrevolution, 13, 20–24, 32, 46

Creole oil installations, 155

Creole Petroleum Corporation, 154

Cuban artists and writers, 101–4

Cuban exiles, 2–3, 12, 21–23, 30–34, 36, 46, 50, 187–95

Cuban Revolution, 2–3; Bay of Pigs invasion, 31–36; and communism, 14–17; Council of the OAS, 66; and democratic traditions, tensions with, 123–28; demonstrations for and against, 145–46, 156–57; domestic opposition to, 20–24; early responses to, 11–14; export of revolution, 29–30; foreign supporters of, 17–20, 82, 85–86, 104, 197; Latin American public opinion of, 47; and multilateralism, 37–41; overview of, 9–11; public declarations on stance toward, 132–36; self-determination and nonintervention, 25–28; US-Cuban relations during, 15–17

Cuban Revolutionary Council (Consejo Revolucionario Cubano), 188–95

*Cuba Nueva* (Coral Gables), 182

Cuba's Federation of University Students, 155

Cueva de los Portales, 96

Czechoslovakia, 81, 200, 220–21

Dager, Jorge, 86

Dantas, San Tiago, 28, 75, 76

Decade of Spring (Guatemala), 80, 81

"Declaration of San José," 30

defensive weapons, 51–52, 71, 189

de la Guardia, Ernesto, 29–30

demilitarized zones, 74–75

Democratic Action party (Venezuela), 13, 85, 126–27

Democratic Republican Union party (Venezuela), 126

Democratic Revolutionary Front, 21–22, 32

demonstrations, 1–2, 21, 29, 35–36, 138–40, 143–57, 217

denuclearization, 74–78, 232–35

MARA (Movimiento Argentino Revolucionario Anticomunista), 140–41

Maracaibo, Venezuela, 35

*Marcha* (Montevideo), 216

Mar del Plata, Argentina, 91, 137

Mármol, Armida, 104–5

Marshall Plan, 37

Martí, José, 19, 21, 27

Martin, Edwin, 52, 56, 190, 201, 209–10, 233

Martin, John Bartlow, 80

Martínez Sotomayor, Carlos, 123

Masetti, Jorge, 34, 105

Matos, Huber, 106

Matthews, Herbert, 11

McClintock, Robert, 90, 92–93, 153, 203–7

McCone, John, 54–55, 166

McKinley, William, 9

McNamara, Robert, 160, 166, 189

Melo Franco, Afonso Arinas, 74

*Memories of Underdevelopment* (film), 106

Mexico, 23, 25–26, 28, 52, 70–71, 197–99, 217, 233–34

Mikoyan, Anastas, 17, 21, 215, 221–26, 231

Mikoyan, Sergo, 221–22

Milicia Nacional Revolucionaria (Cuba), 31

MIR (Movimiento de la Izquierda Revolucionaria, Venezuela), 85–88, 154, 219

Miró Cardona, José, 16, 188, 190, 194–95

MNR (Movimiento Nacionalista Revolucionario, Bolivia), 132, 199–201

Moncada army barracks, 10–11

Monge, Luis Alberto, 193

Monroe Doctrine, 182

Montalvo, José Antonio, 114–15, 118

Montevideo, Uruguay, 35–36, 145–46

Moore, Carlos, 99–100, 172–73

Mora, José Antonio, 63, 67

Moraes, Vinicius de, 128

Morocco, 68

Mothers of the Plaza de Mayo, 151

Movement of Revolutionary Action (Panama), 29

Movement of the Revolutionary Left (Venezuela), 85–88, 154, 219

Movement of Unity and Trade Union Coordination (Argentina), 136

Movimiento Argentino Revolucionario Anticomunista. *See* MARA

Movimiento de Acción Revolucionario (Panama), 29

Movimiento de la Izquierda Revolucionaria (Peru), 184

Movimiento de la Izquierda Revolucionaria (Venezuela), 85–88, 154, 219

Movimiento Nacionalista Revolucionario (Bolivia), 132, 199–201

Movimiento Universitario de Renovadora Orientacion (Mexico), 23

multilateral approach, 26, 37–41, 64, 66–67, 70–71, 89, 108, 126–28

multilateral organizations, 63, 182–83

Muñiz, Carlos, 90–93, 203–6

MURO (Movimiento Universitario de Renovadora Orientacion, Mexico), 23

mutual security agreement, 47–48

National Action Party (Mexico), 23

National Anti-Communist Organization (Bolivia), 139–40

National Autonomous University of Mexico, 23

National City Bank (Venezuela), 153

National Civil Defense Commission (Panama), 109–10

National Commission of Solidarity with the Cuban Revolution (Argentina), 135–36, 138

National Confederation of Stevedores (Brazil), 147

National Defense Council (Venezuela), 154

National Front (Colombia), 37–38, 113

Rio de Janeiro, Brazil, 147–49, 181
Rio Treaty: blockade or quarantine
of Cuba, 56–57; and Chile, 123;
and Colombia, 114; and Council of
the OAS, 64–65; and Guatemala,
82; Kennedy's speech, 59; MAP
agreement, 205; and Mexico, 70; and
multilateralism, 39–40, 182; signing
of, 15; Soviet buildup in Cuba, 52; and
Venezuela, 126–27
Roa, Raúl, 175, 233
Robles, Marcos A., 108–12
Rojas Pinilla, Gustavo, 37, 113–14
Rojo, Ricardo, 227
Roosevelt, Franklin, 10
*Rosales* (destroyer), 91
Ruiz Novoa, Alberto, 114
Rusk, Dean, 33, 41, 53–57, 63–66, 75–76,
88, 93, 183, 189, 194, 203–4, 209–10
Russell, Richard, 57

Sagua la Grande, 164–65
Sánchez, Celia, 170–71
San Cristóbal, 53, 106, 118, 164–65
San Cristóbal de Huamanga University,
218
Sandinista Front of National Liberation
(Frente Sandinista de Liberación
Nacional), 20, 104
Sandinistas, 128
Sandino, Augusto César, 19–20, 35, 101
San José, Costa Rica, 30, 40, 143, 192
San Marcos University, 35
San Martín Anti-Communist Youth
Organizations, 138–40
San Nicolás Commission of Solidarity
with Cuba, 135, 138, 150
Santacruz, Luis, 116
Santa Cruz de los Pinos, 50, 53
Santiago de Cuba, 10–11, 172
Santiago Ruiz, Antonio, 192
Sanz de Santamaría, Carlos, 114
Schlesinger, Arthur Jr., 13
security, 4–6; and Argentina, 89–93;
and Bolivia, 54; and Brazil, 78;
and call to arms in Cuba, 99–101;

and Council of the OAS, 65–67; of
democratic traditions, 123–28; of
denuclearization project, 74–78,
234–35; editorial representation of,
62; Inter-American Quarantine Force,
84, 88; and international law, 224;
and multilateralism, 40; opposition
to communism to ensure, 15; Soviet
buildup in Cuba, 46–47; US-Argentine
relations, 205
Security Council of the UN, 59, 67–69,
74, 123, 161, 176
self-determination, 25–28, 64, 125–28,
136, 138, 149, 218
Sendero Luminoso (Shining Path), 218
Senegal, 104
Shen Jian, 220
Silva, Albino, 77–78, 176, 209
Sino-Soviet struggle, 52, 118, 219–20
Socialist Party of the National Left
(Argentina), 216
socialization program, 210
Sofocleto, 183–84
solidarity, 4–6; and Argentina, 91–93;
and Bolivia, 201; and Brazil, 25–28;
and Chile, 123; and Colombia,
115; Council of the OAS, 64;
demonstrations for, 144–49; in
editorials, 62; as foreign support to
Cuba, 30, 35, 104–5; and Panama, 113;
public declarations of, 133–38; Soviet
buildup in Cuba, 46–47
Solís, Galileo, 30, 51–52, 108, 193
Somarriba, Rafael, 20
Somoza Debayle, Anastasio, 19–20, 51
Somoza Debayle, Luis, 19–20, 28–30,
83–84, 194–95
Somoza García, Anastasio, 19–20, 36
South Africa, 104
sovereignty, 4–6; Bay of Pigs invasion,
36; call to arms in Cuba, 99–103;
Council of the OAS, 64–67; and
Cuban democratic traditions,
123–28; and Cuban Revolution, 9,
13; Cuban-Soviet relations and,
227–29; and denuclearization project,

74-78, 234-35; editorial support of, 62; and international law, 224; and multilateralism, 40-41; and Panama, 112-13; public declarations of, 133-38; as self-determination and nonintervention, 25-28; Soviet buildup in Cuba, 46-47; UN inspections, 174

Sovereignty Day, 153

Soviet May Day slogans of 1963, 226

Soviet Presidium, 167-69, 225

Soviet Union, 2-3; attacks on US planes, 164-69; and Bay of Pigs invasion, 30-37; and Bolivia, 201-2; Council of the OAS, 64-67; Cuban-Soviet relations, 221-30; Cuba's alliance with, 14-17; fight against Castro, 186-89; and foreign brigade for Cuba, 104; and Inter-American Quarantine Force, 81-83; Khrushchev's retreat, 169-73; and messages of peace, 71-78; mobilizations, 95-98; Sino-Soviet struggle, 219-20; Soviet buildup in Cuba, 45-53; Soviet-Cuban trade agreement, 17, 31, 226-27; standing in the Americas, 214-21; support for revolution, 220-21; transnational networks in, 81; UN resolution, 67-70

Spain, 9

Statsenko, Igor, 175

Stephansky, Ben, 201

Stevenson, Adlai, 67, 161

Stewart, Charles Allen, 86

Sukarno, 200

surface-to-air missiles, 50, 165, 168-69

tactical nuclear weapons, 224-25

Tacuara, 152-53

Taylor, Maxwell, 166

Tello, Manuel, 26

Thant, U, 67-69, 77, 160-61, 171, 173-78, 183, 188

Third Position, 18

13th of November Revolutionary Movement (Movimiento Revolucionario 13 de Noviembre), 81-82

Thompson, Llewellyn, 56

Timerman, Jacobo, 181, 205-6

tin dumping, 63, 200-201

Tito, Josip Broz, 200

Torrijos, Omar, 29

trade fair in Mexico City, 219

Treaty of Tlatelolco, 232-35

Treaty on the Non-Proliferation of Nuclear Weapons, 235

*Trinchera* (bulletin), 21

Trinidad and Tobago, 79

Trotskyist Revolutionary Workers' Party, 132

Trujillo, Rafael, 13, 28-29, 79-80, 126

Tupamaros, 146

Turkey, 170, 186, 229-30

23 de Enero neighborhood, 12

26th of July Movement, 10-11, 15-16, 228

Ubico, Jorge, 80

*Última Hora* (La Paz), 60, 157

UNEAC (Unión Nacional de Escritores y Artistas de Cuba), 102-4

Unión Republicana Demócrata (Venezuela), 126

United Arab Republic, 68

United Fruit Company, 81

United Nations (UN), 2-3, 38, 56, 67-70, 73-78, 123-24, 174-78, 181-86, 232-34

United States: Bay of Pigs invasion, 30-37; and Colombia, 114-20; Council of the OAS, 63-67; counterrevolution in, 22-23; and Cuban and Soviet attacks on US planes, 164-69; Cuban exiles in, 22-23; Cuban Revolution, 9-11; and democratic traditions, 124-28; demonstrations for and against, 143, 149, 151-54; denuclearization project, 233; fight against Castro, 187-95; Inter-American Quarantine Force, 79-84; messages of peace toward, 71-78; mobilizations from, 95-98; and Panama Canal, 29, 107-12; public declarations as critical of, 132-33, 135-37;